BECOMING

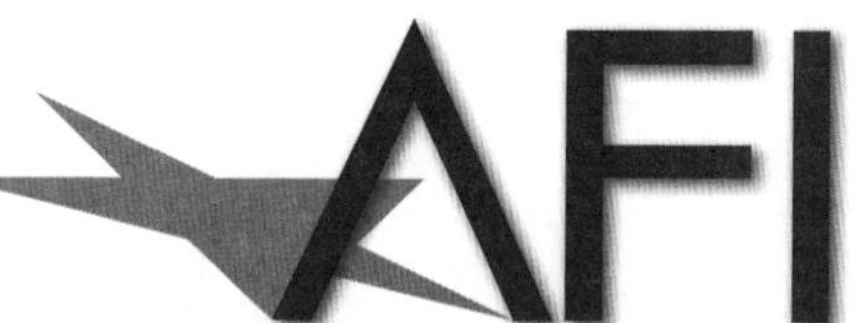

50 YEARS INSIDE THE AMERICAN FILM INSTITUTE

BECOMING AFI

50 YEARS INSIDE THE AMERICAN FILM INSTITUTE

JEAN PICKER FIRSTENBERG

AND JAMES HINDMAN

FOREWORD BY DANA GIOIA
PREFACE BY PATTY JENKINS
AFTERWORD BY DAVID LYNCH

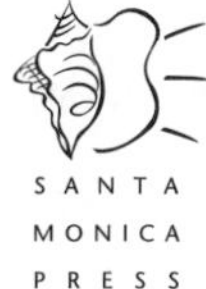

SANTA
MONICA
PRESS

Published by:

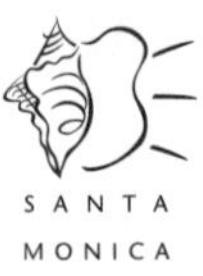

Santa Monica Press LLC
P.O. Box 850
Solana Beach, CA 92075
1-800-784-9553
www.santamonicapress.com
books@santamonicapress.com

Printed in the United States

Santa Monica Press books are available at special quantity discounts when purchased in bulk by corporations, organizations, or groups. Please call our Special Sales department at 1-800-784-9553.

This book is intended to provide general information. The publisher, author, distributor, and copyright owner are not engaged in rendering professional advice or services. The publisher, author, distributor, and copyright owner are not liable or responsible to any person or group with respect to any loss, illness, or injury caused or alleged to be caused by the information found in this book.

ISBN-13 978-1-59580-094-7

Library of Congress Cataloging-in-Publication Data

Names: Firstenberg, Jean, author. | Hindman, James, author.
Title: Becoming AFI : 50 years inside the American Film Institute / by Jean Picker Firstenberg and James Hindman.
Description: Solana Beach, CA : Santa Monica Press, [2017]
Identifiers: LCCN 2017020377 (print) | LCCN 2017031395 (ebook) | ISBN 9781595807946 | ISBN 9781595800947
Subjects: LCSH: American Film Institute--History.
Classification: LCC PN1993.5.U6 (ebook) | LCC PN1993.5.U6 F54475 2017 (print) | DDC 791.4306073--dc23
LC record available at https://lccn.loc.gov/2017020377

Cover and interior design and production by Future Studio

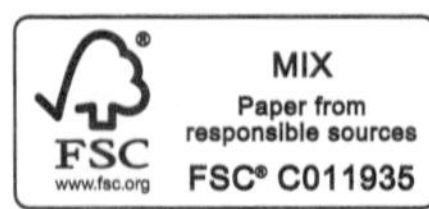

*Dedicated to all those who celebrate the past
and create the future of the movies*

"We will create an American Film Institute, bringing together leading artists of the film industry, outstanding educators and young men and women who wish to pursue the twentieth-century art form as their life's work."

—President Lyndon Baines Johnson
White House Rose Garden, Washington, DC
September 29, 1965

"No matter how divisive life in this country may become, the movie theater has always been a place where we can discover what unites us."

—Vernon Jordan Jr.
New York Times
February 18, 2017

CONTENTS

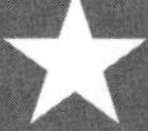

FOREWORD

DANA GIOIA

Everyone acknowledges that the vitality of a culture depends on creativity. Society rightly celebrates its art and artists. What fewer acknowledge is that culture also depends on the ongoing preservation and presentation of those artistic achievements. The music of operatic classics remains silent on the pages of their scores without the elaborate and expensive expertise of an opera company. *Otello* and *Don Giovanni* are masterpieces of the human imagination, but the Metropolitan Opera is also a sort of masterpiece—a triumph of pragmatic vision that has sustained itself through wars, depressions, and social change to present works at the highest level of execution. The arts depend on institutions to curate and advance their expanding legacies.

In the rich contemporary culture of the United States, we often take these institutions for granted. They exist, and we enjoy them as a natural part of the artistic landscape. We often forget how recently they have arrived and how precariously they continue. Our country did not have a National Gallery of Art until 1941. It happened only because of the dogged efforts of Andrew Mellon, a private citizen who was—ironically—the target of a politically motivated investigation by the federal government at the time. How easily Mellon could have abandoned his costly philanthropy. The "venerable" Chicago Lyric Opera began only in 1955, and the Los Angeles County Museum of Art opened in 1961. Even the National Endowment for the Arts, the official arts agency of the U.S. government, did not come into existence until 1965. The American Film Institute emerged in 1967.

Art institutions are also fragile. Even vibrant organizations need constant work and renewal. Although most major arts enterprises are essentially public/private partnerships, which enjoy special tax and legal privileges, they are far from secure. Organizations as large and important as the New York City Opera, Martha Graham Dance Company, Philadelphia Orchestra, and Detroit Institute of the Arts have faced possible bankruptcy. Surrounded by the immense but philistine wealth of Silicon Valley, the San Jose Symphony went bankrupt in 2002 after sixty-five years of performances, and the long-established San Jose Rep disappeared in 2014. The wealth existed in Santa Clara County but not the cultural leadership or local traditions of artistic philanthropy. On a national level, the National Endowment for the Arts has repeatedly faced extinction by Congress, though it has always survived. The arts thrive in the U.S. only through the constant efforts of thousands of leaders, administrators, and patrons as well as millions of audience members and voters.

There is no art more characteristically American than the motion picture, and no medium more fragile than film. The movies grew with such speed, glamour, and ubiquity that almost no one considered what happened to last year's hits. More than half of the American films made before 1950 have been lost. Experts estimate that between seventy and ninety percent of silent films have vanished. Some prints were destroyed deliberately by the studios themselves. Before television, cable, cassettes, and digital media, the studios saw little commercial value in old releases. Why pay for the storage and preservation of worthless and highly flammable reels of aging film?

Other prints deteriorated through the brittle and unstable nature of celluloid. Still other films vanished more dramatically in fires caused by early nitrate film, as in MGM's famous vault fire of 1965. Even the films that survived often contained gaps or damaged sections. It seems odd that our archetypal modern American art form resembles ancient Greek drama or Elizabethan theater in that so many works survive only as evocative titles. Theda Bara's *Cleopatra* (1917) and Lon Chaney's *London After Midnight* (1927) are now as lost as Shakespeare's *Love's Labour Found* and Sophocles's *Daedalus*.

The creation of the American Film Institute in 1967, therefore, represents a hugely important moment in both American culture and the history of motion pictures. For the first time, a national organization existed for the preservation of America's cinematic legacy. The institute's birth was properly theatrical. The AFI was first announced by President Lyndon Johnson in the Rose Garden ceremony to sign the Arts and Humanities Act of 1965, which created the National Endowment for the Arts and its sibling agency, the National Endowment for the Humanities.

The new federal arts agency understood the urgent need to save the legacy of American film. One of the NEA's first large grants was for planning the new film institute. Meanwhile, the Arts Endowment helped create a public/private partnership involving the Ford Foundation and the Motion Picture Association of America to fund the new organization's establishment and early operations.

With this powerful sponsorship, the American Film Institute was born like Athena, who sprang fully grown and fully armored from the head of Zeus. By 1971, only four years after its founding, the AFI had recovered 4,500 films. The organization's good works have never stopped—not only in conservation but also by supporting training, education, presentation, historical documentation, and scholarship. The AFI has changed the history of American film by saving the history.

The story of the AFI also shares the glamour of Hollywood. How many boards of directors started with Gregory Peck, Sidney Poitier, and Francis Ford Coppola? Few organizational histories are so much fun to read. Jean Firstenberg and James Hindman's *Becoming AFI: 50 Years Inside the American Film Institute* is a significant addition to the literature of Hollywood.

The importance of this book also extends beyond the film industry. The story of the AFI currently has an urgent relevance for the broader culture. The AFI emerged at a key moment in American political and cultural history. Its creation, survival, and success reflect a democratic vision and social optimism that the nation has subsequently lost.

The AFI grew out of the same legislation that not only created the NEA and NEH, but also expanded the state arts councils and the Kennedy Center. (Two years later, Congress passed the Public Broadcasting Act, which effectively created Public Broadcasting Service and National Public Radio.) The Arts and Humanities Act was a bipartisan bill enthusiastically supported by a Southern president. At the center of this ambitious legislation was the conviction that America's greatness depended not only on its superior wealth, technology, and power but also on its leadership "in the realm of ideas and of the spirit."

The AFI's transformative work grew out of this period of broad political consensus. The AFI and thousands of other cultural organizations across the country demonstrated that a small but steady investment of federal dollars combined and multiplied by state and private money could enrich and expand American culture. Firstenberg and Hindman have told the Institute's story in its full political and cultural context. The book is not only a fascinating account in its own right; it is a timely commentary on our present cultural and political moment. The nation no longer feels the confidence that it enjoyed half a century ago.

In Billy Wilder's *Sunset Boulevard*, the silent film star Norma Desmond explains her career's failure by declaring, "I am big! It's the pictures that got small." This splendid history of the American Film Institute evokes an era when America's cultural vision was as big as the nation. It's a story our smaller moment needs to hear.

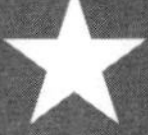

PREFACE

Patty Jenkins

The AFI represents a very special place and time in my career. The one and only pocket of time where I was able to steal all of my focus away from making a living and all of the other realities of survival and focus solely on the kind of filmmaking I loved and the kind of filmmaker I wanted to be.

The best thing about it was that, as close as AFI is to the industry, we really felt sheltered from any corruption of thought that might pollute a developing artist for the sake of calculating ambition. Instead of wasting precious time calculating how to play the current Hollywood industry or how to get agents and win film festivals—an approach I truly believe squelches creativity and voice—we were encouraged to deeply pursue great filmmaking and storytelling, first and foremost. As a result, the process spawned many truly great and international filmmaking voices of every kind and for every market, but great voices of filmmaking most of all.

And though we had plenty of limitations and problems making the films we wanted to make, many of them were issues you will always face in filmmaking: money, schedules, the politics of getting the best crew, and then receiving the ultimate criticism by your peers and mentors.

I'm so grateful for my years at AFI. I deeply believe they helped me find my voice and defining principles of story and craft that inform me to this day.

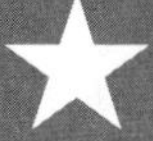

INTRODUCTION

Bob Gazzale

It was a sunny September day when the President of the United Stated planted the seeds for the American Film Institute in the White House Rose Garden. And it was there that the AFI story began to blossom and grow. Calendar pages fly off the wall—fifty years of them—fifty years of preserving the heritage of the motion picture, honoring the artists and their work, and educating the next generation of storytellers. And AFI stands tall and proud today.

But how? The answer to that question lies in the memories of many. And only through collaboration—as is the case with this most powerful of art forms—can these stories be told.

The director and producer of this story is Jean Picker Firstenberg, who led AFI for a peerless tenure of twenty-seven years. Her creative ensemble is an army of artists—friends and colleagues who helped shape the story of AFI. They show that AFI is an organization that not only *invented* itself at its founding, but has *re*-invented itself time and again to adapt to a changing cultural landscape.

It is upon that foundation of evolution—and on the shoulders of the great men and women who have come before—that we look to the art form's next fifty years. After all, tomorrow is another day!

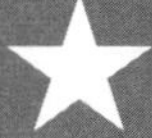

AUTHORS' NOTE

Our friends have asked us: What's your book about? Is it a history of AFI? Or a memoir? Are you going to tell the real stories? Or is it a collection of anecdotes?

We had to ask ourselves those questions many times over the past few years. We started out looking at our years leading AFI—1980 to 2008—and found many fascinating aspects to the Institute's evolution. At least, they were fascinating to us, years later, perhaps because now we see them in a historical context enlightened by perspective, and because, when you step back, you see things far more clearly than when you are in the middle of the fray.

So what we've put together is AFI's history, as we experienced it personally. As we structured the book with the stories we wanted to tell from those years, we realized that some of those stories really belonged to other voices. So we went to several former colleagues and asked them to join our band.

Each chapter tells a stand-alone story about an aspect of AFI. Together, they add up to a full picture, but they are not strictly chronological. So feel free to read from front to back—or jump in at the middle.

Since this was our story of AFI, we decided to provide our own perspective on what came before and after us, thereby bringing AFI's fifty-year mark into fuller focus. (Apologies to George Stevens Jr. and Bob Gazzale for usurping their venues, but we feel comfortable providing our own context for the entire fifty-year adventure.) We hope this explains the various voices included and not included in the book. And we hope you agree that it has been a heck of a journey.

—JEAN PICKER FIRSTENBERG and JAMES HINDMAN
Los Angeles, CA

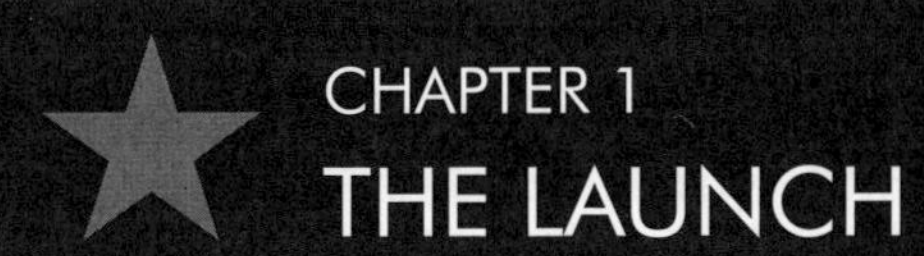

To Begin at the Beginning

Jean Picker Firstenberg

What does reaching fifty mean? Numbers mark our lives, from childhood to adulthood. By fifty, we have been around more than half the average life expectancy—a real milestone. And it is the same for an entity that was created fifty years ago.

Looking back, what was our country like? Sociologist Todd Gitlin called the 1960s "years of hope, days of rage." It was a decade of enormous change, creativity, upheaval, and accomplishment in American life. College campuses erupted with anger at the Vietnam War. The Women's Movement arrived, again. Three American leaders were assassinated.

President Lyndon Johnson's Great Society initiatives, announced mid-decade, promised federal support of the arts and humanities, which also galvanized support from the private sector. This set in motion a cultural agenda that reshaped the landscape, literally and figuratively. In 1965, he signed the legislation that planted the seed for AFI. That was the same year that civil rights protesters marched from Selma to Montgomery, the Beatles played Shea Stadium, Bob Dylan went electric, *The Sound of Music* dominated the Oscars, the Mustang became Ford's best launch since the Model A, and Sandy Koufax pitched a perfect game.

President Johnson's 1965 declaration that "we will create an American Film Institute" was bold. For the first time in U.S. history, federal funding was dedicated to supporting a broader cultural agenda that included film, and this simple declaration signaled a new recognition of motion pictures as an art. But as we all know, many good ideas from the 1960s did not survive. It turns out that the strongest institutions unfold over time. Fifty years later, scholars suggest that long-form storytelling with moving images is now viewed as the literature of the twenty-first century. Indeed, on the day Bob Dylan's Nobel Prize for Literature was announced in 2016, Dana Gioia, who was chair of the National Endowment for the Arts from 2003 to 2009 and now serves as Poet Laureate of the State of California, commented to me: "We've been waiting for an American to win this again for some years. Will Martin Scorsese be next?"

In 1967, AFI was launched and, over the decades, it found its footing as a voice of enduring quality and artistic standards. What started with a concept was followed by formal documentation including a corporate charter, bylaws, and board members who led the way through growing pains into adolescence and adulthood. Enduring and thriving for fifty years is remarkable. Even more remarkable is an institution that continues to evolve and renew itself.

This book tells the story of AFI as it reaches that fiftieth anniversary. It is not a historic recitation in the academic sense; rather, it is a personal memoir from several of us who were there, primarily during the middle three decades, but with a perspective that honors the remarkable first decade-plus and delights in the achievements of the fifth decade.

Fifty years ago, George Stevens Jr., at thirty-five, was asked to lead this new creation. He had never been a CEO before. While everyone knew he was talented, no one could have predicted what a brilliant writer and producer he would become, nor what an astute political competitor he would be. George's life and career have been devoted to the arts, arts institutions, and telling stories worth telling.

When I succeeded him in 1980, at forty-three, I had never been a CEO either. But I also had a promising background, with useful educational and political experiences. I, too, was passionate about the cause. Both George and I brought our knowledge and instincts to bear on a new idea that had no models and no roadmaps. Our life experiences, personal tendencies, and professional inclinations took us to places no one had ever been before.

Late in 2007, I was succeeded by Bob Gazzale, then forty-two, who also had never been a CEO. As a devoted film historian with brilliant writing, producing, and entrepreneurial skills, he has taken AFI through some precarious economic circumstances with grace and tenacity. And now, thanks to Bob, the AFI is strong at fifty.

This book brings us through to AFI's fiftieth anniversary in 2017, by looking at the original goals, the programs that have prospered, the programs we wished had succeeded, and the programs that have passed the test of time. I joined AFI in 1980 as director and CEO. That same year, James Hindman started as a consultant for AFI in DC before moving to Los Angeles, where, within a decade, he became AFI's deputy director and COO, and then co-director, COO, and provost of the AFI Conservatory. In all, we worked together for twenty-four years.

When he and I started thinking about the AFI at fifty, we wondered what story we could tell. And over several years writing this book, we found our voices and, gratefully, the voices of several colleagues. Over time, we found a story that makes us proud, because I know that we—as well as George and Bob—cared about every project we conceptualized and every activity we planned. Reality often had to balance our emotional energy and, in telling this history, we have not avoided the hard moments over the decades. I can also attest that we have always felt honored to support the moving image artists whose insights and genius have contributed to so much culturally, and whose visions and voices are essential to our nation and our world.

First Steps

The elaborate tale of how the National Endowment for the Arts was itself initially established and how it, in turn, established the AFI is quite complex. The first National Council on the Arts, appointed by President Johnson in 1965, was chaired by the respected theatrical producer Roger Stevens, who went on to chair the AFI board briefly before becoming the founding chair of the Board of Trustees of the John F. Kennedy Center for the Performing Arts when it opened in 1971. The council included three artists of the film world: actress Elizabeth Ashley, acclaimed director George Stevens, and distinguished actor Gregory Peck. (Among the first council were artists from many disciplines, as well as heads of the leading cultural institutions in the nation.) The council immediately allocated $91,000 for the Stanford Research Institute (SRI) to advise the endowment on how to organize an American Film Institute. Two years after the endowment itself was organized, the NEA accepted the SRI report.

A young George Stevens Jr. was asked to lead the new American Film Institute. He had come to Washington, DC, in 1961 to head up the Motion Picture and Television Service for the U.S. Information Agency, led by Edward R. Murrow during the Kennedy Administration. Stevens's division produced 300 documentaries a year and distributed them to more than 110 countries. NEA chairman Roger Stevens worked with George Stevens Jr. on the purpose and structure of the new American Film Institute. Then there was the question of funding. The NEA committed $1.3 million each year for three years for the soon-to-be AFI—*if* a matching grant could be confirmed. In fact, in the 1960s, the Ford Foundation, a very strong NEA partner at the time, had become the largest private entity making grants to the arts in the U.S. It is probably fair to say that, because of Ford Foundation vice president McNeil Lowry's leadership, the AFI launch was actually made possible. George Stevens and Roger Stevens met with Lowry and described the concept for a film training center in Los Angeles. As a result, Ford then matched the NEA's $1.3 million (over three years), funds that had been pledged even before AFI was legally incorporated. The Stanford Report clearly stated that "an advanced study center should be established in or near Los Angeles to take advantage of the major resources of the theatrical motion picture industry concentrated there." Thus, AFI was to have a bicoastal identity from its inception.

> "The first National Council on the Arts was stellar. It was comprised of Agnes de Mille, Leonard Bernstein, Isaac Stern, John Steinbeck, Yamasaki the architect, David Smith the sculptor, my father, and Gregory Peck. It was this blazing assembly of real artists. And they knew what to do about grants. They gave grants to dance companies, symphony orchestras, and playwrights. But as we said at the time, you can't give a grant to Warner Bros. So the question became, how do you develop film within the endowment idea?"
>
> —GEORGE STEVENS JR., writer, producer, and AFI founding director

The third angel in the birth of the AFI was the indomitable Jack Valenti, who had moved from LBJ's White House across the street to run the Motion Picture Association of America, and who corralled the major studios to provide a $1.3 million match over three years that got AFI underway. In addition, Roger Stevens wrote to

The Context for an American Film Institute

James Hindman

Fifty years ago, the American Film Institute emerged from a unique confluence of cultural and political energies at a particular moment in American history. While the U.S. had never subscribed enthusiastically to government support for the arts, early attempts in the 1930s New Deal to help artists survive the Great Depression yielded such remarkable results as the Federal Theatre Project, Federal Writers Project, and Federal Art Project. Congressional discomfort and the war effort ended these experiments but left memories and a belief in the ideal of government support for the arts as a public good.

Postwar European cultural reconstruction was the source of interesting models for public art as a national identity builder, especially through the support of major flagship institutions like museums, orchestras, and performing arts centers. Under President Kennedy's triumphalist New Frontier, supporting the arts directly was seen as a natural part of the agenda for developing a mature America, holding its own with the European nations it had rescued.

At the same time, interest in movies as more than ubiquitous popular entertainment began to grow. Sparked by the importing of brilliant international art films in major media centers like New York City, Boston, and Washington, DC, renowned critics like Andrew Sarris and Pauline Kael gradually promoted a new image of movies as *cinema*—art with profound insight into the world's cultures and the human spirit. The arcane processes that brought films to the screen were fascinating and of growing interest to a movie-infatuated public. The French obsession with *auteurisme*, authorship in movies (nevertheless truly a collaborative art) focused on the director, suggesting that he (not many "she's" out there) could achieve the status of a film artist—and even America might have a few of these remarkable creatures, like John Ford and Orson Welles.

How to study this phenomenon? How to recognize movies and cinema as real art? How to have access to the best examples? How to preserve them, like great paintings? How to prepare the best and brightest for careers here?

According to Deborah Jae Alexander's 2010 dissertation, "A History of the American Film Institute," as far back as 1935, a call came from American educators to support the use of film as a learning device for students, leading to a proposal for a so-called American Film Institute to garner government support of film in the classroom. And in the summer 1961 issue of *Film Quarterly*, Los Angeles editor Colin Young joined critics and educators to explore the possibility of establishing a national organization dedicated to film. "An American Film Institute: A Proposal" set out his concept of the goals and opportunities for such an institution, based on government-supported film institute models in Britain and Sweden. Support existed among major film critics and a small group of academics, but it wasn't until 1965, when the U.S. government took up its mantle as the nation's primary art patron, that the American Film Institute came into real focus.

George Stevens Jr. in February 1967 that further funding would be forthcoming if things proceeded as expected, with $350,000 more in fiscal year 1968. He also believed that AFI should receive ten percent of the NEA budget on an annual basis. Unfortunately, neither would come to pass.

The minutes from those first AFI board meetings create a fascinating look into the challenge of starting a national institution from square one. Founding trustee Arnold Picker (my uncle) alone took on the challenge to raise the required $1.3 million in matching funds by AFI and reported on that progress at every meeting. Valenti worked with his member companies at the MPAA while Arnold reached into the wider filmmaking community to companies like Eastman Kodak, Technicolor, Deluxe Labs, Consolidated Film Industries (Sid Solow), and exhibitors like Sherrill Corwin and Michael Forman and their National Association of Theatre Owners (NATO). Arnold also enlisted the support of Charles Benton, lawyers, the guilds, and his close friend and leading Hollywood agent Charles Feldman. (When Feldman fell ill and passed away in 1968, Arnold raised $150,000 in his memory to fund the Feldman Library at Greystone.)

The television networks were reluctant to lend their support because of the name American *Film* Institute. At the time, the businesses of television and film did not mix. But Arnold suggested putting the head of CBS at the time, Jack Schneider, on the AFI board. It was a brilliant recommendation; from day one, CBS was an extraordinary partner of AFI, with every subsequent CBS chair/president having a major influence on the life of the institute over five decades.

Those first years were a fundraising bootstrap operation. But soon it became apparent that creating a new national institution—as well as raising those matching funds—were together too much of a challenge. A handful of trustees, a young director, and a thin staff could not build the AFI fundraising apparatus on their own. The board understood the need for fundraising co-chairs in New York and L.A., with a greater delegation of responsibility for recruiting support from different constituencies. Rudimentary means had already accomplished an incredible amount, but to be sustainable, the AFI also needed to have a professional staff structure. It needed to act like an organization that planned to be around for a while.

A Brilliant Array of Programs

On the programming side, there was plenty of energy, daring, and courage at the newly emerging AFI. Everything was uncharted. Nothing had been done before, so there was a blank page, and good people filled in the lines. Those first formative years were a rush of trying out many diverse ideas, learning, and adjusting quickly.

Those efforts and the priorities they represented gave AFI the contours of its first institutional identity. It was, in fact, a difficult task to embody the range of aspirations set by the NEA and other original funders. It was all so new, and everyone had a different opinion about what AFI should or should not do. For example, film preservation was seen as an urgent issue, especially because traditional combustible celluloid film was fast decaying. Over those early years, AFI's archival team included Sam Kula, Larry Karr, David Shepard, and Anthony Slide, a most respected group. So the AFI "Nitrate Won't Wait" campaign drew widespread support, but the film preservation community itself was fraught with intrigue, suspicion, and competitive instincts. Initially, the *AFI Catalog of Feature Films, 1921–1930* was welcomed warmly, but due to a confluence of reasons, the 1961–1970 volume took twice as long to produce, at double the cost. Just after it came out in 1976, the *Catalog* entered a multi-year hiatus that would create considerable ongoing resentment and hostility toward AFI within the archival community.

None of it was easy, but George was not deterred and did not allow AFI's prospects to be denied. As he described that first decade in his own words in *The First Ten Years: The American Film Institute, 1967–1977*:

"We have done a lot over these ten years. We have encountered criticism for being over-ambitiousness, for sometimes straining our capacities and funds, and there is no question that when faced with a choice between 'doing' or 'not doing,' we, more often than not, chose to do. This led us to launch a range of programs, only one of which initially received hearty approval from all quarters: the coordinated effort to preserve America's films. Other programs had their advocates, detractors, enthusiasts, and skeptics. Nevertheless, we invested our full commitment into each enterprise—a professionally equipped facility to train new filmmakers, a unit to train minority filmmakers, a directing workshop for women, internships with leading filmmakers for aspiring directors, a repertory film theater at the Kennedy Center, a scholarly catalog of motion picture data, grants for independent filmmakers, a quality magazine on the film and television arts, an annual Life Achievement Award, and a program of national membership for the public."

CENTER FOR ADVANCED FILM STUDIES

Establishing the Center for Advanced Film Studies was an early priority. The decision to locate it in L.A. was the first sign that AFI's center of influence must go to filmmaking's capital of the world—Hollywood. The 1969 negotiation to lease Greystone, the Doheny Mansion in Beverly Hills, was remarkable—$1 a year for ten years, in a time when the going rate was well over $200,000 a year. Even with $50,000 in renovation costs, I'd call that one heck of a deal.

September 23, 1969, was Opening Day for the Center for Advanced Film Studies. George Stevens Jr. outlined his vision: CAFS was to focus activities intensely on filmmaking, functioning as a bridge between the study of filmmaking and the profession. The

"I have the fondest memories of Greystone. We came from all over the country and, actually, all over the world. I came from my apartment in New York, and my best friend came from the Netherlands. We converged on this magnificent mansion in Beverly Hills, where the bedrooms were converted to office space and the kitchen, which looked like the kitchen in *Upstairs, Downstairs*, was used to make the bologna sandwiches for our cycle projects. The beautiful wall-paneled living areas were there to host the guests at the Harold Lloyd Master Seminars: King Vidor, John Cassavetes, Sydney Pollack, and so many others. It was the first time in my life that film was regarded as an art form."

—ROBERT MANDEL,
filmmaker and AFIC dean (class of 1977

education was to be interdisciplinary, because "film is the most complex of all the arts, demanding that one be versed in many arts—acting, writing, music, design, and photography." It would offer an atelier-style, mentor-driven program characterized as follows: "An ecumenical attitude will make Greystone a harbor for many different styles and artistic points of view." Stevens summed up the height and limitations of what CAFS would offer: "I believe that while it may not be possible to train people to make films, it is possible to create a climate in which people can learn to make films." Harold Lloyd and Elia Kazan gave opening seminars, setting a very high mark for both the moment and the outlook for the experience and artistry CAFS would field.

THE DIRECTING WORKSHOP FOR WOMEN

The Directing Workshop for Women was founded in 1974. Its fuller history is told in Chapter 4. As far ahead of its time as it was forty-three years ago, it is still—sadly—needed as much today as it was then. The DWW was my first introduction to AFI's work, and the program has remained a passion of mine ever since.

EXHIBITION

Exhibition is a strength in AFI's legacy, and it should be high on the list of universally applauded programs, as AFI's commitment started from day one and has never wavered. It wasn't until John Ptak provided me with verbatim transcripts of the NEA AFI panel discussing each AFI program in 1983 that I read that one of this country's most distinguished nonprofit exhibitors argued that the AFI Theater in the Kennedy Center in Washington, DC, was inappropriate because there was no filmmaking community to interact with—a nonsensical argument given that film is for everyone. Washingtonians and young government employees grew up seeing

The MCA-Based Film Library-Museum Proposal

Imagine how different today's AFI would be, had this idea, considered in the August 8, 1969, executive committee meeting and recorded in the minutes, been pursued:

> "A proposal, written by AFI archivist Sam Kula and circulated to the committee in advance of the meeting, was concerned with an invitation by MCA for AFI to establish a film museum and film library on MCA premises at University City, California. This kind of relationship with a major studio was deemed by the committee as not suitable for the Institute to pursue at this time."

film history at the AFI Theater, just as New Yorkers did at MoMA. And now, Washingtonians experience film history at the AFI Silver Theatre and Cultural Center, while New Yorkers frequent the Film Forum and the Walter Reade Theater at Lincoln Center. At the same time, the arrangement that brought the AFI Theater and office space into the Kennedy Center (in unused space below and above the Eisenhower Theater) was incredibly creative.

AMERICAN FILM

American Film magazine, starting in 1975, was a bold, expensive proposition that would have great impact and influence but, in the end, was not sustainable economically.

LIFE ACHIEVEMENT AWARD

In 1973, AFI, CBS, and the film community joined together to celebrate a movie icon, John Ford, the first recipient of the AFI Life Achievement Award. That inaugural LAA event was the only one that included a sitting U.S. president, as Richard Nixon presented John Ford with the Presidential Medal of Freedom after Charlton Heston and George Stevens Jr. honored Ford with the first AFI Life Achievement Award—a venerable way to launch a tradition that continues to this day.

Marking the First Decade

It is hard to capture in a few pages the tone and spirit of AFI's first decade, let alone identify the dozens of women and men whose energy and dedication were responsible for so many creative efforts. Their efforts culminated in AFI's Tenth Anniversary celebration in 1977, a twelve-day series of events throughout the Kennedy Center, crowned with a White House reception and gala benefit at the Kennedy Center for the Performing Arts. For the first time,

> "Nothing that happens in this democracy could alter the power and magic of this extraordinary thing, the American movie. And for me, the American Film Institute stands, more than any other organization in the world, for the best that America has to offer."
>
> —SIR HOWARD STRINGER, corporate executive and AFI board of trustees chair (2000–present)

leading members of the film community—from in front of and behind the camera—were invited to the White House and received by President and Mrs. Jimmy Carter. The Kennedy Center gala was attended by Hollywood luminaries and Washington leaders saluting the ten greatest American movies as selected by AFI members. The gala was also telecast in an edited version on CBS. The evening was such a success and the light shone so brightly on George Stevens Jr. that it opened a new path for him, as the masterful Roger Stevens invited him to think about an equally exciting awards event for the Kennedy Center. The following year, indeed, marked the beginning of the Kennedy Center Honors, brilliantly conceived by George and Nick Vanoff.

With that new chapter opening up, it was no surprise when George announced his resignation in June 1979 to move into a full-time creative producing career. He had put this idea, this American Film Institute, on its feet and felt it was strong enough to survive and thrive. I was deeply honored to take up the torch.

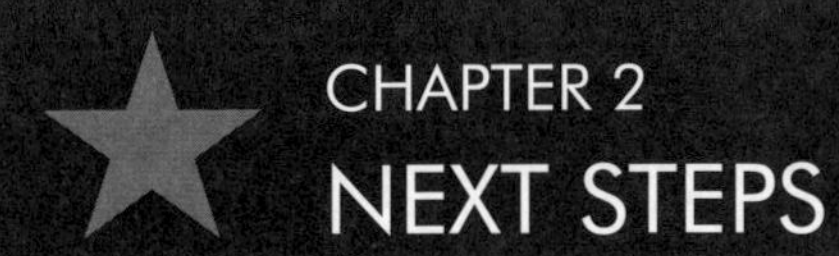

AFI in 1980: A New Decade, A New Director, A New Home

Jean Picker Firstenberg

This is a story—my story—of one year in the life of the American Film Institute. It was 1980. The nation was in the throes of a heated presidential election that would usher in the Reagan era. After the turmoil of the Vietnam years, there was also backlash against "artists on the federal dole." The politically precarious fate of the National Endowment for the Arts became a serious campaign issue, in turn putting AFI's very survival at risk.

This was the year that we first experienced the twenty-four-hour news cycle. John Lennon would be killed that fall. The first personal computer was still a year away; the invention of the World Wide Web was still a decade away. The Cold War was coming to an end but still played out in the headlines—at the Winter Olympics, a young U.S. team defeated a heavily favored Soviet team, the "Miracle on Ice." The Summer Olympics became a non-event as the U.S. boycotted the Moscow games to protest the Soviet invasion of Afghanistan. Politically, socially, culturally, economically—change was in the air.

The AFI was also in transition, beginning in 1980 with a new director and CEO, about whom the movie editor of the *Washington Post* asked, "Who is this mystery woman?" Six months earlier, in the June 9, 1979, issue of the *New York Times*, the resignation of AFI's founding director, George Stevens Jr., was announced, but he would stay on until his successor was at the table.

As soon as I read that article, I knew that I wanted to be that person. I had never run anything in my life. Pursuing that position was a leap of faith, as well as a leap up an organizational chart to even be considered for the position. But I knew I wanted it, and I did have one undisputable asset: I was a Picker.

The Pickers and "The Flickers"

In 1912, my Russian-born grandfather's New York City clothing business went bankrupt. For reasons no one ever explained to me, David V. Picker (my brother would be named after him) took a gamble on "the flickers." He borrowed money from his brother and opened a nickelodeon in the Bronx. He built a small chain of nickelodeons and then merged them with his friend Marcus Loew's company, establishing the real estate basis for part of the Loews Theatres chain.

My grandfather was an honorable man. He repaid his previously forgiven debt plus fifty percent interest to his creditors, and I have the thank-you letters and news articles to prove it. He had four sons—Eugene, Sidney, Leonard, and Arnold—who all went into the film business. My dad and namesake, Eugene, was the oldest. When my grandfather died in 1928, my dad left college to work for Loews Theatres, watching over the family property.

My childhood was anchored at the movies, seeing every film that played in a Loews theater and going every weekend with my dad as he visited theaters to be sure everything was working properly. He took exceptional pride in the quality of each theater's projection and sound, in the attractiveness of the concession stand and the cleanliness of the restrooms.

I would ride with him to different New York boroughs on the weekends, to the Brooklyn theaters on Saturday and to Queens on Sunday, for example. We would visit those great movie palaces, many on the locations where my grandfather had built his original nickelodeons. While my dad was checking on the theaters, I slipped in to watch the movies, albeit in fifteen-minute segments. Can you imagine a more wonderful childhood? It was the world of the MGM musical, the Warner Bros. drama, the Columbia film noir, and the spectacle from Twentieth Century Fox. Opening nights at the Loews State or Capital Theatres in Times Square were unforgettable.

For as long as I can remember, I was the Picker maverick. Even as a youngster, I was interested in story rather than spectacle, in content rather than fluff, in art rather than commerce. My uncle Arnold would say, "If Jeannie likes a movie, it's sure to be a bomb at the box office." And, believe me, a bomb at the box office was the most painful thing you could discuss at the dining room table. As it is today, box office returns were a measure of a film's success, though not necessarily of its quality.

Nonetheless, I grew up in a family that respected movies and moviemakers. Honesty and quality counted. When it came to business, they believed that you made a commitment with a handshake and not a contract. I was taught that you should spend your life doing what you love every day, so you always look forward to Monday.

The Road to AFI

I started adult life in the manner traditional for the era. At twenty, after my sophomore year in college, I married. My husband, Paul Firstenberg, was at Harvard Law School, so I transferred to Boston

University. My parents wanted me to graduate college because they hadn't. At what is now called the BU College of Communications, I majored in radio and television and was director of WBUR, the 20,000-watt FM radio station that's still a powerhouse today. That was a great gig! I had dreams of being a sports broadcaster (I was decades ahead of my time, before women were allowed into dressing rooms), but life had other things in store. In 1958, I felt like I got two degrees, because my husband graduated at the same time. At twenty-two and twenty-four, I had children.

In 1962, we moved to Washington, DC, to work in the Kennedy Administration. As a woman, it was eye-opening. Women were more involved in every aspect of life than I had ever seen before. Meeting people from all over America, all extremely smart and deeply committed, was exhilarating. In that wonderful New Frontier atmosphere, we really did believe we could save the world.

While in DC, I became a protégé (one of many) of the late, great Lindy Boggs. Marie Corinne Morrison Claiborne Boggs, known as "Lindy," succeeded her husband, Hale Boggs, as U.S. Representative for Louisiana's second district and served for eighteen years. Hale was Majority Leader of the House when he died in a plane crash in Alaska on a campaign trip in 1972. In her final role in public service, Lindy served as U.S. ambassador to the Holy See. Lindy taught me an enormous amount about politics, connections, family, and public service. I raised my children and worked part-time on projects, including the Democratic National Committee's "Get Out to Vote" campaign for Lyndon Johnson's presidential campaign. That resulted in one of my proudest moments, when I was honored to travel with Rosa Parks to black churches in Ohio and Maryland in an effort to get out the vote.

In 1965, Lindy was chair of the Presidential Inaugural Balls. Demand was so high for tickets that four balls were added to the six originally planned, just days before the January 20 inauguration. Lindy asked me to chair one of the additional balls. A fantastic five days followed, with no time for sleep or fatigue. The honorary chair of my ball was Gregory Peck. I was twenty-nine years old.

Next, in New York City for a few years, I worked for what would be the only for-profit employer in my career, J. Walter Thompson. My dearest friend, Marie Luisi, was in charge of media at this pioneering advertising agency. If you watched *Mad Men*, you have a sense of the atmosphere, but JWT did move with the times. On the same day in 1970, JWT made seven women vice presidents, including Marie.

In 1972, my husband became chief financial officer of Princeton University. This would be the next eye-opening phase in the executive education I didn't realize I was getting. In those days, private universities would often find a role for the spouse; I was assigned to work for a grand gentleman, William Weathersby. Bill had been at the State Department and joined Princeton as their first-ever vice president for communications. Princeton had become co-ed in 1969 and was still figuring out how to attract a more diverse student body. He asked me to start up a publications office to help tell the Princeton story. (Princeton appears to have been successful in that effort, with Michelle Obama '85, Sonia Sotomayor '79, and Elena Kagan '81 among their illustrious alumnae.)

I was preparing for something, though I didn't know exactly what. The entire nation was confronting the changing role of women in American life—at home, work, and play. In a few years, I would be divorced. In 1972, the Senate passed both the Equal Rights Amendment and Title IX legislation. The ERA eventually stalled as some states refused ratification, but Title IX gained steam, changing the world forever for women and girls with just thirty-seven words:

> *No person in the United States shall, on the basis of sex, be excluded from participation in, be denied the benefits of, or be subjected to discrimination under any educational program or activity receiving Federal financial assistance.*

It ensured equal access to programs, including athletics, for girls and women at schools and colleges. It took years for Title IX to be implemented across the country, but I think it was the most significant legislation for women since we got the right to vote in 1920.

After four years at Princeton, my last career adventure before AFI was as a program officer at the John and Mary R. Markle Foundation. My admiration and respect for its president and visionary leader, Lloyd Morrisett, was and remains boundless. Morrisett was far ahead of his time. He was among the first to recognize the profound influence of mass media on society and the power of technology to amplify that influence. He also believed that mass media could be a source of great educational value. From this insight and relentless commitment came the Children's Television Workshop and its flagship program, *Sesame Street*. He was CTW chairman for decades and is now chair emeritus.

Over four years, he showed me the power of sound, business-based philanthropy, as well as the transformative effect of having confidence in a vision. Morrisett never sought the spotlight. Unassuming and humble, but extremely focused, he didn't get lost in ungrounded ideas and grand ideals. Rather, his energy went directly into effecting change. For me, it was an exhilarating experience that redefined the role and possibilities of philanthropy. He liked to say that he ran Markle not like a foundation but like a venture capital company that measured the success of an investment by social benefit rather than by financial profit. Fifty years later, we call this kind of effort social innovation or impact investing. He didn't need a special name for it. That was just the way he did it.

The Search Committee

As soon as I read the *New York Times* article about the AFI director stepping down, I set my sights on getting that job. So I focused on being a strong candidate for the AFI directorship. I certainly thought I had a number of advantages, despite my limited executive experience. My family connections were a huge asset: my uncle Arnold had been a founding AFI trustee and my brother David was on the board in 1972. (Following in the family tradition, David had a remarkable career that started during the heyday of United Artists, where he rose to president of production and marketing by the age of thirty-one, a story he tells in *Musts, Maybes, and Never: A Book About the Movies.*) In addition, Richard Brandt, who had been chair of the executive committee and was on the board search committee for the next director, was a longtime friend of the Picker family. Richard had been brought onto the AFI board at the suggestion of my uncle Arnold and, over the years, served in many leadership positions, including a strong stint as board chair during particularly hard years. His tireless efforts throughout many decades made AFI what it is today. Along the way, he became and is today a very close friend.

At the time, I cautiously used my married name—Firstenberg—to downplay my family connections. While I knew that my maiden name had opened the door for me to be considered for the position, I really wanted to win the job on my own merits (imagine that). The family connection, though, did have a way of dispelling doubts about my potential. Once someone made the Picker connection, their response was always something like, "Well, why didn't you tell me that first?" People who knew my brother said, "Oh, she's David Picker's sister. She'll be fine." Film still remains a field where relationships and family connections matter, at least to open the door.

As the interview process began, I thought I did well with board members on the East Coast, but those on the West Coast were not as comfortable with me. They thought I only knew film and television from an East Coast perspective, and clearly, I had never lived or spent much time in L.A. I was beginning to sense a coastal divide in the cultures of power and approaches to film.

The search committee narrowed the field to three finalists and called us to L.A. for the last round of interviews on October 12, 1979. This date happened to coincide with the opening day of the first AFI Conference on Education, a three-day program the Markle Foundation had funded with $15,000 at my instigation. The conference included an open meeting of the AFI Board of Trustees. Interviews began immediately after a luncheon at which Congressman John Brademas (D-IN) spoke about his support of the then-beleaguered NEA and AFI. Even before the Reagan years and culture wars of the '80s, it was becoming clear that federal funding would be a major challenge for any nonprofit cultural organization going forward.

I remember telling the search committee that, while I had never raised funds for an organization, I had sat on the giving side of the table and thought I knew what needed to be done on the asking side (why the committee believed such nonsense, I have no idea). My work as a Markle Foundation program officer spoke volumes.

For years, the AFI had been somewhere in my peripheral vision. During President Kennedy's administration, I had briefly worked for George Stevens Jr. when he was at the U.S. Information Agency, arranging the U.S. delegation to the 1965 Moscow Film Festival. In 1976, when I was at the Markle Foundation, we had funded the third and fourth cycles of the AFI's Directing Workshop for Women (DWW). In 1977, because of the DWW funding, I was invited to AFI's Tenth Anniversary celebration at the White House, followed by a gala event at the Kennedy Center for the Performing Arts. It was a glamorous event, with the worlds of Hollywood and DC coming together. It also felt like a return to what I knew. Where I had once worked for George, now I hoped to succeed him at the AFI. As I look back on it now, I cannot believe how audacious I was to even envision such a huge leap.

The Friday interview ended, and then the waiting began.

Mostly, I remember sitting in my hotel room waiting for a call, an answer one way or the other. But in fact there were two more days of the conference to attend. I moderated a session on the topic of giving with officials from the NEA, Ford, and Rockefeller Foundations and the young documentarian, Barbara Kopple. One of the early recipients of an AFI Independent Filmmakers Grant, Barbara received an Academy Award for Best Documentary for *Harlan*

"AFI has had an incredible and lasting impact on my life and career. When I was struggling in the coal fields of Kentucky, filming on the picket lines, in the jails, courtrooms, and the homes of the striking miners for my first film, *Harlan County USA*, I received one of the first Independent Filmmaker Grants given by AFI. That $10,000 grant meant everything—it meant that people cared about the work I was doing, and that funding would be available to carry me and my crew through the production. More than the money, the idea that AFI, an organization so respected, had seen the footage and wanted to support the film gave me the confidence to push on and finish it.

"Years later I was honored to serve two terms on the board of trustees. As an independent documentary filmmaker coming from New York, it was an education to work with educators, heads of studios, corporate representatives, and other filmmakers to ensure AFI's national role would always be at the forefront. I used to take a deep breath and just dive in, to push for projects I believed in, and it meant so much to have my voice heard and respected by the AFI board. I continue to be honored to have my films shown at AFI festivals in L.A. and Washington, DC, because I know they will be great events. AFI stands alone as an institution: celebrating filmmakers, teaching the next generation, and keeping the future of American filmmaking strong and inclusive."

—BARBARA KOPPLE,
documentarian and AFI trustee (2001–2010)

County USA, a film named to the Library of Congress National Film Registry of historic films in 1991. It was my pleasure to become her friend over the years and to have her participation on the AFI Board of Trustees from 2001 to 2010.

It was late Sunday night when the call finally came. To this day, I am still confused about what George told me. I think he said I was the search committee's choice, but it was very close, and they didn't want to tell anyone anything without additional meetings with trustees on both coasts before making any formal announcement. *And* I was not to tell anyone—*not anyone!*

Oh, and there was one other thing. One of the finalists had put his name forward very late in the process. Ted Perry was a respected, credentialed leader in the preservation field. He had run the magnificent film program at the Museum of Modern Art in New York and had recently been named director of the British Film Institute. But he had withdrawn after the announcement, because his family decided they did not want to move to London. So, while I was the likely choice of the search committee, they wanted to keep Ted involved and were asking him to immediately become a member of the AFI Board of Trustees. Was this his consolation prize?

I might have been new to executive politics, but I knew this situation was a bit of hedging that could be awkward. I couldn't imagine how you could ask someone who did not get the job to sit on the board. But I'm glad they did, because he served as a very productive member of the AFI board. Despite this beginning, he was a very productive member of the AFI board and became a good friend.

Of course I told my brother, but he, too, was confused by what I thought I had heard. He advised me not to tell anyone—including our parents. He thought they might be too excited not to share the news. As it happened, I deeply regret that I never got to tell my mother. On November 1, 1979, she had a massive heart attack and died in Los Angeles, where my parents were attending a National Association of Theatre Owners Convention at the Bonaventure

Hotel. The next seven weeks, with many meetings on both coasts as my agreement was being finalized, turned out to be more challenging than I could ever imagine.

Finally, a press conference was called for November 26, 1979, at the Kennedy Center. AFI co-chair Charlton Heston flew in, an impressive presence throughout the search process. Chuck was very forceful about his dedication to AFI and how much he cared about its future. He gave me confidence, even as doubt was being cast my way.

New Director for a New Decade

And so, on January 1, 1980, it was in many ways a re-launch for AFI: a new decade with a new director and CEO. After twelve and a half years, the AFI had some amazing accomplishments. I have nothing but admiration for what founding director George Stevens Jr. was able to do in those years. Starting something from scratch is always the hardest.

Based on its own founding mandate in 1965, the National Endowment for the Arts had commissioned an AFI design study by the Stanford Research Institute. Published in February 1967, "Organization and Location of the American Film Institute" proposed a range of ideas on the nature, structure, and activities of an American Film Institute. While the need for such a study was obvious at the time, the resulting document certainly did not create a particularly practical or insightful blueprint from which to build. Nonetheless, AFI was both bold and aggressive in its launch, and its leadership was strong and unflinching.

Founding director George Stevens Jr. described this in his usual bright style in a January 6, 1980, *New York Times* op-ed article. His assessment was that "building an institution is like a war. You plan a strategy and then proceed to make brave sallies, commit tactical errors, win and lose battles and—either win or lose the war." AFI had survived, "taken root and begun to influence our culture," and was primed "to take its place, in the next decade, beside the Smithsonian Institution and the National Gallery of Art as one of our most vital institutions."

Indeed, much had been accomplished. However, what I would find awaiting me as I stepped into my new position was quite different.

First Challenge: The Washburn Report

On January 19, 1980, I headed to California for my first trip in my new role. I was to meet with the West Coast part of the AFI at Greystone, the Doheny Mansion in Beverly Hills where the Center for Advanced Film Studies (CAFS) was situated. I was also to meet renowned director and chair of the NEA-AFI panel Robert Wise, who began his storied career as editor of *Citizen Kane* (1941) and went on to direct, among others, *West Side Story* (1961) and *The Sound of Music* (1965)—both films winning the Oscar for Best Picture and Best Director. I was excited and resolute (who wouldn't be?). I also had no inkling of the shock that was just around the corner.

On my way to L.A., I had stopped in New York City to meet with Joseph E. Levine, a major AFI donor and producer of *Carnal Knowledge*, *The Graduate*, and *The Lion in Winter*. Joe told me that he broke into the business only because my father played his film, *Hercules*, in the Loews circuit when no other exhibitor would play it. So he immediately thought of me as a friend, and it was mutual. Joe called me "Madam President" over and over again (even though my then-title was director and CEO). He made me feel special.

I arrived in L.A. at 2:00 AM after a delayed flight and, with little sleep, went on to Greystone and then hors d'oeuvres late in the afternoon at Robert and Millicent Wise's condo in the new Century

City Towers. We were joined by two other members of the NEA-AFI panel: agent and former AFI staff member John Ptak, and respected screenwriter and Oscar recipient Dan Taradash. There, they handed me the NEA Washburn Report, a hostile, contentious, innuendo-filled analysis of AFI's spending of government and taxpayer money. This was the first (but not the last) time that the NEA-AFI panel, in formal or informal settings, aggressively put AFI's performance on trial.

They told me that the report actually accused AFI of misappropriating funds. How do you respond to that sort of ambush as a white-gloved butler is offering you canapés? It was four against one, with Millie chiming in with her own opinion of AFI's activities. Bob ended the show after about ninety minutes and took us all to a lovely Italian restaurant a few blocks away on Pico Boulevard. As I tried to sort out what had just happened, Bob sat next to me, chatty and friendly, as if he were a long-lost uncle catching up after not seeing me for years. For a couple of years, I would experience this "split personality." In his official position as chair of the NEA panel, Bob was openly hostile. In a social setting, Bob was utterly charming. One of the best things that happened for AFI was that, in 1982, Bob left the NEA panel and became part of the AFI family. As chair of CAFS and vice chairman of the AFI Board of Trustees, he was deferred to as one of the most respected members of the creative community. He became a dear friend and seemed much more comfortable being a favorite uncle than an adversary.

My predecessor had been sent the Washburn Report in November 1979 but chose not to show it to me. As it turned out, he was right; had I read it then, I might have run for the hills. Now, just weeks into my directorship, I seriously wondered what I had gotten myself into.

It took six months for all parties to agree that the Washburn Report was, in fact, only a politically driven hatchet job and completely inaccurate. A delegation of AFI trustees and I met in DC with the NEA in April 1980 to try to calm their chronic distress over AFI. Executive committee chair Gordon Stulberg flew in from California, Richard Brandt and Ted Perry came down from New York City, and trustee and general counsel Harry McPherson came from across the street to meet with NEA leaders to try to define how the relationship between AFI and the NEA could be more constructive and positive. The NEA's concerns went to accounting, funding, matching grants—complex questions of what programs their funds would or wouldn't support. Everyone tried very hard to turn the page and start anew, but many battles had already been fought and the atmosphere was tense, to say the least.

I quickly bonded with my CFO, Bruce Neiner, during those months. He was the voice of reason and spent many hours explaining to me why there wasn't a shred of truth to the Washburn analysis. Thanks to Bruce and Eamon Kelly, a brilliant consultant whom I brought in to review the report, AFI survived this traumatic moment, but not without a great deal of work and much initial uncertainty.

Second Challenge: Finding AFI's Home

The second huge challenge that loomed over 1980 was the fact that AFI was about to lose its West Coast address, and we needed to find an appropriate location for the Center for Advanced Film Studies in Los Angeles. The identification and acquisition of a home for AFI and CAFS would turn out to be another re-launch of the Institute, and would become both the literal and figurative foundation for defining basic assumptions about the role of AFI in the cultural landscape of America.

As an East Coast native, I was fully committed to the AFI headquarters in Washington, DC. But the AFI-West, as it was called then, was in need of change. On that first fateful visit to L.A., the staff had asked me, "Where are we going to go?" In another revelation that hadn't been clear before my appointment, I saw how crowded and inadequate Greystone had become.

The Doheny Mansion had been home to CAFS for ten years and was beloved by everyone. But its original lease for $1 per year was up, and the city of Beverly Hills offered to extend it—for a low, commercial-level monthly rental fee of $15,000. The original lease had provided a brilliant beginning for a start-up center, but now it was time to "grow up" and settle into a more appropriate and permanent home. Starting in 1976, a board site-search committee had begun to look for a new location, and the search had gone down several trails that led nowhere. At one point, it focused on trying to create an AFI Theatre Center, with a major film exhibition program like the one at the Kennedy Center to establish a larger presence in L.A. There had even been discussions about a joint venture with Filmex, the start-up Los Angeles film festival that presented something of a threat to AFI in 1980. Ironically, AFI would agree to take over Filmex responsibilities within a decade.

From my years at Princeton University, I knew how transformative a campus acquisition could be. As CFO, my then-husband had been responsible for the enormous real estate property Princeton owned around its campus—over 1,000 acres. During the economic downturn of the 1970s, Princeton needed further financial resources, even beyond its remarkable alumni giving. Through an extraordinary process I observed closely, the Princeton Forrestal Center was developed. (I played a tiny part, putting together a slideshow—the analog precursor to PowerPoint presentations—to help convince Princeton trustees of the project's strategic value.) Its long-range goal was to influence the quality of development in the area surrounding the Forrestal Campus and, at the same time, generate substantial, permanent income for its own educational objectives. Princeton Forrestal Center is similar to the Stanford Research Park, both home to extraordinary facilities and companies that complement the institutions' academic objectives while making enormous contributions to the institutions' financial resources. I knew from this experience that finding a home for AFI was about much more than real estate.

The first and only Los Angeles property I looked at was the Immaculate Heart College (IHC) campus in Hollywood, a six-mile drive east from Greystone to Western and Franklin Avenues. The 8.6-acre campus had buildings, landscaping, paths, and views. It had something spiritual and majestic about it. Everyone who went there loved it.

The first time I walked around the IHC campus, I knew it could work. The move would be a transition from a magnificent (but faded) mansion with gardens and stables (serving as editing bays) to the foot of the Hollywood Hills with a view of the Dodger Stadium lights at night. It was an oasis in the middle of the moviemaking capital of the world, with the original studio lots that created Hollywood just down the street and over the hillside.

Founded by the Sisters of the Immaculate Heart of Mary in 1916, the women's non-residential day college had gradually evolved into a co-ed day campus for students who returned to academia later in life. Sister Corita Kent, who headed IHC's art department, was the college's most recognizable figure, known as an energetic anti-war activist-artist and friend of poet Daniel Berrigan. This strong-minded order of nuns had lost the support of the Catholic Church after their Vatican II–inspired reforms caused a public standoff with the conservative Cardinal James Francis McIntyre, Archbishop of Los Angeles.

The sisters were forced to sell the campus to eliminate their substantial debt and to care for their own elderly flock. As we explored the possibility of a sale, I was deeply impressed with the nobility of these women and their leadership. I was humbled by their grace and pride in the beauty of their campus, a spot where you could see the ocean during the day and the downtown lights twinkling at night. (And the respect carried forward. In 2016, at my first meeting as a new member of the California State University Board of Trustees, trustee Douglas Faigin introduced himself and said his late wife, Mary Jane Pew, had been acting president of Immaculate Heart College when AFI bought the campus in 1980. Faigin said she had always spoken highly of me. She had been Governor Jerry Brown's assistant campaign manager during his first election, so when Governor Brown was considering my appointment to the Cal State board, he had asked Faigin about me.)

The campus had become fairly down-at-the-heels and was in need of repairs, but it would give us a prodigious start. It felt right in a way that Greystone's elitist Beverly Hills location and faded grandeur had not. AFI, after all, had its beginnings in LBJ's Great Society, with its vision of democratizing opportunity and access. A mansion in Beverly Hills didn't really embody that message. It would feel a lot more comfortable asking supporters to embrace a traditional campus structure in the heart of Los Angeles, at Western and Franklin, than a reclusive gated landmark in Beverly Hills. And, as I later realized, the NEA really was embarrassed to be supporting a mansion in the 90210 area code, which only added irritation to an already tense relationship.

The Ask

Robert O. Anderson, the chair and CEO of Atlantic Richfield, only spent Mondays in Los Angeles. He lived in New Mexico and didn't like city life very much. His company had built the twin ARCO Towers in downtown L.A. in 1972–1973, with fifty-two floors and a novel underground shopping center. Anderson could see me at 4:00 PM on Monday, March 31. I would just have time to get to the Oscars, being telecast a few blocks away at the Dorothy Chandler Pavilion of the Los Angeles Music Center.

Ninety days after arriving at AFI, I drove downtown in my rental car and entered the ARCO Towers through a private elevator that went directly to Anderson's office on the fifty-second floor. (Patricia Neal did the same thing in *The Fountainhead*, where Gary Cooper was waiting for her.) Anderson heard my pitch: AFI wanted to buy the IHC campus and have a permanent home in Los Angeles. Did he think this was a smart thing to do? Would he help with the acquisition? Forty-five minutes later, Anderson blessed the idea and gave us the credibility, confidence, and sheer bravado to launch a rapid, intensive capital campaign to acquire a spectacular campus in the middle of Hollywood at a very fair price. His commitment: a $1 million loan with interest to be paid by the ARCO Foundation, though this became no small detail when interest rates rose to twenty percent. In addition, the services of a young real estate consultant, C. Thomas Ruppert, were paid for by ARCO. There was one caveat—ARCO would not be the large gift. There was never an easier ask, there was never a quicker response, and nothing would ever be that simple or straightforward again. But what a way to start!

The same private elevator took me down to my car. The Bonaventure Hotel was a few blocks away—the hotel where my mother had had a heart attack and died just months before. I went there to the ladies room, changed into my Oscars dress, and was in my seat at the Dorothy Chandler Pavilion in time for the opening of the fifty-second Academy Awards telecast.

An AFI board and search committee member, Fay Kanin, had given me the tickets. She was the second woman to become president of the Academy of Motion Picture Arts and Sciences. (Bette Davis was elected president in 1941, but resigned after two months because of disagreements about certain Academy policies in wartime.) This was Fay's first opportunity to speak at the Oscars telecast. In a magnificent red Bob Mackie dress, Fay ascended from the bowels of the stage as the announcer said, "Ladies and gentleman! The president of the Academy of Motion Picture Arts and Sciences—Mister Fay Kanin!" If you look at the clip of the ceremony in the AMPAS archives, however, you will not hear "Mr. Fay Kanin." It has been changed for posterity.

Fay didn't hear the intro, because she was below stage level. Just as well. It was another sign to me that, as a woman, I was not even expected to be here. In 1980, it was a surprise to see a woman running a nonprofit entity, whether the long-respected AMPAS or the young AFI. But even today, more work needs to be done to support a diversity of voices and stories in film and filmmaking. Also, Fay made a meaningful remark about the value of movies and the stories they tell: "Movies have become national treasures to be preserved and esteemed as much as a nation's art and music."

Supporters Step Up

The swiftness of the campaign to acquire the campus took everyone's breath away. When potential supporters visited the campus, they immediately understood why the AFI wanted it. Immaculate Heart College hoped to get $6.5 million. The valuation came in at $5.9 million, but there would be considerable renovations, maintenance, and move-in costs.

We decided on $10 million—a nice round number—for the capital campaign. The momentum was palpable. The board was with us, responding to the patchwork development and consultant team. There weren't many turndowns, and, crucially, there weren't many competing offers to acquire the campus. We found new friends, like Roz Wyman, who had been appointed to the National Council on the Arts by President Jimmy Carter in 1979 and also knew people on the IHC board who became our advocates, especially Linda Hope and Martin Gang, chair of the IHC board. They were greatly respected and helped galvanize the community with an energetic enthusiasm that only a new, unwavering optimism can generate.

On May 29, 1980, the board met and authorized AFI to

continue fundraising and proceed to a potential bid. On July 25, a special dinner meeting of the board was held in the pool house of executive committee chair Gordon Stulberg's home on Comstock Avenue in Westwood. Sixteen of twenty-five board members attended.

Making the best case for the campaign was Steve Broidy, one of Los Angeles's greatest fundraisers. Steve was a film executive and active philanthropist who had sold the original Mount Sinai Hospital in Hollywood and built the new Cedars-Sinai Medical Center in Beverly Hills. In 1962, he had received the Jean Hersholt Humanitarian Award from the Academy of Motion Picture Arts and Sciences. Now, he made an impassioned speech about the value of the property and what it would mean to the future of AFI. ("It's only money!" he declared.) Broidy's contacts in the banking world also proved to be significant to the deal. Together with his close friend Harry Volk, then chairman of Union Bank, they negotiated for loans and a mortgage that would be favorable for AFI.

Another major reason for AFI's early progress and its long-term success was the remarkable history of support from Warner Bros., starting with Jack Warner's original gift of $250,000 to build the AFI Theater at the John F. Kennedy Center for the Performing Arts in 1973. Support for the campus acquisition was immediately in play with two advocates: Ted Ashley, chairman of Warner Bros. and an AFI board member, led the way, while Steve Ross, who had bought Warner Bros. and created Warner Communications, lent his imprimatur with a $1.5 million commitment. (Almost immediately, that commitment was raised to $2 million to name a screening room in honor of Ted Ashley.) Bob Daly soon succeeded Ted Ashley as Warner Bros. chairman and became, over time, the most committed board leader in AFI's fifty-year history.

At the time, Daniel Selznick, former AFI trustee and grandson of Louis B. Mayer, was serving a brief stint as chair of the Louis B. Mayer Foundation. In this role, he gave AFI a $1 million gift to name the library after his grandfather. Timing is everything.

Other gifts in smaller denominations followed suit, until a pledged sum of $4.5 million plus the ARCO $1 million loan gave the board considerable security to move forward with a bid to acquire the campus. On August 26, almost six months from the day I had first seen the IHC campus, I walked down its hillside with Charlton Heston, Steve Broidy, and the acting president of IHC, Mary Jane Pew, to announce to the press that AFI had signed a letter of intent to purchase the campus. Bottom line, AFI acquired 8.6 acres of real estate, with an educational variance, for $4.7 million—simply a great deal.

There were many heroes in this effort. The many supporters include Russ Mead, consultant extraordinaire; Kathy Hammer, a brilliant young woman who was on the staff when I arrived; C. Thomas Ruppert, whose expertise was invaluable and whose memos to the files were poetic; Bob Blumofe, head of AFI-West; National Council on the Arts member Roz Wyman, a prominent member of the L.A. political and cultural world; and F. Keenan Behrle, who joined our legal team late in the process, held my hand through the long negotiations, and, when we signed the final papers, asked, "Are you having lender's remorse?" I replied, "No—buyer's fear!"

Despite never having lived in Los Angeles (and never expecting to move to the West Coast) I instinctively knew the AFI campus would work. It was a beautiful campus with proud roots, at a central location between many sectors of the large Los Angeles metropolitan area. Looking at the totality of the opportunity, between its cultural heritage, aesthetic beauty, geographic location, and financial cost, acquiring the IHC campus just seemed the right thing to do. Without explicitly saying so, it was now time to move past the internal AFI cultural divide between East Coast and West Coast.

Transition in Titles

When I joined AFI in 1980, my title was director and CEO, as was my predecessor's. Given AFI's origins, this term was appropriate for the Washington agency culture it emerged from. When I retired twenty-seven years and ten months later, my title was president and CEO. (AFI had only used the title president in an honorific way for Charlton Heston after he resigned as chair in 1983 and held the title president until his death in 2003.)

It was my opinion that the next person running AFI should have the title president rather than director, because we had become a fully accredited academic institution where the title director was no longer appropriate. In 2006, at the first meeting of the search committee, I explained my rationale for changing the title for my successor. The thoughtful Bob Daly interjected that if my successor were to be given a different title, it would seem that he or she was assuming a different responsibility. Therefore, my title should become president and CEO immediately. The trustees amended the bylaws, we printed new business cards, and the title was changed on the stationery and the website. No press release was sent out. No one ever asked me about the change.

So, for twenty-five years, my title was director and CEO, but for the last eighteen months or so it was president and CEO. When my retirement began, the board graciously named me president emerita and a lifetime trustee only because Bob Daly had changed my title.

With its leadership and education mission together in one center, AFI could become more than the sum of its parts. Truly, it could be a relaunch of a national mission and vision.

Sometimes your life experiences combine to prepare you for a certain moment. Looking back, this was the moment I had been preparing for.

A Whole New Identity

As my first year with AFI came to an end, much had changed, and even more changes were on the horizon. The campus made it possible for AFI to plant deeper roots in California. I never thought I would leave the East Coast. I was a New Yorker to my core, loved Washington, DC, and thought the "Bos-Wash" corridor would be the range of my living experience. But the AFI campus was a magnet for me personally, and it is very hard to build the culture and environment for a community from 2,500 miles away. By 1982, I was paying taxes in California, and I haven't changed my zip code since.

Although AFI was and is a national organization, it didn't need to have headquarters and principal offices in Washington, DC, next to the NEA and the federal government. While government support would continue on for eighteen more years, it was, at best, a precarious source of funding, up for renewal (or not) every year. I knew from experience that no organization can confidently program or plan with that financial structure. AFI had to be seen as central to the artistic and commercial community that it represented, while also maintaining its independence. That balance was—and still is—always in play.

Because of this confluence of circumstances, AFI adjusted its position and became an entity with far more credibility. A whole new identity opened up, changing the way AFI was perceived nationally by the creative community, corporate entities, and funding bodies. By taking the future in our own hands, we showed the NEA that AFI was stable, growing, and energized, and it would continue to fight for its part of the media arts budget.

The Center for Advanced Film Studies, begun with such enormous promise, entered a new phase. It had a permanent home and now deserved its own identity as an accredited educational entity. That immediately became my next focus and goal.

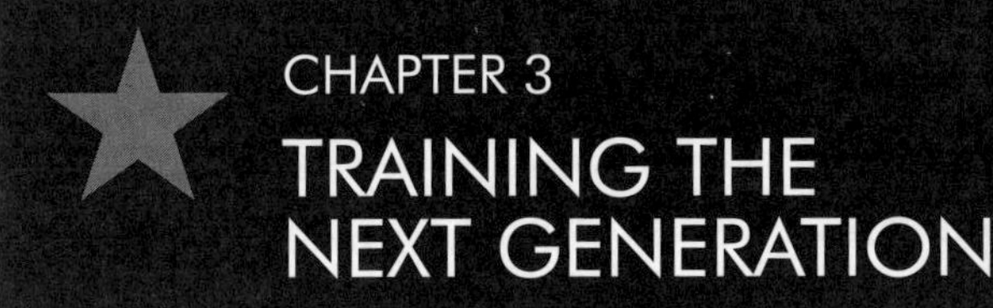

CHAPTER 3

TRAINING THE NEXT GENERATION

From the Center for Advanced Film Studies to the AFI Conservatory

James Hindman

In 1969, just two years after AFI was founded, the Center for Advanced Film Studies—CAFS, as it came to be called—was opened at Greystone, the Doheny estate in Beverly Hills, California. The story of how CAFS developed over the next five decades, quickly becoming an international beacon for serious talent in cinematic arts, is a classic Hollywood tale of adventure, high art, and low comedy.

From its inception, AFI CAFS was never envisioned as a traditional academic institution. Even today, as a freestanding and fully accredited graduate school known as the AFI Conservatory (the title was changed in 2000), it still has neither sponsorship from nor affiliation with any university. Admission has always been based on expressive talent and evidence of creative potential, not on previous academic achievement. With a typical enrolled population of some 250, the AFI Conservatory now has only twelve full-time faculty. The rest of the senior staff of around sixty-five are working professionals who make their rich experience in the field available to AFI on a part-time basis, as adjunct faculty. About one-third of those enrolled are from outside the United States, talented young people from all over the world who have sought out the unusual brand of training that the AFI Conservatory offers. And since its founding, the young people enrolled in the Conservatory have been referred to as "Fellows," recognizing the caliber of those accepted as exceptional, while emphasizing their aspiration to become members of a unique creative community with expectations of advanced and mature work.

> "Our goal in bringing professional artists to the Center is not solely to assist you who will study here, but also to create a tutorial tradition for film such as exists in architecture, music, and medicine—a tradition which can grow to the benefit of universities across the country. Before long, we hope, the finest filmmakers will accept teaching as a rewarding part of their creative lives."
>
> —GEORGE STEVENS JR., writer-producer and AFI founding director

Perhaps the most telling measure of the Conservatory's success in defining and meeting its mission is the professional success of its alumni, whose accomplishments in the aggregate are truly astounding. Now approaching a mid-century mark, the Conservatory's story stands as a tribute to those who founded it and to those who have nurtured it along the way.

Origins

The AFI Conservatory is itself a mosaic of personal stories, requiring more than a simple recitation of the historical record. Certain defining moments and choices have given the Conservatory a resilience and strength that has endured, even as the field itself—moving-image storytelling—has changed beyond recognition. In reviewing my own memories as well as key documents and a detailed timeline, the Conservatory's guiding principles and distinct phases clearly stand out: the Frank Daniel moment, the Toni Vellani decade, Dezsö Magyar's time(s), Frank Pierson's era, and then the Sam Grogg and Bob Mandel (class of 1977) years. Those of us who have been privileged to work in the trenches there on a daily basis will recognize both the pain and the joy of many of those defining moments, and it's a great pleasure to share them with generations to come.

At AFI's founding in the 1960s, with few exceptions, any sort of program in film studies was a radical and new concept in higher education, and certainly academically suspect. Even at their best, movies were understood as a form of popular entertainment; the practice of movie-making was seen as an arcane craft with little relation to the academic disciplines—primarily humanities and sciences—that were the proper purview of a university worthy of the name. When it opened its doors in 1969 with the best of intentions, the AFI and CAFS leadership had to invent every wrinkle and policy of its operation, usually in direct response to some immediate crisis. AFI CAFS was invented out of whole cloth, and it has continued to reinvent itself along the way as circumstances dictated. Only in hindsight does its success begin to look likely, based as it was in a clear mission, sound pedagogy, shared values, and strong leadership.

My Introduction

My personal connection to CAFS began a decade into its existence. In the late 1970s, I was director of the graduate program in theatre at American University in Washington, DC, and had become deeply interested in the emergence of video as a field of study. My friend and colleague, Larry Kirkman, who had run the television program at American University and who had deep roots in the independent and community video world, was recruited by AFI's founding director, George Stevens Jr., to develop a robust television and video program for AFI, which was at that time still headquartered at the Kennedy Center in Washington, DC (with CAFS soon to move to a campus in Los Angeles).

I knew little about AFI or its activities, and Larry's stories about the range of its programs and personalities on both coasts were fascinating. My impression was that AFI was attempting to play on a national stage, to support the development of a deep culture of cinema in the United States—a fairly novel notion at that time. And through CAFS, AFI aspired to create a European-style fine-art training program for advanced, deeply talented filmmakers who were determined to revolutionize American film.

CAFS itself was described as being run by an autocratic Italian grand master, Antonio Vellani, a director who had worked closely with Roberto Rossellini and George Stevens Sr., and who reflected a classic Hollywood perspective toward film aesthetics, grammar, and practice in his teaching. He was also known for his temper and heavy hand with Fellows. Anxiety about his approval or contempt dominated the atmosphere of CAFS. Other AFI staff generally kept their distance.

Nevertheless, by the late '70s, CAFS was already famous for the initial success of its early alumni, particularly David Lynch (class of 1970), who had finished the edit of his distinctive film *Eraserhead* while living secretly in the stables of Greystone. Terrence Malick (class of 1969), Paul Schrader (class of 1969), Caleb Deschanel (class of 1969), and others' strong recent successes had created an enormous mystique around CAFS.

My first visit to Greystone came in March 1981. While on sabbatical from American University, I had gone to work with Larry Kirkman, then ramping up the new AFI program, TV and video services, with a particular mandate (but few resources) to provide support and outreach to the burgeoning independent video community nationally—something of great importance to our prickly friends and funders at the National Endowment for the Arts.

Kirkman and I were asked to visit and address an AFI board meeting about an exciting new venture, the National Video Festival, underwritten with a large grant from Sony Corporation, to take place at the Kennedy Center in June of 1981. The board then included figures like the notorious studio head David Begelman and producers David Brown, Samuel Goldwyn Jr., and Joseph E. Levine. It also marked the first board meeting for Bob Daly, David Lynch, and Bonita Granville Wrather, each of whom have played a large part in the evolution of AFI. Addressing the board was intimidating and very exciting, but my time at Greystone was odd. Despite the shabby grandeur of the shopworn house and grounds, it was clear that CAFS was an island unto itself—isolated and inwardly turned, with little interest in much else that the rest of AFI was up to. We were thoroughly snubbed and ignored, but we weren't daunted. It was clear that the landscape was changing, and the increasing role of video and television in the cinematic arts would not be denied.

Learning the History

I learned what I could about CAFS. Launched shortly after AFI first opened its doors, it was viewed as central to the core mission of the new AFI. The initial policy document purporting to set the direction for the future AFI, the Stanford Research Institute (SRI) Report of 1966, "Organization and Location of the American Film Institute," suggested that the primary purpose and mission of the Institute would be to enhance and improve the quality of American film—a fairly grandiose aspiration. As the report put it, "The training of the artists who create film is perhaps the most important single function which a national film institution could undertake. . . . There is no other function that could have so direct a bearing on the

> "AFI opens doors for the filmmakers. AFI puts filmmakers on the map. AFI informs—inspires—and supports filmmakers. AFI reveres and protects the motion pictures and all those who make them—past, present, and future. I love AFI."
>
> —DAVID LYNCH, artist and filmmaker (class of 1970)

state of the art or so immediate an effect on the quality of the art." AFI's training arm would be at the heart of these activities. It was hoped that AFI's efforts would help establish cinema in the United States as a popular but genuine art form, to be taken seriously, with support from the federal government and the general public. A primary means of achieving this mission would be to have AFI establish a successful training program for future filmmakers, filling a genuine void in the wild and woolly American system.

The SRI report cast about in vain for appropriate models for AFI to follow in establishing such a program. American universities had recently begun to teach film studies, primarily through appreciation courses, with a few classes in practical filmmaking staged initially at the major Los Angeles and New York university campuses. However, the SRI report did not see universities as useful models for AFI because of the absence of professional filmmakers as faculty, as well as the lack of professional standards and conditions in classrooms. There were no film schools that taught through practice, and when they did, they usually followed an industrial film model, rather than a strict focus on narrative storytelling. But after AFI was launched, George Stevens Jr. visited film schools in France, Poland, Russia, and Czechoslovakia to flesh out a perspective on what AFI's Center for Advanced Film Studies should be, a perspective that continues to influence its guiding principles.

Rigorous film training programs existed at a number of European art schools that the SRI/AFI planning team also visited. But these were also seen as ineffective models for AFI, because they were focused primarily on serving and protecting their own subsidized national film industries, and they were directly funded and controlled as government entities.

The major American film studios were ceasing to function as the "producing" structures of American movies and were evolving into financing and distribution entities. This also brought an end to traditional studio training and mentoring functions that had been the entryway for new talent into the professions. For example, Fred Zinnemann had been trained by making shorts on the MGM lot with limited shooting time and budgets that won acclaim and catapulted him into the world of feature films. Many other filmmakers had this same trajectory, but now that entryway was no longer available.

Hence, the AFI film training program was launched in something of a vacuum, without guidance or models for its curriculum, funding, policies, or operations. The SRI report seemed to suggest that the filmmaking community itself would be AFI's primary partner in launching and running such a program. As the SRI report said, AFI should:

> *. . . bridge the gap between the academic and professional realm . . . and, include the active participation of outside film makers in the professional development of outstanding prospective students . . . that would be vital to the success of this concept, the profile and ingredients of training programs that have yet to be defined either in the United States or abroad.*

The Launch

So, from the 1969 opening of the AFI Center for Advanced Film Studies—this new, long-term but open-ended program being launched for eighteen Fellows—was to be tutorial and mentor-driven, as were other serious art schools for music, fine art, and dance. As George Stevens Jr. made clear in his opening remarks, the hope was that these program participants, with oversight and help from major visiting professionals, would develop individual film projects, from script to finished movie.

Within the first three years, CAFS workshops were developed for Fellows in screenwriting and directing (including Directing the Actor). Initially, directors were assigned to recreate scenes from extant movies as exercises; eventually, the new Screenwriting Workshop was asked to supply directors with original scenes, then short film scripts.

But the hands-on teaching-and-learning model could be brutal, meant to mimic conditions in the professional world. The critique and analyses of completed projects was the spine of Toni Vellani's Directing Workshop, and the participation of all Fellows was expected. The creative team that had made a particular film sat in enforced silence in front of the entire group of Fellows, enduring an aggressive critique of their often shaky early efforts, with no provision to respond or defend their creative and practical choices. Tears and trauma sometimes resulted, but mistakes were never repeated.

Constant production and critique quickly became the primary teaching tools of CAFS, supplemented by specialized classes within various production disciplines. The tagline was "Learn by doing; study with the Masters"—the ongoing Conservatory mantra to this day.

Participating mentors from the profession gradually evolved into formal but part-time teaching faculty—for example, Nina Foch for Directing the Actor in 1972, Howard Schwartz for Cinematography in 1974, Lois Peyser, Arnold Peyser, and William Fadiman in Screenwriting in the 1970s, and Bob Boyle in Production Design in 1982. New classes were often added on an ad hoc basis, when faculty or staff felt that some current weakness in the Fellows' work had to be addressed.

Unlike the college or university film training models evolving at the time, CAFS had always been built around a single master teacher, which kept the curriculum and the entire program tightly integrated. Frank Daniel, the first master teacher, had run the screenwriting program of the world-renowned Czech film conservatory, FAMU. He was supported by Ján Kadár, a renowned Polish director, and developed the fundamental elements of the CAFS teaching style during the initial three years he ran the program.

The comings and goings of Frank Daniel must be left for another book. The three years of his leadership were experimental and turbulent, just as those years were throughout American higher education in the late 1960s and early '70s. When Frank and some of the most outspoken Fellows decided that Washington, DC, was just too far away and AFI was not providing enough support for the Conservatory, they insisted that the Conservatory should secede and become independent. The board asked Frank to resign, and he did. He went on to serve as head of film programs at American universities into the 1990s, including the University of Southern California and Columbia University.

Also established in the early years, the SAG-AFTRA Conservatory at the AFI has been a tremendous resource for both filmmakers and actors. Working from a unique contract since 1974, the SAG-AFTRA Conservatory provides SAG-AFTRA talent for all first-year cycle projects at no cost to Fellows. Thesis films may (though they are not required to) cast from the SAG-AFTRA Conservatory; all actors on thesis films work under AFI's unique contract, so there is significant budgetary savings for the filmmakers and a substantial level of talent on AFI thesis films. The SAG-AFTRA Conservatory provides not only casting access to AFI films, but also training and classes to their membership. Kathleen Nolan, the Screen Actors Guild's first vice president, made this arrangement possible for both CAFS and Directing Workshop for Women (DWW) productions. Kathleen herself would soon become the first woman to be elected president of SAG and was also a member of the first cycle of DWW.

Leadership: The Vellani Years

By the late 1970s, the basic structure of the overall curriculum had evolved; it remains essentially intact today. CAFS director and master teacher Antonio Vellani led the Directing Workshop—which was the heart of the entire program—with an iron grip, while specific discipline-based classes were offered by an accomplished professional faculty. Given the strength of his personality and the sheer verbal power of his classroom critiques, Toni Vellani's role as master teacher in the CAFS Directing Workshop eventually became the centerpiece of the entire CAFS' pedagogy. The scene projects developed, shot, and critiqued in Toni's Directing Workshop evolved into three groups of cycle short films, made in teams by specialized Fellows organized into traditional production disciplines.

Toni used his critiques to teach classic cinematic storytelling, and he insisted that every aspect of a production and every decision made by each member of the creative team contribute clearly to the dramatic action and character arc of the film. While his bias was toward the director as the primary creative force on the film, he insisted that all Fellows take responsibility for their own creative efforts as full participants in a collaborative art form. The short films produced in three cycles during the program's first year were subject to lengthy critique sessions from all first-year Fellows, carefully orchestrated by Toni to drive home whatever lessons he felt necessary to illustrate the shortcomings in their work. Alumni still talk of the Vellani critiques with shock and awe; they claim they still hear Toni's voice as they work today.

Other master teachers and major professionals took time from eminent careers and left indelible impressions over the years. The arrival of legendary director Robert Wise in 1982 was pivotal in bringing prestige and a higher profile to the center. He was inordinately generous with his time for individual Fellows with crises and problems, and his calm and kindly demeanor did much to balance the overall tone of CAFS.

Highlighting a series of active filmmakers-in-residence was another major figure in CAFS history, director Dan Petrie. He was passionate and deeply committed to the quality, integrity, and seamless operation of CAFS. Like Bob Wise, he became an active AFI trustee and a strong advocate for CAFS with the board. They joined trustee and executive committee member Franklin Schaffner, who also chaired the Conservatory Board Advisory Committee (CBAC)

"The first day as dean of AFI, I walked into my office and saw the four-by-eight, black-and-white poster from Giant—the one of James Dean wearing a Stetson, reclining in the car with the mansion in the background. This was the same photo that hung for so many years on the office wall of Toni Vellani, my much-admired mentor and dean when I was a Fellow from 1977 to 1980. Certainly, one of the main reasons I accepted the new position was because of the influence Toni had on my life. It was an opportunity to repay Toni's generosity of knowledge, by sharing what I had learned with a new generation of filmmakers.

"How I wish the Fellows I see every day could have spent one afternoon with this slight, elegant man wearing an ascot, smoking a cigarette and speaking in his velvet-tongued Italian accent. The words 'droll' and 'witty' don't begin to describe his hilarious, well-intentioned condescension in Narrative Analysis. We came to AFI for an honest appraisal of our work, and we got it. Many would agree that it made us stronger, ready to take on the abuses and the intoxication of our future careers. A compliment from Toni in the morning meant a huge celebration that evening. And, of course, what endeared him to us most was that no matter how harsh his criticism, we knew he was our partner in the struggle to find our voices."

—ROBERT MANDEL,
filmmaker and AFIC dean (class of 1977)

---

that determined CAFS policies. Wise was CAFS chair for several years, followed by Dan Petrie, who was succeeded by Bob Rehme, a major executive, trustee, and longtime supporter. When Schaffner passed away, he was succeeded by Bob Wise with Jon Avnet (class of 1972) as vice chair, and then Avnet went on to serve as chair of the CBAC for many years.

> "You are your best when you talk about things you know something about. When the inspiration for your work comes from your observation of human behavior—not interpreting somebody else's observation about human behavior. In other words, do not conform to things, and don't talk yourself into doing things that you think other people would like you to do for the sake of success or achieving your goals. It is a hopeless enterprise."
>
> —ANTONIO VELLANI, master teacher and artistic director

Through a competitively selected second year of participation, a much smaller group of Fellows from various disciplines would then team up to make a total of three to five elaborate short films, based on strong scripts green-lit by AFI (read Toni Vellani) and largely funded by the Institute. Master of Fine Arts degrees were awarded upon successful completion of second-year films, which included being cleared for distribution. (The first AFI degrees were awarded in 1982 after NASAD accreditation, the first step toward full academic accreditation.) For many, this opened the door to the more coveted prize: a professional career in American independent cinema and television.

Becoming a Formal Institution of Higher Education

My own professional attention during this time was largely focused elsewhere within AFI: developing an elaborate television and video program; keeping our generous friends at Sony happy through a successful Video Festival; growing international programs in India, Japan, and Italy; launching various competitions for amateur video makers and television writers; and arranging conferences and screening series seemingly without end. Constant fundraising was a necessity, with each new program becoming a springboard for the next venture. This activity raised AFI's profile within the creative community (you always needed more contest judges!), but it was always a struggle to keep the bills paid and provide a financial return to the mother ship. I had moved myself and my family permanently to Los Angeles in 1982 with some trepidation, having resigned from a tenured position at American University to cast my professional future with AFI. (My wife, Elizabeth Daley, quickly launched a very active career as a creative television producer that would eventually lead her to become dean of the successful Cinema School at the University of Southern California, seen by many as the AFI Center's primary peer in the newly emerging field of professional film education.)

In 1980, AFI had named its second director and CEO in its history. One of Jean Picker Firstenberg's first acts was to orchestrate the purchase of a campus for CAFS, moving east from Greystone in Beverly Hills to its present location at the foot of Griffith Park. Soon thereafter, AFI headquarters moved its center of gravity from DC to L.A., putting the Institute and CAFS side by side for the first time.

For CAFS, the impact of the move to the new campus was profound. Suddenly, it had gone from a below-the-radar cinema workshop housed in an extraordinary Beverly Hills estate, to what was clearly a college campus. Had it become a real academic institution, as its surroundings proclaimed? With AFI and CAFS in the same walls, how would the two work together? Would resources, energy, and focus be shared, bolstered, or diluted? In 1981, as I settled into the idea of my new Los Angeles base, it was clear to me that the primary business of the new AFI campus was CAFS, and its operations would take precedence. In fact, a multi-year CAFS identity crisis ensued.

The atmosphere in those years was not always ideal. In the 1980s, my office was next door to Toni Vellani's, and the thin walls did nothing to muffle his regular shouted outrage at some unfortunate Fellow who had dared to cross him. We nodded in the halls, Toni and I, but my sources of CAFS gossip would have to lie elsewhere. He didn't report to me, and he had no interest in what I did.

By the time of the move to the new campus, CAFS had established most of its teaching and learning features. Essentially, it worked as an extended workshop program in the strong grip of Toni Vellani, with only minimal outside oversight. Despite some academic window dressing, CAFS actually had few of the operating features of a traditional college or university. Gradually, additions and embellishments in the mid-1980s had a growing impact on the image and perception of it as an academic institution.

Initial CAFS Accreditation

Early internal memoranda show that, within the first few years of the institute's founding, AFI Director George Stevens Jr. explored the possibility of seeking full and formal academic accreditation for the Center for Advanced Film Studies. (The "Advanced" was always a great source of irritation for film academics at universities. "So what are we, chopped liver?" was a famous rejoinder from a UCLA faculty member.) Professor Ray Fielding, a renowned film academic on the AFI board in the mid-1970s, discouraged an AFI attempt to get definitive accreditation as a graduate school by the Western Association of Schools and Colleges (WASC) because CAFS faculty came with few advanced degrees—which proved to be no barrier at all for WASC in later years, given the eminence of CAFS faculty's outsized professional achievements.

While CAFS's first few classes were essentially free, within a few years AFI management was forced to charge real tuition, making access to student loan funds essential. Compared to private universities, tuition costs were initially low: no rent at Greystone, no full-time faculty, a tiny staff, largely donated equipment, etc. But over the first few years, the normal expenses of any academic venture crept in. After the purchase of the Immaculate Heart campus in 1980, it was clear that AFI needed a different foundation for CAFS structure. The clear academic anomalies of CAFS (few Fellows continuing into second year, admission without bachelor's degrees, and a completely part-time faculty with few or no advanced degrees) made an attempt to secure full institutional regional higher-educational accreditation seem much too daunting. But an exciting alternative was presented by the National Association of Schools of Art and Design (NASAD), who seemed intrigued by the notion of joining forces with a film school. Culturally we were a good fit. Faculty profiles were similar, student aspirations were similar, and CAFS could move into its next phase formally defined as an "art school," which, in retrospect, has had a subtle but profound impact on AFI's directions.

NASAD'S goal was to set and maintain standards for art education by accrediting specific art programs, which usually resided within schools, colleges, and universities; they did not accredit the larger institution, but rather the particular program. As a body of professional arts educators, NASAD followed the usual accreditation processes for a specialized single-discipline program (law or medicine, for example), including elaborate self-studies, visits by teams of arts academics, and detailed evaluations of the sometimes-sketchy CAFS curriculum.

The strengths of AFI's existing program were quickly acknowledged by NASAD: CAFS was practical, hands-on, and performance-based; the emphasis was on collaboration and teamwork; the focus was on creating narrative and fiction long-form works as the highest expression of cinematic art. Despite the excellent survey classes called for by Franklin Schaffner and taught by the charismatic Jim Hosney for many years, there was not much film history, documentary, experimental, or international cinema taught, nor critical theory. The program was not faulted for these limitations. Its strengths were seen to come from the very narrowness of its focus, a truth that would stand it in good stead in coming years.

NASAD accreditation gave a strong psychological boost to staff and trustees, reinforcing AFI's emergence as an actual academic institution. Among many advantages, CAFS Fellows became eligible for federal student loans, which gave us a huge marketing advantage. My colleague Jean Firstenberg was soon able to leverage the political clout of backstage AFI supporters to place AFI into a California state bond issue for higher education. This would simultaneously achieve less expensive financing for the purchase of the new campus while creating further traditional academic legitimacy for something as outré as a film conservatory. Thankfully, that also resulted in further assets to remodel the fairly decrepit AFI "house on the hill." (The former owners of the campus, the good, liberal, and outspoken Sisters of the Immaculate Heart, had been under assault by their local reactionary Cardinal McIntyre and had let things go on campus until they were forced to sell the "old home place.") And, sharing the higher education bond issue pool were Stanford University, the University of Southern California, and Pomona College—lovely company to be seen in.

As part of the first NASAD self-study, we surveyed the Fellows of the last three classes. The range of accomplishments was impressive: Bill Duke (class of 1978) went on to be an AFI trustee; Oscar-nominated Pieter Jan Brugge and Stan Brooks (both class of 1979) have been teaching producing classes at AFI for years (Pieter has also been an outstanding Narrative Workshop leader); Joe Garrity (class of 1979) heads the production design discipline; Robert Elswit (class of 1977) is an Oscar-winning cinematographer; and Robert Mandel (class of 1977) went on to a fine directing career and then became dean of the AFI Conservatory. This amazing array of alumni demonstrates a deep commitment to their AFI experience.

One Fellow, Gary Winick (class of 1986), found his experience so invigorating that he audiotaped all of Toni Vellani's classes and then had the transcription edited and sent it to Jean and myself, hoping we would publish it. It finally became the source of the book we edited and dedicated to Winick after his untimely death of brain cancer at the age of forty-nine. *The AFI Conservatory: Toni Vellani on the Practice of Filmmaking; Compiled by Gary Winick, AFI Class of 1986* (AFI Press 2013) is presented to every new class entering the AFI Conservatory.

AFI Commencement was introduced in 1986 with NASAD accreditation, a symbolic shift in how AFI saw itself. The idea met resistance from strong supporters and good friends of AFI who felt that a graduation ceremony compromised a commitment to artistic attainment as the only measure of the Fellows' success; in this view, a diploma was meaningless—only the film should matter. The formal program event for second-year Fellows who completed graduation requirements evolved into a full-tilt ceremony, complete with live music, caps, and gowns and a carefully staged processional for trustees and senior officers, faculty, and graduates. Suddenly, we were carrying out the rituals of a traditional academic institution. Held in a beautiful glade at the top of the campus, it became a lovely occasion for Fellows to celebrate with family and loved ones, dressed to the nines.

Honorary degrees were added in 1989, presented with full pomp and circumstance, giving CAFS and AFI an additional opportunity to celebrate the careers of a wide range of figures from the moving image arts and major contributors to our culture and society (see this distinguished list of honorary degree recipients in the Appendix). Commencement became, for me and most of the staff, the high point of AFI's year.

"The honorary degree you bestowed on me so many years ago was one of the most important and memorable moments in my life, not just my career. I was seriously considering leaving this work at the time and your recognition—and the institute's inspiration—turned me around. . . . Over the years when I was tempted by fatigue or frustration to move on, I have looked at the AFI citation on my wall and felt a surge of resolve."

—BILL MOYERS,
journalist and honorary degree recipient (1989)

By the mid-1980s, the now NASAD-accredited CAFS had settled into the new campus environment fairly comfortably, but with tight budgets and limited staff, it often struggled operationally. Despite Vellani's heavy dictatorial hand, there was usually a whiff of anarchy in the air. Most of the Fellows identified with American independent cinema and saw themselves as guerrilla filmmakers working from the margins against Authority. Rules were meant to be tested, circumvented, broken, or ignored. If Fellows were lucky enough to get into second year, where only a third of them were invited back, they dragged out the completion of their thesis films for years. Graduation meant becoming the depressing alternative to a promising AFI Fellow: just another out-of-work filmmaker on the hustle.

Recruitment of new applicants, supported through various national outreach programs, was never easy—although it got easier after David Lynch got *Twin Peaks* on the air in 1990. Even though CAFS was a graduate school, we were not terribly interested in recruiting current college graduates. Our targets were older, more accomplished and experienced figures with clear evidence of successful commitment to creative expression. Like most art schools, admission was portfolio-based, and evidence of expressive talent was to be established in the work submitted, of whatever nature.

Because of its reputation and European-style conservatory education, CAFS attracted many foreign applicants, and entering classes typically could be as much as one-third international. When AFI still received substantial federal funds from the NEA (through 1996, and then eliminated completely after 1998), foreign Fellows were deemed ineligible for entry into second year, a huge loss of talent and a problem for morale.

The cabal that ran CAFS—Toni Vellani; the efficient, gravel-voiced, chain-smoking administrator Nancy Peter; and various secretaries over the years whose favors were slavishly courted by adroit Fellows—kept the ship afloat, supported by a small technical staff in lighting and grip and in the Sony Video Center (an on-campus production and post-production resource generously funded by Sony). They were abetted by the infamous Roman Harte, who provided generous servings of vodka in his café-style office to a huge array of Hollywood cronies, thereby keeping CAFS on the receiving end of many favors: costume and prop access, sound sweetening, specialty lenses, and lights—elevating the Fellows' projects to a high degree on production value. Roman's memorable curse, delivered toward colleagues who frequently annoyed him, was simply "AMATEURS!" The central teaching model was still the fine arts atelier, dominated by a master teacher but administered as a production center with teams from the various Fellow disciplines in constant production of short films, mostly shot and edited on industrial-grade video equipment generously supplied by Sony Corporation, with superb acting talent.

The actual quality of the Fellows' work remained high. Vellani's rigorous teaching of classic Hollywood cinema dramaturgy and narrative technique was supported by a series of filmmakers-in-residence, notably Wise and Petrie but also the accomplished directors Robert Ellis Miller and Dezsö Magyar, who came to succeed Toni at the end of the decade. These working filmmakers volunteered to meet with Fellows struggling with original scripts to give them avuncular advice. Their mentorship seriously raised the bar on finished pieces.

> "In every artist's life there is a time or a place, or a teacher or a class, that marks you, bequeathing a tradition and a set of skills, and at the same time imparting the confidence to develop your own voice. For me, as for so many others, AFI was that time, that place, and that teacher."
>
> —EDWARD ZWICK, filmmaker (class of 1975)

While the three first-year projects were not required to secure intellectual property and music rights and, therefore, could not be distributed, second-year thesis films were so required. These films, often widely distributed, helped with CAFS promotion and recruitment. Many played festivals, winning major awards and launching careers for alumni. Thanks to an early and brilliant policy designed at CAFS's opening by the young attorney Tom Pollock, AFI always retained the copyright to finished thesis films; this allows AFI to secure inexpensive group production insurance and to aggregate and bundle packages of thesis films for the ever-diminishing market for shorts. Pollock, straight out of law school and with the august title of business manager, assisted George Stevens Jr. in setting up Greystone and CAFS, then went on to a stellar career while remaining continually involved with AFI in ever-expanding leadership positions.

Leadership: The Magyar Years

In 1986, CAFS changed its name to the AFI Center for Advanced Film and Television Studies—CAFTS—a needed acknowledgment of the small screen in the real world. By 1988, the otherwise indefatigable Toni Vellani had fallen seriously ill, and I was asked to take on overall responsibility for CAFTS with institute-wide responsibilities as deputy director. Since it was the crown jewel of

AFI's many programs, I was frankly intimidated but excited, knowing CAFTS would need nurturing and new long-term thinking about its future. Given the similarity of their teaching approaches, Dezsö Magyar was asked to take over Vellani's most visible role, conducting the Narrative Workshop (the evolution of Vellani's Greystone Directing Workshop). It was the foundational structure for the whole first-year experience; there, primarily a place to critique the narrative shorts shot in three cycles during the year, filmmaking technique could be teased out and discerned from the sometimes painful, often brilliant efforts of first-year teams. The discussions and critiques focused on what worked as narrative on the screen, what didn't, and why. Lessons publicly learned in the Narrative Workshop were often brutal, but the strong survived and flourished.

Magyar was an enormously articulate, voluble Hungarian director with some interesting credits. He loved to talk about movies, with great passion and strong opinions, and was a powerful force in the Narrative Workshop. But he was not a natural administrator, nor was he much interested in the delicate nuances of first-year admissions, "casting" a new class, or walking the political high wire to separate the sheep and goats for second-year continuation.

Several months after Toni Vellani passed on November 13, 1989, 500 CAFS alumni gathered at the DGA to remember him. Everyone agreed that Vellani left his signature on the Fellows and their films. Marshall Herskovitz (class of 1975) spoke candidly of Toni's ability to terrorize, but "he had purpose in doing so, a vision . . . that I am thankful for every day." Caleb Deschanel said he "never really thought of Toni as a teacher, so much as someone he learned from." Bob Mandel said, "Just as any great institution takes on the character of its leader—Bob Brustein at Yale, John Houseman at Juilliard—so did AFI for twenty years take on the spirit and humanity of Toni Vellani." Mandel never imagined at that time that sixteen years later he would fill Vellani's shoes.

Without the Vellani presence and with the invaluable Nancy Peter choosing to move on, I slept badly in fear of imminent catastrophe. And there were a few dreadful moments over the next few years as untended fires set off minor conflagrations. But Dezsö quickly became a masterful master teacher. Still focused on career opportunities, he came and went several times to other positions and projects, usually with little notice. As a friend with a genuine passion for the highest quality cinema, he was delightful company, and Monday mornings always held the promise of a lengthy, extraordinary exchange about the weekend's movies.

The eight years I had spent working in graduate education at American University stood me in good stead, particularly in trying to corral the suddenly fractious CAFS faculty. Having spent as much as fifteen years under Toni's relentless thumb, many felt that it was time they took over its administration. The management style we assumed made the faculty feel loved and appreciated, but still aware of boundaries. Several left, but there was never a problem finding others who wished to be part of the heady ambience of AFI. Initially these were part-time positions that paid only a token honorarium, and tenure was certainly not part of the picture; nevertheless, a number of faculty had been part of the organization since well back into the Greystone era, believed in its unique teaching style, and wanted to help forge its future. Squabbles over limited scheduling time and resources were endemic, and they usually reflected the postures and rhetoric of a movie set—cinematographers vs. directors, screenwriters vs. everybody. The battles were stimulating, and I actually looked forward to faculty meetings, until a new CAFTS dean some years later decided he wanted the floor to himself. Deemed "too busy" to attend thereafter, I nevertheless missed that stimulating collegiality with the faculty.

Because CAFTS management had felt it could only afford to produce a small number of second-year films (later called thesis films), it admitted only a small number of second-year Fellows

> "From its inception, AFI has always attracted extraordinary people—the most gifted, the most curious, the most passionate. This has been true about its leadership, its staff, its faculty, and certainly about its Fellows, the young filmmakers, seeking a transformational creative experience at AFI. No matter where life takes us, none of us will ever leave AFI; its spirit, its passion for excellence will always be a part of our lives."
>
> —DEZSÖ MAGYAR, director and CAFTS director (1989–1994)

(in teams, with semi-approved projects), meaning that only some of the first-year Fellows could stay on and actually complete a degree. The bottleneck and related competition for second-year admission became a growing structural and morale problem for AFI: many were called; few were chosen. This structural limitation created a negative atmosphere that would eventually explode into threatened lawsuits, furious and alienated alumni, and an ugly competitiveness among Fellows in the lead-up to possible second-year admission. The path through was just too traumatic for many and, until the mid-1990s, two-thirds of all Fellows had to leave, even when they had had a successful first year. To be only a one-year "graduate" of AFI seemed like failure at the beginning of one's dreamed-of career.

Expanding the Curriculum

As a senior administrator responsible for CAFTS, I was determined to find a way to solve this structural dilemma, and expanding the second-year curriculum seemed to be the only way through—while trying desperately to keep the budget balanced and tuition affordable. That meant more classes, more faculty, more equipment and facilities, and even more parking! But I had strong support from

AFI trustees; the renowned directors Robert Wise and Dan Petrie in particular pushed me to find a way to allow all Fellows to have a second-year experience. By the mid-1990s, we had begun to experiment with various alternative tracks the Fellows might follow into a second year, also raising tuition along the way to comparable levels with our closest academic peer programs.

With the CAFTS faculty's active engagement after Toni's passing, it was now possible to take on the curriculum's weaknesses and absences. For example, we soon launched editing as a full discipline within CAFTS. Without editing Fellows, the task of editing first-year cycle projects, or even the few second-year thesis films, had usually been done by the directing member of the creative team, leading to fierce battles and uneven outcomes.

The arrival of a new, advanced level of Sony-donated professional video equipment provided the impetus to develop a serious editing program. Ron McRae, head of the Sony Video Center, was a crackerjack editor in his own right, able to take chaotic footage of a poorly documented event and turn it into a miraculously coherent, snappy short clip we could present at a board meeting to the leading American film and television executives gathered there. I had faith that he could spearhead this new program, and we reached out to ACE (American Cinema Editors, the national editors' guild) for help and support. Sadly, Ron soon left AFI under unfortunate circumstances. His successor, Phil Linson, expanded the initial program at CAFTS.

The rapid computerization of the art of visual effects led me to consider the creation of a seventh discipline, made possible by the developing relationship with Intel Corporation, whose products were powering a new generation of lower cost computer work stations that rivaled the industry-leading products from Silicon Graphics. As part of an arrangement negotiated by AFI's new technologies guru Nick DeMartino, Intel donated a computer lab worth more than $1 million. Initially, the lab was run as part of the

AFI's non-degree extension program, but as AFI Fellows started using the facilities to create effects shots and more elaborate title designs, a new degree was launched, the M.A. in media arts—not a full-scale program discipline, but one that supported every film made at AFI. The program only lasted a few years, in part because of the cost of keeping up with the rapidly changing technologies, as well as difficulty in attracting students.

We also periodically debated establishing sound as a separate discipline. AFI thesis films were notorious for unevenly mixed and weakly designed sound scores—offset by clever, sophisticated cinematography, first-rate acting (thanks to AFI's fortunate long-term relationship with the Screen Actors Guild), and inventive directing. Since sound mixing was usually the last post-production element addressed in cash-starved productions, Fellows' budgets were typically exhausted, and sound became an afterthought in the finished film. Major sound houses provided generous discounts to the Fellows, but AFI did not have the resources nor the personnel to give an in-house sound program the proper foundation. So, we punted. A fully developed sound discipline still remains a goal for the future.

Other areas were strengthened in the 1990s. Production design was fleshed out as a discipline, and a larger number of recruited Fellows allowed more cycle and thesis films to receive the active support of a committed designer. Thanks to the extraordinary leadership of the renowned production designer Bob Boyle—famous as Alfred Hitchcock's designer on *The Birds* and *North by Northwest*—graduates of this program have done exceptionally well professionally. Boyle continued to meet with AFI Fellows past his one-hundredth birthday. They loved his vision and passion. Bob was brilliantly succeeded by Joe Garrity, a CAFS alumnus who continues the Boyle legacy of true visual storytelling through production design.

The limited facilities of the AFI campus only allowed for one sound stage, usually needed as a teaching space for lighting and cinematography. Interior sets were at a premium, and the Fellows' apartments did constant double duty as locations. We fielded many cranky calls from irate landlords regarding the wear-and-tear of student shoots.

Over the years, I had come to see the producing discipline as lying at the heart of any serious advanced training program in moving images. It is the producer who must integrate and preserve the creative vision underlying any project, recruiting and managing a creative team that can fulfill that vision balanced with a deep understanding of business affairs, deft administration, a talent for tracking every detail—the list goes on. The CAFTS producing program had stressed production management as the major responsibility of the producer, a practical foundation that supported the work of the ever-privileged director. We added faculty and classes that fleshed out the many roles of a great creative producer, at a time when the rare major figures who could do this work brilliantly were disappearing. The rise of the showrunner in premium television has made the need for first-rate producers with creative skills ever more pressing.

Certain programs had always been strong and just continued to improve—especially cinematography. From the Greystone era, DP Howard Schwartz (succeeded later by the great teacher Bill Dill and then brilliantly led by Stephen Lighthill) had established a resilient program and managed to make it nationally unique and robust, despite the limitations of the early video production equipment. Graduates of the CAFTS cinematography program typically have active and energetic careers, and a number have risen to the top of their field. The secret in cinematography seems to have been the stress placed on the visual image as servant to the narrative. As outstanding alumnus Janusz Kamiński (class of 1987) said, the work of the cinematographer is not about the camera lens—it's about the story. Screenwriting was always special, with Leonard

Schrader at the helm for many years. Successful alumni kept coming back, like Tom Rickman (class of 1969, who chaired the discipline) and the revered Gill Dennis (class of 1969, who taught a special workshop for every new class during their first month on campus and was a creative thesis advisor for second-year Fellows).

It was clear by the mid-1990s that CAFTS was no longer quite as unique as it had been at its founding, when its rigorous hands-on training process, with major professionals mentoring exceptional talent who competitively struggled for entry, reflected the best European models. Public universities were moving into media education—the UCLA film and television program had begun even before AFI was established—but the funding and flexibility of the best private universities gave them an edge. And the generosity of their major alumni (for example, George Lucas's support of USC programs) might attract endowment and facilities AFI could only dream of. Nevertheless, CAFS had unique strengths: it was small, focused tightly on fiction film, and unencumbered by traditional academic processes, structure, and governance. Top-down management at CAFTS was autocratic but nimble. Resources were thin, but senior management was responsive.

Paying the Bills

The financial health of a growing conservatory made recruitment and tuition income deeply important. NASAD accreditation made federal financial aid easier to come by and worthy incoming Fellows more able to pay tuition, but vanishing support from the National Endowment for the Arts during this period put pressure on AFI as a whole. Separate fundraising for CAFTS was not encouraged, since it might drain off possible financial support for other AFI efforts. Since two-thirds of the alumni left feeling angry and rejected after failing to get into the second year, they were unlikely supporters in the future. More Fellows, hefty tuition, and larger classes seemed to be the solution. But we were acutely aware of the crushing, mounting burden of the Fellows' tuition debt, aggravated by the temptation to sneak personal money into cycle and thesis film budgets. The infamous example was the probably an apocryphal faculty complaint that the usual Fellow fix for a potentially weak film was to rent a crane for some fancy camera work, as opposed to fixing the script itself.

Despite the power and resources of its board and principal supporters, AFI simply did not have the wherewithal to compete with what had emerged as the top few American film schools—despite AFI's own national mandate, enviable reputation, and resonant alumni names and careers. History and reputation alone could not guarantee the future. Outreach regionally and internationally helped.

During the '70s and '80s, AFI had developed National Education Programs, which were basically extension-style professional training classes and workshops offered in conjunction with regional media centers in such active media hubs as San Francisco, Minneapolis, Chicago, Atlanta, and New York. These programs brought well-credited specialty teachers into communities that had only limited access to the profession. Talented participants in these programs often applied to CAFTS over time, raising AFI's profile regionally.

Just as it is now, Hollywood was a magic beacon to cinema aspirants worldwide, and extraordinarily talented would-be filmmakers from around the globe polished their English for a shot at CAFTS, often with funding from their home governments. Tuition dollars from the subsidized foreign Fellows was more than welcome, though CAFTS enrollment, often as much as one-third foreign Fellows, suffered after 9/11, as securing student visas became a horrendous adventure. The mix of cultures and perspectives in entering classes made for a heady brew, although certain Asian countries became infamous for applicants who cheated on TOEFL

"I can still remember the first week at AFI as if it was yesterday. Probably the memories are so crisp because there were so many dreams, so many creators yearning to create and get started. And the faculty bombarded us with tons of information. They kept saying this one word over and over again, and that word was 'collaboration.' . . . I left AFI with two of the great collaborators of my life—the cinematographer Matthew Libatique, who shot everything I have done since AFI, as well as my business partner, my best friend, and my producer, Eric Watson."

—DARREN ARONOFSKY,
filmmaker (class of 1992)

exams and came to their first shoot speaking virtually no English.

Creative collaboration was among the most valued skills a Fellow had to learn, and the struggle to work together in order for all to make the same movie was one of the primary learning experiences Fellows would have. Teams could not break up or expel a member; like traditional Catholic marriage, there was no possibility of divorce. I came to realize that relationship counseling was how Toni, Dezsö, and subsequent leaders spent much of their day. And, in fact, many professional relationships were launched while at AFI, and these teams tend to hire other AFI alumni because they are confident that they have learned how to be part of a collaborative group and have a sophisticated grounding in narrative storytelling.

Consolidating Leadership

By the mid-1990s, personnel changes in CAFTS management required a new master teacher. Beginning with Frank Daniel, the charismatic but obstreperous Czech screenwriter (and well-regarded script doctor) recruited to lead CAFS at its opening, the director of the program had always been its master teacher—establishing the pedagogy, leading the major workshops, and spearheading the critiques of the Fellows' work. Administration had been dealt with as something of an afterthought, which helps to explain the slightly anarchic spirit that often prevailed. Toni Vellani perpetuated this schizophrenic and heavy-handed leadership model, and Dezsö Magyar quickly made it clear that management was not his primary interest.

When Dezsö left for the Canadian Film Centre in 1993, we replaced him with a good friend of Dan Petrie's: Ron Silverman, an old-line Hollywood producer who had no educational experience but who would, more or less, keep the operation moving along. But the Narrative Workshop, the centerpiece of the first-year program, required a master teacher of exceptional skill—articulate, sensitive to the balance between thoughtful critique and aspirational standards of excellence, and simultaneously tough-minded and generous.

In 1995, after several unhappy experiments, we were able to recruit the extraordinary writer-director Frank Pierson, which changed the AFI world altogether. Famous for such films as *Dog Day Afternoon*, *Cat Ballou*, and *Cool Hand Luke*, Frank's career included many writing and directing masterpieces. But his ability to talk about filmic storytelling with precision, clarity, and passion was unique. Frank became a superb artistic director who was gentle in his critiques, kindly with Fellows in crisis, extremely smart, and funny as hell. His many years leading the Narrative Workshop, plus his generous mentoring of thesis films and availability to Fellows, made him truly a legend among the Fellows and a source of cohesion and inspiration for the faculty. Frank came from the old three-martinis-at-lunch school of Hollywood; when it was appropriate to treat him accordingly at Musso & Frank, I would worry exceedingly as he zipped off afterward in his turquoise Mercedes two-seater sportster. But Frank was made of sterner stuff, and he always seemed to have a whale of a good time wherever he was. He was finally a rare combination of great storyteller and galvanizing teacher.

Formal Academic Accreditation—Finally

Now my attention was fully focused on building the CAFTS structure for the long term. As CAFTS stabilized and grew—with new disciplines, more Fellows, effective administration, larger and stronger faculty, better production and post-production equipment—the painful exodus of those Fellows who didn't get into the second year became ever more problematic. Second-year admission had been a two-pronged affair. Initially, first-year Fellows had to be approved to go forward; then they had to team up around a short film script that the program head wanted to see made. AFI budgetary limitations meant that perhaps only three to five films could be approved, since AFI heavily subsidized their making. Fellows might be approved to make a thesis film, but their film might never be green-lit.

The situation had come to a head in classic Hollywood style in 1990, when a team led by a particularly pugnacious directing Fellow had their script turned down for production. The team found an aggressive attorney who threatened to sue AFI for damages, but thanks to the oversight of Robert Wise, Dan Petrie, and attorney Susan Grode, we tiptoed into an embarrassing compromise that allowed them to make a project.

The CAFTS chair at the time, Dan Petrie, had developed his own annual evaluation system each spring when he interviewed a random selection of Fellows across all disciplines, keeping precise written notes on each interview. From those, he developed recommendations about what needed the most attention at CAFTS. His recommendation from that year's interviews: all qualifying Fellows needed to be able to attend the second year. Dan (two of whose children had attended CAFTS) insisted we find a way to change the program into a full two years (or, more realistically, three years) for all qualified Fellows. We struggled with various ways to make it all work, but within several years we were on our way to becoming a genuinely rigorous, thorough, and unique full graduate degree program for everyone who entered—except we were not a regionally accredited institution of higher learning as yet.

For an aspiring independent graduate school, AFI and CAFTS was still oddly nontraditional. This was reflected in our rhetoric: *Fellows* as opposed to *students* (though always a source of contention for female "Fellows"), a conservatory within an institute as opposed to a school within a university. Even the board advisory committee avoided academic trappings and had only professionals and no academic members (until I shoehorned in professor Rick Jewel from USC's Cinema School, my wife's associate dean). My sense was that the board of trustees, senior staff, and even the faculty prided themselves on the fact that university film programs offered lots of cinema history and theory, but the AFI and CAFTS were hands-on, dedicated to the practicalities of making the best narrative moving image art. Remember the motto: *Learn by doing; study with the Masters.* Until the end of the 1990s, we had not bothered with traditional academic procedures like exams, or syllabi, or even a real credit hour system for our classes. As Toni Vellani was known to shout at the Fellows, "Either it's on the screen or it's not, and nothing else matters."

Because AFI did not have formal regional accreditation, a strong case could be made that such academic accreditation would only strengthen CAFTS. Graduates with a fully recognized accredited MFA degree could teach, foreign Fellows could more easily get their government's support, and other paths to financial aid might become possible. And AFI could compete fairly for the cautious but talented applicants who hedged their bets by also applying to the ever-stronger MFA film programs at NYU and USC. When AFI was young and unique, such competitive perspectives did not enter in, but in the words of Bob Dylan, the times they were a-changin'. I now felt I could clearly make the case to everyone who needed convincing that the future and health of CAFTS could only be secured

> "What I believe has worked with the people I've seen come through AFI is the more courageous you are, the more you somehow tap into what is uniquely your own, the better off you are. Keep your own voice. Everybody's got something unique to say in his own experience. Tap into it!"
>
> —CARL FRANKLIN, filmmaker (class of 1986)

through full regional academic accreditation—as daunting as that would prove to be.

Raising the Accreditation Bar

Ironically, the tipping point for seeking regional accreditation came in the mid-1990s, when Rod Merl, AFI associate director and campus administrator from 1981 until 1997, decided to go back to graduate school for a PhD in higher education policy. I suspect that he wanted to use the AFI accreditation attempt as a dissertation project. As a former academic myself, I was intrigued by the notion that we might be able to take this wildly idiosyncratic institution through the eye of the academic needle, convincing the gatekeepers that, as a blatant, successful arts venue, we were just as worthy of academic respect as Stanford. There was little guarantee we could pull it off, but as the holder of a PhD myself, I was not going to be stopped by what I imagined was the equivalent of a gatekeeper keeping the riffraff out.

My first stop was the office of Neil Hoffman, the head and chief administrator at the time for the Western Association of Schools and Colleges, the regional membership body that oversees accreditation for California and the Pacific Region, then housed on the charming campus of Mills College in Oakland. I found him welcoming and very interested in the unique beast that was CAFTS. Most importantly, he did not see obviously insurmountable obstacles in the way of our journey to the promised land. He was cautious but encouraging. Midway through our six-year journey to the finish line, he left WASC to become president of the newly reorganized Otis College of Art and Design. Fortunately, he agreed to help us from the outside as an accreditation consultant. His knowledge of the "deep woods" at WASC and his awareness of what went on there was invaluable. He even led an all-day retreat for CAFTS faculty and staff that made a crucial difference in securing buy-in for the entire messy accreditation process.

The next major assignment was an institutional self-study—a rigorous, exhaustive, self-reflecting, and deeply critical analysis of what the place did and why it did that. We had done this for NASAD accreditation and for all its subsequent renewals, but a WASC self-study was another order of magnitude. Most importantly, the self-study required the institution to define standards of excellence and clearly demonstrate how they were or were not met. CAFTS had never been subject to that kind of close scrutiny, and the procedural holes that showed up were large enough to disappear into. On the other hand, the unique strengths of the conservatory approach—rigorous hands-on teaching, constant practice and critique, creative collaboration and emphasis on teamwork, narrow focus on narrative, professional faculty—became clear as well.

Rod Merl made the first attempt to write up the exhaustive self-study, but he was in the throes of his graduate program and could not help being more academic than the rest. The results were utterly impenetrable. Debra Henderson, who had succeeded Ron Silverman, took it on next. She started in 1995, as did Frank Pierson, with the title of director of education and training. But as a non-academic Canadian, she could not quite get the hang of the necessary language and rhetoric. So I weighed in. The final result after a lengthy process was a comprehensible and painfully honest assessment of what the CAFTS aspired to be, what it actually was and how it hoped to move into a better future. The final document was 600 pages in length, and the entire process took a year. Another order of magnitude, indeed; the NASAD first self-study was sixty-six pages long.

Finally, we girded our loins for our first team visit in February 1997, a consultation by senior academics mainly from major schools considered to be peer institutions: Marilyn Chapin Massey, president of Pitzer College; Brigitte Kueppers, head librarian and archivist at the University of California, Los Angeles; Lewis Cole, chair of the film program at Columbia University; Beverly O'Neill, provost of the California Institute of the Arts; and Stuart Wiener, executive vice president of finance and administration at Western University of Health Sciences.

From backstage, Neil Hoffman made it as easy on us as possible in his casting of the team, but at least one member of the team made it clear that he harbored the deep hostility to AFI that George Stevens Jr. had inadvertently stoked among academics in some early days of intense campaigning for more federal funding from the NEA. Team members met with Fellows, faculty, senior staff, and some trustees. The latter made me the most nervous, since some of them were not convinced this whole process would be good for AFI in the first place. But everyone was well-behaved, and the atmosphere was pleasant. A few skeletons fell out of the closet—why, exactly, doesn't CAFTS raise funds directly for better facilities, more scholarships, and so on?—but there were no nasty surprises.

In 1998, the efficient Debra Henderson had decided to return to Canada, but we were able to recruit Sam Grogg back to AFI from his post as founding dean of the film school at the North Carolina School of the Arts. Sam had a PhD and traditional academic and professional chops, and he knew AFI well, having been head of the AFI National Educational Programs back when it was headquartered at the Kennedy Center. Sam was invaluable in preparing for the final WASC visit resulting in developing the policies and procedures that would finally satisfy WASC, while preserving the space and passion needed to grow strong filmmakers in all disciplines. Sam took the title of dean while I hovered in the background with the newly coined, traditional title of provost of the Conservatory. We were well on track to safely transition into the fully realized, freestanding graduate school we had always aspired to be.

> "Collaboration is the mantra of AFI, and we saw it at all levels of the institution. It is evident in its mission, pedagogy, practices, and in the relationships between and among Fellows, faculty, staff, administration, and the board. It is what perhaps best defines what AFI is and does."
>
> —WASC-NASAD CAPACITY VISIT TEAM

Responses to the team visit, embellishments to the self-study, yet another and different team visit with responses necessary . . . the drama dragged on. Four years into the process, it was 2000. We took the moment of the new millennium to evolve the institution's name; the wieldy Center for Advanced Film and Television Studies became the AFI Conservatory, a more accurate reflection of the style of institution we were known to be.

After an AFI presentation at a large WASC convocation in 2001, we began to be hopeful. We were notified that we would achieve formal institutional candidacy in June of 2002, six very long years and three site visits later, after we started the formal process. During that time, we had been scrutinized by an impressive group. Just consider the WASC contingent visiting AFI in March 1999: Lorne M. Buchman, WASC chair and president of California College of Arts and Crafts; Ken Dancyger, professor of film in the undergraduate film and TV department at NYU's Tisch School of the Arts; Joyce M. Gattas, dean of the College of Professional Studies and Fine Arts at San Diego State University; and Heather Kitchen, managing director of the American Conservatory Theater. In February 2002, the WASC contingent was Ruben Armiñana, WASC chair and president at Sonoma State University; Stephen Beal, provost at the California College of Arts and Crafts; Heather

Kitchen, managing director of the American Conservatory Theater; Thomas G. Schatz, Philip G. Warner Regents professor and chair in communication in the department of film and television at the University of Texas at Austin; and Marilla D. Svinicki, director of the Center for Teaching Effectiveness at the University of Texas at Austin. While WASC collectively still remained somewhat dubious of AFI's intentions and integrity in the Conservatory, they grudgingly opened the gates.

I was utterly delighted, not only that the gatekeeper hadn't thrown us out, but that the entire process was actually useful and even wisdom-inducing. The Conservatory is not only better regarded and much more fully developed as a result of its struggles for full regional accreditation, but the quality and depth of so many elements of the program are much stronger because of the process itself. I consider it perhaps the crowning achievement of myself and my colleagues in my time at AFI.

The Conservatory Era

Once accreditation had been achieved, a great deal of practical work had to be undertaken to turn our glorious rhetoric about the Conservatory's unique educational model into more traditional academic practice. The trick was to find ways to accommodate academic structure while retaining our unusual degree of flexibility and responsiveness to the Fellows' immediate needs. If the Conservatory became as procedure-bound as most academic institutions, we could damage its soul fundamentally. That meant that every policy and practice had to be argued through, resulting in endless faculty meetings and abrupt changes in course.

Finally, having embraced the heady experience of achieving full regional accreditation from WASC, I felt free to think about the future in a new way. Within two years, I had decided to move on from my twenty-four years at AFI to look at other chances to build new schools and institutions in the United States and internationally. These projects would also be deeply daunting and highly exciting but, frankly, nothing could quite match the profound

Franklin J. Schaffner Alumni Medal

Alumni achievements are celebrated by the Franklin J. Schaffner Alumni Medal, established in 1991 and awarded annually, presented at the AFI Life Achievement Award ceremony. The list of recipients over the years is an honor roll that suggests both the remarkable quality of the education they received and the talent, rigor, and outstanding achievements of the graduates themselves. Established shortly after his death, the Schaffner Medal also celebrates the deeply generous contributions of Franklin to CAFS through his magisterial chairing of the board advisory committee.

1991 David Lynch
1992 Edward Zwick
1993 Randa Haines
1994 Martin Brest
1995 Jon Avnet
1996 Carl Franklin
1997 John McTiernan
1998 Amy Heckerling
1999 Mimi Leder
2000 Terrence Malick
2001 Darren Aronofsky
2002 Todd Field
2003 John Dahl
2004 Patty Jenkins
2005 Paul Schrader
2006 Marshall Herskovitz
2007 Gary Winick
2008 Mark Waters
2009 Steve Golin
2010 Janusz Kamiński
2011 Steven Rosenblum
2012 Wally Pfister
2013 Stuart Cornfeld
2014 Anne Garefino
2015 Caleb Deschanel
2016 Lesli Linka Glatter
2017 Frederick Elmes

satisfaction of supporting the AFI Conservatory through a wobbly adolescence into a robust young adulthood. We did it together as a shared dream, sensing the future but never quite sure how to get there. I am deeply grateful to my colleagues for the journey—especially to Jean Firstenberg, who trusted me and shared the vision. Nearly fifty years after its founding, the Conservatory's improbable survival and blooming success is a profound tribute to so many farsighted, film-crazed people who came along for the ride.

Thanks to strong leadership, the Conservatory has gone on to grow and thrive. When Sam Grogg departed in 2004 soon after I did, Bob Mandel was selected as dean in 2005 after an exhaustive search. Mandel had a substantial directing career, and he was reporting to a new COO with filmmaking and academic experience. Frank Pierson continued for a few years as artistic director, joined by Roger Birnbaum for several years. Mandel was a natural educator, despite limited experience in the classroom, and he was especially effective in creating a nurturing environment for the Fellows and in building an eminent faculty that he continued to recruit from his substantial professional network.

Future choices and directions for the Conservatory raise interesting questions. AFI's teaching, learning and work model is incredibly well-tested and clearly successful. Such a narrow, strong emphasis on professional practice, constant hands-on work, creative collaboration, and a fairly classical approach to large-screen narrative fiction remains relatively unique among the leading media arts graduate programs in the United States. But the range and technical foundations of all the moving image arts have undergone radical changes and continue to do so. The field has expanded in a breathtaking way, and novice filmmakers must be prepared for jobs and types of work that do not yet exist. Onscreen narrative will occur in shapes, formats, and circumstances that we do not imagine. It may well be that the Conservatory's profound commitment to the moving image as a public art, and to strong narrative as the key to effective cinema, is in fact exactly the right ground to stand on as it moves into the future. As NASAD noticed more than thirty years ago, the very narrowness of the Conservatory's focus could well prove to be its most enduring virtue.

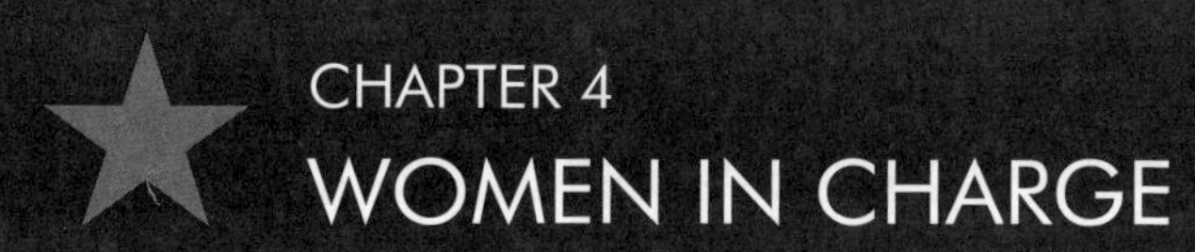

AFI Directing Workshop for Women: Give Them a Chance

JEAN PICKER FIRSTENBERG

Every program proposal that surfaced during AFI's first decade (starting in 1967) emerged as a unique and often original initiative. The majority of projects, activities, and programs had not been attempted before. Everything was new, and it is remarkable that so many exemplary projects were generated so quickly. However, it was also clear that these programs were truly needed.

In retrospect, the late-1960s was one of the most difficult times in American history to start a serious educational, cultural institution. At the same time that there was unprecedented grassroots creativity and learn-by-doing experimentation, popular anti-war, civil rights, and women's liberation movements harbored little trust for institutional solutions. Institutions had to adapt to reflect the changing face of America.

Each step in the Directing Workshop for Women's (DWW) early process highlights the issues and challenges involved with starting something without models or blueprints. It also outlines early steps in the continuing story of a remedy for a problem—the problem of women being given the opportunity to direct major films and television programs in the male-dominated filmmaking capital of the world—that still plagues the entire field (and many other aspects of equality of opportunity for women in American society). Women's opportunities in other film careers are no easier, but control arguably begins with the director; DWW sought to address the problem from the top down. DWW has responded through evolving technologies and opportunities to continue to help women showcase their skills to tell stories across multiple platforms.

Noticing the Gap

Mathilde Krim wasn't the first person to notice that there were no women directors in Hollywood. But she was one of the few to do something about it. A humanitarian and research scientist, she had moved from Israel to New York when she married United Artists co-chair Arthur Krim and continued her research at Sloan Kettering and the Rockefeller Institute. This great leader would go on to devote decades to fighting the AIDS virus, founding American Foundation for AIDS (AMF) in 1983, then asking Elizabeth Taylor to join her when she became founding chair of American Foundation for AIDS Research (amfAR) in 1985. Over the years, they raised hundreds of millions of dollars to fund research that has saved many lives.

But in 1973, Krim's focus was on women in Hollywood. She wrote a letter to AFI saying she wanted to find a way to help women become film directors. Her letter was circulated around AFI and reached the Center for Advanced Film Studies team at Greystone. Toni Vellani, head of CAFS Production Programs, encouraged his colleague, Jan Haag, to fly to New York City to meet with Krim and Michael Novak, program director for the arts at the Rockefeller Foundation.

Haag had developed a proposal for a series of movies to be directed by women and aired on PBS. Everyone liked the idea, but it would take a very long time to go through the standard foundation process for funding the budget of $200,000 to $300,000. If a smaller program could be developed, Novak could immediately provide a start-up $35,000 as a program director's discretionary grant. Done.

Haag's next step was to figure out how to use $35,000 to help women become Hollywood directors. AFI CAFS had launched in 1969 and was the first production-based educational entity that embraced videotape in learning. In those days, 16mm film stock was such an expensive learning tool that it was rarely used in the few production-based courses taught in U.S. colleges. Because of the typically poor quality of the screen images, the use of videotape was very controversial in educational circles, but CAFS had done just that.

Vellani suggested that the women use AFI's videotape equipment during the summer, when CAFS was not in session. This simple idea opened the door for the DWW, but sometimes simple ideas are not simple to implement. Practical reality intruded: it was the early days of video technology, and the equipment continually broke down. Since video editing was time-intensive, the DWW program would need to purchase its own editing equipment. The first discretionary grant from the Rockefeller Foundation did not arrive in time for a summer production schedule, so now DWW and CAFS projects overlapped, causing scheduling nightmares.

One huge benefit of the delay was that AFI Center Fellows could now be available to be members of the DWW crews. Fellows supported the production of DWW short films by working in formalized production roles as cinematographers or producers. They wanted as much production experience as possible, so they volunteered for all the DWW projects. Professional relationships were forged, and over the years many careers were the beneficiaries. Stuart Cornfeld (class of 1975) is an outstanding example. After he produced Anne Bancroft's DWW short in 1976, she recommended him to husband Mel Brooks when he was setting up his production company, Brooks Films. One of the first movies they made was *The Elephant Man*, with David Lynch (class of 1970) directing.

The First Cycle

In designing the selection process for the first cycle of women directors, Jan Haag made a truly insightful decision. She wanted to create the highest profile and attract the most attention for the program as possible. That would be easier if the first cycle of women directors were already well-known, highly respected individuals.

In order to invite the most prominent women in Hollywood to apply to DWW, Haag developed a network of relationships with women across all sectors of the Hollywood community. Martin Manulis, a respected television producer and the new head of AFI-West, suggested Haag call up what he termed the "Big Ladies." That she did, and when she got them on the phone and pitched the program, she asked them to send her a bio (in these days before IMDb). That was their application.

The next step in the process was casting the selection committee for the first cycle. Sitting on these types of committees or panels is an extremely intense process and responsibility. The chair needs to have enormous patience and must be extremely diplomatic to ensure decisions that are fair for the applicants and the organization. Experience is also an asset in this particular artful exercise; apparently Jan Haag was not dubbed "Ms. Machiavelli" without reason. The exact story of how the first cycle of fifteen women were selected shall simply be explained by the list, which included Maya Angelou, Karen Arthur, Ellen Burstyn, Juleen Compton, Lee Grant, Margot Kidder, Kathleen Nolan, and Susan Oliver. "Big Ladies" indeed.

The Second Cycle

The second Rockefeller Foundation grant fully supported the second cycle of DWW, this time with $100,000. Late in 1976, I had just joined the Markle Foundation as a program officer. Jan Haag learned from my brother, David Picker, who was on the AFI board at that time, that perhaps I could be helpful in getting another grant for DWW.

Although I was new at Markle and new to the world of funding cycles, sometimes a good idea rises above inexperience. When I put the proposal on the table, Markle head Lloyd Morrisett immediately said, "That sounds like something worth doing." Markle gave AFI $154,000 for the DWW, just like that. The program's goals were in fact perfectly in keeping with Morrisett's objectives. As Lee Mitgang noted in *Big Bird and Beyond*, "The point for [Morrisett] was to widen the foundation's circle of outsiders and mavericks of all stripes who might act as change agents in the media world."

Two years later, Morrisett asked if we could show one of the DWW shorts at the Markle trustee dinner he hosted every year. Dyan Cannon flew to New York City to show *Number One*, the 1976 Oscar-winning Best Live Action Short Film that she wrote, produced, directed, and edited. The staid members of the Markle Foundation board, many of whom had been serving for years, were rather overwhelmed with the glamorous Ms. Cannon (recently divorced from Cary Grant). The charming short was about adolescent sexual curiosity. The next morning, Morrisett got a call from one of the oldest trustees telling him he thought the movie was pornography. This conversation continued for months.

Actually, there was some irony in this story. Dyan Cannon had asked me what she should wear to the dinner. I told her it was the foundation's annual trustee dinner, an older and conservative group of husbands and wives. Dyan dressed in a pantsuit, with a bodice that zipped all the way to the top—an appropriate choice, from my perspective. Morrisett described it differently, remembering that Dyan "arrived in a tight gold lamé pantsuit with a zipper that was down to her navel." But Lloyd was strong in the face of his trustees' concerns when he wrote in a lengthy letter that the films "have clearly passed the tests of taste, good judgment, and high moral intent." Looking back on it though, Lloyd said, "It was a yoke around my neck that I thought I would never get rid of—but now it's all very funny."

Moving Forward

When I was named director of AFI in 1980, DWW was one of my priorities. Because of my contacts in the foundation world through Markle, we fortunately secured funding from the Ford Foundation for DWW for three years ($100,000, $50,000, and $50,000) and from other funders as well.

Jan Haag must be acknowledged in launching this program, for her dedication, insightfulness, and amazing accomplishments, with a huge assist from Toni Vellani for conceptualizing and implementing this first-of-its-kind program. Haag knew women were not part of the directing world, and she wanted to give them voice, so their vision could be told through moving images. She continued to run the program until 1982, when she left the AFI and moved to India. Much of the DWW's early history is documented in her unpublished autobiography, *Vol. 3: Token Woman*, archived in the Special Collection section of the Blagg-Huey Library at Texas Women's University in Denton, Texas.

Reporting the Conditions

By 1980, others in the community were also concerned about the issue. In 1979, six brave women directors—Susan Bay, Nell Cox, Joelle Dobrow, Dolores Ferraro, Victoria Hochberg, and Lynne

Littman—had convened to form the DGA Women's Steering Committee and conduct a comprehensive study on the facts about employment of women directors. Littman (class of 1974) and Hochberg (class of 1981) were also DWW graduates. The committee statistically substantiated the lack of employment opportunities for women in film and television between 1949 and 1979. The bottom line of the report was that women weren't getting the first shot—the point in the process where the opportunity is greatest—and because of that, weren't getting any shot at all.

This report validated the necessity of a DWW, but dependable funding was always a challenge. There was an unfortunate hiatus, caused by lack of funding support, from 1985 to 1987 (at that time, a cycle covered two years of productions).

Then a new leader stepped forward after reading an article in the *Los Angeles Times* about the DWW funding shortfall. Gale Anne Hurd, today one of the most successful Oscar- and Emmy-winning producers, showed early in her career that she would be a leader in the community when she pledged $60,000 as a matching gift with the commitment to raise the necessary matching funds. Hurd provided leadership and funding for many years, including serving as an AFI trustee from 1989 to 1996. Her leadership spread across the entire community and is still formidable.

Over the next two decades, DWW continued its passionate role in reminding the creative community of the many talented women who, given the opportunity, make compelling, effective, and successful movies. The "Big Ladies" became less identified with the program after the first few cycles, though talented actresses continue to participate. Currently, the backgrounds from the participating talent is spread across a wide range: writers, producers, editors, and cinematographers from film, television, documentary, theater, and the independent community.

The principal oversight for running the day-to-day activities of DWW over forty years was handled by very talented and dedicated individuals including Jan Haag, Martha Carrell, Kay Cooper, Terry Lawler, Tess Martin, Joe Petricca, Patty West, and now Tessa Blake (the first former participant to take time from her burgeoning career to lead DWW and the first director to run the program). DWW alums like Nancy Malone, among others, maintained a lasting interest in the workshop and made significant contributions.

A measure of the character and quality of DWW can be seen from the alumnae who have gone on to strong careers as well as become members of the Directors Guild of America (DGA). Two—Randa Haines and Lesli Linka Glatter—received the Franklin J. Schaffner Alumni Medal. This brief historic description doesn't do justice to the more than 300 women who, as of 2017, have participated in the program.

Nor does it do justice to those legacy funders that made the workshop possible, including the Rockefeller Foundation, the Markle Foundation, and the Ford Foundation, as well as early funders like Gale Anne Hurd, Peg Yorkin, the Academy of Motion Picture Arts and Sciences Foundation, the Los Angeles County Music and Arts Commission, and even the NEA (which continued to fund the DWW for several years after it stopped funding the AFI). Among the most important legacy funders were the McMurray and Gihon Foundations through the generosity of Michael Nesmith, a unique figure first known as one of the Monkees. Michael was the son of a single mother who invented Liquid Paper, which she initially produced in her garage with the help of her son. She sold the company to Gillette for $47.5 million a year before she passed away, and supporting the DWW was a way that Michael continued her philanthropic support of women's issues. As an original thinker, Michael has always been ahead of the curve. He knew where the world of screens and storytelling was going before it got there. As an AFI trustee (from 1992 to 2004), he was able—in most distinctive ways—to articulate AFI's relevant role within the changing digital world.

More recently, Jada Pinkett Smith's family foundation has made a significant, ongoing contribution to DWW, as have Donna Langley at Universal, Google, Broad Focus at Lifetime, and Twentieth Century Fox Film franchise properties, thanks to Stacey Snider.

Work to Be Done

The success of the DWW actually highlights the failure of the mainstream community in this arena. And women directors have been failed by executives who are unwilling to consider giving a "big" movie to a woman director. The individual successes we cherish and cheer have made only a small collective difference so far.

Women directors rarely make the short list, and frequently don't even make the long list. Women who could be directing are still only active "below the line." And that's the bottom line. How ironic—Hollywood, of all places, where movies have been synonymous with memorable heroines for nearly a century's worth of moviegoers. But in real life, women haven't been given the chance to get into the action. Fay Kanin was quoted by *New York Times Magazine* in January 1981 on "The Struggle of Women Directors": "It's going to be two steps forward and three back for a while, but

---

"When I was selected for the AFI Directing Workshop for Women, I was a modern dance choreographer with a story that I needed to tell but no background in film. AFI not only gave me the tools to capture my story on film but showed me what it takes to be a true storyteller. AFI is a unique place that offers that elusive combination of constantly challenging one's self and never settling for less, with learning how to trust one's own voice and tell one's own stories. There is no other place like it."

—LESLI LINKA GLATTER,
filmmaker (DWW class of 1982)

About Those "Girl Directors"

For several decades, Steve Broidy and Martin Gang were two of L.A.'s most influential figures and the best of friends. Steve, in his role as an AFI trustee, and Martin, as chair of the Board of Trustees of Immaculate Heart College, were both crucial to AFI's acquisition of the IHC campus. They cared so much for AFI's success that I thought of them as part of the AFI "family"—Uncle Steve and Cousin Martin. In 1983, I joined them for lunch at the Hillcrest Country Club, where Steve spent most of his days playing cards and raising money for the various causes he supported. My purpose was to thank these dear elderly gentlemen (Steve was seventy-eight and Martin eighty-two at the time) for all they had done—and I hoped would continue to do—for AFI.

We were seated in the large main dining room, which was mostly empty and very quiet. In the headlines that day was the DGA's announcement of a class action lawsuit against Warner Bros. (and against Columbia, later that year) alleging discrimination against women and racial minorities in hiring practices. Across the table from

it will come. Sherry [Lansing] says we'll get to the day when none of us will have 'woman' as (an automatic) prefix stuck in front of our title." Well, it's 2017, and we're not there yet.

As my retirement in 2007 was approaching, the ever-present Nancy Malone invited me to a farewell lunch that turned out to be a surprise party attended by some 100 women who had been in DWW, with several members of the AFI Associates, our women's support group. It was a beautiful moment, and I was deeply each other, Martin and Steve tried to make sense of the news. Being hard of hearing, their conversation was loud to begin with, but indignation rose until I found myself sitting in the middle of a screaming match. The conversation went something like this:

"Did you see that DGA suit in the trades today about *women* wanting to be *directors?*"

"Can you believe it?"

"Do women know anything about directing?"

"Don't they know it's a really hard job? Physically, really hard!"

"Why in the world would a girl want to be a director? Makes no sense."

"Makes no sense" summed it up, but the pitch of their anger pointed to the deeper sense that this violated something fundamental in their beliefs about how the world should work. Their incomprehension about "girl directors" wasn't about any woman in particular, but the idea that moviemaking is a man's world. There was no arguing with them, and it became clear to me that bringing more women into filmmaking would require a generational shift—one still being fought for forty-plus years later.

touched by their expression of appreciation. Truth be told, I felt it should be the other way around. These women were so talented and smart and their stories so compelling that their voices must be heard. I thanked them for never giving up and continuing to tell stories that can make a difference, because talent comes in all shapes, all colors, and all genders. After Nancy's death in 2014, her estate gave DWW the largest individual gift it has ever committed. In 2017, a $500,000 contribution was received which ensured that this still-needed program would continue its leadership role.

At the April 2016 DWW Showcase, the keynote speaker was Sarah Gertrude Shapiro, a participant in the DWW class of 2013. The short she wrote and directed, *Sequin Raze*, became the basis for her award-winning series *UnReal* on Lifetime, for which she is co-creator and executive producer. Sarah Gertrude Shapiro shared her comments with a standing-room-only audience at the DGA theater:

> *I started writing when I was five years old. I figured out I was a director at sixteen. I never wavered once. This is my calling. But it has taken me this long, twenty-two years, to stand before you and say that I will be directing my first episode of television in a week. . . . But I didn't give up. It hasn't been easy for me. And it hasn't been easy for any woman I know. Since the critical acclaim for* UnReal *began, I've been called an overnight success. I've been told I'm living a fairytale. But what I want to tell you is that it feels more like a death camp most of the time. I've worked my ass off, continue to work my ass off, and I am really proud that I've survived. And I want you guys to survive out there, too. . . . The most powerful thing that I've learned in these past three years is the incredible magic trick, which is that you can give yourself the benefit of the doubt! That doesn't mean arrogance. It doesn't mean overselling yourself. It means just refusing to let the acid of institutional sexism induced self-doubt to systematically cock-block you from your life's work. . . . And we can give it to each other. . . . We were not made to give up. If you've come this far, gotten into the program, finished your film—you are already on your way. We were made to take care of each other.*

Let's hope so, because times do change; they will remember that Jan Haag, Mathilde Krim, Lloyd Morrisett, McNeil Lowry, the DGA Women's Committee, and all those who attended the

AFI's Directing Workshop for Women showed that there was always a reason to have women directors. Sometimes it just takes much too long to happen.

"In 1972, I wrote a screenplay, which was produced in Sweden. I was not even considered to direct, although I had directed dramatic stage plays and the music. The production company hired a Swedish man, who had never even shaken hands with a black person, to direct my play. What he produced garnered both bouquets and brickbats, and I did not deserve either.

"After the opening in New York, I went back to Sweden and took a course in cinematography from friends I had made at the Svenska Film Institute. I tried to gain entrance into universities to study the art of directing, without success. In 1977, I was offered, along with eight other women, a chance to make a short film at the American Film Institute. I read every book I could find about directing, on directing, by directors, and about directors.

"I made a short film called *All Day Long*. Without the sanction and support of the American Film Institute, I would have thought that everyone was right, except me. . . . I am proud of the American Film Institute for what it has done for me and others who would never have had the delicious experience of saying 'action' and 'that's a wrap.'"

—MAYA ANGELOU,
poet (DWW class of 1977)

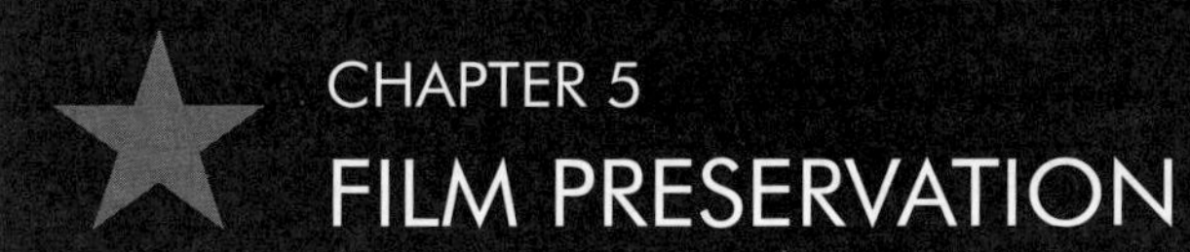

Finding America's Film History

Jean Picker Firstenberg

The American Film Institute's role in the preservation of American films is one of the most complex stories to tell. Fifty years ago, few people appreciated the value of American film history, and that included the individuals and corporations who owned the film rights. Why was there a need to preserve American films? After all, movies were just popular entertainment and not yet recognized as a reflection of American culture, let alone, at their finest, as an art form. The studios, in their shortsightedness, did not even think there was any long-term economic value to their film libraries. Except for a couple of rare instances, they couldn't have cared less. Disney was the notable exception. They were smart enough to realize that every subsequent generation would respond to their timeless family classics. And Roger Mayer at MGM was a staunch preservationist.

In January 1894, when Thomas Edison wanted to apply for one of his first motion picture copyrights for the film *Edison*

Kinetoscopic Record of a Sneeze, more commonly known as *Fred Ott's Sneeze*, the copyright law at the time had no provision in place for depositing celluloid materials into the Library of Congress. So some inventive person, whose identity is lost to history, decided that films deposited in the Library of Congress should be submitted as photographic contacts paper, just like still photographs. Edison and all of the earliest filmmakers who wanted to register their films for copyright protection submitted strips, rolls, or cardboard sheets. The practice continued until 1912, when the Townsend Act changed in U.S. copyright law to enable filmmakers to submit their products in their original celluloid format. Sadly, from 1912 on, the new celluloid submissions were not kept, because there were no storage facilities for film.

As strange as it may seem today, these early paper copies, now known as the Paper Print Collection, were a godsend to film preservationists in that they preserved the images and were not volatile like nitrate film. Decades later, these paper prints had to be transferred, frame-by-frame, onto film stock, but thanks to that initial decision to print these early films on paper, the Library of Congress has been able to preserve over 3,300 of America's earliest films.

Before the NEA and NEH were established, preservation work was being done by passionate visionaries, mostly at museums and archives, toiling with little funding. The Museum of Modern Art (starting in 1935), Library of Congress (starting in 1942), George Eastman House in Rochester, New York (starting in 1949), and UCLA TV and Film Archives (starting in 1965) were the early guardians of film history.

There was a sudden shift once the NEA and NEH included moving images and media in their mandates and the American Film Institute was established. Suddenly, there were national voices declaring the value of finding and saving American film history. Finally, the huge influence of popular culture on our society, our culture, our country, and the world was being recognized. In fact, movies

"Back then [in the 1960s and 1970s], it was a really strange world for film. Many people feared that movies were dead, and they were going to disappear forever. And, in fact, a great many of our classic films really were disappearing. They were becoming lost—negatives were fading, deteriorating, eating themselves, and turning into glop in front of our eyes. It was sort of a time of the plague, really. Some of us feared that our grandchildren weren't going to be able to see the movies that we had seen growing up—the movies that meant so much to us and shaped our attitudes and visions as Americans."

—JEANINE BASINGER,
film historian-academic, author, and AFI trustee (1979–1997, 2010–present)

and electronic media have become the principal delivery of American culture. Our films tell the story of America reflecting everyday life, but then contribute to the shaping of America itself. And now, the endowments finally seemed to be providing the wherewithal to fund and preserve America's cinematic heritage.

That growing cultural awareness, however, was not just theoretical. In formulating an effective and feasible response, the fledgling AFI also had to face the complications that film is a physical medium. From silent films to the talkies, from big screen to small screens, from film to video and then to digital, film preservation is dependent on shifting technologies, with all the difficult and costly decisions that go along with both moving forward and also preserving crucial components of the past.

Film technology has always contained the seeds of its own destruction. Nitrate film stock, invented in the 1890s, was chemically unstable and dangerously flammable, especially as the film stock aged. Triacetate safety film became the standard in the 1950s, which no longer exploded but had other issues, including vinegar syndrome and color fading. Once videotape was introduced, it was initially erased and reused, creating a new kind of preservation problem, subject as it was to degrading and hardware obsolescence as new standards evolved.

Then came the world of digital technology and its own particular and very complex issues. Every era brings its own problems, but at that early moment in AFI's history, the fragility of nitrate film stock and impending loss of early works set the agenda for AFI's preservation focus.

Nitrate Won't Wait

The most exciting AFI preservation project came about in 1996, with a simple phone call to the AFI switchboard that was referred to my office. The caller, Bill Buffum from Portland, Oregon, had a nitrate print of a 1912 silent feature. He was moving and needed to find a home for it. He wasn't even sure what it was, but he knew it was important. Would AFI be interested in seeing it? Would we ever! How do you ship unstable nitrate film stock? The folks at UPS knew exactly how to do it, and the bill was all of $76.

That's how AFI received the oldest surviving feature-length film in American film history, a near-mint print of the 1912 Shakespeare's *Richard III.* William and Margaret Buffum are true heroes of film preservation. Bill had once been a projectionist who would show his personal collection of silent films to friends, family, and anyone who would watch. He came by *Richard III* in a collector's trade in 1960. He knew a lot about nitrate film stock and the explosive nature of nitrate fires, so every year, he and his wife would hand-rewind the films with a pencil in the middle of the reels. They did it by the open kitchen window, in case there were any sparks. He had tried over the years to get someone to take his collection, but no one wanted the entire archive. The Buffums were selling their home and moving into a mobile home, and Margaret didn't want to take the last two films they had. Bill was down-to-earth and so unassuming; his story was irresistible.

After verifying the film's authenticity (and getting over the initial disbelief at such a find), we sprang into AFI action mode. We wanted to make this find a national story. We estimated that it would cost $50,000 for the necessary restoration and transfer to safety stock for a major screening to share this earliest-ever feature film. We learned that it starred Frederick C. Warde, one of the leading Shakespearean stage actors of the period. In those days, Warde would often attend screenings and present readings from the play prior to the movie. It was a gigantic production for its time, costing over $30,000 and shot on location on City Island in Long Island Sound and in Westchester County, New York.

The newly restored *Richard III* premiered October 29, 1996, at the AFI Los Angeles Film Festival in the Los Angeles County Museum of Art's Bing Theater. The evening was all that we hoped thanks to friends Joe and Nancy Kantor, who underwrote the project as soon as they learned of it. It was eventually screened around the world in several venues. The screening in Ghent, Belgium, on June 9, 2000, featured Ennio Morricone conducting a live orchestra, playing a score he composed for the event. What a special moment!

To put it all in perspective, this "lost" film came to AFI almost thirty years after the first "Nitrate Won't Wait" call to action for film presentation. Here it was, the oldest surviving feature film ever made in America. But in the late 1960s, America was just waking up to the value of its film heritage, because old films were spontaneously combusting or deteriorating from being stored in poor conditions. America's heritage was literally burning up or fading from view. What could AFI do? How could AFI address the pressing nature of the problem? AFI's budgets were nowhere near sufficient to do the physical work of film preservation or to build a film archive. But as an organization with national standing, AFI was in a good position to rally the public and cultural institutions as well as film studios to address the problem.

"Nitrate won't wait!" became the rallying cry that began the effort to collect first films and then tapes of television shows from wherever they might be lingering, depositing them with the Library of Congress and other existing archives. AFI used its position and influence as catalyst and facilitator to raise the profile and value of film preservation, an effort that requires the collaboration and combined efforts of multiple institutions over time. No single entity can do this work; it had to be shared among entities, many of whom had very different notions of how to go about it. Navigating the differences, AFI would focus public awareness, rally support, and organize the NEA's grants to film preservation organizations, entities that had the established expertise and commitment to accomplish the considerable day-to-day work of film preservation and archiving. In effect, the example of a national campaign of shared focus, bridging national, academic, and private institutional interests, was the beginning of the modern media preservation movement.

> "It isn't only film but theater buffs—and anyone who cares about American culture—who should celebrate this week's news that the American Film Institute has recovered a near-mint print of a 1912 silent movie of *Richard III*. . . . The first feature-film adaptation ever of a Shakespeare play, this *Richard III* is not merely an artifact from the dawn of movies but a rare photographic record of the vanished American theater of the century before."
>
> —FRANK RICH, film critic

When one looks back at its history, the NEA served as film preservation's first Andrew Carnegie, with $12,725,000 distributed among America's leading and smaller archives from 1967 to 1996. This total does not include separate funding of $9,780,000 for the *AFI Catalog:* $860,921 from NEA, $4,379,533 from NEH, and $4,540,560 raised by AFI. Truth be told, so much more was needed.

The NEA 40th Anniversary Report, published in 2005, explained how proud it was of its central role in the history of the American preservation movement:

> *The National Endowment for the Arts arrived on the media scene at a time when problems with films were particularly pressing, and it quickly made those problems a top priority. By creating the American Film Institute, issuing a mandate to the field to restore imperiled works on films, and investing millions of dollars in the preservation effort, the Arts endowment fundamentally altered the "picture" of one of America's most important and widely appreciated art forms. The challenge was monumental, but by successfully taking on the problems as early as it did, the agency prevented thousands of works from being lost forever. Four decades later, this is still among the NEA's most important achievements.*

The AFI Collection

In its first fifteen years, the AFI preservation staff created the AFI Collection, which was placed primarily at the LOC. They found and acquired more than 18,000 titles through donation, trade, and purchase (at a nominal fee). The staff worked with major studios, foreign archives, labs, and more than 1,000 individuals across the country to acquire these films, many of which were unique copies or the best surviving copies.

Compared to the major film archives, the AFI Collection is admittedly modest, but the nationwide attention this effort gained lifted the prospects of all those advocating for film preservation. With every film added to the AFI Collection, there was a cultural shift that added momentum to the case for finding the next film, so that the AFI Collection stands as a testament of what AFI has done best for fifty years: drawing attention, knowledge, and respect to—and shining light on—the history of the movies.

AFI Catalog and the Decade of Preservation

While AFI was engaged in the early years with sending out the clarion call that gathered thousands of lost movies, others wondered how it was even possible to organize and study America's film history if there was no master list of the films that had been made. To even consider this massive question meant that the *AFI Catalog* would be a hugely ambitious project, but it was launched just to fill that gap. It was a singular and monumental project no one had ever attempted—that of cataloging all films ever made in America (and the scope would soon be expanded to include all films ever exhibited in America). The *AFI Catalog* has become a foundation of film scholarship, archives, and preservation work. It is the common ground from which thousands of separate efforts are launched, assured of the authenticity and care behind the film facts.

When I started at AFI in 1980, the *AFI Catalog* had been on hiatus for three years. The *AFI Catalog*'s debut volumes, published in 1971 and covering films of the 1920s, took everyone's breath away—with 6,606 entries and 1,653 pages, the two volumes' signature red covers would become highly respected and recognized. The community was hungry for more. However, the 1960s volume of the *AFI Catalog* was on an altogether different scale. It was finally published in 1976—5,774 entries and 2,244 pages that had, all told, put a great strain on AFI's overall budget. The project had gone on hiatus, a decision that caused considerable anger within the archival community.

As AFI's director, I was told by one and all that my first priority must be getting the *AFI Catalog* back in motion. I took this advice to heart, while also wondering how we could do it differently—decreasing the financial strain on AFI's overall budget and putting this project back on track in a way that could be sustained for the long haul. This project, after all, is the work of generations—not a quick hit. I knew that the project structure would need to support the highest level of research. Funding commitments would need to be secured. And we would succeed, with the publication of each new decade's research providing a new reason to celebrate. Each release of a new *AFI Catalog* volume, in print and later online, would be received with extraordinary excitement and acclaim—proud moments for executive editor Patricia King Hanson and her team. But in 1981, that success was still to come.

We were fortunate to have a preservation ally in Jeanine Basinger, whose insights, experience, and soul have graced the AFI board meetings and process almost continually since 1979. Few trustees have provided stronger intellectual perspective and personal commitment than Jeanine has over the course of AFI's history. A renowned teacher, historian, and author of more than a dozen books, she is godmother to more than 400 Wesleyan graduates who fill the annals of media culture. In 1981, I didn't know just how invaluable her guidance would prove to be, over many decades and on a range of projects.

As I was trying to figure out how to make the *AFI Catalog* project happen, in late 1981, President Reagan appointed Frank Hodsoll as NEA chairman. Frank is another fascinating figure in NEA history. A brilliant man who devoted his life to public service, he was deputy chief of staff for President Reagan's White House and, to the surprise of people around him, requested the appointment as chairman of the NEA. "Encouraging creativity is like being at the cutting edge of human development," he told the *Washington Post*, which recalled his words in Hodsoll's July 26, 2016, obituary. "Maybe I'm crazy, but I think that would be an exciting thing to do. Not being a member of the creative sector myself, I think it would be interesting to help develop a climate within which creative people will find it easier to do their thing." (From time to time, brilliant staff people like to run their own show. I remember Brian O'Doherty telling me that Hodsoll wanted to be a Cabinet member, but this was the closest he could get.)

Basically, Frank knew nothing about the arts other than his appreciation as a patron and member of the audience. So, as chair of the NEA, he did what every good researcher does: talk to everyone and then decide who to believe and what's most important. He had a particular respect for film, believed film preservation was valuable, and wanted to find a way to raise more money for it. He believed he could build a structure that would encourage all the archives to work together to avoid duplication of efforts. Unfortunately, he underestimated the competitive nature of the perennially starved arts universe.

At the AFI, we very much wanted to continue to be a national voice for the preservation cause. With Bob Wise and Franklin Schaffner leading the way in 1982, we proclaimed a Decade of Preservation. (It started as a Year of Preservation, but when someone like Bob Wise suggests it should be a *decade*, you listen to the director.) The NEA gave AFI an additional $25,000 and we produced an exciting seven-minute trailer about the need and

---

"Thanks to the American Film Institute for creating this place where talented, gifted people can come to learn the tools they need in order to help us see better films. I sincerely believe that to see good films—and to see important films—is one of the most profoundly civilizing experiences that we can have. That when we go to the theater and empathize with those people who are not ourselves, it makes us better people—more broad-minded, more able to understand what's right with the world, what's wrong with the world."

—ROGER EBERT,
film critic and honorary degree recipient (2004)

---

relevance of saving film heritage, with Jack Lemmon on camera and doing the voiceover narration. Sitting with Bob and Franklin when they discussed how to edit the trailer was really a moment I will never forget. We got great distribution for it, because Jim Katz was then heading up something called Universal Classics and was re-releasing many Hitchcock titles. He ran the short at theaters across the country during 1982 and 1983.

The Decade of Preservation got off to a great start with a series of dinners across the country funded by RKO Pictures. Herb Karlitz, a superb communications consultant, organized the sponsorship as he did many others for AFI over the years. The first event was at the Beverly Hilton Hotel, with Bette Davis, James Caan, and Jessica Lange on the dais. The goal was to get people talking and thinking about preservation so that more money would be contributed to the cause. When we screened the Jack Lemmon preservation video at these events, everyone was overwhelmed to see the "before" version of deteriorated nitrate images and then the remarkable "after" restored version—the picture said everything.

National Center for Film and Video Preservation

Finally, with Frank Hodsoll's strong help, the *AFI Catalog* project was rolling again, with funding from both NEA and NEH, as well as the David and Lucile Packard Foundation. But it was too soon to take a deep breath, because Hodsoll wanted a louder voice and more attention paid to preservation. To accomplish this, the role of coordinating the funding of film archives was moved outside AFI proper and placed with a new entity called the National Center for Film and Video Preservation at the American Film Institute (NCFVP at AFI).

Beginning in 1984, this new Center had an auspicious board

led by co-chairs including the wonderful Fay Kanin, the distinguished TV executive Elton Rule, and the actor Eddie Albert (husband of the NEA council member Margot Albert, both of whom were beloved by anyone who met them). Most promising of all was that Bob Rosen, a truly great archivist and leader in the preservation world, took a leave of absence from UCLA and agreed to sign on as the director. I was really excited to be working with Bob and put his office right across the hall from mine. During his years at AFI, Bob not only accomplished a great deal, but also always fostered good will within the preservation community.

As Brian O'Doherty wrote to Frank Hodsoll in a memo dated November 7, 1984, prior to an NEA AFI panel meeting:

Center for Film/Video Preservation

- *Robert Rosen's performance has been admirable.*
- *With a board and chairpersons, the Center will be ready to move.*
- *Among key questions are: Will the field fully cooperate with and support this Center? Will the Center raise private monies to give the enterprise a major impetus?*
- *For many years, the panel has called for the completion of the* AFI Catalog.

As usual, Brian O'Doherty was asking the right questions. The NCFVP at AFI now oversaw the AFI Collection, now close to 20,000 prints housed primarily at the LOC, and the *AFI Catalog*, now deep into the research on films of the 1910s. Rosen took over and made all of this work. At the time, I thought to myself that this structure could make a difference. We seemed to be making progress. But in 1986—far too soon for the well-being of the projects—Rosen's leave from UCLA ended, and he had to leave his post at AFI. For him it was exactly the right thing to do, although I tried mightily to entice him to stay. No doubt, UCLA realized what a great leader they had. Subsequently, Rosen was named chair of the Department of Film and Television in 1991, then dean of the UCLA School of Theater, Film, and Television in 1998 upon the revered Gil Cates's retirement. Without a doubt, Bob Rosen did the archival community proud with his accomplishments. As UCLA chancellor Albert Carnesale described Bob's appointment to dean: "Professor Rosen is renowned in the international film and television community for his leadership and scholarship as a historian and preservationist."

Rosen's work at UCLA helped to increase the importance of that institution's archive, a prime position for an archive housed on the West Coast at an outstanding public university. It made a perfect partner with the LOC Collection on the East Coast. Time would demonstrate the wisdom of this symmetry.

Worthy Projects

AFI's preservation efforts created some big moments in the ensuing years, particularly in 1986 with the restoration and re-release of Frank Capra's 1937 *Lost Horizon* around the United States. To be able to show the before-and-after moments of a film restoration is incredibly exciting, and this brilliant black-and-white film demonstrated the value perfectly.

Patricia King Hanson, director of the *AFI Catalog* project, and Alan Gevinson, associate editor, drove up to Palo Alto on February 16, 1990, through a torrential rainstorm to attend David Woodley Packard's Stanford Theatre screening of the film. It seemed like the entire preservation community was there, including Robert Saudek, who had become head of the LOC Motion Picture, Broadcasting, and Recorded Sound Division. I knew Saudek well from my Markle Foundation days, because he was so respected during the early years of television when he produced many of the great cultural programs, including *Omnibus* for the Ford Foundation.

Kevin Thomas wrote an insightful review of the restoration

and its complexities, putting into context why such efforts were so worthwhile:

> *One of the marks of a screen classic is that while it retains its central meaning; you can respond to it differently at different stages in your life. As a child you respond to* Lost Horizon *unquestioningly as it transports you to its awesome, shimmering fantasy world; as a young adult you understand why John Howard finds Shangri-La so suffocating, and you understand his eagerness to get back to the challenges of the real world. But by middle age, Shangri-La begins to look awfully inviting.*

In 1987, the restored *Alexander Nevsky* (1938), directed by Sergei Eisenstein, was screened in the Dorothy Chandler Pavilion at the Los Angeles Music Center for the Performing Arts, with the L.A. Philharmonic playing a score by Sergei Prokofiev as accompaniment. This thrilling collaboration was masterminded by John Goberman, the Emmy-award winning producer of *Live from Lincoln Center.* How he orchestrated the combination of conductor André Previn, 104 members of the orchestra who donated their services (almost unheard of today), 130 musicians of the L.A. Master Chorale, and mezzo-soprano soloist Christine Cairns is a story unto itself. It was a rare artistic challenge to bring life to this marriage of a historic film with its full orchestration, which had been described forty-nine years earlier as tinny, tiny, and far from the composer's alleged symphonic conception. Previn said originally it resembled "six players recorded in a phone booth."

After the loss of Rosen's leadership, the NCFVP at AFI proceeded with several acting directors until the selection of the next director in 1987. Elton Rule recommended a respected television and advertising executive who would bring media savvy to the role, but the appointment wasn't a fit, and we were quickly back to search mode with more acting directors. In 1989, Shirlee Taylor Haizlip was appointed director. Her career included time at

WNET, the primary PBS station in New York City, study at Harvard, and a teaching post at Tufts University. Charming and bright, she made a noble effort to engage the archival community that, at times, is not accepting of those who haven't spent their lives in the film preservation world. Brian O'Doherty had asked the key question: Will the field cooperate with the Center?

While the NCFVP at AFI was laboring on its path, a new threat to film artists caught everyone's attention: colorization of black-and-white movies. This was very controversial and a major moment in the history of film preservation.

The Colorization Controversy

Colorization was a huge artistic and ethical issue for the film community. It pitted the forces of modernization and commercialization against the ethics of artistic freedom and heritage. It had been lurking for some years, as digital technology evolved, but then seemed to break out all at once in 1986.

But black-and-white movies didn't pull the kind of television ratings in prime time that color films did. Business leaders are always looking for ways to leverage their assets. Television had become a great ancillary income for the studios, and they were basking in this newfound secondary revenue stream. Executives asked how to make these black-and-white film assets perform better. The answer was simple: colorize.

It was an answer with no regard for the creative integrity of a classic film or for the director's intentions. The focus of the move for colorization was solely on the bottom line. The response from leading creatives was violent. AFI, as the voice of film preservation, agreed with them. We called a press conference on October 1, 1986, to take a stand against colorization. We had a strong contingent from the creative community that included Jimmy Stewart, Fay Kanin, producer-director Stanley Kramer, and directors Martha

Coolidge and Peter Hyams. It was, from my point of view, obviously and absolutely the right thing to do. But several board members, including heads of studios, weren't thrilled by AFI's position.

Then, in 1986, Gene Siskel and Roger Ebert, at the height of their popularity, did a special episode of *Siskel & Ebert & the Movies* titled "Hollywood's New Vandalism." They went behind the technical wizardry and described what the Directors Guild of America had earlier described—colorization as "cultural butchery." Ebert's 1988 essay "*Casablanca* Gets Colorized, But Don't Play It Again, Ted [Turner]" followed up on the small step of progress made with the National Film Preservation Act passed by Congress. It authorized a panel of experts to designate twenty-five films a year as "national treasures." Anyone altering or otherwise materially changing these films would have to add a warning on the film and its packaging that colorization had been done without the consent of the original filmmakers. Ebert described it as a step in the right direction.

The legislation creating the National Film Preservation Registry placed the responsibility with the Library of Congress, and the librarian and the board have done a wonderful job of bringing

---

"In 1967, thanks to James Blue and George Stevens Jr., I became part of the initial staff of the AFI at Greystone. I've stayed close these many years, watching and often participating as AFI has grown from a simple Rose Garden speech by Lyndon Johnson to become an institution for promoting American cinema, as well as teaching generations of our filmmakers. Through the highs and lows, AFI has always been a valuable beacon for the notion that film is a vital part of our national memory."

—JOHN PTAK,
producer, former talent agent, and
AFI representative on the National Film Preservation Board

---

attention to film history, to "orphan films" that have no affiliation with a copyright owner, and to home movies. Each year, the office announces the twenty-five films that have been added to the National Film Registry, and every year, the press release reminds the public of these movies' meaning for America. John Ptak has represented the AFI on the National Film Preservation Board since its inception, and he rarely misses a meeting. (In late 2015, he became chair of the board of trustees.) An interesting documentary the LOC did about the legislation, *These Amazing Shadows* (2011), explained that while artistic rights and the colorization issue was the impetus, the board quickly shifted the focus to preservation. Orphan films and home movies demonstrated the growing diversity that had no advocacy or home. In looking at the entire range of moving image media, a new challenge was engaged in America's film history.

Special Events

Special events brought attention to the world of preservation, some amazingly spectacular. In 1988, the seemingly indefatigable Bonita "Bunny" Granville Wrather, a friend of the Reagans, arranged for them to be the honored guests at a Preservation Ball in support of the NCFVP at AFI. When the President and First Lady attend, everyone wants to be there. The evening honored another friend, Fred Astaire, with Ginger Rogers in attendance. Associate director Marcia Mitchell, based in DC, was in charge of the Washington office and events. She recalls that the Presidential staff said that the President would attend the VIP reception (forty-five minutes) and make introductions at the event (another forty-five minutes), but he would not sit at the dinner table. That left the First Lady without an appropriate dinner companion—until Mikhail Baryshnikov was moved on the seating chart. Nancy Reagan was absolutely delighted.

One of the most consequential preservation events occurred in

1989, just as the issue was gaining more national traction. Martin Scorsese had taken up the cause and was friendly with Dawn Steel, head of Columbia Pictures. He convinced her to restore and re-release Sir David Lean's *Lawrence of Arabia*, with a big premiere to raise funds in support of the NCFVP at AFI. The studio wanted to make a big splash, and they did, starting with a press conference announcing the project at the then-new Peninsula Hotel in New York City. Scorsese was there, together with Steven Spielberg and some two-dozen cameras for coverage. The premiere at the Ziegfeld Theater in New York City was one of the most electric nights I can remember—outshining even the two additional premieres in DC and L.A. Everyone was there—including Steven Spielberg, Fay Kanin, Elton Rule, director David Lean, actors Omar Sharif and Anthony Quinn, cinematographer Freddie Young, editor Anne V. Coates, composer Maurice Jarre, and preservationists Robert Harris and Jim Katz. I remember that, after everyone was announced, I hugged Jim Katz, because we had just been part of a special moment in film preservation history.

The NCFVP at AFI staff took on some valuable organizing projects like FAAC/TAAC, which evolved into the American Moving Image Archivists (AMIA) to function as a separate, sister organization to FIAF (the International Federation of Film Archives/Fédération Internationale des Archives du Film), jointly founded in 1938 by the Cinémathèque Française, Germany's Reichsfilmarchiv, the British Film Institute, and the Museum of Modern Art Film Library. NCFVP at AFI served as the secretariat and office for AMIA during its first six years of existence (1991–1996) and continued to publish the *AMIA Newsletter* for years. FIAF's mission includes advancing film preservation as well as advancing scholarship, maintaining a database of archival holdings, and setting preservation standards, which it continues to the present day, with over eighty member institutions around the world.

In 1990, Elton Rule passed away, and Marty Scorsese agreed to be co-chair of the NCFVP at AFI. At the same time, he set up his own organization, called Film Foundation. With Margaret Bodde at the wheel, they have played a spectacular role, raising funds and consistently being involved and available, and always espousing the cause.

In 1991, AFI trustee Tom Pollock, then heading up the Universal Motion Picture group, recreated the *Lawrence of Arabia* spectacular with the restoration, re-release, and premieres of *Spartacus* in three cities across America. Flying around the country with Kirk Douglas was a lot of fun because the public was so enamored with what Spartacus represented. And, in many ways, you could say that Kirk has made this a hallmark of his own life.

We introduced the 1930s volume of the *AFI Catalog* in the AFI Theater at the Kennedy Center, with NEA chair Jane Alexander and NEH chair Sheldon Hackney smiling broadly. Star Fay Wray was there in person as we screened the classic *King Kong*. Every time a volume of the *AFI Catalog* was published, it was a big deal, and rightfully so, considering the years of research and accomplishment. The release of the 1930s volume was special, with so many beloved films from that decade.

But it also was symbolic, because it was 1994, and little did we know that within a year, the NEA would stop supporting the archive pass-through funding program. Indeed, AFI's own archive funding was soon phased out as well. What happened were massive restrictions and reductions in funding for both endowments, with new legislative restrictions preventing pass-through funding. When I heard that film archives would no longer receive support from the NEA, I was stunned. The thinking seemed all wrong. We fought for the NEA to continue supporting the archives. In spite of our best efforts, this was the beginning of the end for substantial NEA funding, not only for preservation but also for AFI. AFI's annual general support would be phased out completely in 1998.

Transitions in Funding

Just before the NEA closed the door on supporting film preservation, AFI completed the $1 million AFI-NEA Film Preservation Challenge Grant (NEA provided $1 for every $3 raised by AFI, primarily from a Blockbuster Preservation Fund in connection with the first year of *AFI's 100 Years...100 Movies* telecast, awarding the bulk of $375,000 to the four other FIAF archives across America and other smaller grants to eight specialist archives. This infusion of funds was a major but, in fact, final contribution from the NEA to this effort.

As the NEA funding was fading away, AFI assiduously continued searching for funds for the *AFI Catalog*, because we believed firmly that it was our responsibility to complete the documentation of the first 100 years of American film history. The *AFI Catalog* team, cohesive and focused, was still expertly led by Patricia King Hanson. At Pat's 2009 retirement party, a noted film historian would say that Pat is the most quoted person in film history without attribution. The *AFI Catalog*, universally respected, is rarely cited or given credit in film literature, let alone on the Internet.

We visited with Sir Paul Getty, who loved the *AFI Catalog*, a number of times in London, England. He was a film historian

---

"AFI's contribution to the Library's national effort to preserve our American moving image heritage goes back . . . to the late 1960s with the initial donations of what would become, over the next twenty years, a broad and diverse range of AFI Collection gifts to the Library of Congress. These numerous AFI-donated collections form a cornerstone in the foundation of the Library's film and video holdings, which have grown to become the largest and most comprehensive collection of such materials in the world."

—DR. CARLA D. HAYDEN,
Librarian of Congress and AFI trustee (2017–)

---

himself and immensely respected both Ken Wlaschin, who had been at the BFI for several years before returning to the U.S., and Pat Hanson. Volumes of the *AFI Catalog* had a proud position on his vast bookshelves. He pledged $2.5 million to support ongoing catalog research, then sadly passed away soon after his written pledge to AFI. Even though it had not yet been recorded in his will, his estate honored his pledge and later allowed the endowment to be used to complete the first 100 years of filmmaking. With that commitment, the future of the *AFI Catalog* was secured.

As the new century arrived, the reality of two symmetrical archives on each coast became clear, one at the LOC (including the AFI Collection) and at UCLA (with Bob Rosen's leadership). Both are possible because of the incredible personal philanthropy of one man: David Woodley Packard and his Packard Humanities Institute. This book is not the place to discuss in detail the cultural facilities Packard built for the nation's Library of Congress in Culpeper, Virginia, and for UCLA at the Packard Humanities Institute (known as the PHI Stoa) in Santa Clarita, California. In March 2016, I toured the Santa Clarita facility, where the dedicated Eddie Richmond showed me this remarkable edifice, unique in so many ways. And in September 2016, I walked the aisles of the fantastic Culpeper facility, led since 2003 by Gregory Lukow, chief of the Motion Picture, Broadcasting, and Recorded Sound Division, and where the AFI Collection is preserved. (Greg was on the AFI preservation team for fourteen years, working in an office across the hall from mine.) These are the two largest audio-visual storage facilities in the United States; suffice it to say, David Woodley Packard is undisputedly the most important patron of American film preservation. Retired Librarian of Congress James Billington, quoted in the *Los Angeles Times*, said, "If you want an analogy to David Packard in American history, Andrew Carnegie would be the best." The NEA made a huge contribution to the movement in the twentieth century, and now Packard has dramatically changed the dynamic in the twenty-first century. Anyone who cares about cultural heritage is greatly indebted to this gentleman, who has made such a difference to the history of moving images.

NEA preservation funding ended just as the latest and newest preservation challenge from digital filmmaking was emerging. As technology has moved from nitrate to acetate to digital media, it is clear that while nothing ever gets easier, our film heritage is unquestionably part of our national cultural treasure. It is almost poetic that, fifty years after NEA and AFI launched this era of modern media preservation, the *AFI Catalog* is the authoritative source for film scholarship on academic shelves and online, and the most trusted and respected historical account of American film culture.

NEA

PRESERVATION CONTRACTS

Total:	$12,725,000
To Other Archives:	$ 8,725,000
To AFI:	$ 4,000,000

***AFI CATALOG* FUNDING**

Total:	$ 9,781,000
NEH:	$ 4,379,000
NEA:	$ 869,900
AFI:	$ 4,540,000

The Final Word: *AFI Catalog of Feature Films*

Patricia King Hanson

One hundred and twenty years ago, stories about the birth of the motion picture were front-page news. Within a very short time, projected motion pictures filled venues with people curious to watch these short-duration wonders "reproducing motion" at 2,400 photographs per minute, as the *New York Evening World* reported in May 1891. People were fascinated by the natural, relatively fluid onscreen movement of newsworthy people and events, everyday activities, or fantastic flights of fantasy. But these "living pictures" were initially thought of as transitory snippets that could be watched, perhaps remembered for a while, and then discarded. As early as the 1910s, though, visionaries saw motion pictures as something more significant: lasting historical records, and even artistic treasures. Early film trade papers routinely published letters and feature articles on the historical value of *some* motion pictures and the need to preserve them, as exemplified by one pithy headline in an April 1915 editorial in *Motography*: "Can Films Be Preserved for Posterity?"

> "No source of information is as complete and accurate, and no other source is produced with the scrupulous level of attention to scholarship and research as the *AFI Catalog.*"
>
> —MARTIN SCORSESE, filmmaker

From a practical standpoint, the big question for archivists, filmmakers, and historians was then—and to some extent remains today: How do you decide what to preserve? And embedded in the process is an even more fundamental question: How can you preserve a nation's films without a list, a record of what films were made? And so, as the broader film preservation movement arose in the U.S., a catalog of motion pictures produced in the United States emerged out of necessity. While not formal archival work, the *AFI Catalog of Feature Films* was to become an invaluable tool in film preservation. Unlike most cinema books that are subjective and opinionated, the *AFI Catalog* attempted to be completely egalitarian; whether films were good or bad, box office hits or flops, they were to be included and given equal consideration. For that reason, it isn't unusual to look at any given page of the 1920s *Catalog* and find a great film such as King Vidor's *The Big Parade* (1925) occupying about the same space as John G. Adolfi's less memorable production, *Big Pal* (1925).

In 1971, the 1920s *AFI Catalog* became the first published installment of an unthinkably massive project. The big, red books of the two-volume set marked a beginning. As founding AFI director George Stevens Jr. wrote in the foreword, "One task of the Institute is to recover the surviving films—nearly 4,500 are already in the AFI Collection at the Library of Congress—and another is to recover and organize the data which can document the history of the art." Two decades later, the National Film Preservation Board 1993 report, "A Study of the Current State of American Film Preservation," stated that the *AFI Catalog* had become:

> *. . . the baseline for U.S. film production . . . [which gives] accurate information for identifying films acquired without titles or credits, and verifies the length, technical processes, and versions of features as they were originally released. By recording studio and independent production decade-by-decade, the* Catalog *provides a statistical population against which film survival rates can be reliably calculated.*

That was the founding idea behind the *AFI Catalog*, but like all big ideas, it wasn't easy to implement. It was, and still is, a great deal of work. And the value of the *AFI Catalog* turned out to be so much more, not just for archivists but all sorts of others. Film historians, of course, would predictably find it useful, but the public's increasing thirst for film information since the late 1960s has made the *AFI Catalog* a perfect source for anyone who wanted information on a particular film or actor. Its value would increase over the years to include students and professors working on statistical projects about things as diverse as film production, women's studies, and societal mores.

The Work Begins

Research on the *AFI Catalog of Feature Films, 1921–1930*, began in 1968 at the Library of Congress in Washington, DC. Putting things into perspective, when research was started on the 1921–1930 decade, it had been less than forty years since the end of the 1920s, about the same separation of time we have now from the production of *The Godfather* or *Chinatown*. The seven-member staff, under the direction of executive editor Kenneth W. Munden, was given the mandate to identify and catalog all American feature films, adhering to the International Federation of Film Archives (FIAF) rule that features are films that are four reels (approximately forty minutes) or longer in length. They no doubt were daunted by the task at hand, even more so given that the research was done in the late 1960s and early 1970s, decades before the Internet, IMDb, or any other major published work had tackled a similarly large-scale project on American film history.

The 1920s staff used sources such as the *U.S. Catalog of Copyright Entries*, Maryland and New York census records, *Variety*, *Film Daily*, *Motion Picture News*, and other trade papers to systematically compile a title list of the 1921–1930 films, which in turn was fleshed out with available credits, release dates, companies, cast, and crew, plus plot summaries, genre, and subject terms. Given the lack of previous works on the decade's filmographic output, cataloging 6,606 titles remains an amazing work of scholarship. It prompted no less a scholar than historian Arthur Schlesinger Jr. to write in 1972: "The AFI's '20s *Catalog* is not only a triumph of exact scholarship, it is also endlessly absorbing as an excursion into cultural history and national memory."

With the completion of the 1920s, it became immediately clear that, with the publication of each decade, there would be a sharp snapshot of American filmmaking culture for a moment in time. It also meant that, even in 1971, there were still five decades of feature films to conquer. For reasons that may seem odd now, but made complete sense in the early 1970s, a decision was made not to go back into the more remote decades of the 1910s or 1930s, but to tackle the 1960s—because it should have been much easier to catalog films that had just been released a few years before. Sadly, this turned out to be a poor decision.

There were problems with the 1960s from the beginning. The executive editor who had launched the project, Kenneth Munden, died early in the 1960s decade work, and new editorial direction was needed. There was an agreement with the publisher of *Filmfacts* to utilize the excellent plot summaries it included in that monthly publication. Unfortunately, as broad a canvas as *Filmfacts* was, it was woefully short of the mark in terms of comprehensiveness. Perhaps the largest misstep for the 1960s was its new scope—to include every film released in the United States, not just American-produced films. This will explain why movies as varied as the Swedish-produced Ingmar Bergman film *The Devil's Eye* (1961) is side by side with the American-produced Andrew V. McLaglen picture *The Devil's Brigade* (1968). The inclusion of foreign productions merely exhibited in the U.S. increased the size of the 1960s *AFI Catalog* by at least twenty percent.

Despite the Herculean efforts of second executive editor Richard P. Krafsur, the staff ballooned to twice the size of the staff for the 1920s volume, and the 1960s *AFI Catalog* took six years to complete. While it was another excellent example of dedicated film scholarship, it was a huge blow to AFI's financial stability. The *AFI Catalog* project came to a halt in 1977. The young institution simply could not sustain such an impactful increase in expenses and personnel.

AFI Catalog Goes to Hollywood

Shortly after Jean Firstenberg became head of AFI in 1980, she heard many voices asking for AFI to revive the dormant *AFI Catalog* project. Working with NEA chair Frank Hodsoll, NEH chair William J. Bennett, and philanthropist David Woodley Packard, she made it a priority to re-launch the *AFI Catalog* project. With funding grants from the NEA, NEH, and the David and Lucile Packard Foundation, work was restarted at the AFI's new campus in Los Angeles in October of 1983. I took on the role of executive editor, ready to restart the project with a staff that included Audrey Kupferberg as project manager, and Cathy Root, Marsha Maguire, and Barry Sabath as the initial group of catalogers, followed soon after by Alan Gevinson and Amy Dunkleberger. It was a difficult project to restart. From the previous era's team, we inherited a potential title list of 1910s films, all neatly typed up on three-by-five index cards with copyright information and trade reviews. But in every other way, we needed to start from the ground up, from chairs and desks to microfilm readers.

While film is a visual medium, when the 1910s *AFI Catalog* work began, there was no expectation that we would actually see any of the films. Catalogers hadn't viewed films to create the 1920s or 1960s *Catalog*, but aside from their methodological example, there were very few films from the 1910s accessible at that time. We did see a handful of films that happened to be made available to us, including *The Birth of a Nation* (1915), *Intolerance* (1916), and other D. W. Griffith films, as well as a few unusual titles, such as *Bolshevism on Trial* (1919). Still, the number of films viewed for the 1910s *AFI Catalog* was minute in comparison with the 5,189 films included in the 1910s *Catalog*.

Flashing forward to the late 1980s, when we were cataloging films for the 1930s *AFI Catalog*, America was experiencing a burst of nostalgia and appreciation for those films. It soon became apparent to us that we could not rely solely on the often-sketchy printed materials on 1930s films when an increasing number were becoming available on what were then the reigning standards: videotape and late-night TV. So we made the fateful (and perhaps foolish) decision to watch as many 1930s films as possible, not just to capture accurate screen credits, but also for plot details and to identify additional uncredited actors.

It was a mind-boggling task, especially when it dawned on us that not just some films, but most films, could be seen in one form or another. Word soon got around that we were aiming to watch every feature film, and we were overwhelmed by the kindness and generosity of so many individuals and institutions—from a truculent collector who concluded that "anyone who likes Budd Buster movies can't be all bad" to large studios and archives, video shops, and 16mm distributors. People were rooting for us; they wanted these films to be seen and cataloged, and they trusted us to do it.

True Film Detective Work

Occasionally, a staff member had an inadvertently hilarious interchange with someone who worked on films of the past. The last remaining member of a great family of stuntmen was gracious enough to explain to cataloger Howie Davidson the names and confusing nicknames of his entire family so that every name in the index of personal names was correct. I even contacted the gracious writer-director Hal Kantor to confirm my hunch that he had delivered the satirical narration to the 1958 Dan Rowan and Dick Martin film he directed, *Once Upon a Horse*. As he talked, explaining that he had no memory of narrating the film, I told him that, listening to his voice, I could confirm that he did narrate that little-known gem. Another time, restaurateur Harry Lewis confirmed to a colleague that the Harry Lewis filmography we had amassed for films of the 1940s, which we assumed reflected two different actors of different ages, and possibly neither of them him, were actually all his roles.

There were some funny sides to this quest. Someone, usually associate editor Alan Gevinson, religiously checked the *TV Guide* to see which old films were going to be shown locally. (This was before online searching, after all.) Assignments were made for video recording, and feelers went out to friends and family about anything obscure being shown in other cities. We often said, only half-joking, that when you work for the *AFI Catalog*, your family and friends do, too.

In addition to our own collection of VHS tapes amassed over the years, the San Fernando Valley video store Eddie Brandt's Saturday Matinee was an incomparable source. No doubt to their ultimate chagrin, Eddie Brandt and his family provided free access to their extensive off-air video collection, so invaluable for titles that were never available commercially. Archives were as generous as they were efficient in their offerings. The UCLA Film & Television Archive, Library of Congress, George Eastman House, Wisconsin Center for Film & Television, and occasionally the Museum of Modern Art, National Center for Jewish Film, Cinémathèque Française, and the British Film Institute provided our staff with access to their archival collections.

With limited travel funds, staff members vacationing on the East Coast or in Europe often found themselves (sometimes reluctantly) taking a day off from their vacation to watch a 1930s, '40s, or '50s film in a local archive. I remember a brief New York City vacation in 1986 where I was treated to a private screening room viewing of the Greta Garbo–Clark Gable film *Susan Lenox: Her Fall and Rise* at MoMA, years before it became available on DVD or broadcast on Turner Classic Movies. The BFI staff went a step further in their willingness to help, watching some American films in their collection and sending the information to us. A notable example was *Unashamed: A Romance*, a 1938 nudist film that was inexplicably maintained in their collection. This seemed to be a hot ticket for the BFI staff.

In the late 1980s and early 1990s, studios still maintained libraries of 16mm films that they loaned to us, often sending them from the East Coast, or allowing us to pick titles up at their storage warehouses. Sony, Universal, and Turner Entertainment, with its vast library of MGM, RKO, and Warner Bros. films, were particularly generous. We soon learned that buying up 16mm projectors was relatively easy and inexpensive. As local school districts were switching from 16mm to VHS tapes to show films, several staff members

> "It's too bad that the AFI couldn't give its AFI Life Achievement Award to executive editor Patricia King Hanson, assistant editor Amy Dunkleberger, and the rest of the eleven-person project staff and editorial advisory board. They all worked . . . to produce this nonpareil reference set, and they have made an irreplaceable contribution to American film."
>
> —KENNETH TURAN, film critic

gleefully plunked down $50 to $100 to buy and maintain their own machines. It was not unknown for the then-two-room office to resemble a multiplex, with projectors active in each of the rooms and a cataloger taking notes while attached to headphones.

In retrospect, this embarrassment of riches makes us realize that it was a perfect time to have worked on the 1930s and 1940s volumes when we did. It would be a much more daunting task to watch all of those films today. Certainly archives have identified, acquired, and preserved many more films than were available in the 1980s, but for individual viewers, having the ability to watch the films with ease is much more difficult. TCM (and file-sharing websites) notwithstanding, there simply aren't as many old films available. There are virtually no 16mm houses or studio-held 16mm libraries, and there are more restrictions on viewing 35mm films in major archives, as well as a reduction of commercially available titles. Thanks to all of the opportunity available to us then, we amassed some impressive statistics for viewing the films we cataloged: eighty-two percent for the 1930s, ninety-two percent for the 1940s, and ninety-seven percent for the 1950s. Of course, these were not always pristine, archival quality films, but impressive numbers nonetheless.

Serving our audience was a complicated, ever-changing battle. The *AFI Catalog* started out as a preservation tool, documenting the filmographic history of the United States. Yet we realized when working on the 1910s and beyond that we served other needs: fans (certainly), trivia lovers, scholars interested in statistical analyses of motion pictures, and almost anyone interested in what subjects were covered. A quick search of the *AFI Catalog* database reveals these quirky statistics: How many films deal with seances? Ninety-one. Divorce? Over 1,000. Marriage? More than 4,000. Murder? Almost 8,000. Falls from heights? More than 650.

These diverse aspects of the *AFI Catalog* were both positive and negative. In a sense, we were put in the position of being everything for everyone—an impossible task. While other databases, including the now ubiquitous IMDb, deal with individual films, piece by piece, the *AFI Catalog* always looked at films as a whole. We were often amazed by how seriously people took things. Typos, omissions, or different interpretations of data were completely unacceptable. Plot points interpreted differently were heresy. We received angry letters from fans incensed that we had missed a particular character actor in a film, when we had only been able to watch it once, in an archive, with no way to rewind. But despite that, we were fortunate to have received much more positive feedback than negative, and reviewers proved to be some of our biggest supporters.

> "It's quite an experience to hold two volumes of *Film Beginnings: 1893–1910* and literally feel the weight of the motion pictures produced in the United States during this early period. The books and their substance are a tangible reflection of the import of the work that AFI does and the value of the long relationship between AFI and the endowments."
>
> —JANE ALEXANDER, actress and NEA chair (1993–1997)

Kind Words

When the 1920s *AFI Catalog* was published in 1972, the reaction was overwhelmingly positive about this then-groundbreaking two-volume set. Adding to Arthur

Schlesinger Jr.'s praise, Librarian of Congress Emeritus Daniel Boorstein called it "an unequaled guide to the film sources of our history (and also to film history)." These were lofty words to live up to. But when the 1910s, 1930s, and 1940s *Catalogs* were published, AFI and the *AFI Catalog* team were more than happy with some of our own reviews. Richard Koszarski wrote in *Film History*: "For the first time one source can provide hard answers for some of the period's most basic historical questions. . . . Information that previously had been scattered in various hard-to-locate sources has now been compressed into a pair of hefty volumes (one of them an index)." Aljean Harmetz of the *New York Times* noted, "This book is a lifesaver for detailed information about movies that otherwise I would know nothing about."

Much to our surprise and delight, when the 1940s *AFI Catalog* was published, it was named one of the top nonfiction books of the year by the *Los Angeles Times*, whose film critic Kenneth Turan wrote, "These volumes add up to nothing less than an authoritative *Oxford English Dictionary* of American film. . . . The great pleasure of these books, as any reference addict knows, is what you stumble upon while you're on the way to what you think you're looking for."

And that is exactly what we had hoped—that every person interested in film, whether an archivist, film scholar, or casual fan, would find what they were looking for, and much more. Of course, not everyone was so gracious. Over the years, we received a few cringe-worthy, sometimes hilarious complaints.

Filling Out the Picture

In addition to work on American feature films, the *AFI Catalog* staff compiled two standalone publications during the 1990s: *Film Beginnings, 1893–1910* and *Within Our Gates*. While the staff in Los Angeles worked on the 1910s, 1930s, and 1940s, *Film Beginnings* was compiled in Washington, DC. Elias Savada, who had been a cataloger on the 1960s project, toiled alone to compile data for the thousands of short films released in the U.S. between 1893 and 1911. After more than a decade, archivists and film historians began to suggest that the field would welcome the publication as a work-in-progress, rather than wait for a fully cataloged set of volumes that would require many additional staff and years to complete.

So in 1995, after the finishing stages were completed in Los Angeles, *Film Beginnings, 1893–1910* was published. Although subtitled *A Work in Progress*, a large percentage of the more than 17,000 entries contained as much information as could be known about these early films, and the volume continues to be an invaluable tool on early silent films.

The other major *AFI Catalog* project that was not part of the decade-by-decade march through the twentieth century was *Within Our Gates: Ethnicity Within American Feature Films, 1911–1960*, edited by Alan Gevinson. It was the only published *AFI Catalog* project focusing on a specific topic, and the only one to combine entries from decades previously published with some from decades not yet completed. *Within Our Gates* focused on American productions about ethnic groups within the United States and illuminated many films not previously well-known. Independently produced films made by African Americans, Asian Americans, or Hispanic Americans and Yiddish films were placed alongside mainstream Hollywood productions. And as a new wrinkle, in addition to the normal indexes, such as subject and personal names, *Within Our Gates* included an exhaustive ethnic and tribal index.

The Stakeholders

During the twenty-six years I headed the *AFI Catalog* project, we rarely had the opportunity to interact with the filmmakers we researched and wrote about. Most were either deceased or retired in remote places. Sometimes, though, we had the joy of being able to meet or speak with them, as at the February 8, 1994, event celebrating the publication of the 1930s *AFI Catalog*. Despite a snowstorm that night that threatened to close Washington, DC's Kennedy Center, where the event was held, we had the wonderful experience of meeting and spending time with *King Kong* star Fay Wray, who delighted the audience that night with her post-screening recollections.

On March 22, 2000, after the 1940s *Catalog* was published, AFI hosted a wonderful dinner at Morton's restaurant in Beverly Hills, attended by some of the great stars of the 1940s—Maureen O'Hara (still beautiful and fiery at eighty), Janet Leigh, Virginia Mayo, June Haver, Eddie Bracken, Laraine Day, and André de Toth among them. *Los Angeles Times* film critic Kenneth Turan spoke after the dinner, and the event was livened by a rather heated discussion between O'Hara and Mayo over residuals for older films.

Going Online—Goodbye to the Big Red Books

In the late 1990s, when the Internet was just starting to take off, it became apparent that the *AFI Catalog* project had reached the point at which an online presence was a necessity. As much as the *AFI Catalog*'s loyal followers loved the big red volumes that had become so recognizable, the cost of typesetting, printing, and publishing those multi-part, hard-copy volumes was becoming prohibitive.

Since the late 1980s, the *AFI Catalog* staff had been reliant on a proprietary database using CuadraSTAR software system, with records for each decade maintained as a distinct subset. Making the entries accessible online required several years of meetings and discussions on how to design, map, and convert the decade subsets into a fully integrated, cohesive, relational database suitable for online access. Accommodating the needs of a database that includes millions of personal names, dates, and subjects as well as lengthy text fields was an enormous task that took almost eighteen months to complete. KPMG Consulting, working with AFI, donated the time and personnel to effect the data conversion and set up a new SQL-based software.

By 2001, the *AFI Catalog* was officially online through an agreement with ProQuest-Chadwyck-Healey. To broaden the user base even further, subsequent versions have become available on

The AFI Catalog and IMDb

On their way to researching films, people may wonder about the difference between the *AFI Catalog* and IMDb (Internet Movie Database). On the surface, they may seem similar but in fact serve quite different purposes.

The *AFI Catalog* is the authoritative, expert source focused on American films, while IMDb is an aggregator of crowdsourced information about films, television shows, video games, and people from around the world. Where AFI goes deep, IMDb goes wide. Where AFI prizes professional standards of accuracy, IMDb prioritizes the dynamism of crowdsourced content.

Crowdsourced sites like IMDb and Wikipedia bring a vast amount of information to our fingertips, but verification of that information always lags. It trades off quality for quantity. The professionally curated content of the *AFI Catalog* prioritizes depth and quality. This direction was set in the *AFI Catalog*'s beginnings as a traditional, scholarly project with professional researchers and writers. The amount of information included in the *AFI Catalog* entries is staggering, covering not only the film but also its broader context, showing how it relates to the careers of cast and crew, as well as its place in American motion pictures as a whole. As one reviewer succinctly

AFI.com as well as Turner Classic Movie's website, TCM.com. More than twenty-five years of updates to earlier *AFI Catalog* entries, previously only accessible by outside users who called or wrote the *AFI Catalog* staff about specific films, were now available online. Corrections could now be made very quickly, and new data updates were ready at a much faster pace than hard-copy volumes. These timely improvements only make me appreciate even more

put it, a film listing from the *AFI Catalog* "is like IMDb on steroids."

As the *AFI Catalog* migrated from print to online, those high editorial standards have continued. With every entry, AFI's reputation is on the line. By contrast, IMDb makes no claim for the accuracy of its listings. IMDb relies on voluntary, unpaid contributors who submit credits, film summaries, quotations, and trivia. Readers must take this at face value. By contrast, the *AFI Catalog* aims to give readers a path to retrace the source of details, whether from the films themselves, archival sources, reviews, or news items. These citations, as well as documenting original production and publication dates for underlying source materials, make the *AFI Catalog* a definitive research tool for film scholars and film buffs.

IMDb is a dynamic tool for keeping up with the diversity and speed of new releases, and serves the entertainment community in ways that go beyond film research. When it comes to definitive information and insight on American feature films, the *AFI Catalog* is still the gold standard. The real difference and unique contribution of the *AFI Catalog* compared with IMDb might just boil down to the overall vision of the two projects when it comes to American motion pictures. IMDb gathers the data, but the *AFI Catalog tells the story.*

the kindred soul of film historian Jeanine Basinger. When we met in October 2015 to talk about the AFI's role in the history of film preservation, she said to me, "I still like to touch those big red books, every day, with respect and affection."

The 1950s and Beyond

Compared to the 1930s and 1940s, the 1950s seemed like a breeze to catalog. The first half of the 1950s entries—1951 through 1955—went online in 2000, followed by yearly installments. At the end of the 1950s, as the 1960s had already been cataloged and published in 1976, the *AFI Catalog* staff shifted to the decade of the 1970s, starting with 1971, with the intent of adding a year every six to eight months. The 1970s brought in new areas of complexity: the studio system was gone, international co-productions comprised a large segment of U.S. film production, and lines were just starting to blur between film, television, and video. Soon the first 100 years of American feature films would be available. Additionally, since 2000, the ten films annually recognized by the AFI AWARDS have been cataloged.

As we approached more recent decades, another even more monumental change started to shape the *AFI Catalog*. No one could have predicted such a radical—and rapid—change a few years before, but by 2000, additions to the *AFI Catalog* moved away from the old model of typeset, hard-copy volumes to an online, widely accessible database. The world of large scholarly books was shaken in a few short years, and there was no turning back.

AFI Catalog by the Numbers

Volume	Published	Films Cataloged
1911–1920	1988, print	5,189
1921–1930	1971, print	6,606
1931–1940	1993, print	5,525
1941–1950	1999, print	4,315
1951–1960	2000–2006, online, published in installments	3,285
1961–1970	1976, print	5,774
1971–1980	Online	2,306
1981–1990	Online	2,166
1991–2000	Online	3,046
2001–2010	Online	4,310
2011–2015	Online	2,507
2016	Online, in progress	31
Film Beginnings 1893–1910: A Work in Progress	1995, print	17,752
Within Our Gates: Ethnicity Within American Feature Films, 1911–1960	1997, print	2,464

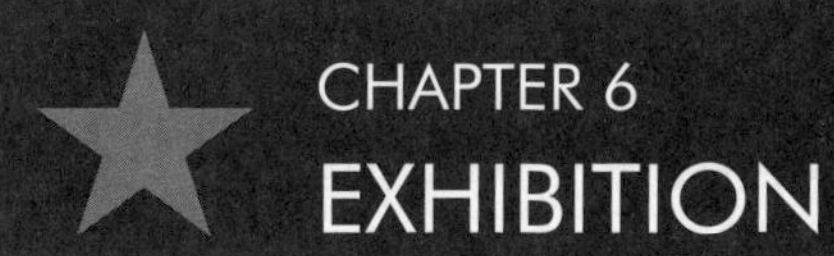

CHAPTER 6

EXHIBITION

AFI's Commitment to the Silver Screen: As Films Are Meant to Be Seen

JEAN PICKER FIRSTENBERG

A **chapter about AFI and exhibition** must start at its historical roots—the AFI Theater at the Kennedy Center for the Performing Arts—because this is one of AFI's most successful areas of accomplishment. AFI's founding director, George Stevens Jr., made it a priority from day one. And with my family's exhibitor genes, there was no way I was not going to continue that involvement.

The first site of the AFI theater program in Washington, DC, was at the National Gallery of Art's 300-seat auditorium from January to June 1970. It then moved to an 800-seat theater at L'Enfant Plaza. It was not easy to find venues in those days, but it displayed a commitment to wide public access to film in many different genres and styles. Remember that, before videocassettes, seeing a movie in a theater setting was the only way to see American or foreign films, studio films or independents, whether current or from the archives. With the dedication of the John F. Kennedy Center for the Performing Arts in 1971, George got Jack Warner to give AFI $250,000 to build an AFI Theater in the Kennedy Center.

The Kennedy Center AFI Theater had to be shoehorned into an odd space, but architects Hardy Holzman Pfeiffer Associates did a brilliant job (though some people felt otherwise). The architects designed a 224-seat black box that was basically dropped into the rear of the large Eisenhower Theater, not attached to any walls. The classic box office in the Kennedy Center lobby was an original 1920s box office restored in Kansas City and acquired by AFI—a genuine aesthetic gem. It's now in the AFI Silver Theatre lobby. AFI was also able to occupy office space above the Eisenhower.

The theater's site lines were wonderful, and it served as a forerunner to stadium seating because of the requirements of fitting seats into this block-sized space. The walls were decorated with funky '73 Chevy car hoods, which handled all the acoustical issues—no small matter, since the bare walls of the site were basically an industrial space in the back of the Eisenhower Theater. Large trucks would drive in between the entrance to the theater and its lobby, delivering sets for the next production. Timing of deliveries had to be arranged around shows in the AFI Theater. On some days, it wasn't easy for the trucks to get in and out as required.

With the consistent support of then–Kennedy Center chair Roger Stevens, the AFI Theater opened in 1973. There were twenty-two opening night films, and the third film was originally slated to be Costa-Gavras's new film, *State of Siege*. Given his standing as a distinguished international filmmaker, the choice seemed fine until someone realized that the movie was about the assassination of a political leader—not necessarily appropriate for the Kennedy Center. And so, the opening night movie was replaced amidst a great deal of angst reported in the *Washington Post* and the *New York Times*.

Because the AFI Theater was housed in a huge performing arts complex, it had certain challenges: there was no marquee, no concession stand, and no public transportation. No one walked by the Kennedy Center unless they were going to a performance at one of its theaters. This, by definition, changed the nature of the experience. It made it hard to attract an audience and hard to generate sufficient revenue. (It is a fact that commercial exhibitors make their money at the concession stand, not at the box office.) Though I loved the notion of a movie theater in a performing arts center—because that enhanced the concept of moving images as an art form—it challenged the effectiveness of the enterprise. While the realities were often painful, AFI was later offered an opportunity that allowed the Institute to take a new and bold exhibition step, making the viability of AFI at the Kennedy Center a moot point. (Read about the AFI Silver Theatre in the next section.)

Those first years at the Kennedy Center were filled with exciting screenings of film classics, both American and foreign, as well as new releases and independent screenings. The theater was programmed and run by young enthusiasts who were open and energetic and willing to try anything. George Stevens hired bright, devoted young people and let them do creative and exciting projects. Sometimes they went up to the edge, and usually they pulled it off.

The annual arrangements with the Kennedy Center were incredible, to say the least. AFI paid no rent for the theater and only $25,000 for its offices. The rent for the theater would be free unless the box office proceeds were in excess of its costs, in which case the revenue would be shared with the Kennedy Center. In addition, maintenance for the theater and the offices was fulfilled by the National Park Service. They were responsible for the entire Center, because it was on government-owned land. What a deal! And, by the way, there never was any theater revenue to share.

Exhibition Activities

Starting in the 1970s and continuing into the early 1980s, programmer Michael Webb organized events in both DC and L.A., as well as a very successful touring program, Best Remaining Seats, that included prints of films restored in the AFI Collection.

In addition to the regular programming at the Kennedy Center in Washington, DC, AFI established an Exhibition Services division in 1981 that organized impressive touring programs across America, including:

- New American Cinema: A Showcase of Premiere Films, co-sponsored with the Independent Feature Project, went to four cities.
- Jewish Film Festival—Independent Filmmakers: Looking at Ourselves, co-sponsored with the Judah L. Magnes Museum, toured New York, Los Angeles, San Francisco, and Washington, DC.
- China Film Week, films from the People's Republic of China, went on a seven-city tour, extended to thirteen additional cities and a second year.
- New Hungarian Cinema, featuring the best of contemporary films from Hungary, went to sixteen cities.
- AFI Presents the British Film Institute: Independent Film 1951–1982.

In the early 1980s, there was simply no way for Americans to see these outside-the-mainstream movies except in special exhibitions or festivals. There were repertory theaters around the country, but they were not able to secure prints of these kinds of movies to show in one location. Over the years, the exhibition leadership included Mike Clark, Nancy Sher, Eddie Cockrell, Ken Wlaschin, and Ray Barry.

In Washington, DC, AFI hosted many glamorous premieres, primarily held in the 1,100-seat Eisenhower Theater, for which projection equipment had to be rented every time. In the early '70s, Ina Ginsburg, a socially prominent woman, brilliantly organized a Film Club where a foreign film would be screened, often with the leading actor, actress, and director speaking before or after the screening, followed by a reception at the appropriate embassy. Access to embassies was not easy unless you were at certain levels of government service, so this was a welcome addition to the Washington social calendar. Ina was soon invited to join the AFI board in 1979, where she served effectively until 2008.

The 1994 Eisenhower Theater premiere of *Clear and Present Danger* (the second movie in the Tom Clancy bestseller book series) was one of my favorites. Given the spy genre and CIA connection, everyone in Washington wanted to attend. Producers Mace Neufeld and Bob Rehme were both AFI trustees, so it was a win-win for everyone. I left the pre-screening reception early and went down to the theater. Two other people had also already gone to their seats: Supreme Court Justice Ruth Bader Ginsburg and her husband, Martin Ginsburg. I introduced myself and welcomed her to the event. She told me she loved the AFI Theater and went to it often, because they lived next door in the Watergate apartment complex. The next day I sent her a letter with a pass to the AFI Theater, and she sent back a handwritten thank-you note that hangs on my wall today. That correspondence—and their attendance at the theater—continued for several years.

In 1982, a new series emerged to showcase European films. To this day, it continues and is one of the highlights on the fall calendar.

The West Coast Story

In the 1970s, over the course of several years, an AFI board committee had searched for a permanent Los Angeles exhibition site that might be shared with Filmex, the organization that ran a very successful film festival led by a real showman, Gary Essert. Gary was revered by many in the community for his strong commitment to every genre and for having a dramatic sense of show

AFI European Union Film Showcase

Ray Barry

In the early '80s, as the AFI Theater increasingly expanded its vision to encompass the exploration of contemporary world cinema, we began discussions with what was then known as the European Economic Community to launch a showcase for European cinema in Washington, DC. Out of those discussions, in 1982 we launched the European Community Film Festival in collaboration with the ten member states of the European Economic Community: Belgium, Denmark, the Federal Republic of Germany, France, Greece, Ireland, Italy, Luxembourg, the Netherlands, and the United Kingdom.

Little did we know that the launch of what is now known as the AFI European Union Film Showcase would be the start of our longest and most enduring collaborative undertaking. In 2015, we would present an AFI EU Showcase that represented twenty-eight member states, with more than fifty new films coming from a European community of 500 million people.

Our work with the European Union Delegation to the United States led us into a broader connectedness with Washington's diplomatic community. We collaborated closely with embassy staff, cultural counselors, and ambassadors to bring hundreds upon hundreds of films to Washington. Over the years, the Showcase always business. But he was also known for his excessive exuberance that sometimes could go too far. After I arrived in 1980, discussions turned to a tri-party relationship, including the Center Theatre

focused on inclusiveness and diversity, featuring works ranging from international award-winners and U.S. premieres to debut works of promising new talents.

In 2003, with our new home at the AFI Silver Theatre and Cultural Center, we were suddenly able to expand our reach. We had multiple screens, entertainment space, food service capabilities, and a bright, shining marquee facing the street. We could be far more expansive with our programming and could host events in our own space. Ambassadors could hold small private receptions for filmmakers in our spaces, then attend screenings in our large, beautifully restored theater and enjoy a post-screening drink and chat with the crowd. We always enjoyed the presence of ambassador João0.Vale de Almeida, who in 2010 became the first Head of the European Union Delegation to hold the rank of ambassador.

Not only did the EU Showcase flourish at AFI Silver, we were also able to re-energize our Latin American Festival (which grew out of a long collaboration with the Organization of American States) and with that energy make it as large and lively as our EU Showcase, with even Spain and Portugal joining in the mix. Today, AFI Silver is building programs around new African and new Caribbean cinema that is growing fast and connecting us with new filmmakers and new audiences, connecting people with the best in visual storytelling from around the world.

Group (CTG) which had two successful venues, the Ahmanson Theatre and Mark Taper Forum at the Music Center (Performing Art Center of Los Angeles County) in downtown L.A. The creative leader of CTG, Gordon Davidson, wanted a black box theater to put on smaller productions. I was certainly the new kid on the block, and as impressed as I was with Gordon, I was wary of a joint project with Filmex, let alone having three organizations living together in one facility. The focus on acquiring the campus for the Center for Advanced Filmmaking soon took precedence, and the idea of permanent exhibition space on the West Coast was pushed to the margins.

At the same time, a change in the fortunes of Filmex provided a new opportunity for the AFI. In 1983, the Filmex board leadership changed, and they grew disenchanted with Essert's fiscal management and a deficit that grew from $150,000 to $700,000. It was an acrimonious divorce that played out in the press over several days and resulted in Essert's removal. But the Filmex board agreed that while it would continue to run Filmex, Essert had the right to establish a year-round cinematheque—the same idea he had been discussing with AFI for years.

The new Filmex board chair was William Magee, CFO of Atlantic Richfield, the company that provided a $1 million loan to AFI. The loan was interest-free for three years, but the loan was due on October 7, 1983. Needless to say, it was in AFI's best interest to have a good relationship with Mr. Magee. We held a series of meetings with Magee, myself, and various AFI trustees over several months to see what kind of a relationship might evolve between Filmex and AFI. Magee hired two brilliant individuals to lead Filmex: Suzanne McCormick (from the Chicago Film Festival) as executive director and Ken Wlaschin as artistic director (from the same position at the BFI). We were struggling at the time to find strong leadership for the AFI Theater in the Kennedy Center, and we hadn't been able to identify anyone with the qualifications of either McCormick or Wlaschin. George Stevens Jr. was very busy with other projects at this time. When he was able to come to meetings, he was deeply concerned about how this relationship might work and how AFI might be seen as the lesser of the two organizations. But at this point in time, AFI clearly had the stronger exhibition program; we could control the evolution of the relationship. And that is exactly how it worked. An agreement resulted in Wlaschin and McCormick initially programming and planning the exhibition space for the AFI in exchange for free rental space on the new AFI campus.

The exhibition program was back on track. In less than two years, Wlaschin became the only employee of Filmex and then became director of AFI's exhibition program. At the June 1986 board meeting, Ken Wlaschin and the deputy director at the time, James Hindman, made a passionate presentation about the history and current strength of the entire exhibition program. They had some compelling statistics:

- Since the AFI Theater at the Kennedy Center had opened in 1973, it had averaged 600 films per year, with around fifty-five thematic series.
- Total attendance had reached 1 million patrons since 1973.
- There had been seventy-five director and actor retrospectives with special guest appearances from national and international filmmakers.
- In 1985, four major exhibitions had toured forty-eight cities in the country, with 300 individual screenings reaching 25,000 people in the U.S. and Canada.
- Future plans included a major five-part Soviet film series that would tour nationally for two years; national tours from Ireland, Iceland, Romania, and Spain; and a series devoted to films made by black artists for black audiences.

Wlaschin expressed his hope that AFI could find some kind of ongoing L.A. exhibition presence and that it would soon come to pass. Because when it came to Filmex, with or without Gary Essert, nothing was simple. Essert had gone on to found the American Cinematheque (AC), and while it still wasn't up and running, he was still trying to get other organizations into his tent. By early 1986, Magee was no longer chair of Filmex, though he remained committed to finding a resolution. Jerry Weintraub was the new chair, and this larger-than-life producer guaranteed that meetings were always entertaining. But Filmex still had a $300,000 deficit. Weintraub was a dealmaker, and all he wanted to do was either merge Filmex with AFI or give it back to Essert. To complicate matters, the AC was chaired by Ken Kleinberg. Ken was a wonderful lawyer, but he was also Weintraub's lawyer, and he taught a very popular course at the Center for Advanced Film Studies. How incestuous can you get? And, I forgot to mention, the most prominent individual in these negotiations was Tom Pollock, who had chaired Filmex for ten years (before Magee) and was now a member of the AFI board.

One way or another, after a multitude of meetings and intense discussions and negotiations, six months later Filmex went quietly out of business—with its bills covered. Because of Tom Pollock's strong voice, AFI took on the role of mounting a Los Angeles film festival in the spring of 1987. It took a long time to decide whether or not to keep the Filmex name that had been so meaningful to so many, but we decided to call it the AFI Los Angeles International Film Festival.

It took a number of years for the festival to establish a clear identity and become a major Los Angeles event. There was a residual trauma to the end of Filmex, and the new festival had a hard time finding sponsors. Because AFI ran on a relatively tight budget, there was never enough funding to have substantial public relations

"In 1984, I had left England, where I headed the London Film Festival, to come to Los Angeles to direct Filmex with Suzanne McCormick. Together we made it a success for two years, but accumulated debt eventually sank what had been L.A.'s only real window on world cinema. It was a time of despair for local film lovers. But amazingly—just like in the movies—the cavalry rode to the rescue. Tom Pollock asked the AFI board to assume responsibilities of Filmex, and AFI FEST was launched in the spring of 1987 with a star-studded tribute to Hal Wallis. It was an unforgettable evening and notable launch to AFI's flagship film festival."

—KEN WLASCHIN,
film historian and AFI FEST director (1986–1992)

for the festival, and it took many years to find the right time of year to present it. Festivals held later in the year were meant to coincide with films focusing on the awards season. In 1995, the event was moved to the fall to be able to show films that had been successful at Cannes.

Today it is known as AFI FEST presented by Audi. While the festival has never reached the level of mainstream buzz as Sundance or Telluride, it has found its footing and, with great guidance by my successor, is now in a strong niche. Over the years, some well-regarded festival directors succeeded Ken Wlaschin, including Christian Gaines, Jon Fitzgerald, Rose Kuo, and now Jacqueline Lyanga (class of 2001).

During his years at AFI, Ken Wlaschin's presence as AFI's programming guru in DC as well as at the AFI L.A. Festival was a great asset. Because of his decade at the BFI, he was well-respected and incredibly knowledgeable. He knew American film and world film history, he wrote books about opera on film, and he loved and was admired by filmmakers.

The East Coast Evolution

Meanwhile, whenever Kennedy Center leadership changed, it was time to reintroduce the AFI relationship and myself. In some ways it was an odd arrangement, because AFI was not a performing entity that was housed at the Kennedy Center. There was always some tension at the staff level between the operating personnel for the KC and the AFI. Those who succeeded Roger Stevens were always distinguished executives, including Ralph Davidson (1988), James D. Wolfensohn (1990) and his president Larry Wilker (who later became a good friend with whom we worked when he came to L.A. as CEO of the new Kodak Theatre at the Hollywood & Highland complex in 2001), and James A. Johnson (1996) and his president Michel Kaiser (who had no interest whatsoever in AFI's role at the KC). George Stevens Jr. maintained his strong relationship with the Kennedy Center through his role with the Kennedy Center Honors, so it wasn't as if AFI wasn't part of the KC family. But starting with Ralph Davidson in 1988, there were discussions about the AFI staff space being needed by the Kennedy Center, and the AFI Theater not generating revenue for the Center. AFI staff moved out in 1989 to an expensive office space down the street at the Watergate (with a cost of $170,000 per year); although the theater staff stayed in the KC, there was always a sense that the AFI Theater would not be permanent.

Other options came into view. Initially, AFI's Washington friends and supporters Ted and Jim Pedas, respected local real estate owners and independent exhibitors, hoped to provide an option at a site they owned and wanted to develop into an AFI Theater with street access and a marquee at 21st Street and Pennsylvania Avenue NW. But for a variety of reasons, it never came close to being a viable option. In 1996, the Kennedy Center leadership went to Congress to start a fund to renovate and make major changes, and it was clear that the AFI Theater's days were numbered. Indeed, in 1998, the AFI Theater stopped running seven days a week and became a special screening venue until it closed later in 1998. Fortunately for AFI, while one door was closing, an even bigger exhibition opportunity was opening. Soon AFI's East Coast presence would shift from the Kennedy Center to Silver Spring, Maryland.

The chance to continue my family's strong tradition in film exhibition as leader of AFI was something of a dream for me. Whenever I was working in DC, I was especially aware of being a part of the Kennedy Center's national arts scene. At night, when I would leave my office above the AFI Theater, I would see people waiting to go into the theater or milling around outside, talking about film. That commitment to the moviegoing experience is why the AFI exhibition program continues to this day in truly exciting ways, always rooted in the history but also focused on where film exhibition is going, today and into many tomorrows.

AFI Silver Theatre and Cultural Center: 21st Century Exhibition Vision

James Hindman

The story of the AFI Silver Theatre and Cultural Center is probably one of the most compelling and positive memories of my time at AFI—dramatic, exciting, improbable, and scary as hell. In some ways, it is best captured by describing the one day that was the wildest ride of all: the day we fired and rehired the extraordinary Ray Barry, AFI's long-serving head of the Kennedy Center (KC) theater program. It is quite a story to tell.

As Jean describes in the first part of this chapter, the stability of the AFI Theater at the Kennedy Center operation had been shaky for some time, given the absence of most of the amenities that make a commercial movie theater successful—great concessions and popcorn, a snappy marquee and poster display, and a vibrant commercial neighborhood with good street traffic and transportation. Since we had none of these, it is actually a tribute to first-rate programming and a sophisticated local audience that the AFI KC screen had survived as long as it had. Going to the Kennedy Center was a serious commitment to High Art, quite different from going to the movies.

Making matters worse, moving most AFI programs to the Los Angeles campus in 1984 left those remaining KC programs and staff fairly isolated. Jean and I spent much time on airplanes to keep our hands on things, but it often felt a bit lonely in our formerly dynamic base of operations.

Yet Ray and the KC theater staff continued to present first-rate events, drawing strong local press and great loyalty from committed, often-small audiences of cinephiles. In addition, Ray was also a remarkable networker, deeply interested in local politics and government and well-loved and respected in the suburban Maryland community where he lived. Ray understood how the various levels of county and state government worked, what the current issues were, and who had what to gain in future planning.

By the mid-1990s, Ray had told me that plans were afoot to revitalize (with serious funding) the eastern end of otherwise-wealthy Montgomery County, reinvigorating a large unincorporated area of more modest suburban communities of Silver Spring, Maryland. This huge, largely residential community had fallen on hard times. Its twenty-five-acre commercial sector, once the vital engine of the area, was becoming blighted with vacant stores and failed businesses. Typical of suburban growth, it itself had sucked the life out of commercial downtown Washington, DC, when it opened in the 1930s. By the 1970s, it was in turn being cannibalized by shiny new malls opening farther out in the county. By the mid-'90s, Silver Spring's commercial economic blight was giving rise to crime and fear—impacting the otherwise charming surrounding residential areas.

Lying at the center of the decaying commercial zone was the long-shuttered Silver Theatre, a brilliant example of art moderne architecture that had opened in 1938 and once been the heart of the neighborhood. Designed by famed theater architect-designer

John Eberson, it was slated for some sort of eventual redevelopment by the county. How to make downtown Silver Spring work? Clearly, a great movie theater had once succeeded in being its heartbeat, and this now-ghostly reminder of past glories needed to play a central role.

Doug Duncan, a rising and charismatic young politician, was elected Montgomery County Executive in 1994 on a platform that committed the county and state to revitalize Silver Spring, and he had a tax base and enough popular support to actually make it happen. Ray Barry tracked these developments through his local county network, and he had spoken to Duncan about the possibility of AFI becoming involved in a revitalized Silver Theatre. Given the risks of involvement in totally unknown territory like urban renewal, it is likely that no more than polite expressions of interest by AFI senior management would have occurred, but then the deteriorating situation at the Kennedy Center changed the picture.

With the end of NEA funding approaching and the constant struggle to find new ways to pay the bills in the mid-1990s, endless recurring deficits at the KC theater were clearly unacceptable. Finally, in 1998, the painful decision had to be made to close the operation. Jean set a meeting with KC senior management to discuss various options, and we prepared to give Ray an appropriate severance package with gratitude for his more than two decades of AFI service. Jean met with Ray to explain things (he was deeply saddened but gracious as always).

Then Jean met with KC management, who promptly upended things by offering to accommodate AFI with a very generous part-time usage package for the theater. The next meeting on the calendar was with Doug Duncan, who outlined his plans and hopes for Silver Spring and his intention to subsidize AFI to operate a lavishly restored Silver Theatre as the cultural anchor of the whole project. Jean rehired Ray just after the Duncan meeting.

It had been quite a day for all of us, especially Ray. While we had no idea what the future might actually hold, we were all on board for an amazing ride.

The Meeting with AFI Silver's Destiny

Jean Picker Firstenberg

The first meeting with the county executive and his team was a big deal. Ray Barry knew the county's intentions, but they were otherwise hard to comprehend. Since this was basically a real estate proposal, I asked my son Doug Firstenberg, a Montgomery County resident and real estate developer with projects in the county, to attend. He sat next to me at a large table in the county offices.

Doug Duncan began directly: "We're prepared to make AFI an offer it can't refuse." In detail, he explained the county's intention to revitalize downtown Silver Spring with investments of at least $400 million. The centerpiece would be a restored Silver Theatre, to be named the AFI Silver. To make this happen, Montgomery County would spend $5 million to bring the Silver back to its original glory *and* would pay for any deficits that AFI incurred on an annual basis. It was quite an offer. Overwhelming, really. But I knew the AFI board would have many questions that would need to be answered before any offer could be accepted. After the meeting, my son said, "You sure were cool in responding to this amazing offer." Only cool on the outside. And on the inside? Absolutely thrilled.

The Silver Theatre Becomes a Cultural Center

I'm leading here with yet another hoary old adage: Be careful what you wish for! The notion of taking responsibility for a substantial urban cultural operation, which this sort of cinematheque certainly would be, did give us pause. This also came at a time when AFI was changing its very nature, trying to go from a federally supported national arts entity into a self-supporting champion of the enormous and wildly diverse field of moving images. Did we really need another potential source of liability? And we did not really know these new allies and supporters, nor did we deeply understand the geography and community we would have to become an integral part of. Becoming a highly visible entity in a region in transition posed obvious risks, and our overall reputation would be on the line.

Doug Duncan quickly became a reassuring ally and sympathetic supporter as we wrestled with the decision to go forward. Any question or request was answered positively. Who would own the facility and be responsible for its upkeep and maintenance? *The county, of course.* Could AFI walk away from the deal if it deemed it necessary at any point? *Of course.* A one-screen theater was impractical to program—how about adding two new screens constructed on adjacent county property? *Of course.* The original lobby was too small for good concessions and retail—how about a larger one to support the new screens? *Of course.* In the future, movie theater projection must include video as well as 16mm and 35mm film, and soon will include new digital projectors—pricey equipment. *Of course.* How about a liquor license, so beer and wine can be served? *Of course.* The old 1,100-seat main auditorium was absurdly large for modern audiences—could it be reduced to 400 while still preserving the beautiful interior as John Eberson designed it? *Of course—let's talk to the architects.* We eventually ran out of blue-sky requests.

Duncan and his staff were prepared to make this all work and were creative and encouraging at every point. Particularly helpful was a staff member with responsibility for the county's role in the overall Silver Spring revitalization project: Bill Mooney. He had a long history in county government and was ingenious in devising ways around an endless series of crises and obstacles, always with modesty and unfailing good humor. He did retire from government shortly after the Silver Theatre opened, and I always hoped we had not drained his life's blood in the process. But he seemed enormously proud of what was eventually accomplished.

AFI Board Approves the Concept

A decision point for AFI's commitment was reached by mid-1998, when Doug Duncan was invited to Los Angeles to present his overall plan for Silver Spring to the AFI board's executive committee with a specific proposal for AFI to operate the Silver Theatre. He explained that AFI would have no operational liability and that AFI's expenses against revenues would be subsidized by Montgomery County to a break-even point. All expenses for the construction and outfitting of the renovated theater would be borne by the county. (His original budget at this point was $5 million for all construction; by opening in mid-2003, this number had grown to $25 million, with nary a word of complaint.) AFI would have a 100-year lease, renewable every ten years at $10 a year, which could be exited at any point as necessary.

The discussion at the board level following Duncan's appearance was fascinating. While there was some fear of possible financial and reputation exposure, there was palpable excitement at the possibilities. Finally, AFI could have a real movie theater in metropolitan Washington, DC. Interestingly, some of the strongest support came from AFI's founding director and trustee, George Stevens Jr. George argued that this could be a new facet of AFI's commitment to film preservation, a national model for how movies were meant to be seen, as opposed to videocassettes with poor sound and images on a home screen. Others argued for the value of a clear AFI footprint in the Washington, DC, area. With the likely disappearance of the Kennedy Center presence, AFI might be seen as a regional Los Angeles organization. Permission was unanimously granted for AFI management to go forward in finalizing arrangements with Montgomery County.

Meanwhile, building the support within Montgomery County that would be needed to get legislative approval of the Silver project was underway. Ray had gone fully on the county payroll as soon as we had agreed to try and develop the project, and he was generously housed in county offices for several years. Ray applied his considerable political skills to help rally the local citizenry, under the expert tutelage of Doug Duncan and his staff. Strong and consistent support came from county staff, who were always professional and patient with us. I particularly recall that Susan Hoffmann, Don Scheuerman, and Jerry Pasternak did tireless work on this project.

Ray Barry vividly described to me how he spent several years' worth of weekends and evenings within the community, working with the civic organization Friends of the Silver Theatre, which had struggled for many years to have the county remake and re-open the Silver as a local performing arts center:

> *I spent an enormous amount of effort to get Friends of the Silver Theatre on board, or at least to not be a roadblock. I remember very vividly sitting with Doug Duncan and Bill Mooney in the living room of Alice Gilson—the Friends of the Silver president, being cross-examined, harangued and put through the wringer by her and her supporters. Earlier at the county offices I remember Bill and Doug saying we were going to do this and everyone hopping into the van and just heading over there. I had no idea what we were getting into, and for the life of me, I couldn't grasp how Doug Duncan, the County Executive*

of Maryland's largest jurisdiction (nearly 1,000,000 people), who was responsible for a $5 billion budget, was heading to have tea in Alice's living room at 8:00 at night to be grilled. In any case, we sat there and took it and answered every question and accusation as honestly as we could. As we walked out I didn't realize that we had won, but the next day I started to get calls from several people who were in the room saying that they were on board with us. It was an amazing lesson in grassroots, retail politics and community relations, and those lessons, and others like it, have stuck with me and served us well.

Ray was just warming up for years of similar work in the trenches. With our cautious approval, the county had retained the services of a large international architectural firm, Gensler, which had done a number of major cultural edifice overhauls and quickly put a top-notch team together to take on this complex design issue. The Gensler team included Richard Logan, Diane Hoskins and Michael Darner. Government funding and approvals required a rigorous restoration of the original theater structure, a dilemma because modern exhibition had changed the nature of much of the needed materials and configurations. Retaining original design elements like a beautiful proscenium arch and a gorgeously embossed plaster ceiling would be crucial, but clearly, they were an obstacle to decent sightlines and modern theater acoustics.

The Gensler team and the construction company Foulger-Pratt, led by the thoughtful and charming Bryant Foulger, eventually wrestled each problem to the ground with ingenious solutions. For example, the fantastic original plaster ceiling had largely fallen down due to water leakage and years of freezing and thawing, but the team was able to recreate it, using acoustically appropriate, sprayed-on material dyed to match the original colors, then used massive stencils to paint the swirling lines—a fantastic engineering feat. The huge original tapestries hanging on the side walls had been made opaque by forty years of audience cigarette smoke (then allowed in the theater), but they were carefully copied and brilliantly restored. Even the original carpet pattern was rediscovered at the mill and rewoven for reinstallation. In comparison, designing the new construction for the theaters and 32,000 square feet of offices adjacent, housing the two new auditoria and screens as well as a large lobby, café with beer and wine, retail and exhibit spaces, was a walk in the park. Gensler's skill was in making the overall building seem a single entity that honored its history while functioning beautifully as a state-of-the-art, three-screen multiplex theater.

But the planning process underscored the need to define the AFI Silver as a cultural entity as well as a movie theater. What would happen in the offices, conference areas, library and service areas that were also a part of the new construction? AFI's exhibition program had an illustrious history in presenting a wide range of festivals, panels, conferences and special screenings hosted by filmmakers and specialists. Special events of various kinds happened on a weekly basis. What had worked so well at the Kennedy Center, however, would have to be expanded and reimagined to serve a new and largely unknown community audience. Programming movies—AFI's branded mix of classics, independents, foreign, retrospectives and premieres—must also be supported by programming that had local relevance and appeal. And that, ultimately, could only be known by trial and error, our usual method of feeling our way into the future.

Clearly much of Montgomery County's attraction to AFI at the Silver had to do with our national profile and impact in Washington, DC. However, our value as an educational resource became a major selling point. Ray and I began meeting with various officials in the county education offices to see what might be viable for K–12, up through the local community college level (Montgomery College). Many options were explored and abandoned because of limited resources and scheduling difficulties, but a robust program would emerge, including field trips to the movies and customized curricular materials. This planning occurred just as various screen education initiatives were being developed at AFI in Los Angeles, and we got financial support from Pepsi with the help of the redoubtable David Weitzner, a brilliant marketing consultant from the studios. Large and active programs with Montgomery County schools continue to be a central part of the AFI Silver's cultural function and, to date, more than 100,000 local and regional students have come to the theater on these programs.

The design of the AFI Silver complex proceeded within the context of the larger development of Silver Spring revitalization plans. Montgomery County would pump more than $187 million into the initial design and then added more than $138 million in a new transit structure and close to $70 million in a magnificent new library. The early dream was that Silver Spring would have a dynamic downtown that was accessible from all over the region, filled with the street life that had characterized it in decades past. If it worked, the regional economy would strongly rebound, and more than pay for the investments that the county and state must make. The initial forecast was for a $400 million redevelopment program, but in fact it has grown to more than $1 billion—a redevelopment success story.

An Impressive New Neighbor Arrives

Central to the redevelopment of Silver Spring was the wish to attract major new businesses to the area. Discovery Communications, then a rising cable giant, was looking to create a new world headquarters that would make them, in essence, the anchor tenant of the new Silver Spring. As the county put together a package of lucrative incentives for a vacant twenty-five-acre lot sited diagonally from the Silver, it became clear that AFI's visible presence was also an incentive for Discovery to come in.

Doug Duncan was trusting enough to unleash Ray and me on Discovery senior management to develop a series of possible future collaborations. By good luck (their children went to the same school), Ray knew Judith McHale. Judith was happy to consider working with AFI, and I found her to be one of the most impressive, thoughtful, and decisive executives I had ever dealt with. (McHale's career has been distinguished, appointed undersecretary of the Department of State during the Obama administration and, in 2016, named to the reconstituted board of Viacom controlled by Shari Redstone, who succeeded her father after fighting for her vision of the company.)

Don Baer, a recently retired speechwriter from the Clinton White House who was now Discovery's senior vice president for strategy and development, was assigned to work out details. Given Discovery's roots in documentary, we proposed the presentation of a world-class documentary festival as an annual anchor event at the AFI Silver, programmed by us and sponsored by Discovery. After some months of meticulous negotiations, Discovery would commit to a five-year sponsorship of what we called SILVERDOCS: AFI Discovery Channel Documentary Festival (ever-sensitive to branding) for a total of $6 million—truly a lovely way to inaugurate a relationship as neighbors and friends. They proved to be excellent partners, and Discovery CEO John Hendricks soon joined the AFI Board of Trustees, serving energetically and generously from 2003 to 2012, then returning in 2013 to serve into the present.

> "It's a wonderful thing to have a theater like [the Silver] where the art of film is preserved and where it lives. For that, I thank AFI."
>
> —WILLIAM FRIEDKIN, filmmaker

Our original hope that the completed AFI complex would open shortly after the new millennium began was not remotely realistic. As construction costs mounted and the complexity of the project became clear, visible progress slowed. A simple example: the world supply of steel had dried up because China had acquired most of it for its aggressive rebuilding and industrialization campaign. Then, China got most of the world's cement for the Three Gorges Dam. Such stories from Bryant Foulger kept us informed and on edge for many months.

As construction proceeded, however, we saw the risk of being the first kids on the block in the hoped-for newly dynamic downtown Silver Spring, which still had the reputation of being a place to avoid after dark. Coupled with the absence of attractive parking options, we worried about drawing audiences. New amenities such as cafés and clubs were promised, but leases had to be negotiated and spaces rebuilt.

AFI staff started to move into the partially completed structure in the fall of 2002, as we cautiously parked in a nearby bank lot. It seemed like we were working in a construction zone. And then, like the first breath of spring, things quickly began to change. An edgy comic book store opened nearby, and a young and hip crowd perfect for us began to show up, followed by large and well-lit parking garages. The infamous wig stores (a colleague said you could always tell how badly a neighborhood was doing by the number of wig shops per block!) were boarded up and moved away. Other amenities, including restaurants close by, began to materialize.

With final construction and equipping of the three theaters and the two state-of-the-art projection booths underway, AFI's upstairs offices began to be occupied. Cardinal Systems and Boston Light and Sound, two premier theater outfitting companies, started the process of setting up first-rate projection booths while creating a contemporary technical infrastructure. Ray could also begin to build a theater staff, after working mostly alone for several years.

I had been splitting my time between Los Angeles and Maryland for several years to keep things thought-through and focused.

I actually had deep roots in the area, having spent years there as an undergraduate and graduate student, and later teaching for a number of years at nearby American University. I even had vague memories of seeing movies at the then-decrepit Silver in the 1970s. Seeing the area come back to life was therefore something of a personal epiphany for me. We could clearly see what the AFI Silver would mean to the process of regrowth there—it would provide the life, energy, and fun that would draw the community together again.

Building Out a Cultural Center Staff

Ray had been a brilliant project manager, without whom this venture would never have been more than a twinkle in Doug Duncan's eye. Now his focus had to turn to establishing an elaborate and newly invented overall AFI operation itself. We needed a real showman as well, we thought, someone to "front" the Silver to its audiences. Through a friend and former colleague, we were introduced to Murray Horwitz, a recently departed National Public Radio figure with roots in music and show business. Part of Murray's claim to fame was that he had finished college and gone on to be a clown for Ringling Brothers for three years, a work history I found irresistible. Murray was charming and lively. While he knew little about the movies, he was a quick study. For five years, he and Ray worked together closely: Murray as the onstage, front-door guy, and Ray as the backstage genius who also nurtured ever-stronger relationships with the county and local community.

Ray built a strong staff of programmers to handle the regular movie schedule, including Mike Jeck, Gabe Wardell, and a number of other interesting characters over the years, and now headed up by the gifted Todd Hitchcock. They sometimes had eccentric tastes and weren't always easy to manage, but Ray's genius was his instinct for his audience, which grew and evolved as he and the Silver did. Working gently from backstage, Ray controlled the show. And he focused strongly on front-of-the-house issues and personnel, working constantly to make the audience's experience as warm and welcoming as possible.

The Next Door Actually Opens

By the fall of 2002, it became clear that we could actually plan a date to launch the emerging AFI Silver Theatre and Cultural Center. So we began to plan for an opening on April 4, 2003. Facilities were nearing completion, staff was being identified and hired, programs were in place, and movies and special events could be booked. A large national chain, Consolidated Theatres of North Carolina, with support of its erstwhile leader, Herman Stone, was opening a giant twenty-four-screen multiplex in the nearby shopping center that would draw huge foot-traffic, some of whom might actually be interested in AFI-style programming. Consolidated Theatres proved to be warm and wonderful neighbors, and we did a number of programs together in later years. We even had some lively competition soon after we opened. The Landmark chain, a small national company that specializes in art films, foreign films, and edgy independents, opened an eight-screener not far away in upscale Bethesda, Maryland. (In 2003, Landmark was purchased by AFI trustee Todd Wagner and his partner, Mark Cuban. Ted Mundorff has run the chain for them, after twenty years at Pacific Theatres and creating the ArcLight concept with another AFI trustee, Christopher Forman. The exhibition world Jean grew up in is truly a small circle of devoted cinephiles.)

Clever movie series and programming were designed for the first spring season, such as Films of 1938: The Year the Silver Theatre Opened, Trilogies from Francis Ford Coppola to Marcel Pagnol, and a new 35mm print of *The Greatest*, the film about Muhammad Ali. But it was crucial to open with a bang, to attract the media necessary to get on the map—and to just begin to say thank

"AFI Silver is where filmmakers feel they have died and gone to heaven. You pinch yourself thinking this can't be real, but it is—one of the best places on the planet to share your work and to see the work of others."

—KEN BURNS,
documentarian

you to Montgomery County and the many supporters who had invested so much in this vision of a true model community theater. We invited Clint Eastwood to present the opening film—one of his choice—to a spectacular invited audience. He chose *The Ox-Bow Incident*, a classic black-and-white Western from 1943 starring Henry Fonda and Dana Andrews and directed by the master, William A. Wellman. It featured major moral dilemmas in traditional Western formulas, which very much appealed to Eastwood as he said in his eloquent introduction. Jean, Ray, and I got to pose with Doug Duncan and Eastwood for a formal ribbon-cutting before the program, and the neighborhood seemed thrilled that we were there. We certainly were!

Quickly following, in June 2003, was the very successful opening of SILVERDOCS, which more than justified Discovery's investment. Their magnificent new world headquarters hosted some of the week-long festival. A highlight was the premiere of a skateboarding documentary featuring Tony Hawk, who appeared in a live demonstration on a closed-off street next to the AFI Silver, drawing thousands of old and young spectators from the community and strongly raising the profile of the Silver as a community resource. The newly formed partnership between AFI and Discovery to showcase documentaries came to the attention of the Corporation for Public Broadcasting (CPB), which had become a significant sponsor of the AFI Digital Content Lab program at the AFI campus in L.A. After some delicate negotiations with all parties, AFI was able to bring CPB into the SILVERDOCS family as sponsors of a conference held during the festival that continued for many years.

One other remarkable event stays with me as emblematic of our success that first year. AFI had often collaborated with various embassies and their cultural affairs operations to stage small festivals and tribute events to honor their national cinematic achievements. Such events were quite logical at the Kennedy Center, but we were not certain that they would easily translate to the AFI Silver. However, the French embassy approached us to support a tribute to the legendary film composer Michel Legrand. The highlight would be a screening of a slightly obscure 1963 black-and-white masterpiece directed by the equally legendary Jacques Demy, *Bay of Angels*. Not only did it star the extraordinary Jeanne Moreau, but the French embassy offered to have her introduce the film and take questions from the audience afterward.

The Silver event quickly sold out, and Ms. Moreau arrived in fine form. After the riveting screening, she paced restlessly in front of the screen, chain-smoking (despite requests to the contrary, but who wanted to argue?) and answering polite questions from the audience with fierce observations about the vulgarity of American movies and the mendacity of the mainstream Hollywood studio system in general. Sitting in front of me toward the back of the audience were two older local gentlemen; as Ms. Moreau carried on, one whispered delightedly to the other, "Can you *believe* we're in Silver Spring?" That moment alone made everything that had come before worthwhile.

There would, of course, be bumps in the road, but the first two years of the AFI Silver quickly lived up to the promise Doug Duncan had seen in it. In a report to the AFI board in 2005, the Silver could claim 160,000 admissions that year, nearly $1.5 million in ticket sales and concessions, and a thriving education program that saw more than 6,000 local students visit the theater for activities. And it has continued to grow from there. More than

100,000 students have participated in AFI Silver's education program; over 1,500 filmmakers, actors, musicians, thought leaders, subject experts, educators, ambassadors, and people from around the world have graced the stages of AFI Silver's three theaters; and some 2.5 million people have attended the shows and events that take place every day at AFI Silver.

Commercial Silver Spring's economic turnaround has become legendary. I wandered the streets around the Silver recently and was overwhelmed by the transformation. While AFI and the Silver cannot take credit too widely for all this, the energy and spark we have provided to the neighborhood and region continues to reverberate. And the Montgomery County government continues to be pleased—AFI's lease has been renewed and, over the years, they have provided an aggregate of many millions of dollars in subsidies to cover the deficits that a mission-driven nonprofit theater must inevitably accrue.

Despite our joy in what was improbably accomplished there, what is the value, ultimately, of the relatively small AFI Silver to a national arts organization charged with supporting a huge, enterprise-driven field like movies and movie theaters? Actually, quite a bit of value, looking at it from a bit of distance now. The AFI Silver Theatre and Cultural Center continues to be a model, often copied in various ways, for everything from the successful urban renewal of decayed commercial centers, to arts-driven education, to the value of strong cultural curation of popular culture.

Most important, however, is its glaring success as a true community theater, with a passionate and loyal local audience with whom it is constantly in tune. Ray Barry, the last one standing and still making it happen there, day in and day out, described it well:

> *The AFI Silver Theatre and Cultural Center changed everything, yet preserved the very best of the AFI Theater at the Kennedy Center's legacy. By that I mean: with the advent of the AFI Silver, our long-standing commitment to programming*

Lunch with Jeanne

Jean Picker Firstenberg

Jeanne Moreau—there are few actors I respect more. Twice previously I had met her, first when she participated in the event to present the 1984 AFI Life Achievement Award to Lillian Gish. Moreau had just completed a documentary about Gish, and the next day they came to the AFI Mark Goodson Screening Room, where she showed their interview to Gish for the first time. I sat in the dark theater behind these two artists and thought I was the luckiest person in the world.

In 1996, the producer-director team Ismail Merchant and James Ivory brought their Jeanne Moreau-starring movie *The Proprietor* for a Harold Lloyd Master Seminar. During the seminar, Moreau was asked by one of the Fellows, "What is the difference between French and American cinema?" Without blinking, Moreau responded, "Commerce."

Then, in 2004, Moreau was guest of the French embassy and agreed to come to the AFI Silver Theatre and Cultural Center. Ina Ginsburg, AFI's grande dame in DC, sprang into action. Knowing the French ambassador, she asked if he and his respected guest would like to be invited to have lunch in the U.S. Senate Dining Room. Believe it or not, Republican Mississippi senator Thad Cochran hosted the luncheon. We were seated at a round table in the center of the room, with everyone staring at Jeanne Moreau. She controlled the entire lunch conversation, charming everyone at the table and the entire Senate dining room, too.

integrity and excellence, to not just honoring the well-known canon, but also to exploring the new and the unknown, to taking chances and embracing the world of possibilities, this all was given space to grow, breathe, and experiment and given access to a new and much-expanded audience—not only in terms of numbers, but in terms of ethnic, racial, and socio-economic diversity. That combination allowed us to fly. To enter a world where unknown new films from Africa would draw vast audiences and huge responses, where silent films came with non-traditional musical accompaniment, and little-known documentaries about 1970s Cambodian rock musicians packed the house, shown alongside masterpieces of American and world cinema—all thrive and all come to life before large and enthusiastic audiences, on the big screen, shown as they were meant to be seen, in outstanding theaters that adhere to the highest technical standards. In a nutshell, the AFI Silver is one of the world's leading film centers, whose hallmark is consistently producing authentically community-based programming of national stature.

The AFI Theater at the Kennedy Center always had a commitment to outstanding programming and technical excellence in presentation. The AFI Silver Theatre and Cultural Center took those two commitments, pushed them both to the limit (at its opening, the AFI Silver was the most technically advanced film center of its type anywhere, and remains at the cutting edge today), and then added a third ingredient that completed the recipe—it took a stance of total commitment to engaging with, and embedding itself, in the Washington community. Those three ingredients have become the defining features of AFI Silver. It is why it has such a strong and authentic sense of connectedness with its audience, it is why it is such a much-beloved Washington institution, and it is why it is the hub of Washington's film culture.

We collectively believed that AFI was founded on the premise that movies and screen entertainment of various kinds are a *public* art. To be truly successful, a community-based theater must be in a kind of dialog with its audience, connected in a two-way communication about what's important, what works, and what is of value. AFI can work to set the standards for cinema and the moving image as art with its programs and screenings, but the audience is the final judge. The beautifully tuned dynamic at the AFI Silver works to find this balance every day. Given all the things I worked on at AFI over these many years, the Silver stands out as a vital long-term success.

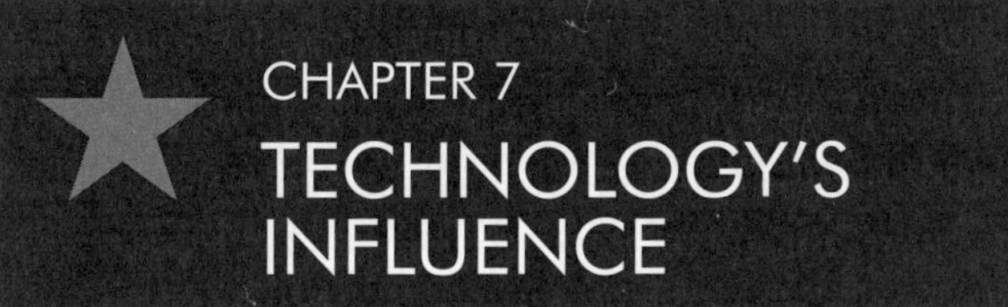

CHAPTER 7
TECHNOLOGY'S INFLUENCE

As the World Turns: From Video to the Digital Revolution

James Hindman

The cinematic arts are perched on a three-legged stool: creative work, commerce, and technology. During its first decade, AFI focused programs primarily on classic film, building an entity to serve the field and be a national voice for it. While the business of film has contributed to AFI's overall context, the direct way to promote moving images as an art form was by honoring, supporting, and teaching the *creative*—AFI's reason for being. The technology side of things had changed very little since the introduction of sound, and technical issues were carefully overseen by trade groups.

However, by 1980, change was in the offing—as usual, coming from the margins and from the least expected directions. AFI provided a highly visible platform for newcomers to be seen in the ever-attractive universe of entertainment, and AFI's aura was enticing to the creative and business community. Soon, technology-oriented corporations would come calling, and we would launch a series of partnerships that gave AFI a unique and prominent position within the creative community and the wider public. Through these partnerships, AFI would become synonymous with innovation.

Most importantly, AFI's technology relationships would have a profound impact on not only the Institute's programs and agendas but also the entire world of storytelling. As the following chapters indicate, most corporate partnerships we formed were driven not by philanthropy but by companies' strategic and marketing objectives. When corporate priorities changed, budgets for partnering would come and go. Looking back through AFI annual reports from these years, I am struck by the number of "first annual" programs that are reported: festivals, contests, workshops, conferences, and special events. Our corporate partners would eventually change direction and move on, launching other new products aimed at other markets. Without continued external funding, these programs could be folded into other areas. But in a resource-thin era, these sponsorships were in fact life rafts for various AFI initiatives. They also provided the means to reach AFI constituents—independents, artists, students, neophytes—who had little or no access to new technologies and to masters of various disciplines and fields. With NEA funding in the 1980s and early '90s, there were clear expectations that AFI would find ways to serve these groups. Sponsorships provided the answer.

Beginning with the transformational Sony relationship and running through Apple, HP, Intel, Microsoft, and many other partnerships, AFI was able to address a huge range of issues for large and small screens and to welcome such innovations as small-format and high-definition video, DVDs, and computers as a creative tool for digital image-making and delivery, well before their implications were fully understood in the creative community. AFI was able to serve its various constituencies in a profound way, while it provided a welcoming nursery for nurturing new applications and hungry creatives.

In the aggregate, over the many years AFI followed and led these developments, AFI technology-driven programs created a compelling research and education mosaic that really helped to define a new field: moving image arts. Rooted in a deep commitment to cinematic history, AFI's programs exercised real authority in identifying new work, new directions, new techniques, and a new perspective on what might constitute the art of the screen.

The Sony-sponsored National Video Festival in 1981 was my first full involvement with AFI, and it was by far the most outsized event the field of independent film and video had experienced. In fact, the festival issues and topics originally identified and documented by my colleague Larry Kirkman would become central to AFI's programmatic agenda for the next decade. The 1990 arrival of Apple was orchestrated with incredible savvy by Emily Laskin. Like Sony, Apple sensed the importance of the entertainment community to its immediate future, which turned out to be a miracle of timing. Through the restless brilliance of Nick DeMartino's experimenting and networking, AFI's new technology programs provided critical leadership for a national creative community eager to understand the potential.

Timing is everything, and the series of dances between AFI and its technology partners was truly fortunate for all parties. While we were never successful in building properly funded permanent structures within AFI, we exploited every opportunity to investigate constantly breaking innovations. And the flexibility which short-term and one-off funding required was really the best way to stay current and responsive to the field. As a result, AFI was able to be a unique bridge to a remarkable future. This section describes that bridge.

Large Screen to Small Screen: AFI Enters the Video Age

LARRY KIRKMAN

It all started with a cold call to AFI from Sony in fall 1979. Would AFI be interested in presenting a student video competition and event at AFI's home in the Kennedy Center in Washington, DC? When AFI director George Stevens Jr. asked me to suggest some ideas for Sony, I proposed a National Video Festival, rooted in my experience as a producer, educator, and activist across the spectrum of video innovation.

At the time, I was a professor at American University, recruited to introduce video into the film program in 1976—part of a movement of independent documentary producers on public television whose productions pushed the envelope of video technology and public affairs formats. And I was an editor of *TeleVisions*, a quarterly journal inspired by the potential of the new media of video, cable, and satellites. *TeleVisions* was founded by Nick DeMartino at the Washington Community Video Center and funded by the National Endowment for the Arts and Rockefeller Foundation. Each issue was filled with high expectations for video's impact on education, democracy, work, and health. Our mission was to support a dynamic and participatory communications environment, one now becoming commonplace in the digital age. The watchword was *access.* We wanted to create new media services and reinvent professional roles.

Television historian Erik Barnouw would define this unique revolutionary moment when he gave the keynote address "The Role of the Independent" for AFI's first National Video Festival in 1981. Speaking to a full house in the Kennedy Center's 500-seat Terrace Theater, he said:

> *Throughout history, new media have always been an offshoot of new technology, and every such shift has brought with it shifts in society—shifts in power, values, and ideas. . . . Now suddenly, once more, a monopoly is undermined by new technology. This is the historic fact, the possibly explosive historic fact that brings us here. Its ramifications are far from clear, but evidence of their possible reach and complexity exists in this very festival.*
>
> *Videotape, on which images and sounds of all sorts and in all manner of combinations can be readily implanted, is a medium—a canvas, palette, sheet of paper, typewriter, new wad of clay, synthesizer, what you will—it is all these and more. Those equipped to use it can feed into our television system, but also bypass it; already the medium is creating a world outside that system. It can feed into our cable systems but also bypass them. It can reach out through satellites and optical fiber channels but need not. It is itself a delivery system. The final delivery points are television screens, already available in home, office, school, museum, library, church, community center, hotel room, party headquarters, or what have you. Each has its own needs.*

> *The high wall that has separated a gigantic Entertainment industry, with a capital E, from individuals in their homes and communities, shows signs of crumbling. Entertainment becomes the business of many, including ourselves. I am reminded of the words of Walt Whitman: "Henceforth I seek not good fortune. Henceforth I am myself good fortune."*

A few months before the call from AFI, I had co-produced a public television special on the Three Mile Island nuclear meltdown demonstration, a "live documentary" distributed on the new PBS satellite. A review in the *Washington Post* that called it "a landmark . . . for the technology revolution in broadcasting" got George Stevens Jr. to hire me as a consultant. "I don't know anything about video," he said, but he knew enough to see the potential in a relationship with Sony, the leading manufacturer and primary innovator in television and video technology.

A year later, when Jean Firstenberg succeeded George Stevens at AFI, she established a substantial new program, Television and Video Services, and hired me to create the National Video Festival, manage the relationship with Sony, and participate in the National Association of Media Arts Centers. We began with an ambitious goal for the first National Video Festival: to celebrate the pioneers of the 1970s and look forward to directions emerging in the 1980s.

AFI and Sony: The Right Time, The Right Place

In November 1980, Koichi Tsunoda, president of Sony Video Products and vice president of Sony Corporation of America, made the commitment to sponsor the National Video Festival. Sony's $400,000 contribution included $100,000 in equipment prizes for the student competition and $30,000 to install its new video projector in the AFI Theater. The National Video Festival served Sony's marketing and political interests. Celebrating small-format video, a field it dominated, at the Kennedy Center in Washington, DC, in partnership with AFI clearly asserted its contributions to our culture and economy.

The AFI board was elated with the Sony partnership, but a major new corporate sponsorship would be a new thing for AFI. After a presentation on festival plans, chairman Charlton Heston said, "Sony's support is important to the total Institute funding picture," and, "The corporation's commitment to the Institute is quite genuine."

So, why did AFI embrace the relationship with Sony? Why did their stories merge in the first National Video Festival and lead to a partnership for the next decade? Looking back, it makes complete sense in the context of the times: technology developments, innovations in production, roles of broadcasters, growth of media arts centers, and the nonprofit funding environment.

Sony launched the video era with its Portapak, introduced in the U.S. in 1967, and fueled innovation in technology and programming throughout the '70s and '80s. Consumer trends and social pressures had created an appetite for the new video tools. By 1970, television in the home was at ninety-five percent. This was the TV generation, and viewers were ready to make it themselves.

In 1972, the new Sony U-Matic was used to cover Nixon's trip to China. In 1975, KMOX, CBS in St. Louis, was the first to replace film with video for its news programs. By the 1976 annual convention of the National Association of Broadcasters, video was mainstream.

In 1979, AFI was still all about film; a self-invented institution, it had not focused on the emergence of video. Despite its base in Washington, DC, AFI was publicly defined by the L.A. presence of its Conservatory, Life Achievement Award, and Hollywood-royalty board of trustees.

Jean Firstenberg knew public television and the video landscape and understood NEA's commitment to media arts centers, independent video producers, and public television labs. She came to AFI from the Markle Foundation, whose president conceptualized and initially funded CTW, Children's Television Workshop, which brought us *Sesame Street.* The National Endowment for the Arts, along with the Rockefeller Foundation and New York State Council on the Arts, had been funding the new video pioneers and their media centers in dozens of cities across the U.S. for a decade.

By 1981, there was a substantial body of interesting work and creative figures for a festival to draw from. Visual, conceptual, and performance artists had seized the new consumer technology. As early as 1965, video arts pioneer Nam June Paik was using a Sony Portapak from Japan before it was on sale in the U.S. Video art came to decode and reinvent the television experience, deploying new tools such as synthesizers in multi-monitor installations for museums and galleries. PBS, which began broadcasting in 1970, became a major force in bringing video to TV, and independent production organizations across the country built relationships with their local public stations.

The First National Video Festival

The first festival asserted the scope and diversity of video innovation. More than 350 video evangelists came to share their work and explore the future in presentations and panel discussions for five days, June 3–7, 1981. During the festival's fifteen-hour days, 185 video works—more than fifty hours—were showcased.

James Hindman took a sabbatical from American University to join me at AFI. I took the title of festival producer and Hindman festival director, and we worked hand-in-hand to mount the conference and exhibition at the Kennedy Center.

We imagined an epic event, and we felt that the otherwise huge scale of the festival and its wide peripheral vision would be necessary to define the field. It was a three-ring circus that featured independent videomakers, visual and performing artists, public and commercial broadcasters, community video and cable access centers, public information and business applications, and the national student competition winners, all congregating in the Kennedy Center's theaters and public spaces.

Was it overreaching for a brand-new program at AFI, with limited staff and resources, to set such an ambitious agenda? Of course, but as curators and conveners, we served the historical moment. It all came together because, as the *Los Angeles Times*' Connie Koennen said of the festival, ". . . the cumulative effect is that an art form is emerging."

Jean Firstenberg's program notes caught the mix of experience and perspectives that defined the festival: "Where else can one find, in a single symposium, ABC's president of broadcast operations and engineering (Julius Barnathan), a founder of The Kitchen (Steina Vasulka), an artist-professor from Chicago (Dan Sandin), the director of video for the New York State Council on the Arts (John Giancola), and the engineer responsible for *Live from the Met* (Mark Schubin)?"

Sony's aspirations for the market were relayed by Tsunoda in his remarks: "Videotaping equipment is now a part of our daily lives, expanding from television stations to schools, industries, and homes. The festival includes leaders from all sectors of technical and production areas, and the diversity is very significant."

I came into the festival with high expectations. I could see that with the tremendous growth of developing technologies, the communications environment would demand programming in greater volume, sophistication, and specialization. I hoped that the festival (and other AFI activities) could have an impact on those developments. Various panels explored new models of programs that promised new opportunities.

STAKING OUT THE TERRITORY OF THE VIDEO REVOLUTION

The festival poster and program cover by renowned graphic artist Milton Glaser captured our vision for the festival as representing a revolutionary moment in media arts and culture. He created a startling image of a lightning bolt cracking the screen of a TV set on an oversized easel covered in dabs of paint and trailing a thick cable wrapped around its legs, captioned: "The State of the Art."

Because of his prestigious career in television, academia, and government, Erik Barnouw could uniquely endow the festival with a mission statement that reflected Glaser's powerful image. As chief of the Motion Picture, Broadcasting, and Recorded Sound Division of the Library of Congress, Columbia University professor emeritus of dramatic arts, author of the seminal histories of television and documentary film, and former chairman of the Writers Guild of America, Barnouw had the standing to proclaim a revolution.

CELEBRATING INDEPENDENT ARTISTS AND MEDIA ARTS CENTERS

The heart of the festival was its focus on independent documentary makers and video artists, and the media organizations that enabled their work. Barnouw celebrated the role of independents, who "ask the unimagined question and listen to the unexpected answer." He quoted French director Louis Malle: "My role is that of a troublemaker. I want to wake people up and make them rethink their values."

Robert Redford was the star attraction for a panel on the last day of the festival named "Untold Stories: Independent Voices for the New Market," moderated by Barnouw. Redford reached out to the participants, saying, "I hope the Oscar [for *Ordinary People*] doesn't make me an enemy." Redford quickly bridged the gap by introducing his new Sundance Institute for Film and Television, which had opened its doors one week before with a workshop equipped by Sony.

Those principles were showcased in thirty hours, reviewing highlights of the alternative video of the 1970s, the pioneering work in the decade before the emergence of the new cable marketplace, work often supported by media arts centers, museums, and public television. Subtitled "The Range of Video Alternatives," the retrospective included productions, program notes, and presentations by ten production collectives and media centers and five museums and exhibition centers. The fifteen programs ran continuously during the five days of the festival.

The festival centerpiece was the mission-driven Downtown Community Television (DCTV), an emblem for the crosscurrents of the festival. It was a prescient choice. For more than forty years, DCTV's founders and directors, Jon Alpert and Keiko Tsuno, have demonstrated both a profound commitment to empowering people with the tools and skills to speak for themselves and, at the same time, the highest professional standards for documentary production. Alpert was on the cutting edge of portable video and a pioneer in investigative reporting for television news in the '70s. Other highlights included work from TVTV, Videopolis, Optic Nerve, Ant Farm, University Community Video, Global Village, NOVAC (the New Orleans Video Access Center), video collective Media Bus, New York City's The Kitchen, the Long Beach Museum of Art, Whitney Museum of American Art's Film and Video Department, the Berkeley Art Museum, Museum of Modern Art, and WNET/Thirteen TV Lab.

FESTIVAL PREMIERES IN THE "NATION'S FIRST" THEATRICAL VIDEO PROJECTION

Five premieres were presented to great effect on the 220-inch screen in the AFI Theater. In *Afterimage*, Cindy Furlong wrote, "AFI turned the film theater into a video theater. For most members of the audience, including this author, it was the first experience in viewing a large-screen color video projection successfully presented in a formal film theater, the brilliance and glow of the projected video image enhancing the immediacy inherent in the medium."

INSTALLATIONS: THE GALLERY AND MUSEUM EXPERIENCE

Artist installations brought the gallery and museum experience into the festival. Nam June Paik, described in the program as an "electronic artist and media philosopher," was the definition of video art and had to be at the center of the festival. A year later, the Whitney Museum would devote a whole floor to his work. His influence and reputation has endured.

His installation "Kennedy Olympics" was designed for the festival, fashioned from Paik's video, *Lake Placid '80*, commissioned by the Winter Olympics Fine Arts Committee. The video was displayed on a row of five monitors seen through aquariums filled with goldfish. Set up for the full five days of the festival, the installation had an insistent soundtrack, a loop of Mitch Ryder's "Devil with a Blue Dress On," that filled the top floor of the Kennedy Center next to the retrospective's screenings and panels. Sony's cofounder and chairman Akio Morita was delighted when he stopped a tour to look at his monitors through the swimming fish. He was overheard to joke, "Oh my, a whole new market for Sony." The live interaction of audiences with the medium was an essential theme of the festival, experienced in the shock of the new theater projection, retrospective screenings, multi-monitor music video exhibitions, and a video dance party.

MUSIC VIDEOS BEFORE MTV

The sense of novelty and new possibilities was most palpable in music video, which had emerged in the 1970s in clubs and galleries. MTV was on the horizon and would be launched on August 1,

1981. Videos were screened on monitors in two exhibition areas on the top floor of the Kennedy Center and projected in the Theater Lab. A video record party celebrated the creativity and vitality of the music video pioneers in a late-night event in the Theater Lab. *Broadcasting* magazine wrote, "Many thought the Video Record Party, hosted by VJ (video jockey) John Hunt, with a new format was an obvious winner."

BEYOND BROADCAST: ENGAGING, INFORMING, AND EQUIPPING NEW AUDIENCES

The festival gave a prominent platform to community video and PEG (Public, Education, and Government) channel programming in "They Speak for Themselves: The Collaboration of Subject and Producer in Social Issues and Community Video." The panel featured George Stoney, documentary film and video pioneer, who was an inspiration and leader for the community video movement.

Stoney made the case for cable access: "As access develops . . . we'll have a different attitude towards what we put on. The people won't just be the pawns, the butt of jokes, fodder for the media." Stoney raised expectations for access to tools and channels, like Barnouw, and he anticipated the new life forms of participatory media that have been realized in the digital age. On the same panel, Atlanta city councilman James Bond argued the case for diversity, explaining that cable access was the alternative to the domination of Cox Broadcasting, providing the only positive image of African Americans in the market. Needless to say, Bond went on to a remarkable career.

The new landscape was surveyed in "The Art of Information: Issues and Aesthetics in Information Programming," moderated by Bill Moyers's producer Sherry Jones. Robert Northshield showed segments from *CBS News Sunday Morning*, including "The Science of Statistics for Political Reporting," and Jon Alpert presented

DCTV work for NBC. A deep relationship to their subjects and respect for their audiences illustrated the challenges that video documentary was making to broadcast news.

The program notes posed prescient questions for the discussion: With "the new services on cable, the introduction of the home market, and the proliferation of video in the workplace" will "our expectations that television should function as a serious information tool" increase? "Where is the line drawn between fact and dramatic effect," between "public service, advocacy, and entertainment? What is the nature of the dialogue with the viewer? How is the effectiveness of informational programming measured?"

STUDENT VIDEO COMPETITION PROMOTES THE NEXT GENERATION

The Student Competition in Videotape Production—one of Sony's primary reasons for funding the festival—recognized the achievements of young videomakers and the programs that trained them. The five winning videos were screened during the festival and broadcast on WETA in Washington and WNET in New York.

There were 330 entries from 140 colleges, universities, and media centers in thirty-nine states. Entries were judged in six geographical regions, and the twenty-three local winners were announced in the festival program. Students took home $100,000 in Sony equipment as prizes. The educational market was a priority for Sony and reflected AFI's future mission in film education.

Students Alex Gibney and Peter Bull won for their fifty-eight-minute documentary, *The Ruling Classroom*, about a seventh-grade social studies class at UC San Diego exploring the roles of government, business, and journalism. Both Gibney (*Going Clear*, *Taxi to the Dark Side*) and Bull (*NOW with Bill Moyers*, *Dirty Business)* went on to acclaimed careers in documentary.

Tom Musca from UCLA won for a dramatic satire on a student

film competition, *Highlight from the New Directors' Film Festival.* Musca went on to produce and co-write the classic film *Stand and Deliver* with Edward James Olmos and build a career in fiction film.

The student winners were fêted in a reception with festival artists and speakers at the Japanese Embassy. A compilation of highlights from the 1982 festival toured the country as part of PhotoShow International.

The Second National Video Festival in DC and L.A.

Following the success of the first festival, Sony's commitment was deep and lasting, funding annual video festivals for more than a decade, as well as a Sony Video Center on AFI's new Los Angeles campus. For AFI, Sony's long-term commitment and practical support over the ensuing years would become a critical part of achieving AFI's mission. It would have been hard to imagine that the AFI relationship with Sony could have become any stronger at this point in time. But it did happen, when trustee Howard Stringer went on to lead Sony USA and then become the first person who was not Japanese to lead the entire Sony corporation.

AFI's new TV and Video Services program became active in the field, for example, helping to plan NAMAC's conference at Appalshop, serving on the video jury of the USA Film and Video Festival in Park City (which became Sundance), and speaking at a Foundation for Independent Video and Film event—"TV Guides: Critics and Video Artists Meet to Discuss Role of Television in Our Culture," along with Nam June Paik and Les Brown (editor of the magazine *Channels*, funded by the Markle Foundation, where Jean Firstenberg had worked on the project for eighteen months before coming to AFI).

Bringing the second edition of the festival to both DC and L.A. was driven by the move to the new campus and by Sony's interest in planting the video flag in Hollywood. We produced a symposium on "Film vs. Video" at the L.A. campus. And in DC, Robert Altman presented the premiere of *Two by South*, shot and edited in video. These events set the stage for panels and screenings in the second festival that would reflect AFI's links to the creative community. There was a pent-up demand in L.A. for a forum on video. Billboard reported attendance of 600 for the festival at the new campus.

The themes of performance and storytelling were planted in the first festival's focus on theater and video music and predictions for the expansion of cable television channels enabled by satellite distribution. In his opening remarks, Sony's Tsunoda predicted that "electronic cinematography" will "dramatically alter conventional film techniques" and evoke a world of "multi-channel, direct-to-home satellite systems, pay-TV, specialized channels . . . home entertainment centers, video cassette recording systems, videodiscs, and computer terminals."

Broadcasting magazine treated the second festival with the same fervor: "Video enthusiasts, artists, and entrepreneurs assemble in Washington June 10–13 and set out to show that the video revolution is not coming, but has arrived. . . . New-age artists and producers, who used the television screen as their canvas and stage, along with some television pioneers, were encouraged and boosted by hearing filmmaker Francis Ford Coppola tell them that old Hollywood methods of film production are bankrupt and that he was combining video and computers in his screenwriting and filmmaking processes." Keynote speaker Coppola envisioned a low-cost "video studio" that would use "electronic systems" to "free artistic invention."

Making video as accessible as film was the focus of the film/video panel, which included key executives from Zoetrope, Lucasfilm, and Sundance Productions, in addition to NBC and PBS. Predicting the future of non-linear editing, Ralph Guggenheim, editing project head for Lucasfilm, described the new EditDroid, a new computer-managed video editor the production company had developed in-house.

Choreographers Twyla Tharp and Toni Basil, broadcast pioneers Studs Terkel and Jean Shepherd, and television executives Jo Bergman and Ethel Winant brought new perspectives to the festival. *Variety*'s Paul Harris called the festival "a mecca" for video producers to showcase their works and compare notes with colleagues, and highlighted the five-hour survey of video music curated by Jo Bergman, director of TV and video for Warner Bros. Records. Music video directors were now auteurs.

The inventiveness of the golden age of television provided compass points for what seemed so modern in these productions. What we appreciate as free-form today on YouTube and some cable channels can be traced back to the creativity and jazz-like improvisation of the Chicago school of early television, revived at the festival by Studs Terkel and TV writer Charlie Andrews, who wrote for three shows for NBC: Terkel's weekly half-hour *Studs' Place*, with a regular cast of characters in a neighborhood bar performing from an outline; the variety show *Garroway at Large*, with the host wandering between set pieces talking to the crew; and *Kukla, Fran, and Ollie*, an inspiration for Jim Henson's Muppets.

Jacqueline Kain, former curator at The Kitchen, selected works by artists and independent producers under the separate headings of drama, performance, and music. Consisting of 100 thirty-second vignettes ranging from the early TV parodies of William Wegman and his dog Man Ray to Robert Wilson's *Video 50*, the tapes defied traditional television conventions, exploring new formats, narrative structure, and language.

The program essay "Installation Video" by MoMA curator Barbara London chronicled twenty years of video exhibition and performance-based work. Shigeko Kubota's installation, "Nude Descending a Staircase," used stair-stepped monitors to "transcend" Marcel Duchamp.

The engaged audience, with intimations of our digital future, was demonstrated by "Hole in Space: A Public Communications Sculpture." Funded by NASA and NEA, it linked giant outdoor screens in New York and L.A. by satellite that allowed spontaneous interaction between the public on both coasts.

The festival program reflected on the seeds of what would become reality programming and TED Talks: "In the 1980s nearly everyone will think about being on television—not only professional performers, but everyone who prints a leaflet or gives a talk." Moderated by Studs Terkel, "The Role of the Subject" was framed by insistent questions inherent in the new media: Who would have a voice, who would have access to the means of production and the channels of distribution? Do you matter, do you even exist, if you're not on television? These questions anticipated the World Wide Web, YouTube, and Facebook.

Looking back thirty-five years, it's hard to imagine how exciting and fresh it was for all of us involved: how easy it was to get people to come at this magic moment, from giants like Sony and Warner Bros. to the independent documentary makers and video artists; how responsive they were to AFI's role as curator and convener; and how firm our conviction was about the need to collectively map the landscape, a stance that was validated by those who showed up and who stayed around to talk.

AFI Introduces Apple to Creatives

Emily Laskin

The AFI/Apple Computer story begins with my friend, screenwriter Michael Backes. By virtue of always exploring the frontier of technology and being considered a kind of visionary, he had an insider relationship with Apple in the 1980s. Mike was also Michael Crichton's writing partner, and Crichton employed Mike as a creative and technical consultant as well as a co-author and thought partner.

Mike was part of an elite group who would test hardware and software for Apple before products were put on the market. He had come to know and introduced me to a young PR and marketing figure, Daniel Paul. Apple was Daniel's client, and at the time the company was specifically interested in connecting Apple to Hollywood. I believe Daniel's Apple title was Entertainment Industry Evangelist.

Over social dinners, lunches, and many random conversations, Mike and I had spoken of the "dream" possibilities of using Macs to enhance the filmmaking process. Although it now sounds like a reference to the nineteenth century, there was very little interaction or wide use of personal computers by filmmakers at the time—although there were early stirrings like the use of then-nascent screenwriting software and Excel documents for budgeting.

MIT Media Lab was the only other program I could find that was exploring similar interfaces. Documentary filmmaker Glorianna Davenport was a founding member of the Media Lab at MIT. Founded in 1980, MIT Media Lab was at the vanguard of exploring digital media in support of storytelling among other equally ambitious goals in technology and applied use.

After hearing about Glorianna, I called her out of the blue. She answered the phone herself and, after hearing me out on my very loose and not fully formed ideas, she offered to be of counsel. Most important, she offered encouragement. I believe, because of her roots at a research university, she clearly understood the nature of our desire to explore, iterate, and discover, not knowing where the journey would take us or if we would succeed. Because we moved quickly, I never had the opportunity to take her up on her offer of counsel, but the encouragement alone spurred me on.

I knew *nothing* about the computer's technical underpinnings, but was excited and inspired to hear Mike spin what then seemed to be crazy but potent possibilities. I truly had no idea what the possibilities could be for AFI, but I trusted in Mike's vision and Daniel's skilled ability, access, and enthusiasm to take up and advocate for that vision with his client, Apple. Mike's broad knowledge of emerging software for filmmaking far beyond screenwriting—including editing and special effects—made his guidance and generous participation critical.

Daniel had a direct line to John Sculley, CEO of Apple (1983–1993) and well-known master marketer. It appeared that Daniel had been tagged to identify potential partners and ideas and bring those ideas directly to the CEO's office. It was acknowledged in the business community that Mr. Sculley had a particular interest in pitting Apple directly against IBM, which at the time was the dominant hardware player.

Mike and Daniel and I had lots of wild brainstorming conversations and, at a certain point in time, Daniel offered to arrange for a team from Apple headquarters to visit the AFI campus. We did not wait long for their visit, and I remember at least ten Apple folks sitting in Jean Firstenberg's office. We made our pitch, and they listened carefully. The meeting lasted over one hour—so long that Jean had to leave before the meeting was over to attend another appointment.

At the end of the meeting, the Apple representatives asked me to prepare and submit a proposal. They told me we would hear back in thirty days. It sounded like the kiss of death to me; few foundations or companies consider and respond in that time period. I thought I had blown it.

When asked to submit our proposal, I was challenged very directly: "Tell us why Apple, and why not IBM." I had no idea, but Mike did. Although I wrote ninety-eight percent of the formal proposal, I asked (begged) Mike to write the one critical paragraph that addressed that very question. His rationale defied my technical understanding; all I remember is his reference to a Motorola drive. He developed the paragraph in a flash and in return, I took him to lunch. That was his "fee," and he was gracious and satisfied—satisfied, I believe, because he knew he had nailed it and had helped clear a definitive path and vision for what was possible for filmmakers utilizing Macs and not PCs.

Less than thirty days after our submission, we heard from Apple. They loved the idea and would establish a lab at AFI as a beachhead in Hollywood.

When we announced the partnership, Mr. Sculley came to the AFI campus and was gracious and available to everyone—staff, faculty, and Fellows alike. In my enthusiasm (and ignorance), I had made up t-shirts for the occasion with the AFI and Apple logo and the date. Daniel discreetly told me that we did not have the right to reproduce the Apple logo, but that Mr. Sculley had said he would look the other way if we only distributed them to the folks in the room and destroyed the extras.

My lasting memory of that day—other than the Apple team's generosity of spirit, tolerance for risk, and enthusiasm—was the reception outside the Mark Goodson Screening Room after the formal announcement. I was eating my lunch, sitting cross-legged on the floor (the room was packed and there were no more seats at tables) alongside a fascinating, clearly brilliant, and strangely familiar, charming gentleman who seemed to know a lot about everything—especially Macs. After our lengthy informal lunch and lovely far-ranging conversation, I asked his name and he said, "Just call me Tim." It was Timothy Leary—another Mac evangelist and visionary—in attendance at the launch of an exciting chapter for AFI.

AFI and the Digital World

NICK DEMARTINO

The history of screened entertainment could be approached as a succession of technologies, from silent film, to talkies, to color television, to home video, and much more. So it was only natural that a national organization devoted to the moving image arts would periodically explore innovations that could "advance" the art form with initiatives that mainstreamed technologies like non-linear editing, experimental media, home video, music videos, and more.

Starting with the personal computer, digital media technologies would become an unstoppable force, transforming the entertainment world in the 1990s and beyond. AFI leveraged its stature to build a series of partnerships that brought Hollywood and Silicon Valley cultures together, and helped to change the face of entertainment forever.

Cinetex: The Prelude

In 1989, AFI needed somebody to run an event in Las Vegas called Cinetex, a film festival, market, and conference. I had never touched a computer until I borrowed one to apply for the job. And yet, within a few months, computers would become the center of my world at AFI, and a significant force in shaping the direction of the organization.

My association with AFI and its leadership went back a few years. AFI director Jean Firstenberg had funded a documentary I produced when she was a foundation executive. AFI's *American Film* magazine had published many of my articles on the rise of the video movement. My friend and fellow video advocate, Larry Kirkman, led AFI's first video initiative, and was succeeded by our mutual friend and co-producer, James Hindman. I drove onto the hilly AFI campus for my first day—January 20, 1990—without a clue that this one-year gig would last for more than twenty years, a period during which I served as AFI's lead man as Hollywood and Silicon Valley collided and connected.

Cinetex was the brainchild of Sheldon Adelson, who had a grand plan to become a billionaire by transforming Las Vegas. His giant computer trade show, Comdex, had already made him rich, and he hoped that AFI could make Cinetex a similar success for the film business. I was the third guy who tried and failed to create a Cannes-rivaling film festival and entertainment market on the Vegas strip for Adelson.

But the Cinetex conference was another matter. My colleague, Anna Marie Piersimoni, and I convinced some 200 speakers to schlep to Las Vegas in September 1990 and speak at forty-two sessions. We were especially proud of the technology track. Virtual reality pioneer Jaron Lanier and Apple Fellow Alan Kay delivered visionary talks about the future of media and education. Pong inventor Al Alcorn reflected on the social role of video games. Hypermedia theorist Ted Nelson was so hyper about his Xanadu project that he fell off the stage. The *Star Wars* visual effects team let people peek behind their magic curtain. Multimedia publishers like Voyager demonstrated a new medium that was interactive. Consultants Michael Backes and Scott Billups revealed computer tips from their pioneering work in Hollywood.

Adelson canceled Cinetex after his third try and my first outing. A flop for him, maybe, but not for me, since I got to study Hollywood all day long, and learned how to use the AFI brand to attract support. Most importantly, I began to build a network within the tech world, a skill that would serve AFI well as I undertook a new project with Apple Computer.

An Apple for AFI

The AFI and Apple partnership was formally announced as a partnership in June 1990, at an event featuring Apple CEO John Sculley, longtime AFI trustee Charlton Heston, and none other than Mickey Mouse (well, an actor in a mouse suit). "This is the real vision behind the dream," said Sculley, "to be able to bring high technology to the people who can craft with it, use it as a tool, help do creative things that will make a difference in the world." Sculley and Firstenberg announced that Apple was donating $1 million worth of computers for AFI to create a "computer lab for filmmakers" on its Hollywood campus. Photos from the event showed Heston, Mickey, and Sculley gripping the Moses staff from *The Ten Commandments*. As metaphors go, the scene was mixed, but the picture made the papers.

Just three years later, *NewMedia Magazine* would describe the AFI-Apple Lab program in its August 1993 cover story as "a high-profile melding of Hollywood and Silicon Valley cultures that attracts big names in both industries." Digital World founder Jonathan Seybold would put it this way: "AFI has had an enormous influence on the digital revolution in Hollywood, accelerating the learning curve for thousands of creative people." But there was much work to do before those words would be written.

For help building the Apple lab, I turned to a pair of guys who understood both traditional and digital media. Michael Backes (who had had such an influence in crafting the AFI proposal to Apple) had worked on James Cameron's groundbreaking motion picture special effects and was himself a screenwriter and game producer. Digital video wizard Scott Billups learned cinematography at the elbow of the great James Wong Howe, and had produced hundreds of ad campaigns and special effects shots. They agreed to co-chair an advisory board for the new Apple program.

Even though charismatic Apple cofounder Steve Jobs was in exile from the company—his twelve-year "interregnum"—the company's ongoing mythology as the rebel outsider remained a powerful magnet for the creative types we needed to build this lab. Figures like musician Herbie Hancock, advertising guru Robert Greenberg, interactive pioneer Bob Abel, director John Badham, and so many others wanted in on what we had started. They lent credibility to the program and sizzle to our monthly planning meetings.

After four months of frenzied study and networking, it was time to debut the AFI-Apple program at the MacWorld conference. It was my first time on the stadium-sized exhibit floor packed with unfamiliar companies. Backes had explained that Apple alone was not enough to start AFI down this road—we needed the software and hardware products from other companies if we were to build a successful program.

From booth to booth, the message to prospective donors was simple: *AFI and Apple are bringing Silicon Valley to Hollywood, and you can be part of it.* Endorsements from members of the advisory board proclaimed that the lab was a "once-in-a-lifetime opportunity," poised "to give birth to a generation of film people who have computer sensibilities" that would "revolutionize both the process and the form of moviemaking." One member called our new venture "the Bauhaus of the nineties." More than 100 companies donated software and hardware that first year, worth a million bucks.

Both Hollywood and tech types jammed the opening of the AFI-Apple Computer Center for Film and Videomakers in May 1991. A slick catalog announced the first slate of classes planned for that summer, focusing on the Mac in film, video, and multimedia.

A few weeks later, Apple premiered its new QuickTime multimedia software at AFI. The star of the show was ReelTime, computer editing software using QuickTime. Its young developer, Randy Ubillos, gave his demo standing at a keyboard, like Jerry Lee Lewis on a piano. The crowd cheered as he put his product through its paces, showing features that had only been available in high-end post-production suites. The vision of how AFI could help Hollywood see its future was coming into focus.

AFI COMPUTER MEDIA SALONS

Backes and Billups were slated to teach a survey course called "State-of-the-Art Mac Applications in Entertainment." One class featured musician and inventor Jimmy Hotz, whose Hotzbox digital processor allowed users to play along to any song or harmonic scale without hitting a wrong note. Next, LSD guru Timothy Leary shared a trippy CD-ROM project. Before long, Leary had commandeered the Hotzbox and was jamming along with Led Zeppelin's "Stairway to Heaven."

Less a traditional class than a talk show with toys, the sessions became a new program called the AFI Computer Media Salons. Every month, salon leaders Backes and Billups found people to explore what they called "The Cutting Edge," which, on some nights, was more like the bleeding edge, when guests would bring early versions of products that crashed or even exploded.

Within a year, we added three more salons, making it a weekly series. I hosted "Reinventing Hollywood," a salon featuring new digital applications specifically created for the entertainment community. An early episode was entitled "Jobs that Didn't Exist Last Year." Broadcast designer Harry Marks presented interactive creators and game designers in "The Interactive Salon." (Marks would become creative director of the Center in 1992.) Marks had a creator's passion that attracted innovators like Robert Winter, author of elegant interactive music discs; Bob Stein, whose Voyager Company pioneered the "expanded book"; and the Miller brothers, creators of the groundbreaking game MYST. PR pro Allison Thomas hosted "The Digital Highway," a salon that explored networks and distribution at a time when the Internet was just beginning to gain traction. Having worked for everyone from Jimmy Carter to Jerry Brown to Steve Jobs, Allison commanded a monthly conversation that was equal parts policy and technology.

"Convergence" was the buzzword of the era. The line between presenters and the audience at our salons could be blurry—artists, technologists, and executives all came to AFI to meet others who shared a new vision of Hollywood. Some also came out of fear. As I told a reporter: "People in Hollywood who might not have any reason to think about computers, all of a sudden felt the ground shake beneath them. The train has left the station, folks. If you didn't get a ticket, you're going to be in trouble."

The salons gave some shape to an unformed future, now being advocated by the evangelists of digital technology. At the time, none of us realized how much that future would change. We just knew the salons were amazing. And fun. For a brief moment in history, the AFI salons were the only such game in Hollywood, and everyone came.

BACK TO THE FUTURE

The Apple Lab program also offered hands-on workshops and lecture-style classes—digital video, computer graphics, animation, and interactive design were the most popular. One workshop produced some of the world's first QuickTime movies, including a trailer for the previous year's Oscar-winning best picture, *The Silence of the Lambs*, and a lovely meditation on the artist Christo's umbrellas, then unfurling in the mountains north of L.A. It was fun showing off the results to VIP visitors. Robert Wise, the Oscar-winning director who had edited *Citizen Kane* at the beginning of his career, watched nine little 120 x 180-pixel rectangles that looked like live-action postage stamps in the center of our giant computer monitor.

"That's just great!" Wise said. "When I was new, sound was just coming in." The great man understood the implications of early-stage technology.

In between the classes and salons, we put on dozens of special events, such as a technical tour of the groundbreaking *Jurassic Park*, a "Technology Careers for Women" symposium, and custom training for studios, guilds, and others.

We were trying to catch lightning in a bottle, to use whatever structure we could find to connect an eager audience to the transformation that was hurtling before us. The team that made it possible included Beth Taylor Hart, Chris Craig, Harry Mott, and Frank Dutro. By 1994, the program was offering more than ninety classes. Over the life of the program, the salons and workshops together attracted some 7,000 participants, most of them working professionals in Hollywood. Many of them consider their time at AFI a career turning point, what I described as a "personal digital epiphany."

CHANGE AT APPLE AND CHANGE AT AFI

When Apple stock lost two-thirds of its value and Wall Street howled about poor performance, Apple replaced Sculley in 1993 with COO Michael Spindler. Initially, AFI felt limited impact from this change. We had made powerful friends at Apple, principally David Nagel, the company's chief technology officer, and Satjiv Chahil, its chief marketing officer, who loved everything about Hollywood. Chahil and Nagel once tried some show biz of their own by driving a Harley onstage for a product launch held at AFI. Nagel honored AFI with a Golden Master Award for our contribution to QuickTime at a special event in Apple's gleaming new headquarters.

Chahil, the dapper, turbaned marketing wizard, became AFI's great advocate (and would remain so during later stints at Sony, Palm, and HP). With his help, AFI secured a gift of $250,000 and a complete upgrade of products needed for AFI's lab and staff. It was high time for Silicon Valley to be represented on the AFI board. Spindler became the first such executive. Others would follow.

After three years of product and financial disaster, Apple replaced Spindler with tech executive Gilbert Amelio, who also joined the AFI board, becoming a very active, generous trustee from 1996 to 2009 and again from 2011 to 2014. Amelio lasted only 500 days before the notorious boardroom coup that brought Steve Jobs back to Apple. With Jobs's return to Apple, AFI quickly lost whatever special relationship it once had with the company. Starting in 1997, we had to buy our own gear, just like everybody else, and would be on the outside as the Wizard of Silicon Valley developed the iMac, iPod, iPhone, iPad, and all the rest.

Nevertheless, a tremendous impact had been made. In 1992, producer and former Monkee Michael Nesmith articulated the historical importance of the program in a presentation to the AFI trustees: "The implications of this new technology are profound, if for no other reason than they will change forever the way stories are told," he said. "The film and television community are the artists and storytellers of our time. AFI creates a link between them and the technologists . . . to cause both disciplines to grow into something greater than either one alone."

Tech as Strategy

Apple's troubles underscored the need for AFI to broaden its technology base, to turn its attention to other companies with the resources to help advance our agenda. The AFI Advanced Technology Council (ATC) was our first move, a group designed to "attract executives who were committed to advancing the digital revolution in Hollywood." Agreeing to serve as co-chairs were Adobe Systems CEO John Warnock (who became an involved and generous trustee from 2001 to 2010) and writer-director James Cameron—one from Silicon Valley, one from Hollywood.

Cameron kicked off the council's raucous first event in a San Jose ballroom jammed with geeks and fanboys; it felt more like Comic-Con than a fundraiser. Next, we convened a series of high-profile dinners featuring leaders from both communities—among them producer Gale Anne Hurd, director Martha Coolidge, MPAA chief Jack Valenti, venture capitalists Ann Winblad and Stewart Alsop, and the founders of TiVo, Motorola, and Sun Microsystems.

The tech executives loved meeting Hollywood insiders and participating in conversations that both sides could understand. The dinners led to meetings, which in turn led AFI to deals with some of the biggest companies in the technology industry.

This tech push was becoming central to what Firstenberg called "the new AFI," built upon a "commitment to create entrepreneurial joint ventures that would generate funds in support of AFI's mission." And so, I got a new assignment and title—director of strategic planning and, for the first time, associate director of the Institute—just in time for the coming of the Internet, Hollywood's biggest challenge yet.

The Virtual AFI

It's difficult to recall a world before the Internet, even for those of us who were there when it started. Just as AFI was setting out on its own digital journey, the Internet emerged from its academic and technical cocoon to take flight as a new and all-pervading data network that would soon transform all aspects of culture and business. In its infancy, the Internet was simply a marvel—a miraculous new utility that fostered community and created much beauty, rather than the corporate battleground it would become.

My Internet life started with AppleLink, a private email service for companies doing business with Apple. Logging on with a squawky dial-up modem, I felt like a member of a secret society of digital somebodies at a time when just having an email address seemed cool. Soon, we built AFI's first campus email network.

Some in Hollywood heard about the World Wide Web—the graphical component of the Internet—at an "Information Superhighway Summit" in January 1994, organized by Rich Frank, an AFI trustee from Disney, who also chaired the television academy. (Rich Frank's role on the AFI board, serving almost continuously since 1991, has been extraordinary. His Frank Family Wines have been served at many Life Achievement Award dinners, and he continues to chair the TV jury for the AFI AWARDS every year.) Everyone was there: Hollywood moguls like Jeffrey Katzenberg, Barry Diller, and Rupert Murdoch, as well as FCC chairman Reed Hundt and Vice President Al Gore, who would subsequently overstate his role in the invention of the Internet.

AFI's first glimpse of the World Wide Web came a few months later during a campus tribute at AFI to *Wired*, the magazine that gave voice to "digital lifestyle" before anyone even knew what that was. After entertaining the audience with the magazine's groundbreaking graphics and McLuhanesque content, *Wired* founders Louis Rossetto and Jane Metcalfe blew everyone's minds with a sneak preview of the web's first commercial magazine, *HotWired*, which they were preparing to launch in a few months. Projected onto AFI's movie screen using the Mosaic web browser, *HotWired* whipped us from one page to another—from words to images to video and back again—with a simple click of a mouse. This was something completely new, a revolutionary way of publishing, communicating, and connecting, and I knew that AFI had to be part of it.

I spent weeks learning to write HTML in order to launch a primitive website that used a discarded Mac as a server. It sure was ugly—a fact that helped me make a case for the AFI to hire a real web designer.

GOING ONLINE

AFI Online debuted on October 10, 1995, as part of the Web's exploding growth—from 600 sites at the beginning of 1994 to over 100,000 sites by the end of 1995. Our Web address was the inauspicious AFIonline.org. Others had already grabbed snappier URLs like AFI.com, AFI.edu, and AFI.org. (AFI.org was the American Fertilizer Institute, giving rise to a one-liner: "AFI, another kind of bullshit.") In 2002, AFI would eventually purchase the AFI.com domain name and AFI.edu for our screen education program for a well-spent $25,000.

Our first website featured various AFI programs, which we dubbed the "virtual AFI." We even offered a virtual campus tour using the new QuickTime VR software. The most original aspect of the site was "CineMedia," a directory of links to thousands of other websites in the field of film, television, and media, developed by UCLA film studies PhD Dan Harries, who became the first director of AFI Online Media, a web unit that became known for its creativity and inventiveness.

Dan and his staff, including Todd Hughes and Stephanie Nye,

eagerly experimented with new web technologies, especially video. AFI Online Cinema premiered in January 1997 as the first website in the world to stream classic Hollywood films, beginning with Charlie Chaplin's silent film *The Rink*, using software from Israeli startup VDONet. More than 100,000 viewers from around the world watched *The Rink* during its first month on the web, earning AFI significant international press attention. AFI Online Cinema continued with more Hollywood silent films, well-suited for the herky-jerky look of early web video transmitted using slow dial-up connections.

The team also designed elaborate multimedia presentations devoted to cinema icons like Martin Scorsese, Edith Head, Shirley Temple, James Stewart, and Alfred Hitchcock, among others, using AFI's collections of photos, videos, physical artifacts, and publications like *American Film* magazine. We also began to offer selections from AFI's library of short films, which later became valuable as the web became commercialized.

FROM TUBE TO WEB

AFI's 100 Years...100 Movies was a three-hour special that aired on CBS in 1998 and celebrated the greatest American films with short clips of films and celebrity interviews—perfect for AFI Online, providing we could raise a budget and secure usage rights. FasTV, a web video startup owned by Khaled Al Nehayan, crown prince of Dubai, covered our costs and provided technology. AFI trustee and Warner Bros. studio chief Bob Daly helped with the rights; Firstenberg and I were able to convince him that our site was piracy-proof, because we were using streaming technology rather than downloads. We launched a companion website for the CBS program featuring thirty-four Warner Bros.-licensed clips—a third of the total—along with a wealth of other materials about all 100 of the movies.

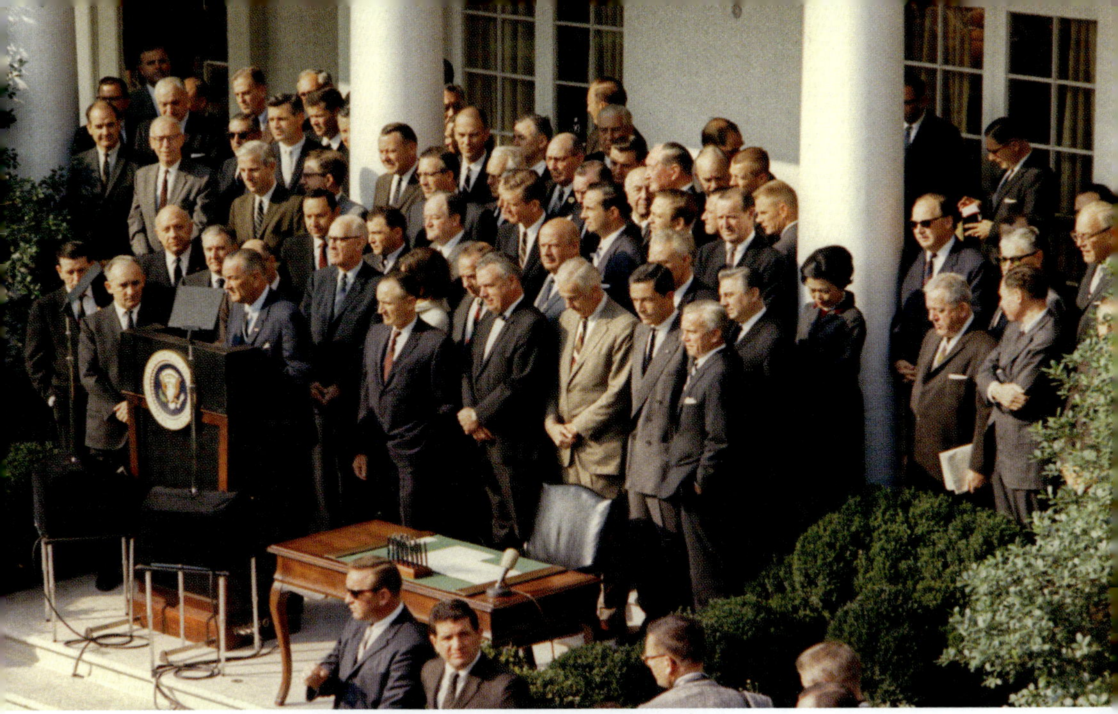

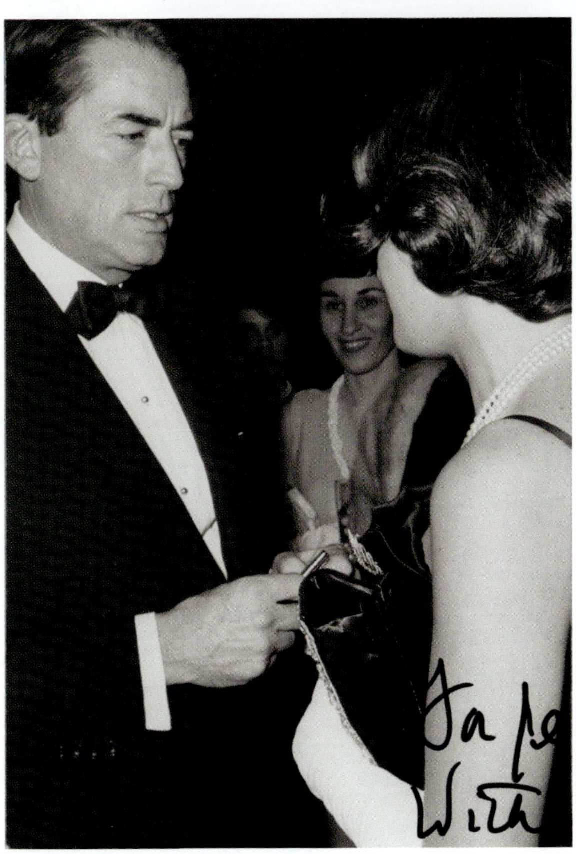

Above: President Lyndon B. Johnson establishes the National Endowment for the Arts (NEA) and the National Endowment for the Humanities (NEH) in the White House Rose Garden, 1965.

Left: AFI honorary chair Gregory Peck and co-chair Jean Picker Firstenberg (*right*) at an Inaugural Ball for President Lyndon B. Johnson, 1965.

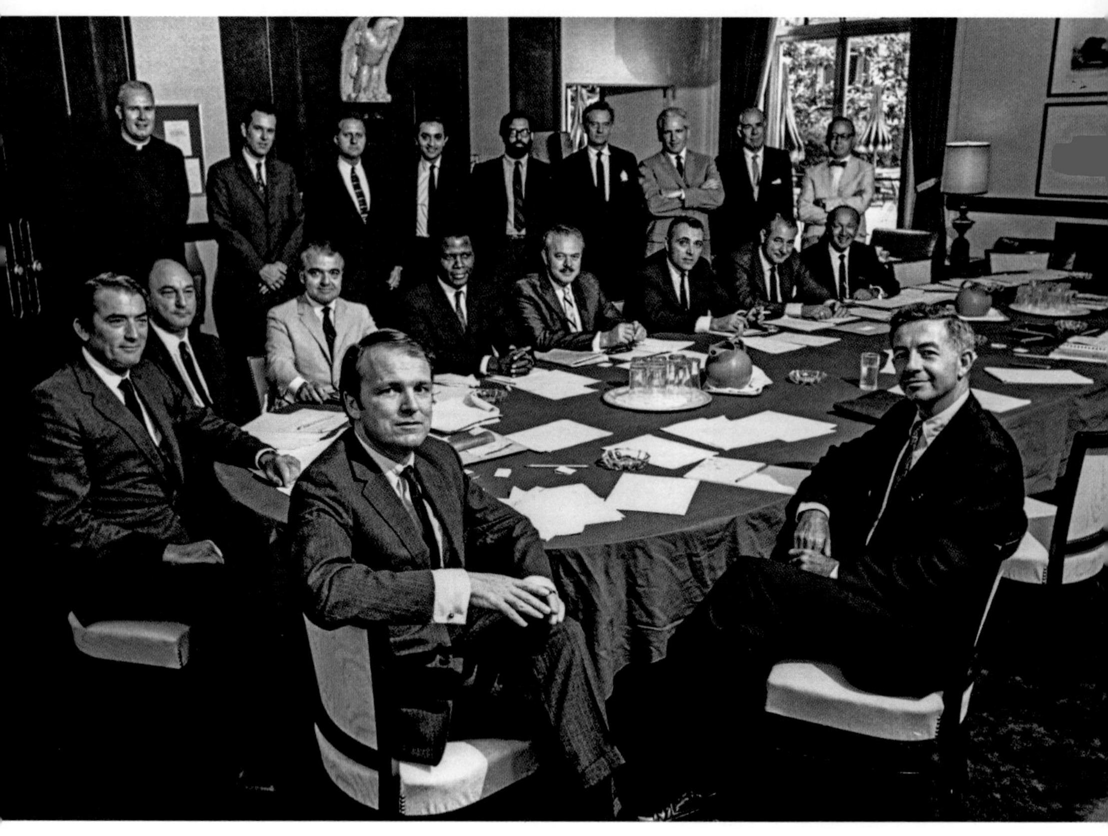

Founding trustees at the first AFI board meeting in 1967, including Gregory Peck (*seated, far left*), George Stevens Jr. (*foreground, center*), Sidney Poitier (*seated, fourth from left*), and Francis Ford Coppola (*standing, center*).

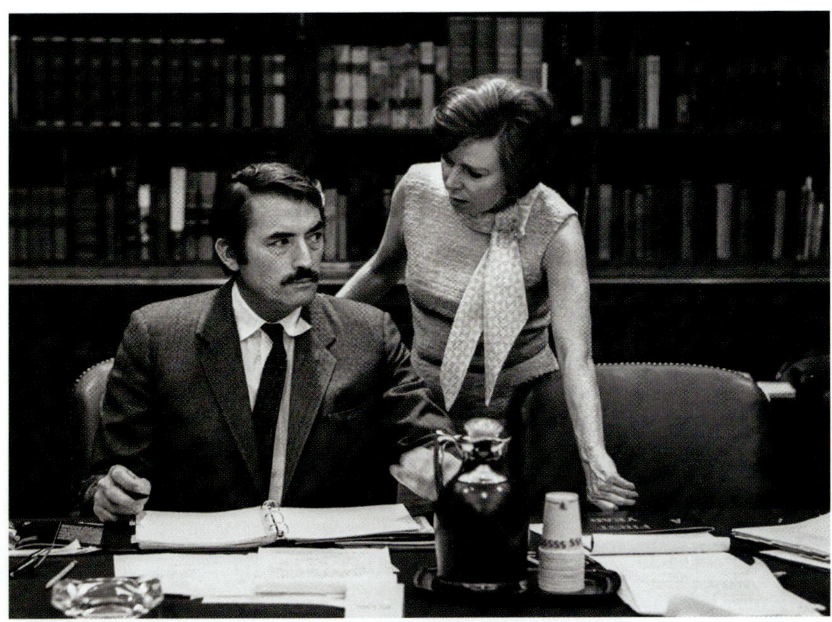

AFI founding chair Gregory Peck with one of the first AFI employees, Adrian Borneman, 1968.

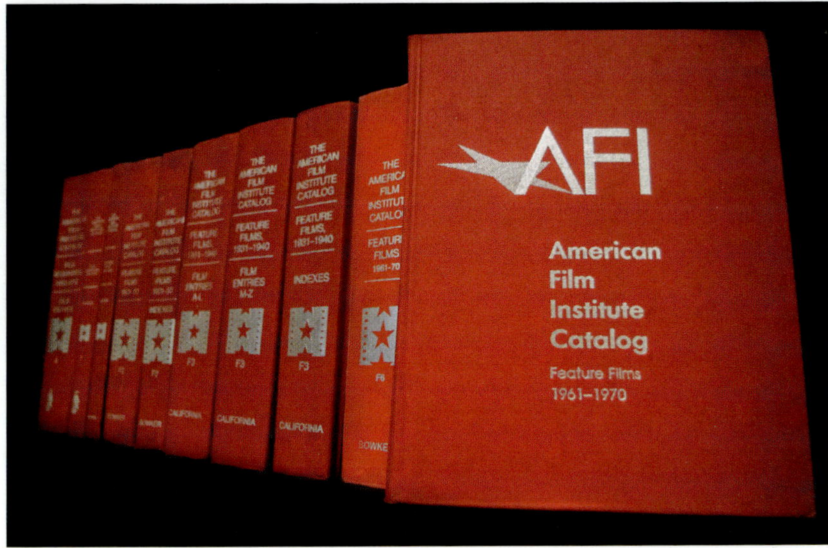

AFI Catalog of Feature Films—the big red books!

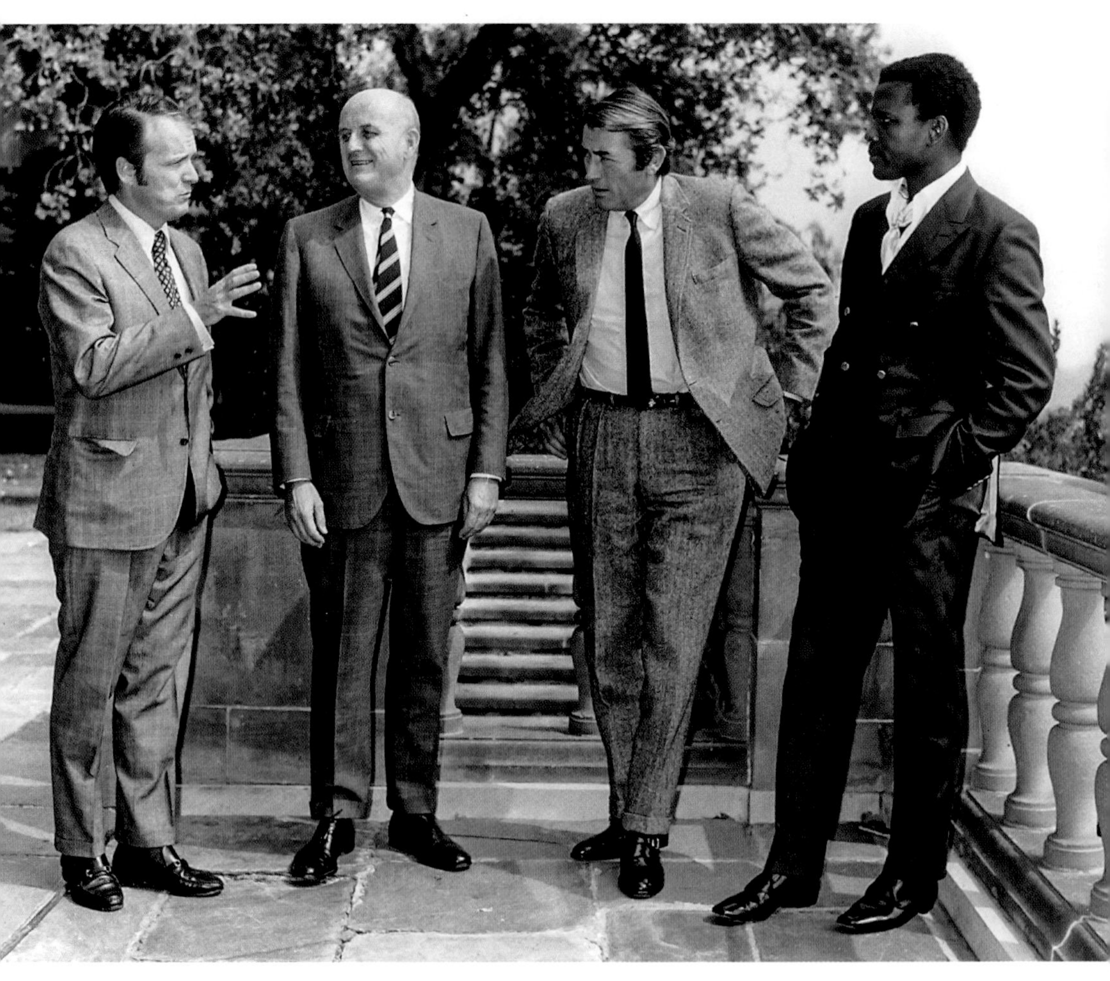

AFI founding chairs and leaders on the terrace at Greystone in 1969 (*left to right*): founding director and CEO George Stevens Jr., founding chair of the National Council on the Arts Roger Stevens, board of trustees founding chair Gregory Peck, and board of trustees founding vice chair Sidney Poitier.

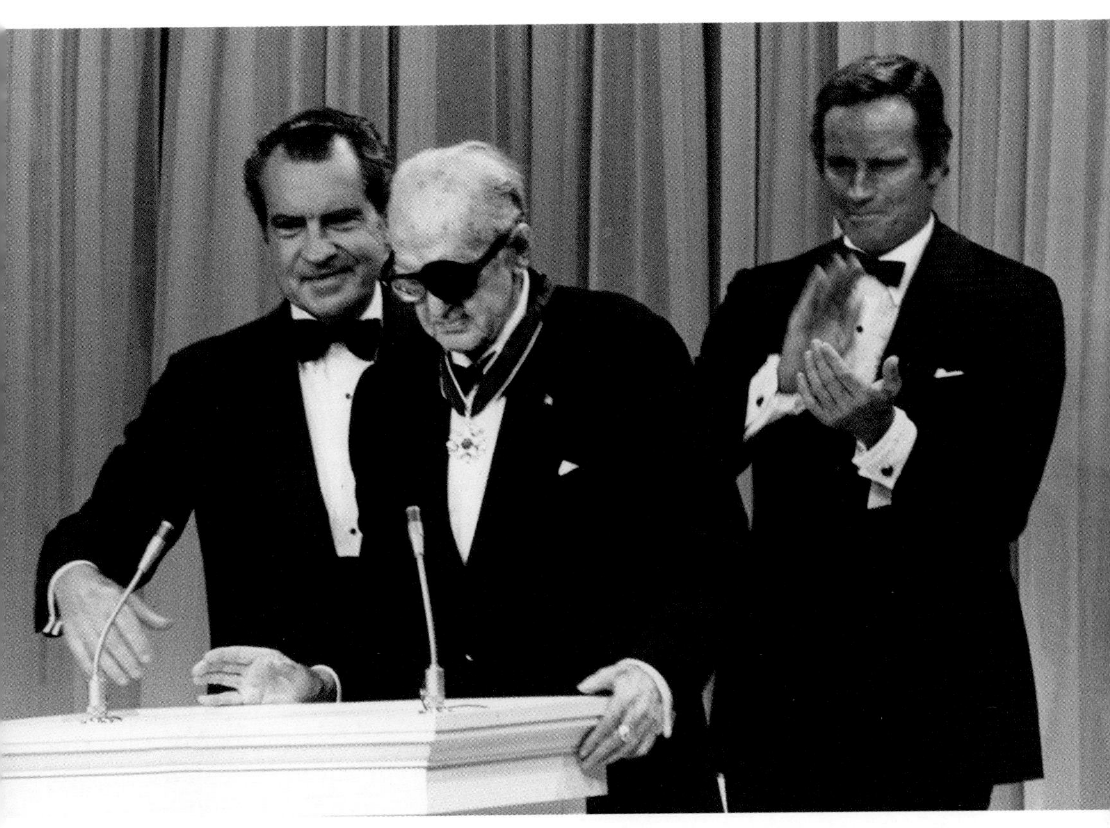

President Richard Nixon, John Ford, and AFI board of trustees chair Charlton Heston at the first AFI Life Achievement Award ceremony in 1973, where Ford received the LAA and the Presidential Medal of Freedom, presented to him by Nixon.

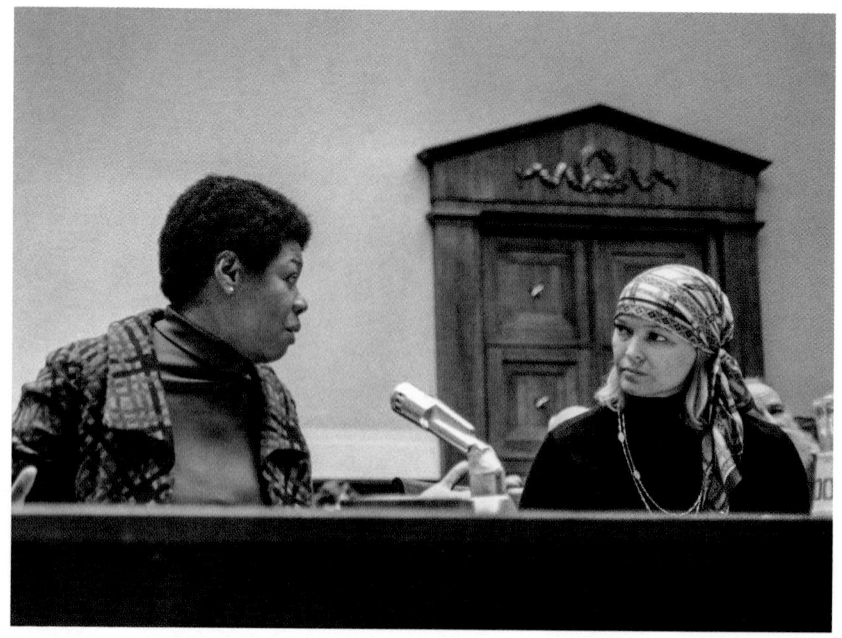

AFI Directing Workshop for Women graduates Maya Angelou and Ellen Burstyn testifying before Congress on behalf of AFI funding from the NEA, 1974.

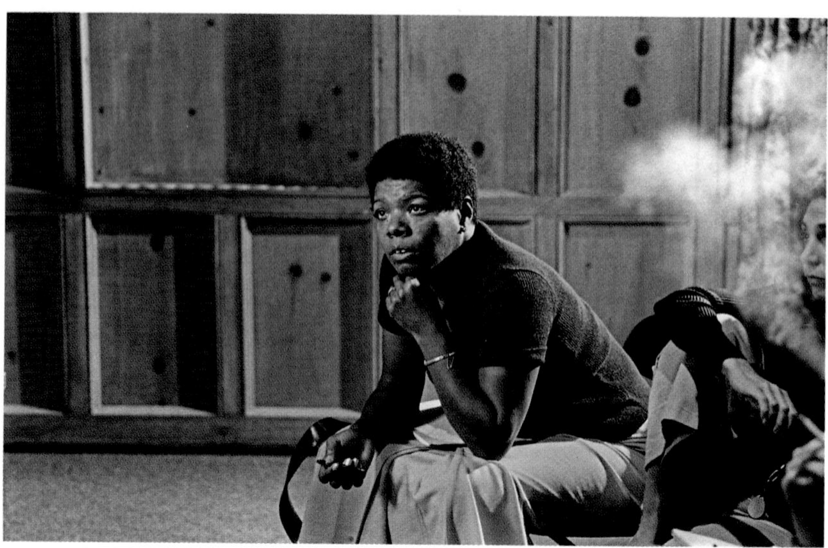

AFI DWW participant Maya Angelou on the set of her first short movie, 1974.

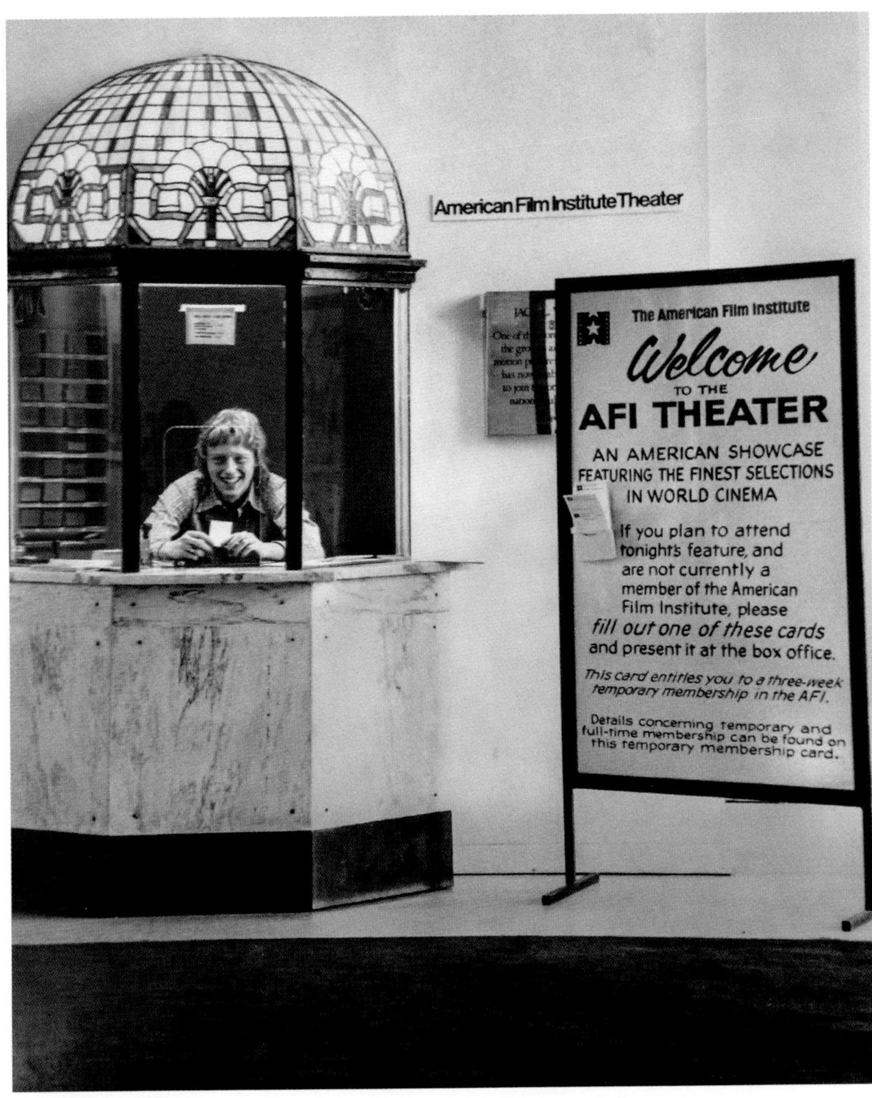

Ray Barry, now the director of the AFI Silver Theatre and Cultural Center, working as a part-time box office cashier at the AFI Theatre in the John F. Kennedy Center for the Performing Arts, mid-1970s.

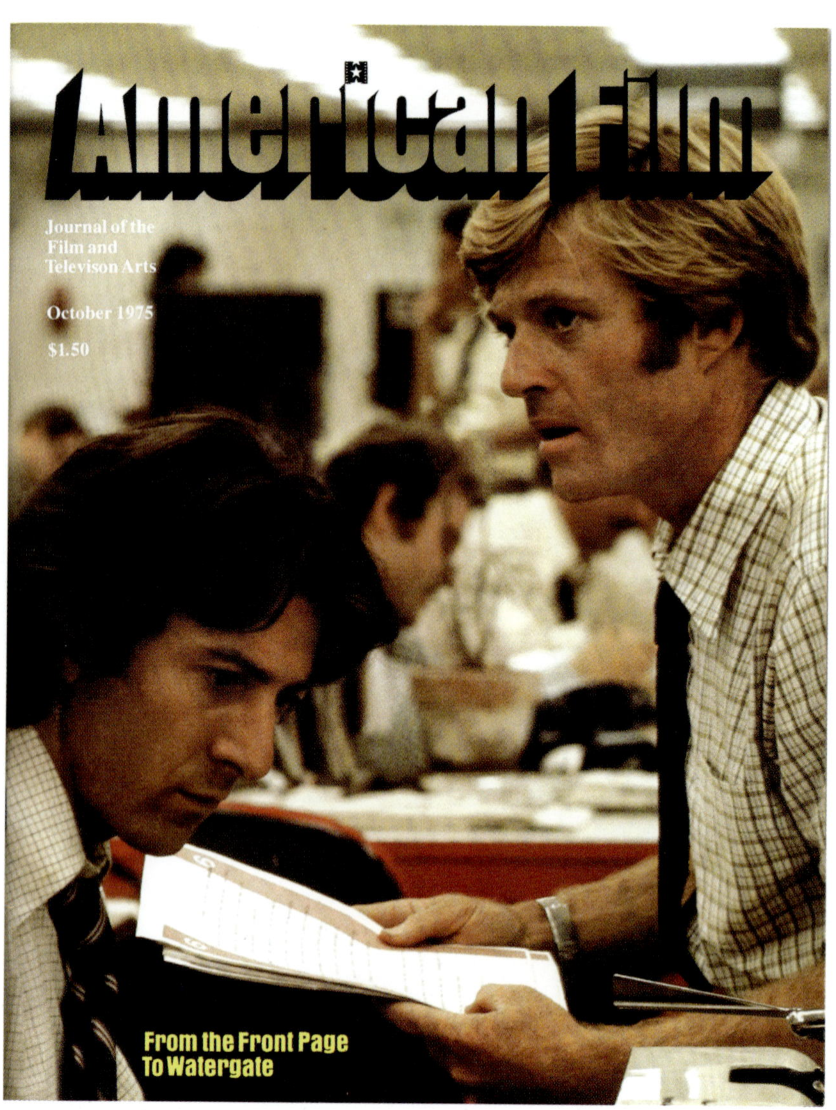

The first issue of *American Film* magazine, featuring Dustin Hoffman and Robert Redford, 1975.

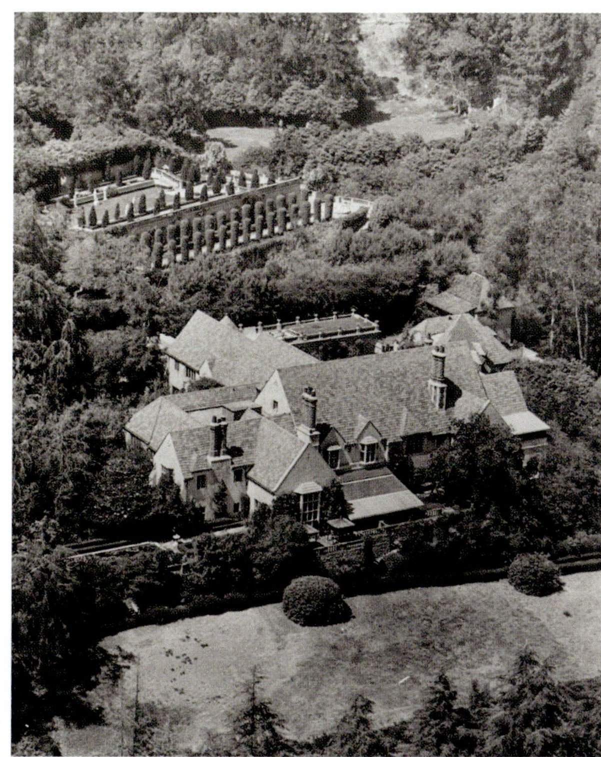

Left: Aerial view of Greystone.

Below: The grand hall at Greystone, the first home of the AFI Center for Advanced Film Studies, 1976.

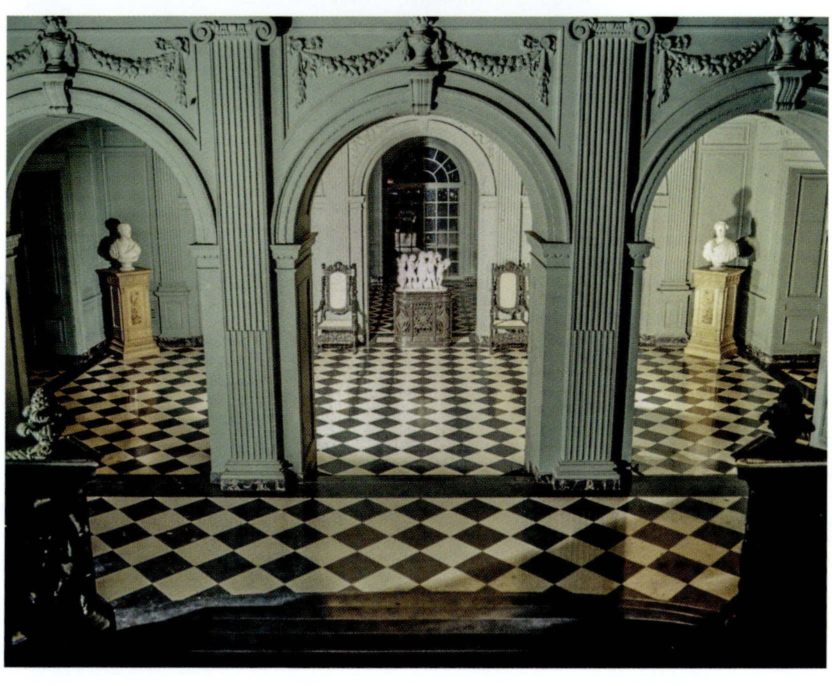

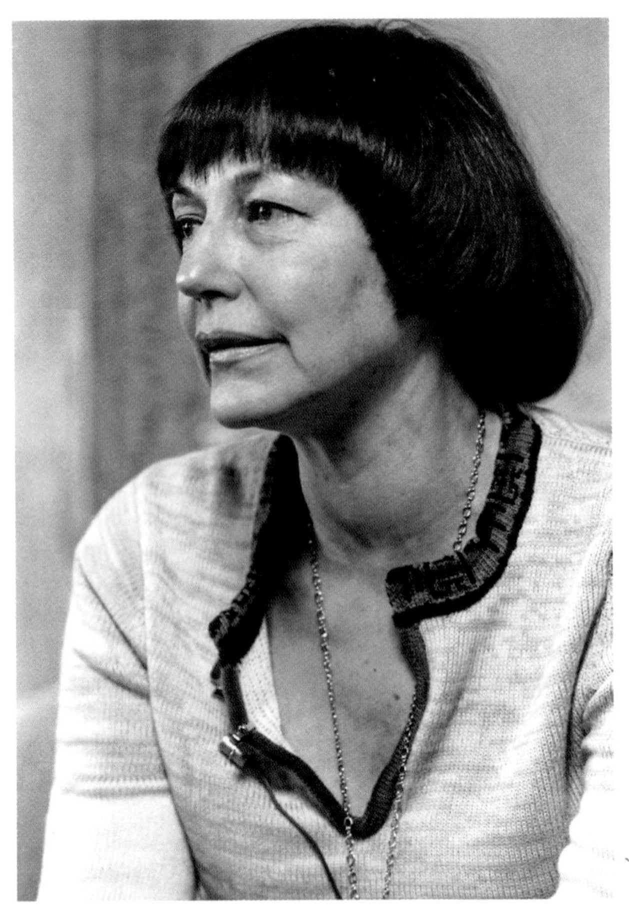

Fay Kanin conducting a seminar at the AFI Center for Advanced Film Studies at Greystone, 1976.

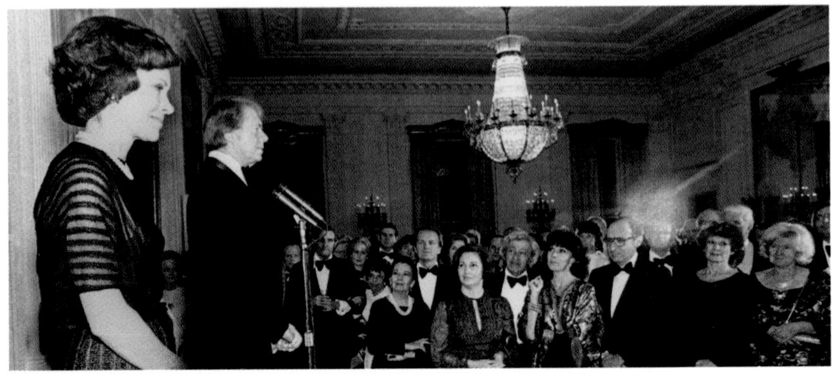

White House reception in honor of AFI's tenth anniversary, with President Jimmy Carter and First Lady Rosalynn Carter, 1977.

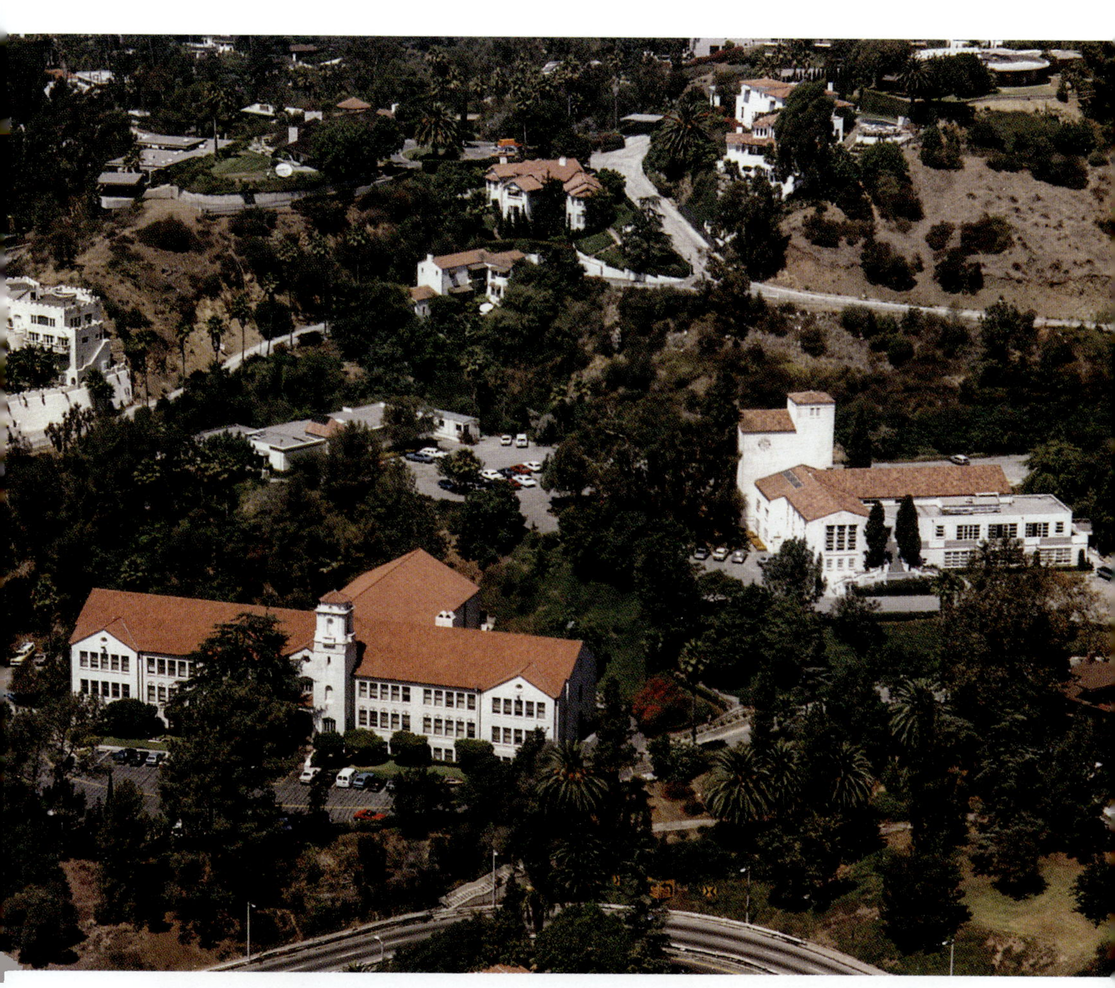

Aerial view of the new, 6.7-acre AFI campus on Western Avenue in Los Angeles, 1981.

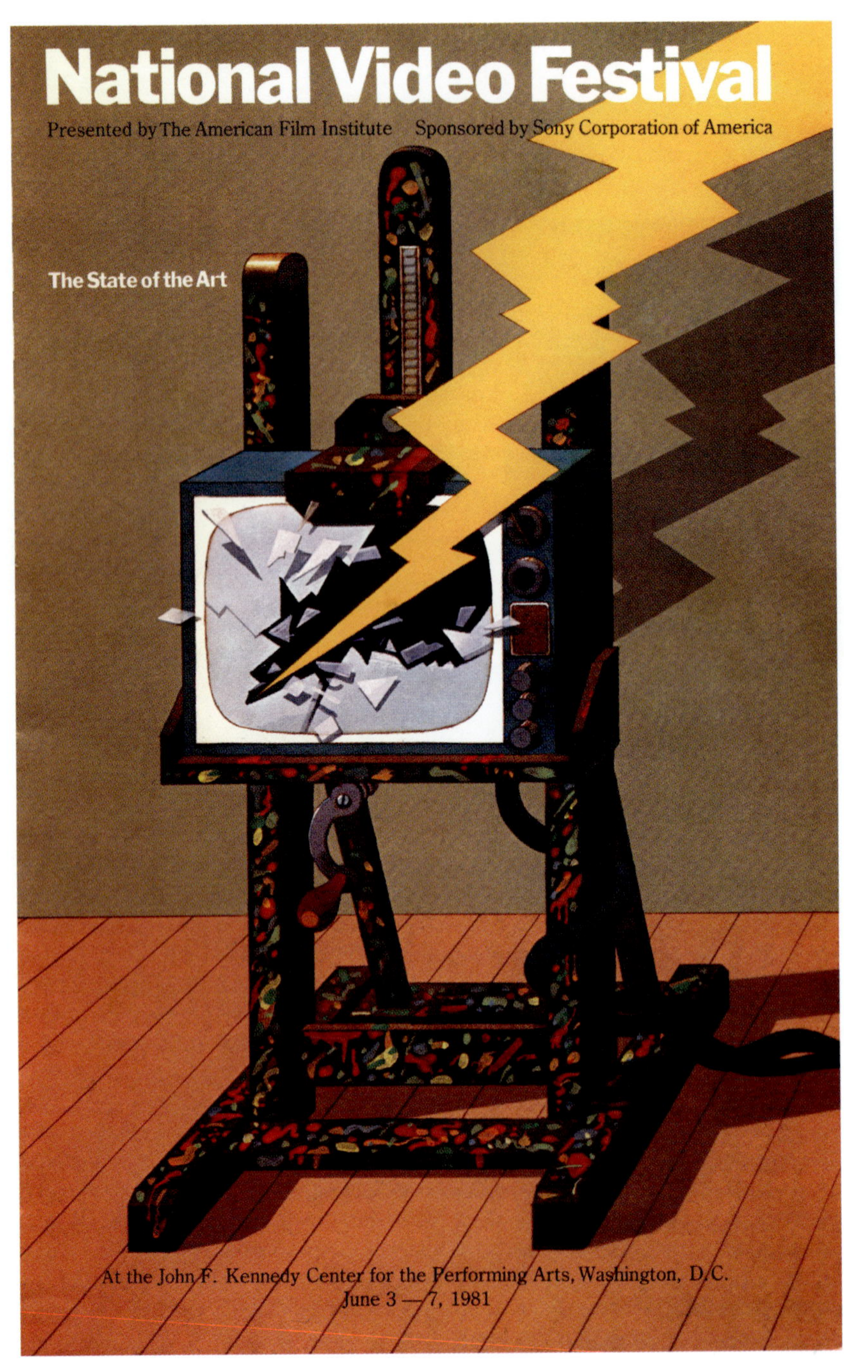

AFI 1981 National Video Festival cover, designed by Milton Glaser.

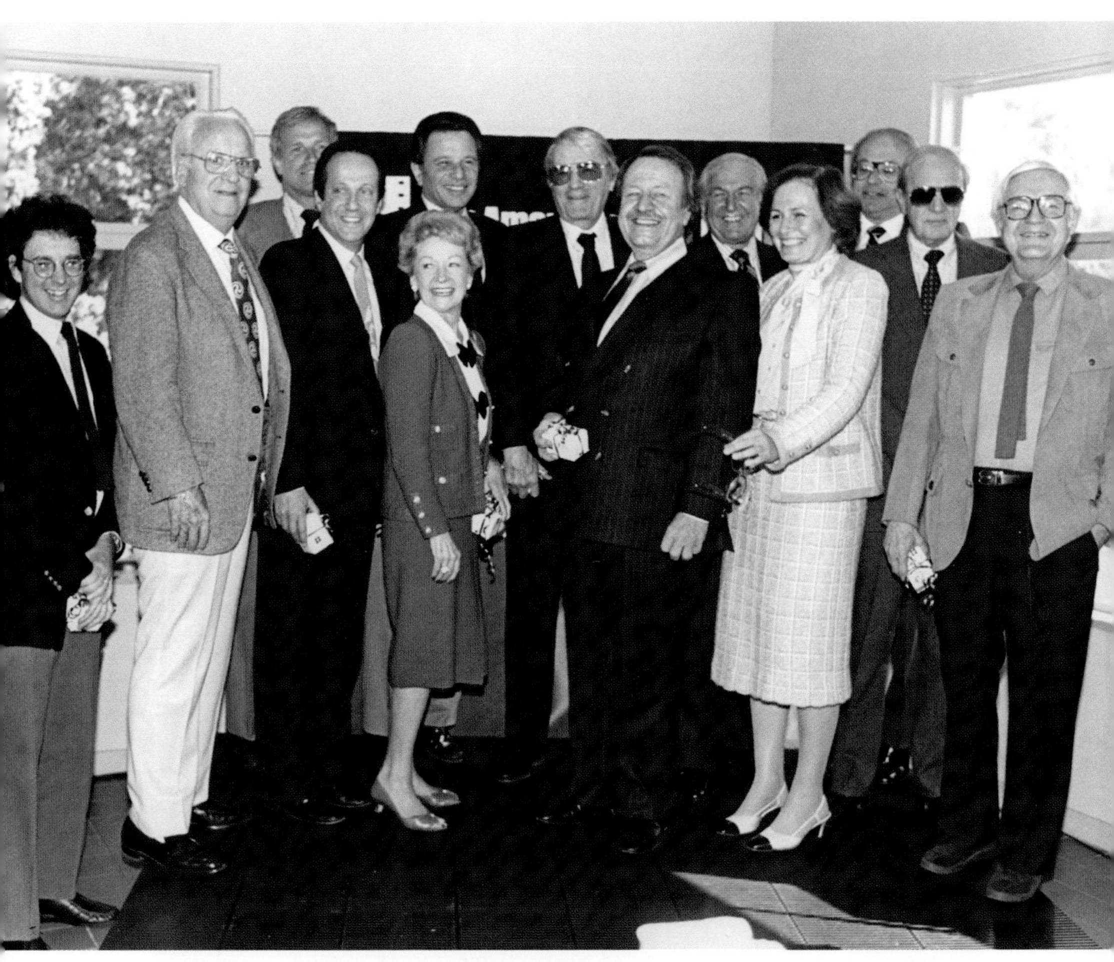

Attendees at the celebration of AFI's inclusion in the California Educational Facilities Bond Issue in 1984 (*left to right*): Michael Pulitzer, Mike Frankovich, Wayne Rogers, Bruce Corwin, Bonita Granville Wrather, Mace Neufeld, Gregory Peck, Jesse Unruh, Henry Rogers, Jean Picker Firstenberg, Alan Hirschfeld, Franklin Schaffner, and Robert Wise.

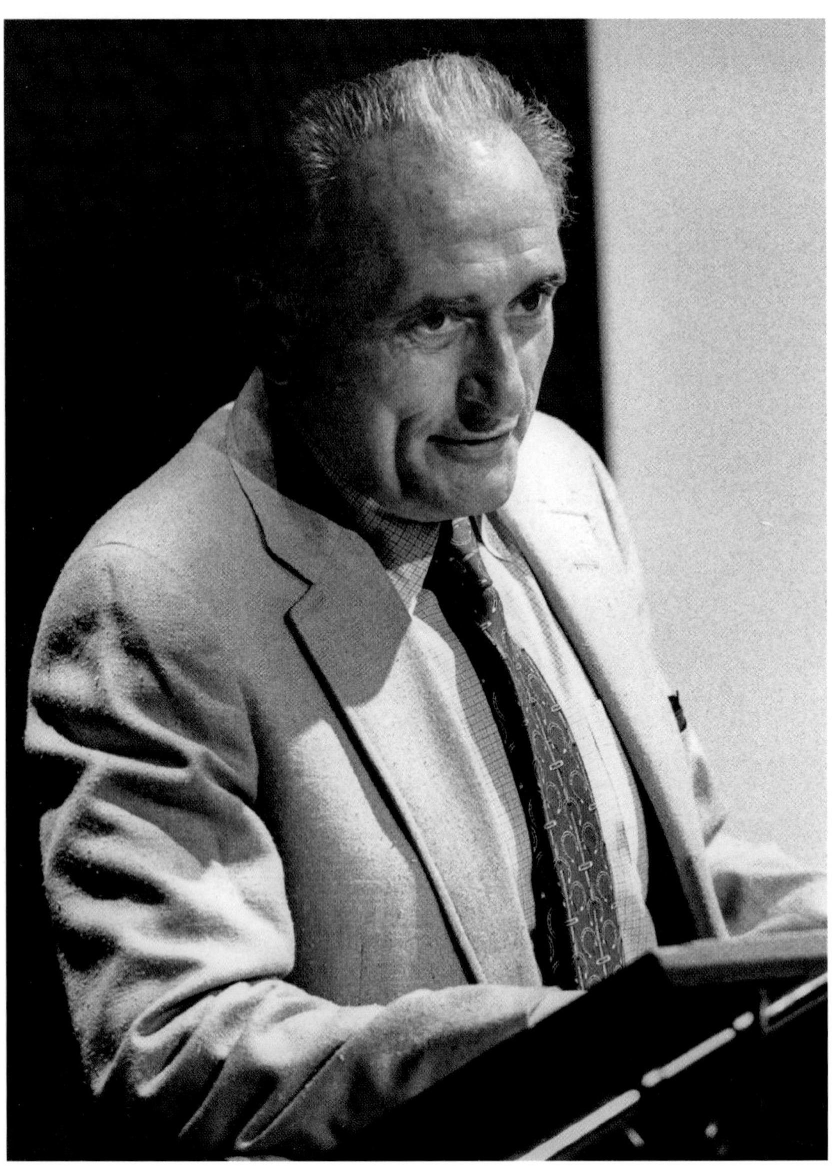

Antonio Vellani, master teacher at the Center for Advanced Film Studies, mid-1980s.

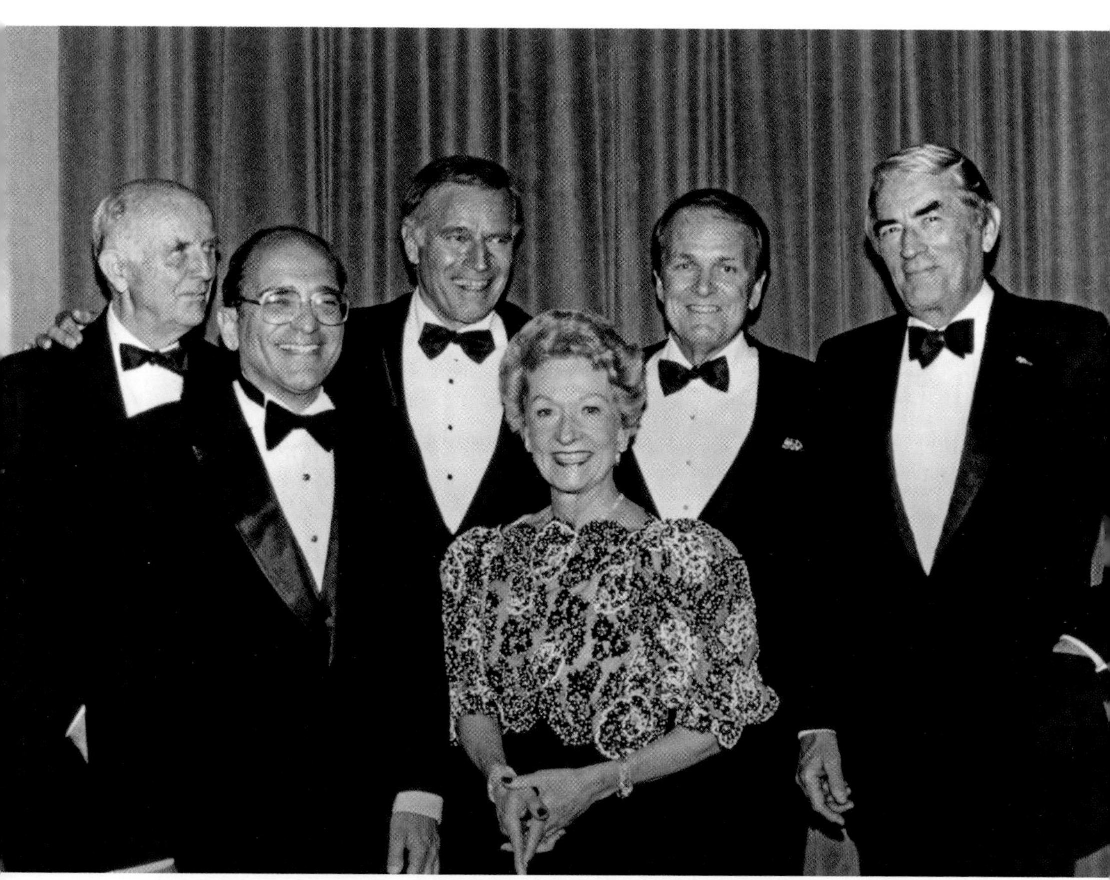

The first six chairs of the AFI board of trustees at the 1986 AFI Life Achievement Award dinner (*left to right*): Roger L. Stevens, Richard Brandt, Charlton Heston, Bonita Granville Wrather, George Stevens Jr., and Gregory Peck.

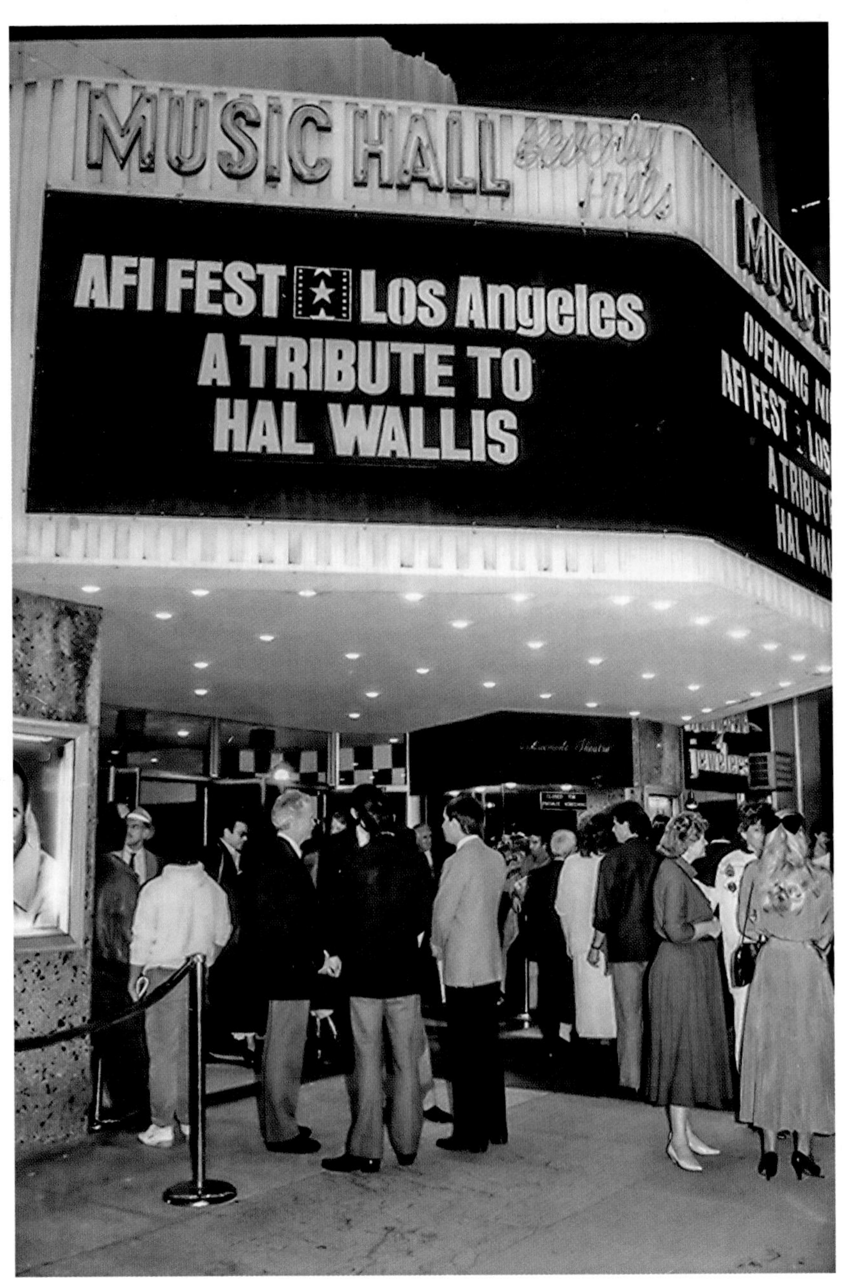

AFI FEST opening night, 1987.

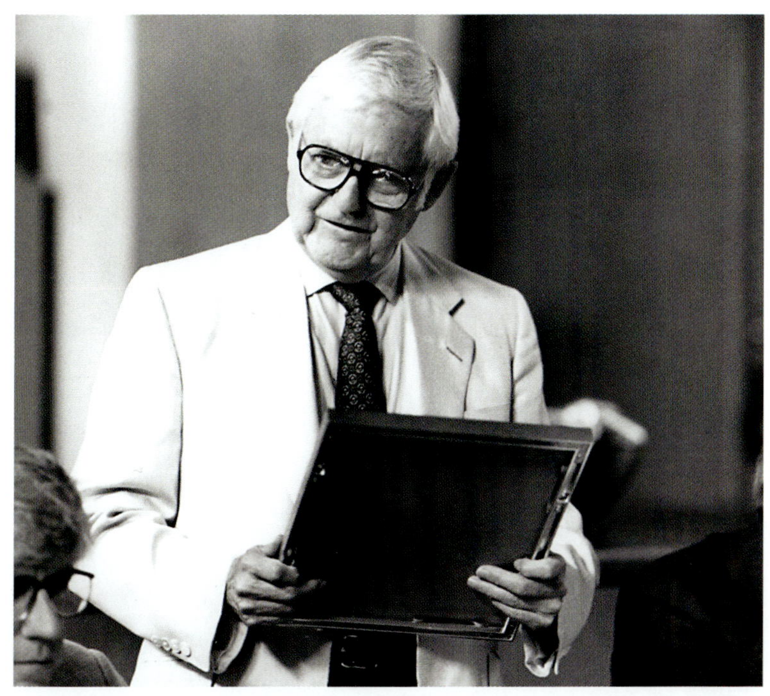

Robert Wise, director and chair of the AFI Center for Advanced Film and Television Studies, at an AFI board meeting, late 1980s.

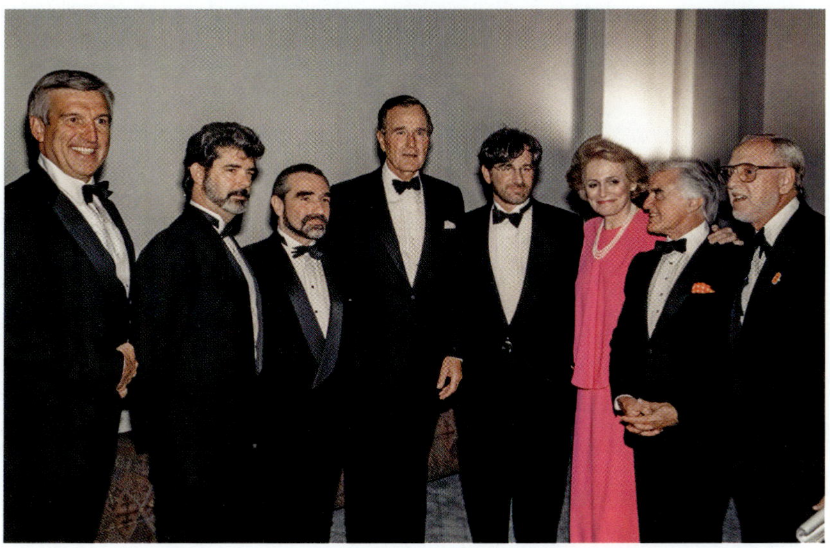

Attendees at AFI's Back to the Rose Garden gala in 1989 (*left to right*): Gene F. Jankowski, George Lucas, Martin Scorsese, President George H. W. Bush, Steven Spielberg, Jean Picker Firstenberg, Jack Valenti, and David Wolper.

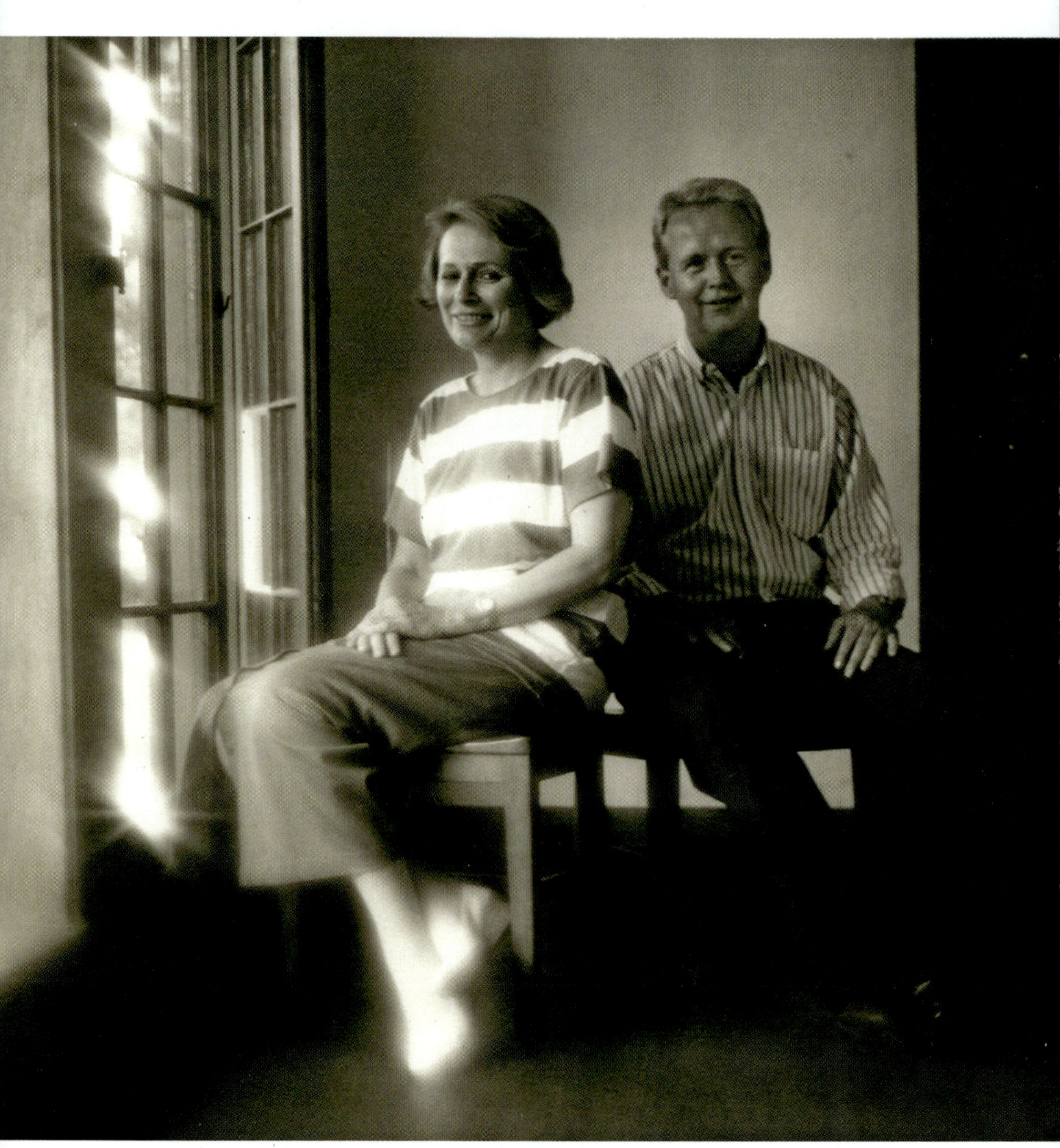

Jean Picker Firstenberg and James Hindman, 1989.

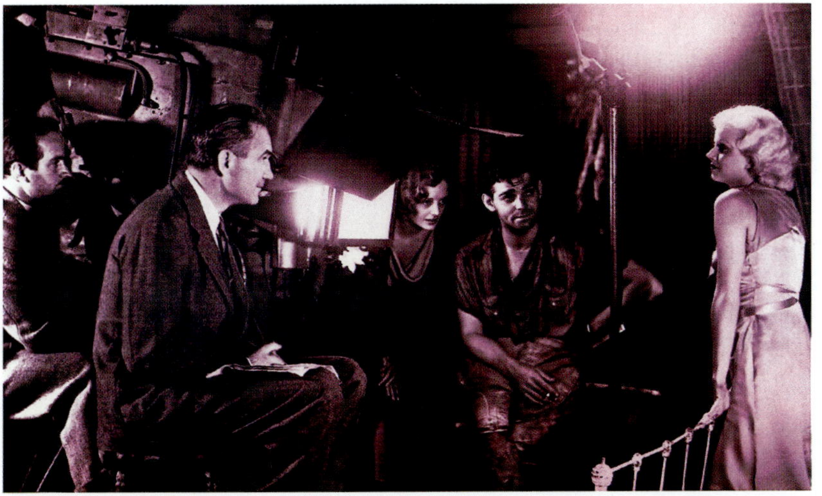

Poster for the 1992 AFI documentary *Visions of Light: The Art of Cinematography.*

M.B. DUDLEY
Presents:
Mr. Frederick Warde
in
Shakespeare's Masterpiece
THE LIFE AND DEATH OF
King Richard III.

Copyright 1912 By Richard III Film Co. Inc.

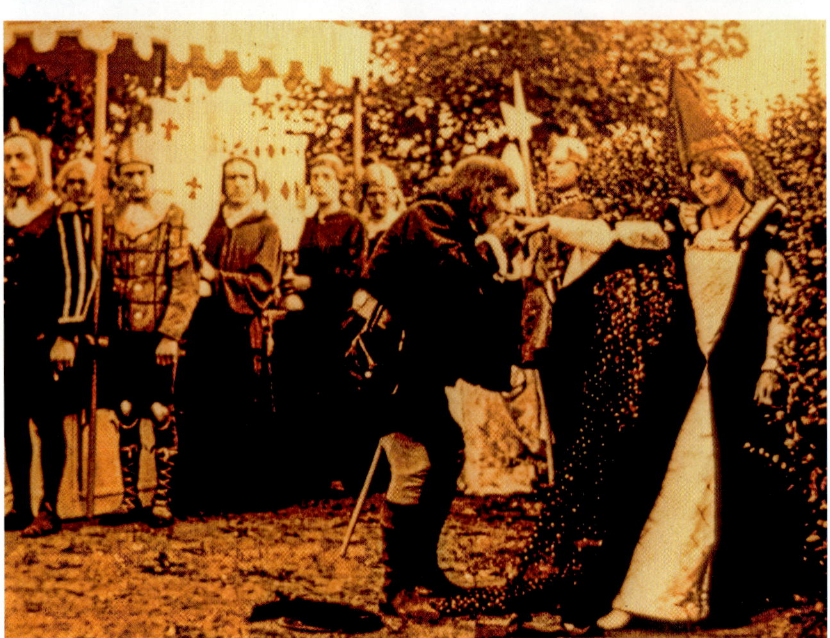

Poster and scene from *Richard III,* the oldest surviving feature film made in the United States, donated to and preserved by AFI in 1996 and now in the AFI Collection at the Library of Congress.

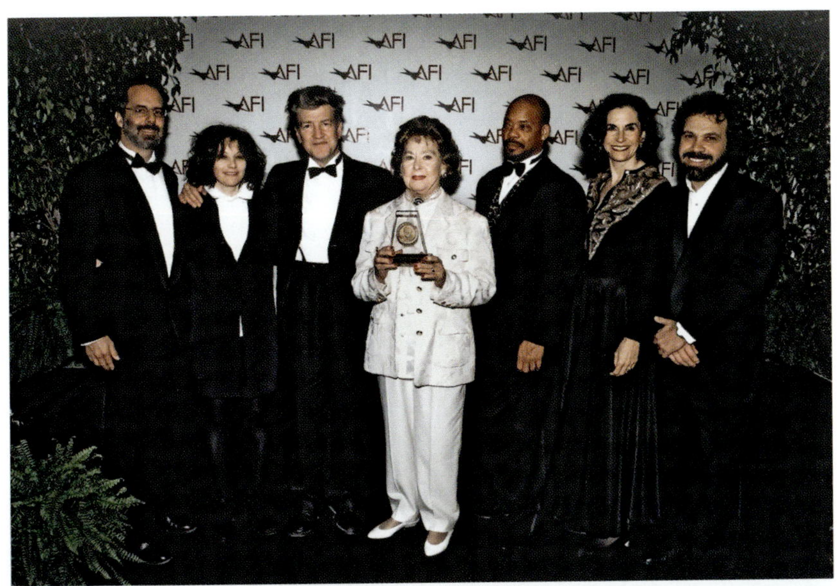

Franklin J. Schaffner Alumni Medal recipients at the 1999 AFI Life Achievement Award ceremony (*left to right*): Jon Avnet, Amy Heckerling, David Lynch, Jean Schaffner, Carl Franklin, Randa Haines, and Ed Zwick.

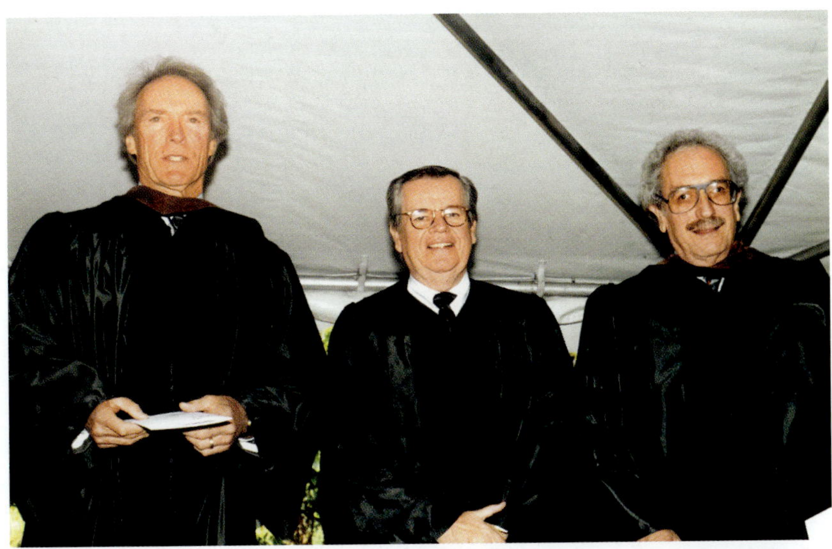

Clint Eastwood, honorary degree recipient Bob Daly, and board of trustees chair Tom Pollock at the 1999 AFI Conservatory Commencement ceremony.

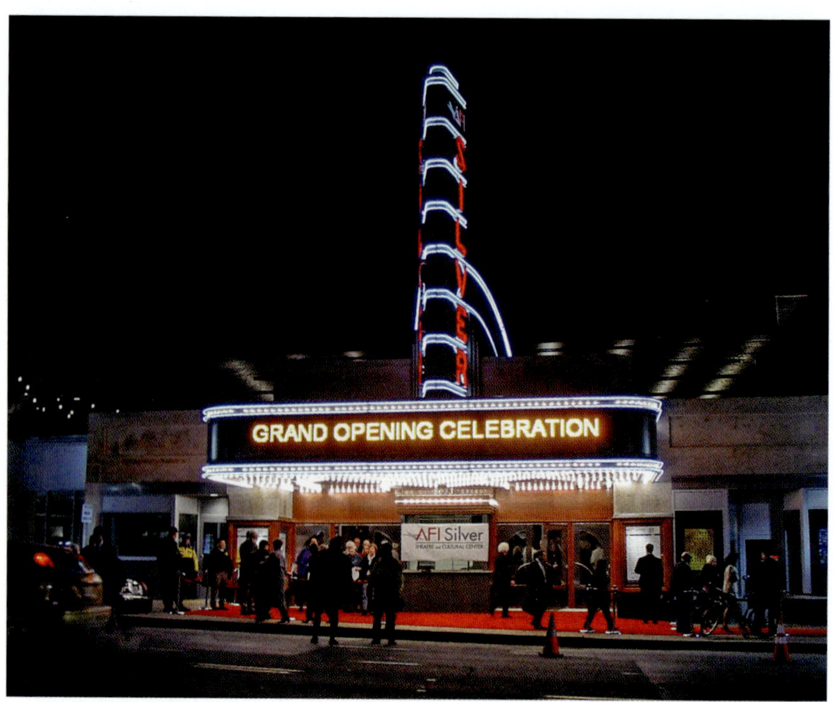

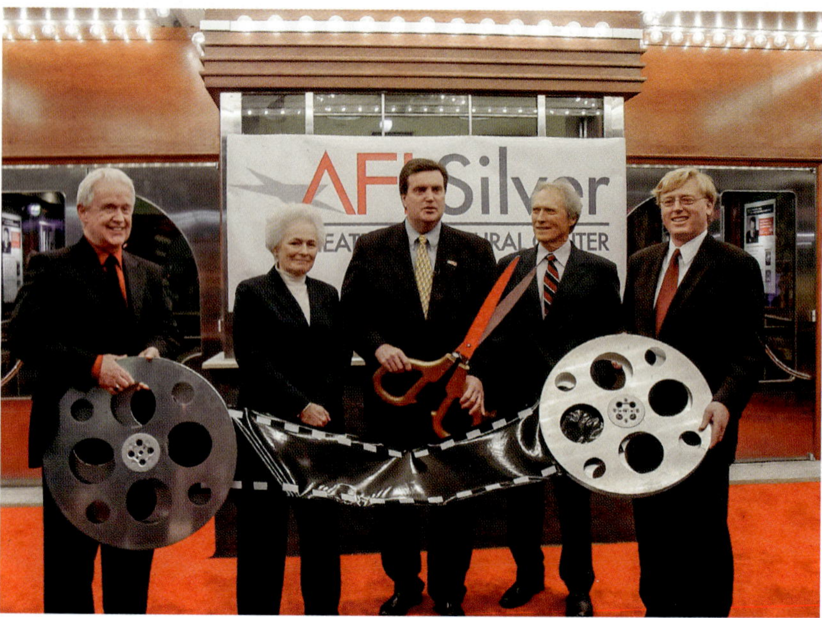

Opening night at the AFI Silver Theatre and Cultural Center in 2003, attended by (*left to right*): James Hindman, Jean Picker Firstenberg, county executive Douglas Duncan, Clint Eastwood, and Ray Barry.

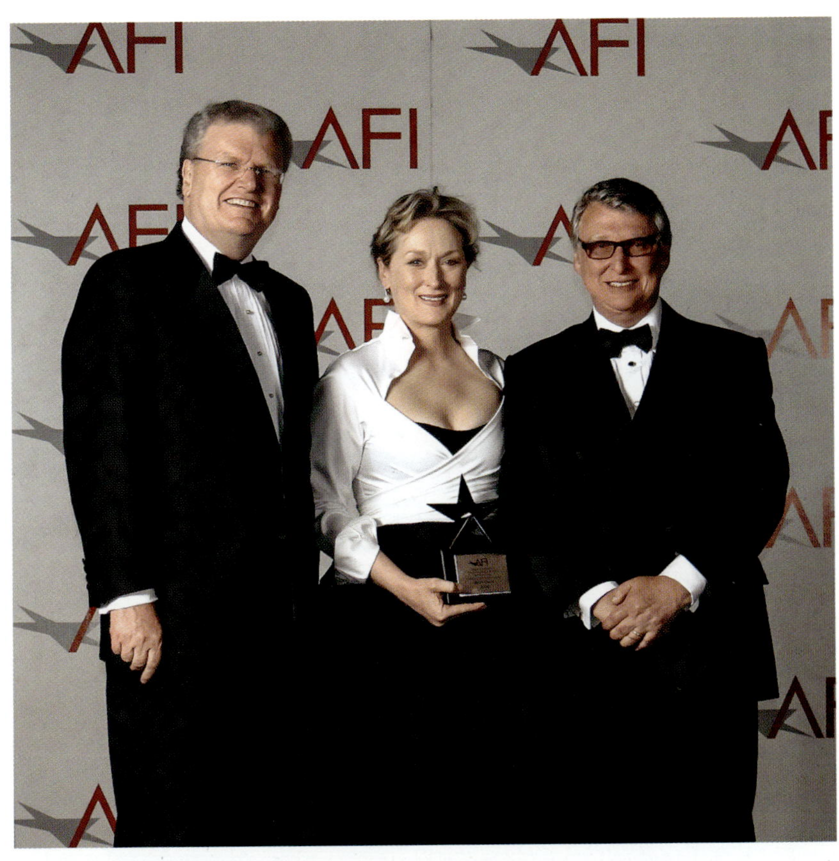

AFI Life Achievement Award recipient Meryl Streep with AFI chair Sir Howard Stringer and Mike Nichols, 2004.

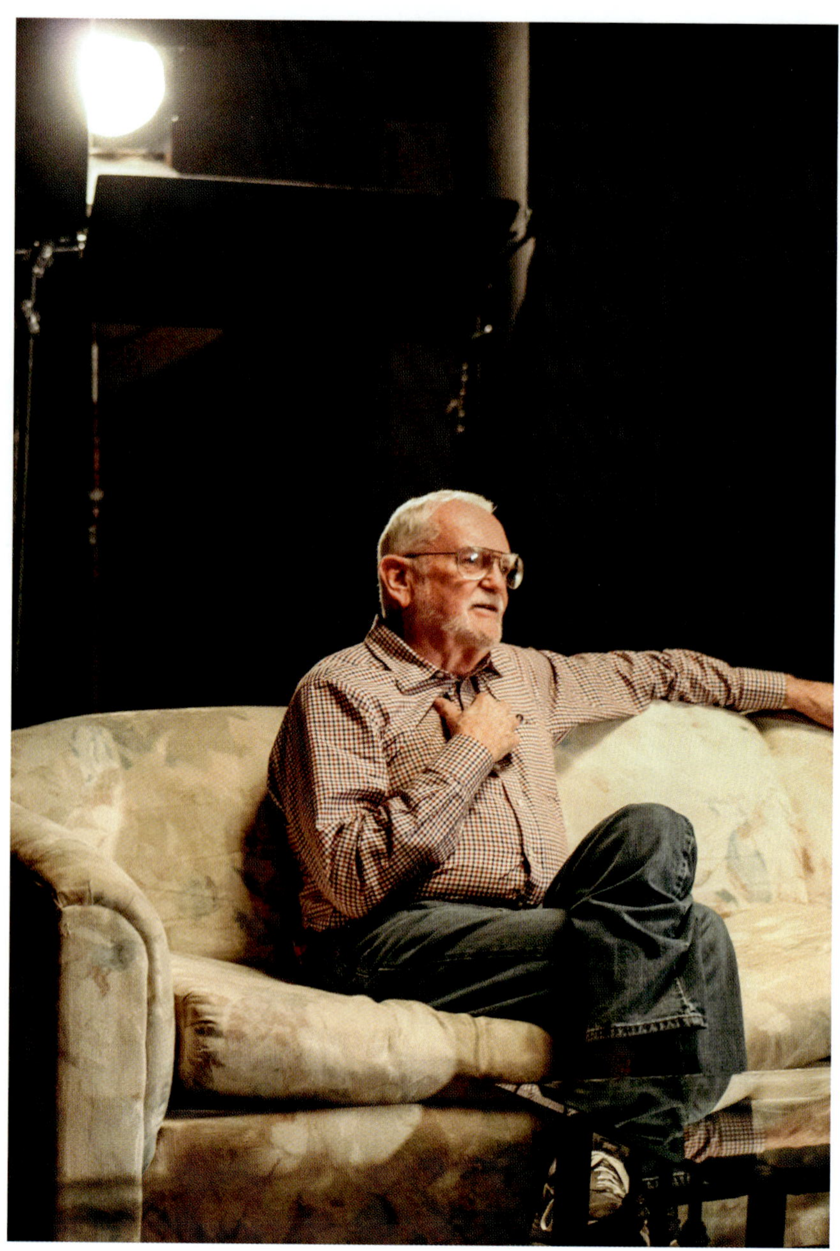

Master teacher Frank Pierson in an AFI Conservatory seminar, 2006.

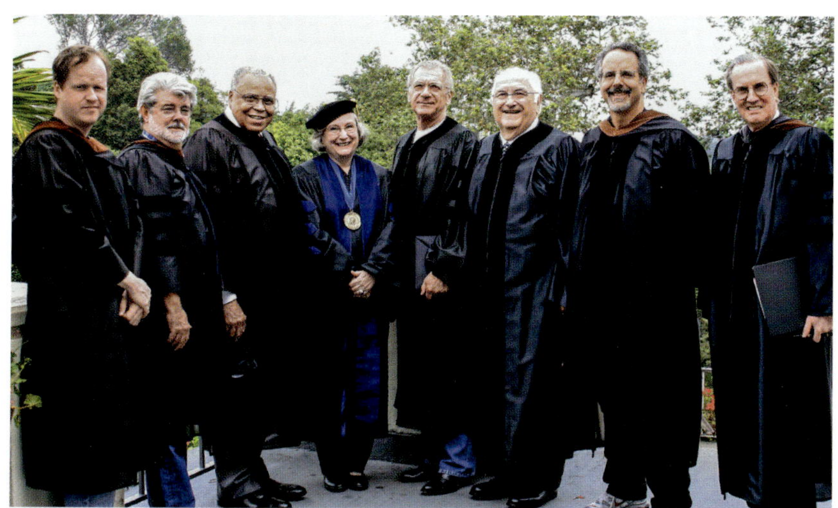

Presenters and honorary degree recipients at the 2006 AFI Commencement ceremony (*left to right*): Josh Whedon, George Lucas, James Earl Jones, Jeanine Basinger, Sidney Pollock, Chuck Fries, Jon Avnet, and John F. Cooke.

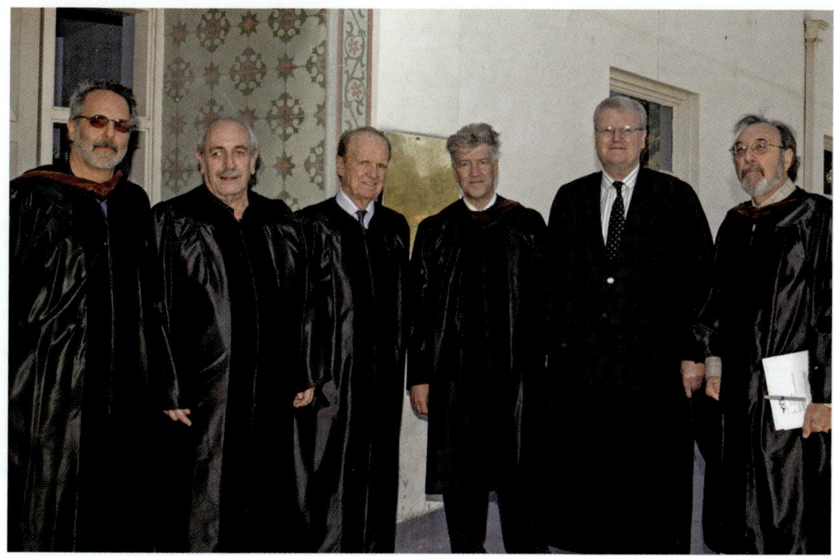

Presenters and honorary degree recipients at the 2007 AFI Commencement ceremony (*left to right*): Jon Avnet, Tom Pollock, George Stevens Jr., David Lynch, Sir Howard Stringer, and James Brooks.

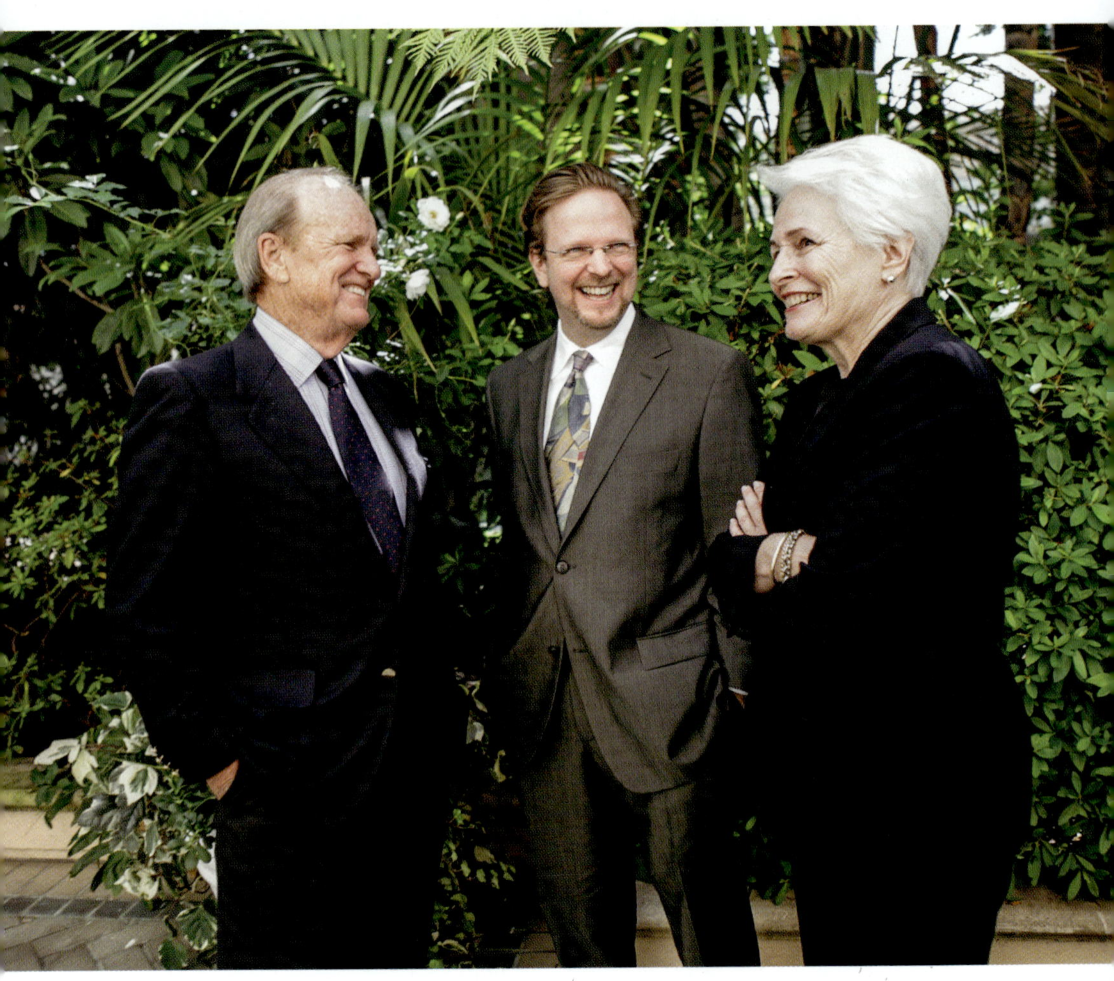

AFI's three CEOs over its first fifty years—George Stevens Jr., Bob Gazzale, and Jean Picker Firstenberg—in 2007, when Gazzale was named as Firstenberg's successor.

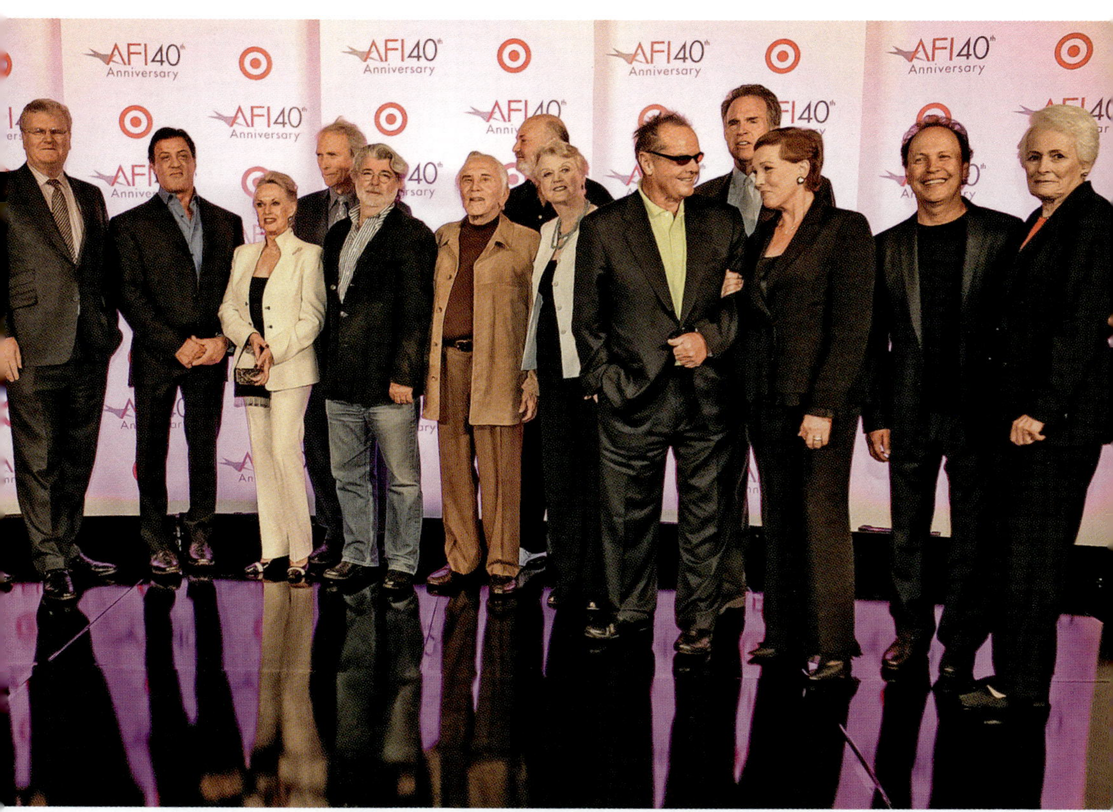

Attendees at *Target Presents AFI Night at the Movies* at the ArcLight Hollywood in 2007 (*left to right*): Sir Howard Stringer, Sylvester Stallone, Tippi Hedren, Clint Eastwood, George Lucas, Kirk Douglas, Rob Reiner, Angela Lansbury, Jack Nicholson, Warren Beatty, Julie Andrews, Billy Crystal, and Jean Picker Firstenberg.

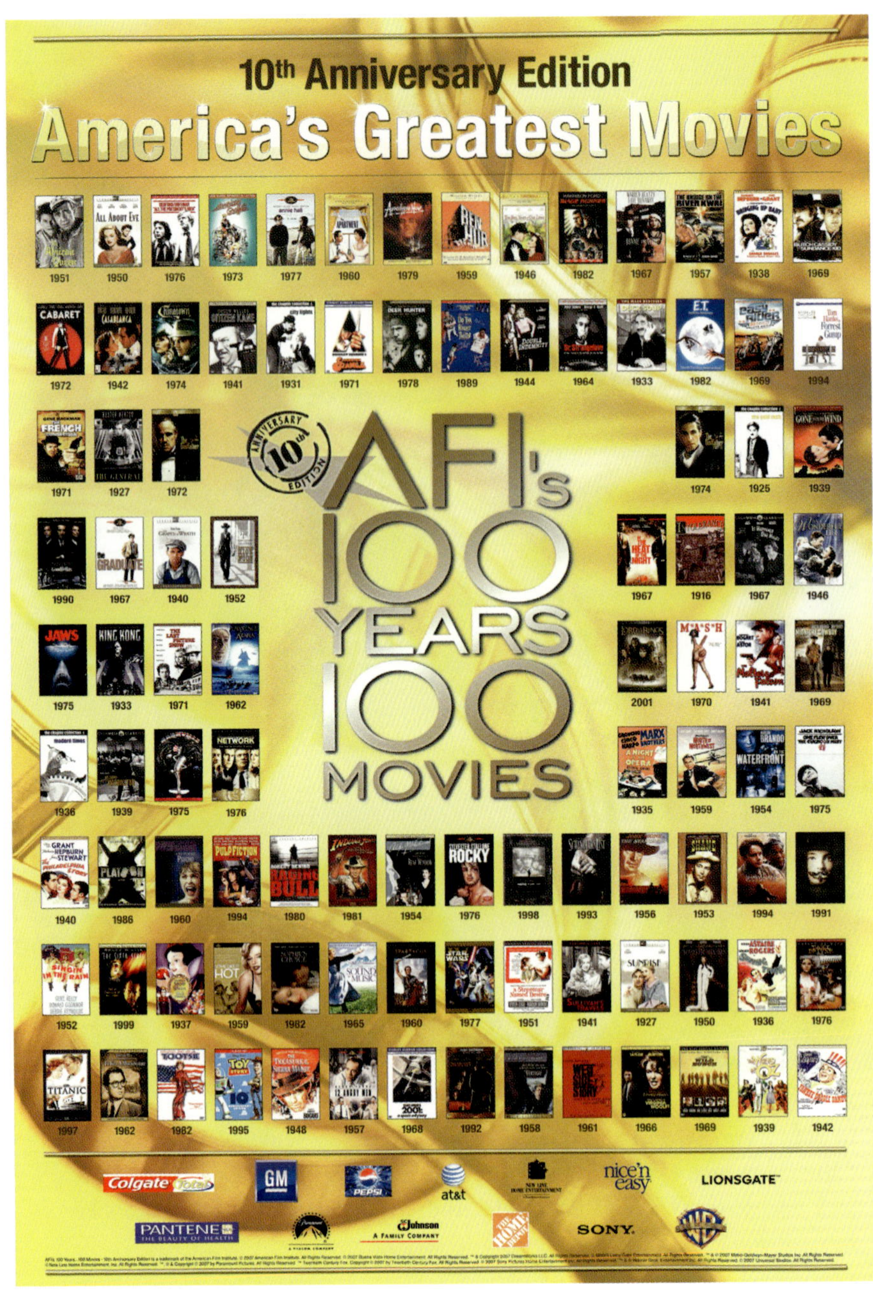

AFI's 100 Years…100 Movies tenth anniversary poster, 2007.

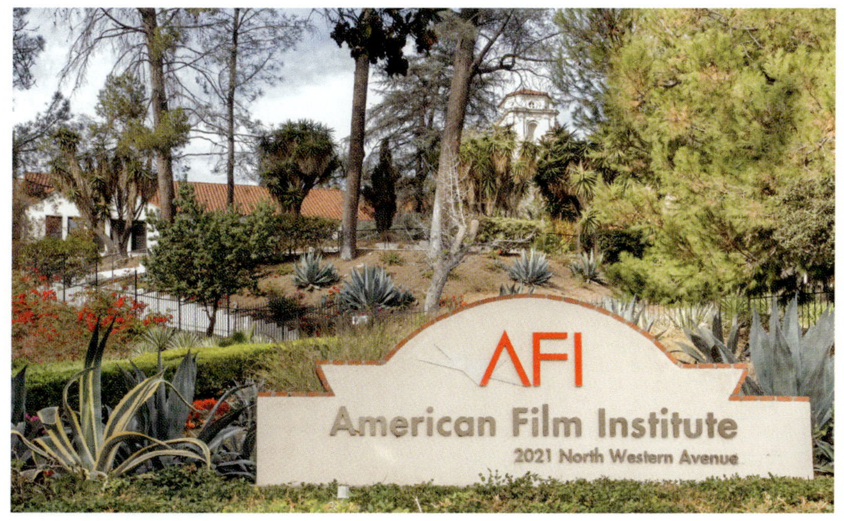

Milestone sign commemorating a major AFI campus renovation that began in 2009.

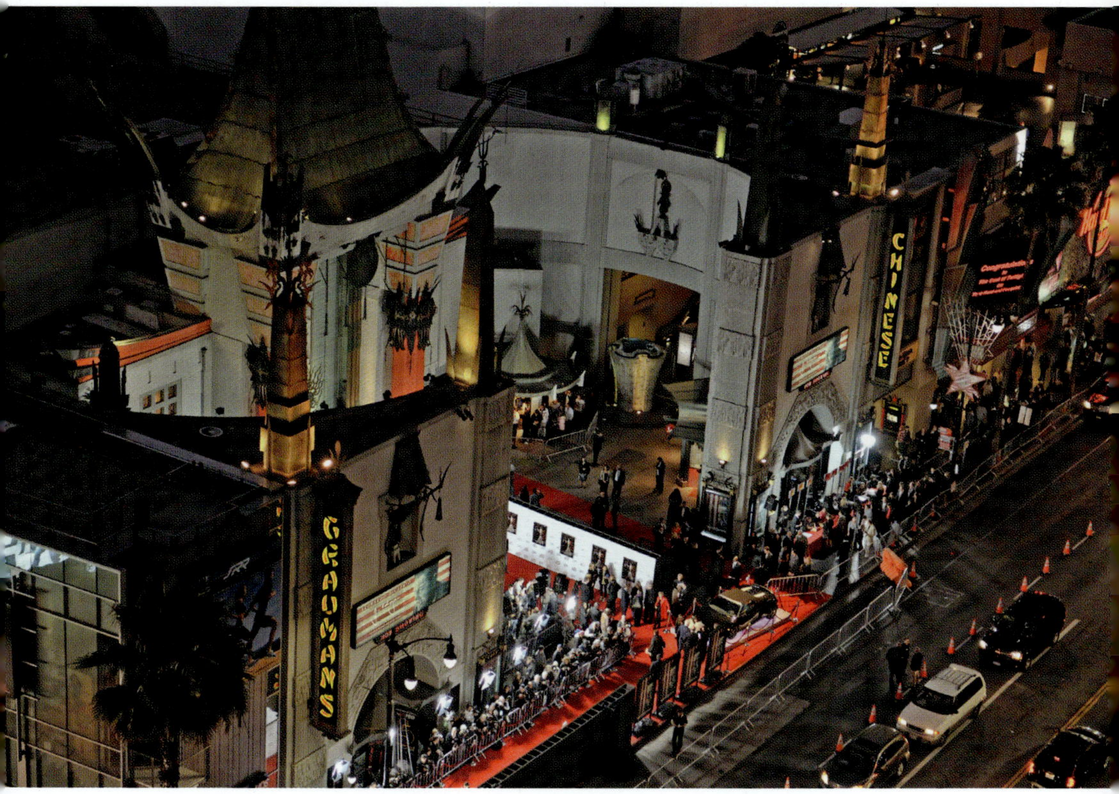

AFI FEST at Grauman's Chinese Theatre, 2011.

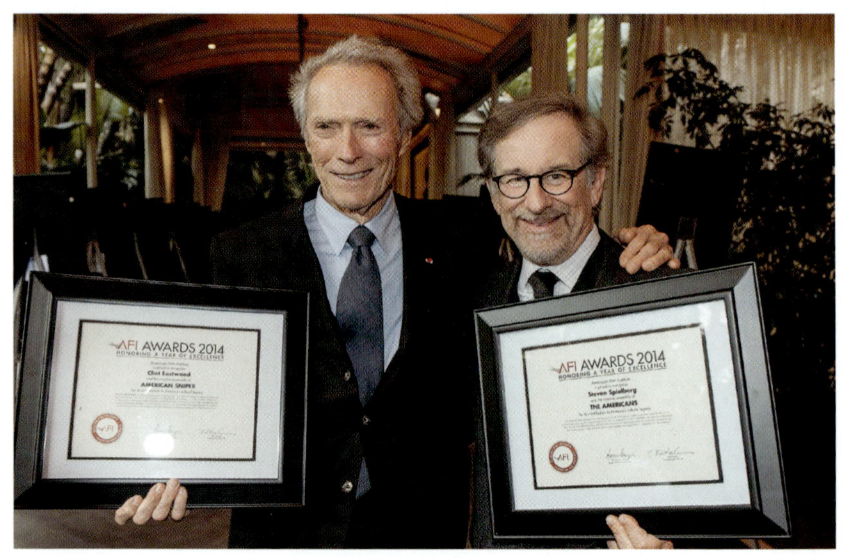

Clint Eastwood and Steven Spielberg at the AFI AWARDS, 2014.

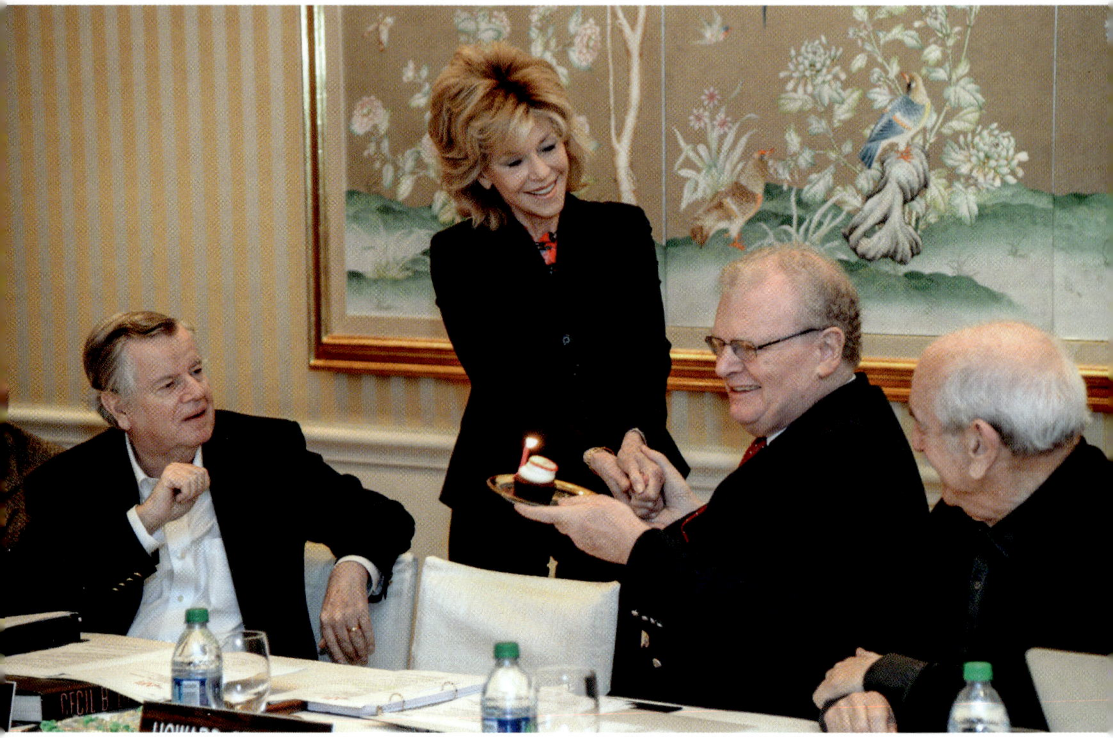

Jane Fonda surprising Sir Howard Stringer with a birthday cupcake at a 2015 board meeting, as Bob Daly (*left*) and Tom Pollock look on.

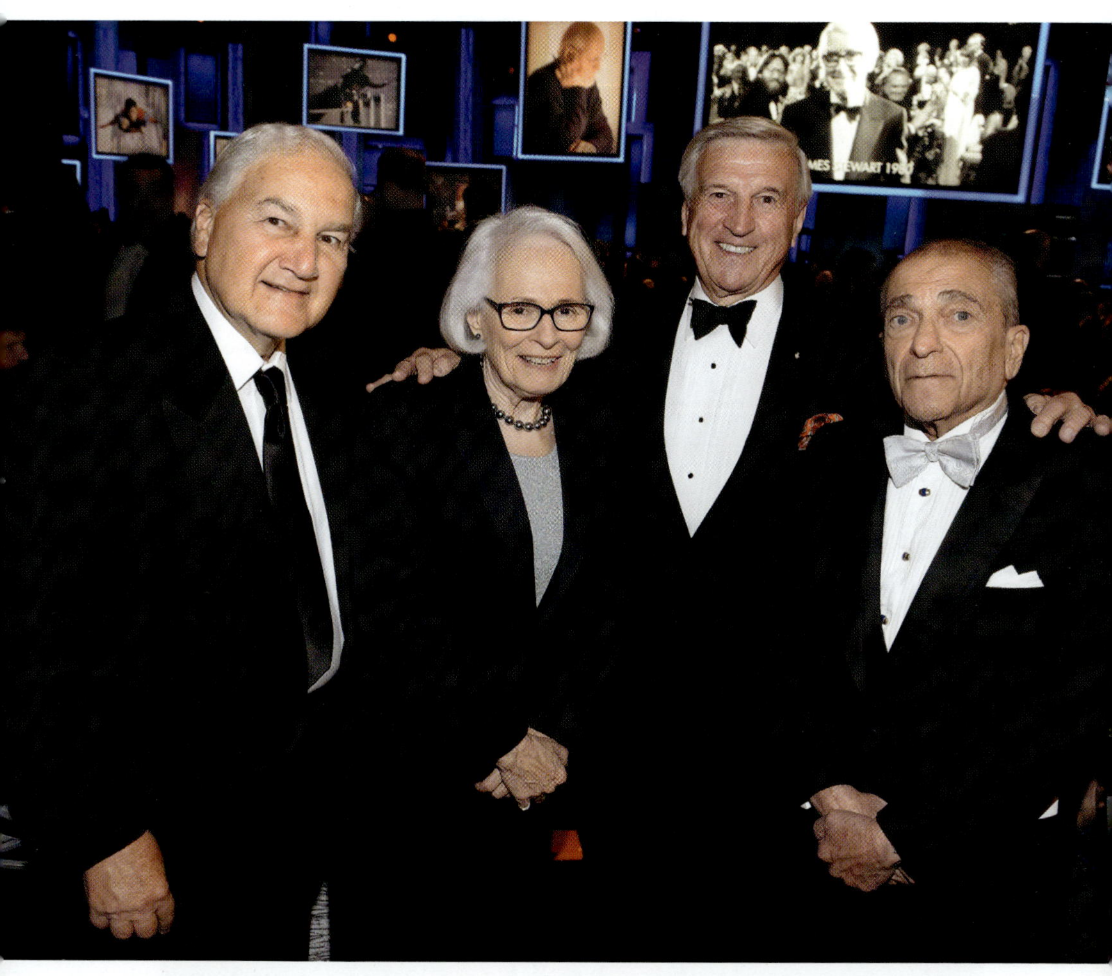

Jean Picker Firstenberg at the 2016 AFI Life Achievement Award tribute with AFI board of trustees chairs emeriti (*left to right*) Fred Pierce, Gene Jankowski, and Richard Brandt.

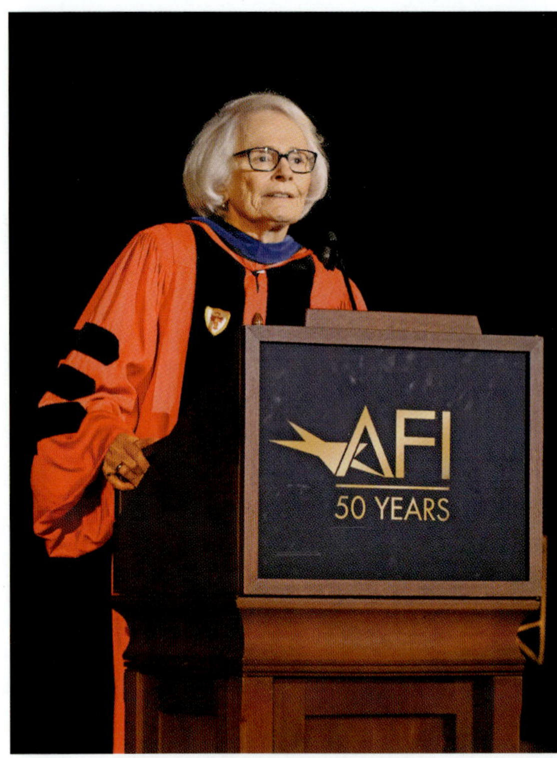

Left: Jean Picker Firstenberg speaking at the 2017 AFI Commencement ceremony, held at the TCL Chinese Theatre.

Below: Bob Gazzale, Jean Picker Firstenberg, and George Stevens Jr. with the graduating class outside the TCL Chinese Theatre at the 2017 AFI Commencement ceremony.

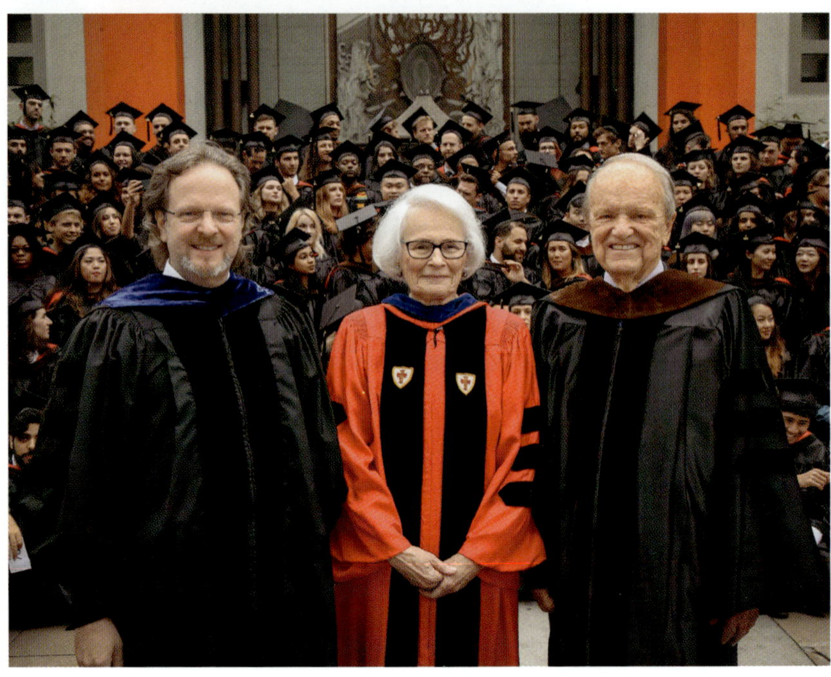

A light bulb went on: the web had the potential for AFI to interconnect the assets it had produced over the course of three decades. We had the data, the photos, the video clips, and the context. With the will and some money, AFI could create the world's greatest movie website. (Ah, if it had only been so!) AFI's early embrace of the web lent depth to our partnership strategy and credibility with companies who were powering the growth of this powerful new medium—companies like Intel Corporation.

The Digital Sandbox

INTEL INSIDERS

Within twenty years of its founding in 1968, Intel had become the largest corporation in the world, as measured by market capitalization. By the mid-'90s, Intel provided the microprocessor chips—the computing brains—that ran most of the world's personal computers and servers. Intel was, indeed, *inside*, as its tagline cleverly asserted. Intel achieved dominance through its willingness to radically transform itself at the first sign of new competitive or technological threats.

The Internet presented such a threat, and a new strategic objective. Intel reasoned that it could sell more chips when media, especially video, was distributed online. Video required an expansion of Internet distribution capacity—so-called "broadband." Intel needed Hollywood to create demand for this broadband video distribution. Intel created a $750 million Content Group, headed by Ron Whittier, to invest in companies that accelerated the delivery and consumption of media (audio, video, and games) on the Internet. Intel also launched its Hollywood charm offensive from a lavish new facility located at the Creative Artists Agency in Beverly Hills.

CAA agent and longtime AFI friend John Ptak arranged for us to meet with Intel executives. Intel quickly agreed to sponsor a live webcast from the AFI Life Achievement Award tribute to Clint Eastwood. A few months later, Intel donated a new computer lab to AFI worth $1 million. But there was more to come. After months of working through the Intel hierarchy of managers and executives, AFI and Intel reached a three-year $1.5 million partnership deal in the fall of 1997. The most important item in the contract was "an AFI-Intel production workshop," which would become perhaps the signature achievement of AFI's emerging technology strategy.

TALK-BACK TV

Interactive television arrived with a splash in 1977 with the launch of QUBE, an elaborate cable system offering new features such as pay-per-view, on-demand movies, special-interest networks, and interactivity. Innovation notwithstanding, QUBE lost a fortune for its owner Warner Cable, which began to phase out the system in 1982. A new round of interactive TV trials in the '90s also failed to find customers or profits, tainting the very term with the stench of failure. Where cable saw defeat, the computer industry saw opportunity. To support web-based technology for interactive TV, Intel and Microsoft organized the Advanced Television Enhancement Forum, which included Intel, Microsoft, Samsung, Warner Bros., Sony, Disney, PBS, CNN, Cable Labs, Direct TV, and NBC. This commitment to web-based interactivity explains how an "AFI-Intel production workshop" morphed into the AFI-Intel Enhanced Television Workshop, which launched in 1998.

How might such a thing work? From a creative standpoint, it was important to adopt the "Learn by doing; study with the Masters" mantra that defines AFI's Conservatory program and Directing Workshop for Women. From a business standpoint, it was crucial that costs be borne by sponsors rather than customers, so that we could recruit the best possible participants instead of running something like a retail business, as we had with our Apple program.

These ideas got a trial run with the California Digital Arts Workshop, which provided a dozen fine artists with the chance to spend an intensive week producing their own original digital projects under the supervision of AFI mentors. Every evening, after spending all day on their projects, the artists attended public events featuring some of the world's best digital artists and web innovators.

THE WHY-BOTHER? WORKSHOP

We employed a similar program model to launch the AFI-Intel Enhanced TV Workshop in 1998. Participants experienced a week-long, intensive production-based workshop with support from digital mentors. Participation was restricted to producers affiliated with TV networks who had permission to experiment with an existing TV property.

For the venture to succeed, we needed to recruit "name" networks. Initially, we talked about the excitement of interactivity and a brand new audience of active viewers, to which some replied, "Why bother?" Soon, we started calling it the "why-bother?" workshop. We selected eight participants, including producers from Fox, ABC, A&E, and E! Entertainment. To help them in the workshop, we recruited a strong roster of mentors. Entrepreneur Ken Locker led the mentor group that included folks from NBC, AOL, Warner Bros., and Viacom; ad agencies RGA, Digital Planet/IXL, Verso Studios, Pittard, and Sullivan; startups Protozoa, Oz Interactive, Inscape, Digital Evolution, Hyperbole Studios, LaFong, Tag Media, Intertainer, Interactive Drama, and Creative Light; and the president of the TV academy, Meryl Marshall.

The disciplines practiced by this diverse group of professionals allowed AFI to create a dynamic engagement experience that might, on any given day, involve such processes as open-design thinking, brainstorming, technology analysis, product positioning, and branding. It was a creative sandbox for participants and mentors alike. The biggest problem was the workshop's compressed schedule; it was too brief for anyone to produce much more than a concept presentation.

The program became decidedly more effective during the second year, mainly because we were able to hire a year-round staff. Heading up the team was Anna Marie Piersimoni, who had performed so well on Cinetex. Piersimoni ran the workshop from 1999 to 2001. Her restructured program devoted a full six months to the design and production of projects, with weekly phone or in-person meetings. During this period, we attracted higher profile networks, established a must-attend aura around the program's showcase events, and survived the conclusion of Intel's three-year deal by finding new sponsors.

The program delivered value to each stakeholder, a virtuous circle built on mutual support and incentives. Networks got a top-notch prototype customized for one of their shows and a team of mentors to build it. Mentors got access to big-brand networks and a rare cross-industry collaboration with peers. Sponsors connected their products to the best and the brightest from old and new media alike, finding developers they could work with. Year after year, people cycled from one role to another within the program, contributing and receiving expertise and pro bono work, networking with new people, and having fun.

For the true believers, the ones I called "interactivists," the greatest incentive was probably the chance to make a difference. "The most exciting part for me is the opportunity to participate in the invention of the future," said one mentor. "I love the new storytelling formats that are being invented, new ways of involving the viewer," added another. "Interactive TV is driven by the human desire to innovate and to become better," said another.

FROM ETV TO DCL

The program's second director was Marcia Zellers, who ran the lab from mid-2001 to fall 2006. An early interactive producer for Warner Bros. Online and MTV, Zellers possessed a finely tuned understanding of commercial media and the people these companies employed. She presided over the workshop at a time of explosive growth in the industry, including the build-out of broadband distribution networks and greater interactive experimentation by the mainstream networks. A new peer group was formed at the Television Academy to capture this interest in interactive media.

A review of the lab's projects during this period reveals a few trends. We attracted a remarkable diversity of genres and program types to the program, including news, kidvid, sitcoms, documentary, awards telecasts, movies, reality series, music programming, games, e-commerce, advertorials, sports, science, drama, education, and finance. We attracted our most diverse set of networks, including PBS, TV Land, USA, Turner Classic Movies, Food Network, SciFi Channel, ABC, Bloomberg, Disney Channel, Washington Redskins, Nickelodeon, MTV, Showtime, Scripps, National Geographic, Telemundo, History Channel, Reuters, and World Wrestling Entertainment. Some of the projects, even those initiated by television networks, ran entirely on non-TV platforms like cellular phones (before they were "smart") and broadband (reaching twenty percent of U.S. homes by 2005).

DIGITAL CONTENT EVERYWHERE

The nomenclature of "enhanced TV" and "interactive TV" began feeling outdated and downright inaccurate. We wanted to find a more appropriate brand for a program that was supposed to be ahead of the pack, not behind it.

So, in 2003, we introduced the world to the AFI Digital Content Lab (DCL), a brand that represented the breadth of what we were trying to do: make digital content a true medium unto itself. The program expanded AFI's commitment to collaboration for a new era, requiring the contributions of technologists, coders, designers, and marketers, as well as artists and storytellers. We built a digital sandbox for the emerging digital media ecosystem.

Internet and interactive TV pioneer Suzanne Stefanac took over as DCL director from October 2006 until March 2010, when the program ended, a casualty of the global financial crisis. She expanded the program to make web-native video ventures as welcome in the lab as broadcast and cable networks. Her focus in the lab during this period reflected both the opportunities and the threats in the consumer media market, from time-shifting devices to social media networks, to video brands like YouTube and Netflix, to the popularity of casual gaming.

Bravo, for example, created a new advertising delivery system designed for viewers using DVRs. PBS created a fundraising app that allowed donors to skip pledge pitches. AOL built a live video switching app within its Instant Messenger platform. NBC's *Law and Order* and the Cartoon Network's *Ben 10* each created companion games on non-broadcast platforms. HBO collaborated with emerging YouTube stars to produce an original, web-only pilot. A

"AFI has done groundbreaking work training the filmmakers of tomorrow, and the recent efforts through the AFI Digital Content Lab are no exception. Setting a standard for innovation in digital media, AFI has brought together the storytellers of the future and technology innovators to explore new forms of how to tell a story in the twenty-first century. It is through this program and all that AFI does for fans and moviemakers alike that they ensure an important legacy for generations to come."

—TODD WAGNER,
entrepreneur and AFI trustee (2003–2012, 2013–present)

---

rock concert promoter created an app that rewarded fans for green behavior with perks from their favorite performers. Hollywood talent like David Lynch (class of 1970), Leonardo DiCaprio, and Kit Carson created products to connect fans to their creative and philanthropic interests. Most of the innovations explored in these and other projects at the DCL would show up in commercial products in years to come.

CONSIDERING DCL'S IMPACT

What was the Digital Content Lab's impact on the world, on AFI, and on the future? How do we measure its success? Consider the numbers: ninety-five productions and forty events over a twelve-year period; more than 1,000 professional mentors, participants and presenters; and fifteen sponsors providing nearly $5 million. Also consider the recognition: ranked among the top leaders in digital media and most influential in broadband by the *Los Angeles Business Journal*; third-ranked digital influencer on a list of fifty by *The Hollywood Reporter*; developed the project that won the first interactive Emmy in 2004; awarded the first TV of Tomorrow industry award; and awarded the "Digerati Award" by the TV academy's interactive arm, in recognition of the AFI's pioneering contributions to the interactive media industry (the only nonprofit entity on the list).

Consider the benefits: the Digital Content Lab provided a remarkable engine for funding, generating overhead revenue, and attracting new prospects to support other AFI programs. The blue-chip list of corporate partners includes Intel (a partner for three years), Corporation for Public Broadcasting (nine years), Microsoft (five years), Adobe (three years), IBM, AOL, AT&T (ongoing), Liberate, and HP (multiple years).

It was a rich experience for most of us involved, largely because of the community we built. The unique circumstances that

> "It's a small industry but the collaborative spirit at AFI has given a certain spirit to the business overall. I've always liked the phrase, 'Leave your guns at the door.' That's been the value and one of the underlying directives of the lab. It's still a new business, and a new industry that's out there. And what AFI has done has really affected that, and created a common sensibility for moving forward."
>
> —DALE HERIGSTAD,
> award-winning graphics designer and AFI Digital Content Lab mentor

facilitated these successes won't come again. But while it lasted, AFI influenced the evolution of both technology and television and, in so doing, cemented its reputation as a leading player in digital media.

Venturing Forth

Even as the AFI Digital Content Lab was helping the entertainment world navigate digital technologies, AFI realized that the Internet presented many opportunities to build its own brand online, and hopefully to generate new sources of revenue. There were three classes of assets that might prove to be suitable for such AFI monetization schemes on the web:

- **Content:** AFI owned hundreds of original short films, segments from broadcast TV shows, and print from its publications, as well as a photo archive.
- **Education:** AFI had produced powerful curricula in film production techniques and film history.
- **Data:** AFI produced high-quality databases like the *AFI Catalog*.

"There is an estimated $90 billion of unspent venture capital searching for investments," I wrote in a 1999 memo proposing an

AFI venture strategy. "AFI should explore if and how it might tap these resources to develop its potential in the dot-com world of e-education, e-commerce, and e-community. Can AFI secure funds to create a new enterprise? If so, what might it do and look like?" This kind of language seemed to play well with the AFI board, fresh off a successful and highly entrepreneurial launch of its *AFI's 100 Years...100 Movies* TV franchise.

I pitched every asset we had to a long list of prospective partners. I also pitched the AFI brand and what it represented: quality, high standards, and respect, as well as Hollywood and glamour. It was still a tough sell, since AFI had almost no development capital of its own. Any AFI partner would have to carry all the costs. The heavens would have to align perfectly. In 1999, they did.

LET ME INTERTAIN YOU

By 1999, everyone was embracing the idea of video as one of the Internet's "killer apps." Warner Bros. and NBC had launched video-based websites. Microsoft, Macromedia, and RealNetworks supported sites to show off their technologies. Startups spent millions to acquire video libraries.

AFI held copyright to hundreds of well-made short films from the Conservatory, some featuring stars and name directors at the dawn of their careers. This provision had been designed in 1968 by a young Tom Pollock, AFI's business manager at the time, with revenues from the sale of a film's rights split between AFI, the filmmakers, DGA and SAG. Plus, it was a library guaranteed to grow as each year's graduating class produced new films. By 1999, a bidding war broke out for this asset among Warner Bros., NBC, Atom Film, iFilm, DEN, Pseudo, Excite, IBM, and others. Atom and iFilm, both well-funded startups, submitted the strongest bids. Each company promised cash, pre-IPO equity, and a variety of in-kind services to win AFI's rights. For once, AFI got to be a chooser rather than a beggar.

At the last minute, a new contender named Intertainer swooped in to win the prize. Jon Taplin, Intertainer's CEO, was a former music manager and film producer who wanted to build the HBO of on-demand video—Netflix before Netflix. Intertainer had raised more than $65 million from a roster of brand-name investors, including GE, Time Warner, Sony, Comcast, US West, NBC, Intel, and Microsoft. The company was negotiating with many of the companies represented on the AFI board. An initial public offering seemed imminent in the go-go market of the time.

Intertainer's offer was three times larger than those of its closest rivals. AFI and Intertainer announced a three-year deal in June 2000 worth nearly $4 million ($1.2 million upon signing), plus in-kind services, plus warrants built into the IPO—an unusually rich deal for an unproven asset like short films. What Intertainer got in return was the right to stream AFI shorts on its premium service and Intertainer.com.

Of course, Intertainer was interested in more than AFI's short films—its business depended upon film rights from the studios represented on the AFI board. With this deal, Taplin had earned access to AFI's world, including a chance to meet the AFI Board of Trustees and participate in a board-level retreat focused on the future of AFI.

ENTRANCE STRATEGY

The Intertainer deal was just one of many partnerships during this era that raised an interesting question: should we create a for-profit subsidiary that could accept investment and earn revenue from AFI's brand and assets? Not just a for-profit subsidiary, such as a museum store or a brand license, but an enterprise that could secure what at the time seemed like boundless venture capital going into Internet startups? Jean Firstenberg invited me to join her and

AFI chairman Tom Pollock at their biweekly breakfast at the Beverly Hills Hotel's Polo Lounge to consider the idea.

"Here's the trouble with your idea," Pollock said, after I raced through my pitch and a cup too many of the exceptional coffee. "These companies want an exit strategy. We want an entrance strategy." Pollock was right, of course. Venture investors hope for big returns on their bets, returns achieved by selling the company or going public. AFI didn't want to sell off its assets; it wanted to use them to stay relevant in this new era.

That settled that. Instead of a for-profit startup, we created AFI New Media Ventures in October 2000, a business unit that consolidated all of my programs and staff and was authorized to tackle a diverse set of goals: to expand AFI's web ventures; to extend AFI's curriculum to K–12; to transform the AFI archive into useful online content; to expand our cutting-edge research and development lab; and to develop sustainable revenue streams for the new AFI.

At its peak, New Media Ventures employed a full-time staff of twenty-two, as well as contractors and vendors to keep all of these goals moving forward. Anna Marie Piersimoni, who relinquished the reins at the eTV workshop to become my strong number two, held the entire operation together as it expanded and became productive.

There is no denying that our enthusiasm for a "venture" approach was inspired by the contagious enthusiasm of the dot-com era, a time of proliferating startups and instant millionaires. At times, working at a nonprofit seemed so old school. Now, with hindsight, it looks like the smart move.

LAWSUIT

AFI delivered more than 100 short films to Intertainer during that first year. We also built a new website, AFIfilm.com, to house the films and to provide a home page for every AFI Fellow, a type of social network that predated Facebook by years.

Intertainer failed abruptly as the dot-com bubble burst. In March of 2001, the company canceled its final payment to AFI, forcing the layoff of eight employees in one day, and halted our most ambitious plans. Though Taplin blamed the market, there was more to the story. Intertainer was in a bitter fight with its content suppliers, all of them studios that sat on the AFI board. Intertainer filed an antitrust suit against three of the studios and Movielink (an Intertainer competitor owned by the studios) in September 2002 and ceased operations a month later, despite its 125,000 Internet subscribers and 35,000 TV subscribers. The case was settled out of court in 2006. Intertainer later sued Apple, Google, and Napster for copyright infringement and settled out of court.

In the years following the collapse of Intertainer, AFI sold rights to its short film library to three different distributors. For a brief time in 2007, many AFI shorts topped the iTunes charts.

Teaching and Learning

DISTANCE LEARNING/DISTANCE EARNING

The web also sparked a land-rush within the gigantic education market. According to *E-Learning: The Partnership Challenge,* the U.S. education market was valued at over $735 billion in 2000. The new online component was predicted to grow from $9.4 billion in 1999 to $53.3 billion by 2003. Universities created new consortia for distance learning. For-profits like the University of Phoenix grew rapidly on the web. Startups like Hungry Minds paid established professors for the rights to distribute their most popular university courses. When the UCLA School of Theater, Film, and Television announced its participation in GlobalFilmSchool.com in 1999, AFI trustees asked how AFI could become part of this distance-learning revolution.

The answer was a deal with Columbia University's Fathom.com, an online education site featuring courseware and other content from a prestigious list of partners including the London School of Economics, the Universities of Chicago, Michigan, and Cambridge, the British Library, and the Smithsonian Institution. Fathom was financed entirely by Morningside Ventures, the venture capital arm of Columbia University.

Fathom was a beautiful site and a worthy effort by some very smart people. AFI produced dozens of short-form courses for Fathom, as well as a full-scale original interactive course, "Introduction to Digital Video Production" with film editor Michael Rubin. The course became a hit for a short time when Columbia's journalism school made it a requirement.

Columbia closed Fathom in 2003, another casualty of the dot-com crash. Although Columbia had invested more than $25 million in Fathom and 65,000 people created accounts, Fathom failed to turn a profit or attract other investors.

FILM AS LITERACY

Although AFI's educational mandate was not primarily focused upon secondary education, a number of middle- and high-school projects dot its history. In the '80s, AFI offered teacher training as part of its National Education Program. In the '90s, AFI ran a summer training program for high school kids in the wake of the 1992 Los Angeles riots and produced (by future AFI president and CEO Bob Gazzale) a course for English teachers, broadcast via satellite, on the novel *To Kill a Mockingbird* and its film adaptation.

The goal of a national K–12 education initiative emerged during AFI planning retreats in the late '90s. Producer-director and co-chair of the board of directors, Jon Avnet (class of 1972), was its strongest advocate. As a Sarah Lawrence undergraduate, Avnet had taken his 16mm film camera into a tough South Bronx neighborhood to help teenagers tell their own stories for the screen. Avnet envisioned a "movie camp" for teens that could generate a curriculum AFI could sell to school districts. While Avnet's exact idea never materialized, it did jumpstart the K–12 education mandate.

Our first step was a white paper that proposed an AFI screen education program composed of K–12 curriculum, teacher training, resources for colleges and universities, and distance-learning. Our focus on K–12 was influenced by AFI's new partnership with Montgomery County, Maryland (described in Chapter 6), that restored a faded movie palace, the centerpiece of redeveloping downtown Silver Spring near Washington, DC. Together, we created "A Novel Look at Film," modeled on the "Mockingbird" project of a few years earlier. *Of Mice and Men*, adapted for film by Gary Sinise in 1992, served as the prototype. A viewing guide helped teachers guide student comprehension of the film and the novel as different modes of storytelling.

The studios should have been good partners for this program, since they adapted so many novels for the screen. Our first partnership was with New Line Cinema: an online student study guide for their first movie based upon J. R. R. Tolkien's *Lord of the Rings* trilogy. The deal did not inspire additional studio funding of study guides as we had hoped.

THE LANGUAGE OF THE SCREEN

Greater success came from a partnership with the educational reform group Workforce L.A., which worked with professionals to teach animation to high-schoolers via satellite. They helped us produce a template for the AFI screen education program, including standards-based evaluation that was required in the data-driven K–12 education market.

The program was based upon two key ideas. First, screens of

all sorts hold a primary place in the lives of students. We asserted that "the language of the screen" was the twenty-first century's primary form of literacy. Second was AFI's time-tested principle, "Learn by doing; study with the Masters"—a real-world enactment of constructivist learning theory, which holds that people construct knowledge through experience and reflection. The pilot started during the 2001–2002 school year, with twelve classrooms in six Los Angeles-area high schools involving 400 students. Our Screen Ed team included Mitch Aiken, a broadcast executive with experience in both education and digital media; Frank Guttler, a charismatic teacher who had worked at AFI's Advanced Technology program; and Bob Jennings, a filmmaker and comic who came to AFI as my assistant and later became a YouTube expert and star.

Screen Ed was not a filmmaking program. It was a literacy program, using the techniques of filmmaking to help students master academic subject matter—any subject mandated by the states. The program included teacher training, student lessons in production techniques, and a website where films uploaded by students premiered and received feedback from AFI's Hollywood experts. English teachers, our largest group, expected the program to improve students' verbal and writing skills and comprehension of literature. And, maybe, their test scores.

At the end of the first year, an independent evaluation reported positive results. Teachers were able to adapt the AFI curriculum to their own classroom assignments—not only for English, but other subjects as well. They reported high levels of student attendance, engagement, discipline, and peer interaction. Student grades and test scores improved at all six pilot schools.

During its second year, the program expanded to fifty classrooms in three regions—L.A., DC, and the San Francisco Bay area. We rethought and redesigned many elements of the screen education program over its eight years of operation, de-emphasizing the face-to-face teacher training and instead using print, video, and the web for greater reach. Materials included a 110-page manual and curriculum for teachers and a video series, *Lights, Camera, Education*, hosted by actor Sean Astin, that streamed from the website and could be used by teachers and students in the classroom. The program was licensed to Apple, Google, and Discovery Communications, which made the program available nationally to more than 70,000 schools. An AFI YouTube-powered site called AFI ScreenNation then added a series of celebrity-powered challenges to make it fun.

SHOW US THE MONEY

The federal government funded Screen Ed through a process of targeted appropriations known as earmarks. The legislators providing the most assistance were from AFI's base states, California and Maryland—Representative Nancy Pelosi and Senators Dianne Feinstein and Barbara Mikulski. In 2003, when congressional control shifted to the GOP, we pitched then-Republican senator Arlen Specter from Pennsylvania. (Trustee Allen Bernstein, a major Republican supporter, introduced us.) After we finished our presentation, he asked in a quiet voice, "So, if you receive this funding, where will the program go next?" Without missing a beat, Jean and I replied in unison, "Pennsylvania!"

On one lobbying trip, we enlisted *American Idol* singing sensation Clay Aiken, whose cousin, Mitch, ran the Screen Ed program. Everywhere we went, throngs of his fans, known as "Claymates," mobbed us, even in the halls of Congress. We distributed hand-fans emblazoned with Aiken's face and the headline, "I'm a Fan of AFI." Altogether, the AFI Screen Education program attracted more than $2 million in federal support, as well as grants from several foundations, Microsoft, and Best Buy. Brad Anderson, chairman and CEO of Best Buy, was a superb, generous, and active trustee beginning in 2001 and continued in a leadership role into

2016, chairing the National Council. Trustee Chuck Fries was a strong proponent of this effort as well, so he and Jon Avnet walked the halls of Congress with us for this project.

HERE'S LOOKING AT YOU, KID

One day in 1997, MIT professor Janet Murray called to see if AFI could help solve a rights problem relating to one of her media education projects. We liked each other so much that we began to brainstorm ideas about how to work together. Our best idea centered on a multimedia website for the study of classic films. Janet and I explained the idea to Jean Firstenberg over lunch. She had only one question: "What movie?" "*Casablanca*," Janet said. "No problem," Jean replied.

Easy for her to say! Two years and dozens of meetings with many lawyers later, Warner Bros. granted us the rights to build a prototype. Murray, by now at Georgia Tech, led a team of graduate students to design the data structure and web interface. AFI's IT team managed the website running on AFI servers. The project was funded by a grant from the federal National Endowment for the Humanities and a software grant from Microsoft.

The "Digital Critical Edition" of *Casablanca* introduced groundbreaking methods for the detailed study of a film. As the term "critical edition" suggests, we sought to apply the scholarship standards of printed texts to the study of film, providing opportunities for detailed analysis and commentary, stop-action and interactivity. Although we were unable to find a way to commercialize a concept that was so dependent upon studio copyright permissions, we were proud of the project's success as an academic research venture, which fueled many years of activity at Georgia Tech. Dr. Murray enjoyed a long relationship with AFI as a mentor in the Digital Content Lab and respected member of the AFI Board of Trustees from 2000 to 2009.

PRINT TO DATA

The *AFI Catalog of Feature Films* is the authoritative database of U.S. cinema, published originally as a series of gigantic red reference books. In 1997, we entered the electronic database market by licensing the *AFI Catalog* to the academic publisher Chadwyck-Healey, which marketed it to universities and libraries in digital formats.

Before offering the *AFI Catalog* to the general public, we needed to solve two problems. First, the database software needed to be upgraded and modernized for the web. Second, our data research and production methodology needed to be overhauled. As it was, the *AFI Catalog*'s small, underfunded staff couldn't keep up with the volume of new movies, much less compete with commercial movie databases like IMDb (Internet Movie Database, owned by Amazon), Baseline, and All Movie Guide (owned by Tribune). This was scholarly research, so it took time to produce detailed summaries, production histories, and other proprietary research for every catalogued film, features which only the *AFI Catalog* accurately provided.

Partnerships with KPMG Consulting and Microsoft solved the first issue. We converted the *AFI Catalog* to a modern SQL database that brought the *Catalog* into the web era. With this base, AFI's programming team, directed by Michael Carter, built customized production tools for the *AFI Catalog* staff and integrated the *Catalog* into AFI.com to enable general access for the first time. AFI was now able to license the data to commercial partners like Turner Classic Movies.

Finally, in partnership with the Baseline movie data company, we developed a plan to consolidate our two staffs and offer a version of *AFI Catalog* data to business customers, including movie studios and web portals like AOL and Yahoo. Before this deal was finalized, however, Baseline was acquired by the New York Times Company, which had no appetite for additional investments in a movie database.

AFI Best

By 2006, Hollywood finally embraced its digital future, making deals and making news. To dramatize the moment for AFI's trustees, I created an animated video presentation using more than 100 headlines that told the story of a business in breakneck transition.

What was AFI's mission in the digital era? With film literally disappearing, what would be the significance of an American Film Institute? Talk about existential questions! Here was one for the organization—and for me as AFI's freshly minted senior vice president for media and technology.

The board set up a media and technology committee to look at AFI's best prospects for success. Warren Lieberfarb and Todd Wagner, two guys who certainly knew digital, held the most sway in the group. Others in the group included former Apple CEO Gil Amelio, producer Kathleen Kennedy, Adobe cofounder John Warnock, filmmaker Marshall Herskovitz (class of 1975), former ABC president Fred Pierce, Best Buy CEO Brad Anderson, AOL president Jon Miller, and former Universal chief Tom Pollock, all AFI board members. Lieberfarb, who had run Warner Home Video, was known as the "father of the DVD." Wagner co-founded Broadcast.com with partner Mark Cuban ten years before YouTube. After selling it to Yahoo for the staggering sum of $5.7 billion, they built a portfolio of film, television, and digital properties.

A consensus emerged inside the committee around the idea of an AFI broadband website business. With AFI's strong brand and assets, why couldn't we create a successful broadband business, too? Lieberfarb brought in the Boston Consulting Group (BCG) to analyze the case for such a venture. Their work began in April 2007 on a pro bono basis, with me as their inside man. BCG presented the case for two different AFI broadband businesses: AFI Best to offer consumers a one-stop destination for great movies to browse, purchase, rent, or stream; and AFI Film School to teach film production techniques online. Both were projected as for-profit ventures. This was a déjà vu moment, since I had advocated similar for-profit web businesses a few years before.

Ultimately, this project was overshadowed by a transition in AFI leadership. In June 2006, Jean Firstenberg announced her intention to retire as AFI president and CEO, and was succeeded by Bob Gazzale late in 2007, just as BCG was completing the first draft of its recommendations. By the end of the year, the board had endorsed AFI Best, committing $200,000 for further development and up to $1.5 million as a potential investment. Todd Wagner argued with memorable passion: "You can't swim to the other shore if you don't jump in the water. It's time to jump in!"

The board told me to develop the business and seek partners. Our team included broadcast and web designer Dewey Reid, who visualized *AFI Best*, and entrepreneurs Richard Cardran and Robert Flynn, who finalized the content plan and financial projections. Hewlett-Packard's Todd Bradley, who had recently joined the board, introduced us to Silicon Valley's most successful angel investor Ron Conway, who told us that AFI could never raise venture funds as a nonprofit. We simply could not deliver a return on investment. These discussions became moot as 2008's financial markets imploded. AFI's corporate partners slashed their marketing budgets, creating a crisis for the new management team. Corporations, nonprofits, and educational institutions across America faced similar problems. AFI programs and staff were eliminated. Priorities were refocused.

Digital Takes Its Place

AFI had thrived during almost twenty years of technological disruption, innovating new programs that helped give birth to a new media-and-entertainment landscape that is still evolving today. In part due to the work undertaken at AFI, Silicon Valley and Hollywood had come together in new ways. What started as a digital revolution had become a fait accompli, not just in Hollywood, but everywhere. All business became digital. All media became digital.

For nearly the entirety of its fifty-year history, AFI, like the storytellers it trains and celebrates, struggled with the role of technology in the creation of compelling works of art and entertainment. Starting with the advent of electronic video capture and editing in the 1970s, continuing with the introduction of computerized tools, and on to the Internet and the full-scale digital industry we know today, a persistent question emerged: Does technology change the fundamentals of storytelling, and if so, what should an organization like AFI do to reflect that change?

AFI's adoption of video production tools within CAFS created a tension: this new technology was at once practical (it was easier, cheaper, and reuseable) and controversial (i.e., video is not film, and therefore betrays the core of the art form). In the 1990s, first with Apple and then with most of Silicon Valley, AFI became a vigorous advocate for computer-based production with training programs that democratized access to the tools of visual storytelling. As the world was devoured by the Internet, AFI found voice as a leader within the Hollywood system for many of the developments that underlie today's world of consumer devices and streaming media. Much of this work was conducted by a bespoke AFI team that was as much a part of the digital subculture as it was rooted in the traditional movie and TV community, whose primary interest, as was the case within the AFI Conservatory, remained the theatrical motion picture and the showrunner-led television series. The digital folks believed that revolutionary platforms like YouTube, Facebook, and all the rest created the opportunity for new story forms that required a different type of creative team. The traditionalists believe that AFI's mission remains constant—to cultivate the art and craft required to tell a story with images. The rest could be sorted out later.

With my own retirement and the onset of the world financial crisis, the tension became moot, since external financial support for AFI's now twenty-year digital strategy vanished nearly overnight. The result was an institution not directly involved with the great struggles brought about by the ever-changing world of technology. Henceforth, AFI's job would be to help each successive generation of storytellers to master the art form as it evolved, so that they could continue to create exceptional work that would endure the tests of both time and the onslaught of new technologies.

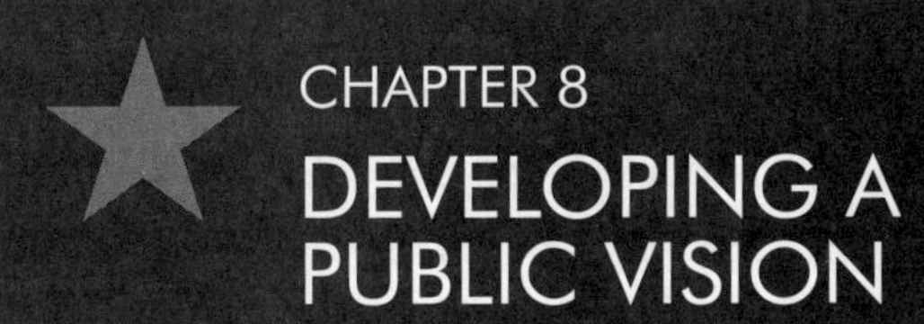

American Film Magazine

Jean Picker Firstenberg

In the '70s, under the leadership of AFI's founding director, the Institute bravely launched an amazing number of programs and projects that were also deeply challenging. Of them all, a new magazine might have been the most exciting. Its editorial content provided a real opportunity for insightful and worthwhile contributions to film knowledge for a wide audience. At the same time, publishing was a tough business to navigate—not an easy undertaking for any entity, let alone a young nonprofit. Five years later, when I became director, *American Film* magazine was going full speed with a circulation of 140,000 subscribers. The question was, could that be sustained?

Launching in 1975 with Hollis Alpert (a well-regarded writer and critic who had written for the *New York Times*) as its first editor, *American Film* grew to be respected and respectable five years later. The first issue was reviewed by Arthur Knight in *The Hollywood Reporter* on October 31, 1975:

> *In short, this magazine is for everybody who has any stake at all in the movie business. On the other hand, it seems to be wide open to anyone with something authoritative to say about films and television. And, on the other, it seems to be genuinely committed to closing the gap between the professional filmmaker (of whatever persuasion) and that vast audience out there that wants to know more about who make the movies and why.*

At its height, *American Film* had a circulation of 140,000 but, depending on how you analyzed it, also carried a significant annual deficit of $150,000 that kept growing over the years to $500,000. When I joined AFI, I was very excited about the magazine, because I had spent the previous eighteen months at the John and Mary R. Markle Foundation, where I had worked on a similar not-for-profit magazine for television called *Channels*. The idea of a monthly journal about movies or television, written with style and substance, was a challenge worth seizing, even if the financial viability of such a venture was questionable.

The model that everyone admired at the time was the incredible launch of *Smithsonian* magazine in 1970. By 1975, it had grown to one million subscribers, one of the most rapid subscriber growth stories in magazine history. American readers found the membership-plus-subscriber model extremely appealing. The Smithsonian is one of our great national institutions, and as a subscriber, I also became a member (and as a member, I became a subscriber). Why was it so successful? My theory is that when people visit the nation's capital for the first time, see the monuments, and visit the Smithsonian museums on the Mall—where entry is free—they want to lend support, because it is such a patriotic triumph.

It seemed a reasonable model for AFI to follow. Like the Smithsonian, AFI is an institution with a national mandate, created by an act of Congress. But the audience for a magazine about film was different from a magazine about museums and the myriad cultural landscapes they encompass. In the early '70s, up to eighty-five film publications arrived at the AFI offices every month. There was a large audience of filmmakers, film educators, film students, and informed moviegoers. These were not commercial ventures attracting the large audience that was reading *Screen Gems* and *Photoplay* (similar in appeal to today's *Entertainment Weekly* or *US*). Most magazines had niche appeal, but the rationale for wide readership was solid: America loves movies. Americans want to know more about movies and moviemakers, and AFI could provide quality insight about the movies from its national perspective. In fact, AFI had a fantastic centerpiece: "Dialogue on Film" was a series of interviews done with filmmakers several times a month at the Center for Advanced Film Studies in Los Angeles.

We strategized that, with a member-subscriber base of at least 100,000, we could begin to attract enough advertisers to cover the budget. The problem was that the only way to achieve that level of membership was through constant and extensive direct mailings, which are incredibly expensive to produce and rarely break even. The return on the investment shows up in renewals, with average renewals coming in at around sixty percent.

As always, there were some AFI trustees who had great expertise to help with the evolution of the magazine. David Brown, a great producer, started his career studying journalism. His wife, Helen Gurley Brown, was the enormously successful editor of *Cosmopolitan* at the time. There was no one more conversant with the current magazine world in 1975. David chaired the publishing committee, and I simply followed his sound advice and guidance.

Unfortunately, two things happened soon after I arrived: the NEA said it would no longer allow its funds to support the magazine (or membership), and editor Hollis Alpert resigned. David Brown led the search committee and found a bright, smart young man as our new editor. Peter Biskind turned out to be first-rate.

Embracing the magazine, I wrote a monthly essay, a regular feature that debuted in the March 1981 issue. The essay was a forum for the AFI director to share matters of interest with the Institute and its members. Indeed, it was a great place to get an AFI point of view across. This feature continued through 1986. My essay topics included technophobia and those who feared that it debased the art form, the timelessness of great TV comedy, TV coverage of major moments in American history, PBS American Playhouse, documentaries and music videos, the renaissance in film exhibition, and how the miniseries was changing TV storytelling.

The NEA panel's negative position on supporting the magazine and membership was consistent with most of their attitudes about AFI programs that served the field. Broad public efforts would not be supported, only targeted ventures aimed at individuals in or entering the field. They were very particular about which programs the NEA grant would support. In 1981, that meant *American Film* and membership were excluded.

I could not understand the NEA panel's disinterest in the magazine. The editorial profile was always the real issue—how to put out a magazine that was intelligent but not obtuse, insightful but not nasty, and smart rather than silly. It was always the editor's job to establish a strong point of view, and to be sharp but not negative, and evenhanded but not boring. The editor had control over content, but both Hollis Alpert and Peter Biskind knew that if they included an article that criticized someone on the board, it would not be well-received. It certainly wasn't a simple or easy situation. There were ten issues a year, and each issue required three to five strong articles to attract and retain a readership. Several dozen such articles every year is a challenge under the best of circumstances.

George Stevens Jr. reached for quite a standard in the premiere issue in October 1975 when he wrote, "With this premiere issue of *American Film*, the American Film Institute reaches out in a new form to people with an interest in film and television, or as the *New Yorker* might phrase it, to those with 'more than a routine interest.'"

But there was much to write about in the '70s—everything from mainstream to independent filmmaking, from narrative to documentaries, from features to shorts, from media arts centers to exhibition, from museum archives to deciding who should be on the cover.

It seemed to me that the NEA panel was really wrong about the value and quality of *American Film*. However, financial pressures on the Institute were severe in the early '80s. As described in Chapter 9, refinancing the campus and then securing the California Educational Facilities Authority bond issue helped, but even after that, the pressure was still intense.

In 1983, the magazine publisher left; this was another troubling sign. Magazines are particularly dependent upon the economy, tied to the ready availability of advertising money and strong levels of consumer spending that make subscription purchases likely. Everyone was looking forward to the magazine's Tenth Anniversary issue in 1985 with the hope that it would attract more advertising dollars and provide enough support to make it a good financial year for *American Film*. The cover was by Andy Warhol, thanks to trustee Ina Ginsburg, who was a good friend of his. This also came at a time when program funding was being reduced, programs were being eliminated, staff was being moved west to reduce costs in DC, and all deficits were being reviewed in detail by the board, who were asking hard questions. By 1984, the magazine deficit had climbed to almost $500,000.

The executive committee discussed every Institute program. Those meetings could get intense. George Stevens Jr. had been bold enough to start the magazine, and he could not understand why the current board would not be bold enough to sustain it, even if it continued to run a deficit. Gordon Stulberg and George argued about this at some length. We looked for a way to keep the magazine going while also—somehow—reducing the deficit. Then Mace Neufeld came up with a powerful idea: ask a donor entity to take on *American Film*, continuing to publish it but eliminating the deficit on the AFI budget ledger. Mace knew a good deal about the AMS Foundation for the Arts and Humanities. Arthur M. Sackler was a fascinating philanthropist, art collector, and medical research scientist. Mace and his wife, Helen, knew Arthur's right-hand representative and attorney Michael Sonnenfeld because of their mutual interests at the Smithsonian, where Arthur was developing his proposal to establish the Arthur M. Sackler Gallery of Asian Art.

So, once again, as these board-level negotiations can magically facilitate, Mace and Michael designed a solid, reasonable structure for *American Film* and AFI. The Sackler empire was then based on MD Publications, major medical journals successful on a worldwide basis. A joint venture was designed through which MD Publications would publish *American Film*, moving the editorial team to New York City. This made much more sense than having a magazine staff in Washington, DC, because so many more writers and filmmakers were based in New York. MD Publications believed they could reduce the deficit and produce the magazine on a break-even basis. Since the magazine was published independently from AFI, this didn't seem to be that different a situation for the Institute. The agreement was for two years, but the Foundation had the right to revoke the agreement if the deficit went beyond its current level.

I don't recall a deal ever being finalized so quickly. It was approved on October 24, 1985, and the editorial team moved to New York City on March 5, 1986. From the get-go, the AFI board was horrified by the apparent change in editorial direction, although it was the same AFI editorial team. A year later, the board tried to establish some editorial guidelines for the magazine. The publisher wanted the AFI board to encourage the film community to buy advertising in the magazine. After the first year, the publisher was optimistic that he could cut the deficit in 1987, based on the interest in AFI's Twentieth Anniversary year. Circulation fluctuated between 125,000 and 135,000. Studios had agreed to advertise, but they weren't used to long magazine deadlines. Some even paid the agreed-upon rates, but never even placed an ad.

Then, on May 26, 1987, Arthur Sackler died suddenly. This brilliant man was gone. Needless to say, the Sackler estate was in a state of shock and disarray. Over the course of a short three years, Arthur and Jill Sackler had become good friends to the Institute and to me.

Following Arthur's death, I invited Jill to join my family on Thanksgiving. She came that year and has come every subsequent year, no matter where we may gather. She is truly a member of my family, having grown to know my children and their spouses and then their children. My family and Bob Gazzale have shared some wonderful moments with Jill at the Arthur M. Sackler Gallery for Asian Art at the Smithsonian Institution. In 2009, I accompanied Jill to China, where I witnessed the University of Peking community's respect and admiration for the Sacklers' work to honor and preserve Asian art at the Arthur M. Sackler Museum of Art and Architecture.

Jill had joined the board in 1986, representing the foundation. But now, with the estate in transition, the joint venture was no longer valid; AFI faced a liability of close to $500,000 to the AMS Foundation and a subscriber liability of $1 million. Graciously, the foundation eventually forgave AFI's magazine liability.

What was our next option? Again, the trustee solution came from Gene Jankowski, who was then consulting for Veronis Suhler, one of the most respected media-focused private equity companies in the country. John Suhler had been head of CBS Publishing when Gene was chair and president of CBS Broadcasting, before forming the firm in 1981. Veronis Suhler took on AFI as a pro bono client, with a $25,000 flat fee. Veronis Suhler knew our objectives were quite specific:

1. Eliminate the deficits. That meant not being responsible for publishing *American Film* anymore.
2. Find someone to assume the subscription liability of $1 million.
3. Find a way to maintain the magazine and the AFI national membership.

Within a few months, Paul Hale, our Veronis Suhler advisor, had two options for the AFI board consideration:

The first option: Murdoch Publications had just started *Premiere* magazine. We met with editor Susan Lyne and *Premiere*'s publisher, two really sharp women. But their offer would only assume the subscription liability and pay AFI $250,000 without any

AFI Film Readers

James Hindman

One of our unlikeliest publishing successes was the AFI Film Readers series, produced with Routledge, a prestigious academic publisher. Given my own academic background, as well as AFI's historically shaky relationship with the ever-suspicious academic cinema community, we hoped to find a project that would be of genuine service to the field. At the urging of several academically based AFI trustees (notably Ted Perry, Ron Green, and, subsequently, Vivian Sobchack), we looked at a series of publications where AFI's endorsement and presence might provide momentum. Bill Nichols, a major film scholar then at UC Santa Cruz, proposed "readers," an anthology series of essays on popular and significant topics in cinema studies. His theory was that, if each one was edited by a major scholar, junior academics way to continue the AFI relationship to a publisher and maintain the membership base. Peter Biskind went on to be executive editor of *Premiere* magazine for over ten years; he has written several books and is a respected cultural critic and film historian.

The second option: Billboard Publications, which covered all three options with a very attractive offer—$400,000 for the ownership, copyright, and liability, but they would also publish the magazine, maintain the AFI membership, and allow AFI to raise funds through them. At that time, we had a very active public service program (short courses and classes for professionals and the general public), and ninety-five percent of their registrations came from *American Film* or festival participation. Billboard wanted to develop a full range of publications with AFI, continuing the successful

and advanced graduate students might compose essays that could give them a leg up through an early publishing credit.

Routledge was looking to do something in the cinema studies area, and Bill Nichols was seen as someone they would take seriously. Bill recruited two extraordinary scholars based at UC Santa Barbara, Ed Brannigan and Chuck Wolf—perhaps the kindest and most patient and persistent souls I have had the pleasure of working with. They took on the Herculean editing and organizing tasks virtually as volunteers, and are still at it. Launched in 1989, the series became a standout success for Routledge and for AFI, featuring ever more specialized topics such as *The Biopic in Contemporary Film Culture and Color and the Moving Image*. To date, the series has published some thirty-five titles and, with oversight from AFI trustee Vivian Sobchack, continues to support and enrich the field of cinema studies in a substantial fashion.

College Guide and a series of books about film. Billboard's corporate entity had just acquired *The Hollywood Reporter*, so they were interested in all aspects of the American film community. It was a very promising affiliation at a time of great stress.

We signed the agreement with Billboard and their president, Jerry Hobbs, and publisher Sam Holdsworth came to the June 1988 board meeting and made an impressive presentation. The name *American Film* stayed with AFI; Billboard only licensed its use. It took a while for the magazine to get going, but the first issue under the new leadership was released in October 1989. Veronis Suhler had made AFI a fine deal, especially with the $400,000 "contribution" to the bottom line. Later the same year, the company sold *TV Guide*, Walter Annenberg's company, in a $4 billion deal. I sent a congratulatory letter to John Veronis, saying that the only difference between the two deals was a few zeroes!

Sadly, the last issue of *American Film* was released in November 1991. This wonderful idea and ideal, launched so boldly fifteen years earlier, could never develop into a viable business. I know this was incredibly hard for George Stevens Jr. to accept, and I shared his deep disappointment. The odds for this kind of venture's success are just too steep. The TV magazine I worked on at Markle was eventually launched and, despite good people trying to make it work, it also proved unsustainable, having worked through a variety of business models.

AFI Guides to College Film and Television Courses 1969–1990

James Hindman

In the twenty-first century, it is hard to remember how *new* the serious study of cinema and media arts actually is. In AFI's founding years, anyone rash and interested enough in taking film and television courses would have had to go to the library to look through the comprehensive national volume that AFI published, almost annually, to find out what colleges and universities offered such exciting pathways to the future.

This pioneering AFI publication was no easy effort to research and compile. Emily Laskin, who edited the volumes after 1980, remembers: "Pre-Internet, the assembly of the AFI Guide was undertaken the old-fashioned way—gathering what information we could via research in libraries and then verifying the timeliness of the date via correspondence by post and a phone conversation with each institution. It took months, but when we went to press, we were confident that it was as complete, comprehensive, and accurate as possible." Indeed, it was an invaluable publication that charted the origins of what is now a huge field, providing a detailed map to those hoping to create its future just at the time when it was needed most.

AFI Productions

James Hindman

During the 1990s, AFI itself produced a number of documentaries that introduced a wider audience to some of the inner workings of filmmaking. Before the "making of" featurette became a standard part of film marketing, AFI gave the public a glimpse into aspects of film art and craft that helped people appreciate watching movies even more.

Starring the Actor

Many of my colleagues and I at AFI had working backgrounds in film and television production, and we were ever alert to opportunities to create new work under AFI's prestigious banner. Shortly after my arrival at AFI in Los Angeles in late 1982, we were approached by colleagues and allies at the Mark Taper Forum, the leading theater in Los Angeles and a source of such major Broadway productions as *The Trial of the Catonsville Nine* and *Children of a Lesser*

God. Gordon Davidson, its renowned artistic director, had begun to develop large-scale television initiatives to utilize the wonderful connections it had with writers, directors, and actors. Gordon Hunt (Helen Hunt's father) was a major director and acting coach with deep ties to the Taper, and he wanted to develop an interview series with serious performers talking about their craft and technique. Of course, what would be critical would be highly prized and generally unaffordable studio intellectual property: clips from the actors' previous work as illustrations of the actors' talking points.

The studios and professional guilds had graciously allowed AFI to use clips without charging license fees or residuals; otherwise, the budgets for projects like the AFI Life Achievement Award or any of the productions described in this chapter would be totally impossible.

Thus, AFI was a highly desirable partner for the Taper, and AFI could also use its relationships to invite many otherwise unapproachable performers to participate in the series. Sony had just equipped the Sony Center on the new AFI Los Angeles campus with broadcast-quality cameras and post-production suites, so much production could be handled in-house. Once serious production funding was secured (from WorldVision, a short-lived premium cable entity looking for prestigious content), the project began to seem possible. We strategized that if we could cover the net and overhead costs, we would justify the request to our major supporters for clip rights. More important than the income, however, was the public education function that *Starring the Actor* could serve, allowing AFI to fulfill its unique role in revealing and defining the art of cinema to a country in love with the movies.

As host and producer, Gordon Hunt did a deeply effective job of opening up the participants in *Starring the Actor*, and such extraordinary talent as Roy Scheider, Blythe Danner, Ellen Burstyn (DWW class of 1974), and AFI trustee Donald Sutherland gave the series a seriousness and sheen that later actor-interview programs like *Inside the Actors Studio* sought to achieve. The thirteen episodes of *Starring the Actor* were critically well–received, but were somewhat lost to the public in the clutter of burgeoning new content on premium cable. They were, however, a real boon in budget-strained years at AFI.

AFI Goes to the Movies

But an appetite for detailed, thoughtful documentary and interview program fare by AFI had been whetted, and several other attempts were made over the next few years to find the funding and outlets to pursue new topics. Several made it to the air, including *AFI Goes to the Movies*, a local Los Angeles production on KTTV, which featured movies with major actor interviews led by the remarkable Jack Haley Jr.

At the same time, as was becoming obvious to all of us in the trenches, technology was in the process of changing the fixed world of American cinema in very exciting ways. Thanks to AFI's deep relationship with Sony, we were tracking the evolution and introduction of high-definition video. Even in its original analog version, HDTV promised to bring some of the qualities of theatrical film to television. In the late 1980s, I was asked to be on the executive committee of the International Electronic Cinema Festival, a very well-funded celebration of the first substantial work done in HDTV from broadcasters all over the world. Held in Montreux, Switzerland, it would showcase the virtues of this new technology. While the obvious commercial interests of the equipment manufacturers like Sony would be served, these were often overshadowed by the intense competition from various national broadcast authorities who wanted their big-budget HDTV programs to win international awards.

In many ways, the Japanese broadcasters were the largest players in this arena, having invested heavily in dramas, variety, and sports programs. Much of the work was made for local sensibilities and did not travel well, but some—like those made by the adventuresome creative teams at Tokyo Broadcasting—were quite extraordinary. The elephant in the room was NHK, the major national broadcast authority in Japan who, like the BBC, had the funds and clout to make elaborate historical dramas in the beautiful, lugubrious traditional Japanese television style. As a regular jury member, I have vivid memories of fighting jet lag, trying not to nod off while admiring the stately pace and sumptuous costumes—as well as constant cutaways to bees and flowers.

NHK Enterprises was established to allow the Japanese broadcaster to do international ventures and co-productions outside of the regular schedule. I had a good relationship with them through Sony and the Electronic Cinema Festival, and they requested suggestions from AFI for a major program they might fund for Japanese and American release. As usual, they were quite interested in AFI's relationships and potential to provide clip rights and access to major figures in our universe—American star power. But NHK did make it clear that there would be no creative interference in the content of the material, which was absolutely critical to us.

Hollywood Mavericks

AFI's TV/Video Services, the department established to continue the National Video Festival and the wide range of programs that evolved out of it over the decades of the 1980s and 1990s, was then led by the creative, solid administrator Terry Lawler. TV/Video would be homebase for any major in-house production. Terry introduced us to Florence Dauman, an extraordinary young French producer-director with a deep passion for and love of classic film. She and her partner, Michael Wilson, drew in the renowned and brilliant chief *Variety* critic Todd McCarthy, and together, in 1990, they concocted for us a very smart feature documentary, *Hollywood*

Mavericks. Using original interviews and archival footage with a liberal dose of illustrative movie clips, they were able to document the eccentric sensibilities and unusual work—highlighting breakthrough films and stylistic masterworks throughout American film history—of seventeen master directors, from Erich von Stroheim, King Vidor, and Sam Fuller to David Lynch (class of 1970), Orson Welles, and Robert Altman. *Hollywood Mavericks* was an original tribute to the true independent creatives, those who operated cleverly within the system while subverting it at the same time. The feature-length documentary was a success of some magnitude, both with critics and at festivals, shaped in many ways by the critical depth and vision of Todd McCarthy and driven by Florence Dauman's directing skills. Well before Peter Biskind's 1998 *Easy Riders, Raging Bulls,* a landmark treatment of the rise of Hollywood independent culture, *Hollywood Mavericks* defined a unique sensibility that had profoundly changed American film.

The success of *Hollywood Mavericks* whetted AFI's appetite for new substantial work. While its limited distribution did not carry large financial rewards to the Institute, the attention and visibility AFI drew was a strong motivator for us to continue looking for other appropriate production opportunities. Yet in all fairness, *Hollywood Mavericks* was something of a mixed blessing for NHK. Its American cinema history focus was of limited interest to NHK's Japanese audiences, most of whom were unfamiliar with the movies and figures being covered. While *Hollywood Mavericks* drew considerable American and international attention, it did not promote the home team particularly.

Nevertheless, as *Hollywood Mavericks* finished post-production, Los Angeles-based NHK executive Noriko Hirai asked us to meet with a new NHK Enterprises producer, Yoshiki Nishimura, who was charged with developing a major American project. They explained that NHK was putting substantial resources behind new special content that would showcase NHK's expanding commitment to high-definition television as a kind of new form of expanded cinema. NHK had done well with sports and lavish, dramatic specials that could take advantage of the sharper, richer image provided by high-definition TV, and it was looking for other content that could reinforce its attractiveness.

Television Writers Workshop

James Hindman

Established in 1983 through the leadership of Grant Tinker, the Television Writer's Workshop was committed to training writers in a different genre in a hands-on, inclusive manner over three weeks each summer. Up to twelve would-be writers met with leaders like Brandon Tartikoff, Chuck Fries, Ted Harbert, Kevin Bright, Peter Chernin, George Schlatter, and Frank Van Zerneck to learn how to develop a television script through tutorial work, case studies, and site visits while they wrote their scripts. The workshop was continued by the AFI Board of Trustees' television committee, chaired by Chuck Fries, over sixteen years in association with the Caucus of Producers, Writers, and Directors. The three networks—ABC, CBS, and NBC—sponsored the workshop on a rotating basis, with particular engagement by Tartikoff. Of the more than 130 alums, any number of careers were launched, and their stories reached the small screen. In 1987, the year Tartikoff chaired the workshop, there was a one-hour primetime special on NBC incorporating the sketches called *The AFI Comedy Special*.

Visions of Light

Visions of Light, a feature-length documentary produced by AFI and funded by Japanese broadcasting authority NHK in 1992, was truly a remarkable achievement for the Institute. Winner of the biggest critical awards of the period, with extensive exposure in major festivals and on public and premium cable television, and beneficiary of two years of national theatrical distribution, *Visions of Light* underscored AFI's emerging role as the major American voice for the art of cinema.

Visions of Light was the culmination of many strands of AFI's mission and programs—honoring classic cinema, saluting and revealing the artistic genius of many great figures within the practice of cinematography, unveiling the potential of a relatively unknown new technology (high-definition video), and fulfilling a public education mandate for AFI in a highly entertaining way. As many critics proclaimed, *Visions of Light* made you fall in love with the movies all over again. And as the uncredited executive producer (Jean and I did not think that senior staff should take titles on large public projects), I had an astonishingly good time and wild ride on the back of this beautiful monster.

It seemed to me that the virtues of the image on the screen were best demonstrated in the work of the cinematographer. As the primary visual storyteller in cinematic art, the best cinematographers combined advanced technical skills with a unique ability to design the framed image, creating meaning and advancing a narrative line. In the words of the master Haskell Wexler, "I think visually." Deeply rooted in the complex technology of film itself, cinematography required serious knowledge of chemistry, optics, and the sophisticated mechanics of the camera. Like editing, the craft of cinematography had always been placed "below the line," appearing in movie credits after the primary creative roles of producing, directing, and writing. Nevertheless, those familiar with successful production knew that serious cinematography was crucial to screen-based storytelling. Great cinematographers were major artists who were rarely given the respect they deserved.

In the creative community, there was a clear distinction between the worlds of film and television, and just prior to the digital era, most major cinematographers would not go near electronics. Film itself held a romance and great history that would not be easily abandoned. The crude and harsh images found on most home TV screens were part of a lesser visual world, the comparison being classic oil painting to commercial graphics. There was something very interesting about bridging these two universes. I proposed to Nishimura that we undertake a feature documentary looking at the history of cinema through the eye of the cinematographer, profiling past and current masters and showing examples of their work as they discussed their personal approaches and particular techniques. An AFI team would conduct the interviews, and NHK (with Sony's support) would provide the HDTV cameras, gear, and technical support to work in this new, largely unknown medium.

Nishimura was interested, and after a lengthy negotiation we agreed to undertake what eventually became *Visions of Light: The Art of Cinematography*. NHK was a tough negotiator; while the budget needed to be generous, given the number of unknowns we faced, many of the terms were stringent. AFI retained U.S. distribution rights in all markets and media, but NHK reserved the rest of the world for itself—a stipulation we would very much come to regret.

The next magic trick was to involve the major cinematographers, who historically and culturally felt chronically ill-used and underappreciated (which is the case with many in the creative community who work for hire on less-than-secure career tracks). I knew the great cinematographer Woody Omens, soon to be retired and then to teach full-time at University of Southern California's respected School of Cinema/Television. He was on the board of the American Society of Cinematographers (ASC), the guild that represented the interests of the profession, an extremely prestigious but fairly insular membership group. Woody proved to be a wily politician, and he was quite taken with the concept of the project. After testing the waters among his colleagues and meeting with some incredulity and resistance, he felt that it would be appropriate for me to address the ASC board directly, explaining in detail what AFI had in mind.

That evening meeting in 1990 at "the Clubhouse," ASC's Hollywood headquarters in a charming old bungalow, was a memorable moment. There was only one female guild member at that time—Brianne Murphy (DWW class of 1977). The rest of the group were older gentlemen extremely suspicious of this outlandish notion. First of all, the history and reputation of their profession was at stake; secondly, this project was being funded through a television authority, and was therefore made for television; thirdly, what in God's name was high-definition video and why should they care; and fourthly, Japan? One elderly board member said, in a not very sotto voce, "I remember Pearl Harbor . . ."

The evening discussion was a lengthy one! The major stumbling block was, naturally, creative control, which the ASC wanted to exert on the final results. We of course refused, and a compromise was reached: Woody Omens would represent the interests of the guild, and he would be involved in the planning process along the way. Woody proved to be a wonderful collaborator and a great facilitator and creative partner. The ASC was on board; they were extremely happy with the final results, despite the internal uproar from non-included members once the project proved to be wildly successful.

Thanks in large measure to Terry Lawler's careful oversight, assembling the creative team for *Visions of Light* really set up the chemistry that led to its final success. The driver was the indefatigable and deeply knowledgeable Todd McCarthy, who had contributed so heavily to the depth and design of *Hollywood Mavericks*. Todd came in originally as the designated writer of *Visions of Light*, with a commitment to do the research and design the interviews with the thirty-seven figures we began with. He became more and more involved with the project, appearing on the set and conducting the interviews personally. His respect for the cinematographers was so clear and his knowledge of their work was so extensive that he quickly built a deep rapport with them, making the subsequent discussions unusually candid and thoughtful. In so many ways, Todd became—forgive me—the vision behind *Visions of Light*. Stuart Samuels, a colleague with whom Todd worked well, served as lead director.

The cinematographer on the project was Nancy Schreiber, handling with unobtrusive care a difficult role, given the nature of the assignment and the complexities of a new camera and technology. She and the creative team hit on an ingenious strategy early on that made many things easier. They invited the master cinematographer/interviewees to come early, play with this unknown electronic camera, light themselves, and frame their own close-up, and then see how they looked through immediate playback on the set. Many of these extraordinary figures had a common weakness: often they were, as Terry put it, "peacocks" and quite vain about their image and appearance. By involving them in the familiar process of set-up, framing, and lighting, they became engaged in the project at a very different level. And they felt taken seriously in their areas of experience and strength. Many went on to become true believers and practitioners of electronic cinematography, often working in HDTV and digital cinema later in their careers. We were indeed doing missionary work.

A central addition to the *Visions of Light* creative team was the eminent editor Arnold Glassman. Shortly after *Visions*, he created *The Celluloid Closet*, the landmark feature documentary about Hollywood's historic depictions of the LGBT community. Arnie's astounding work in piecing together perfect moments from each lengthy interview, with clips that captured the elusive visual concept under discussion, was vital to the success of the finished piece. Given the large number of interview hours he had to sort through, plus the 125 films that were excerpted as illustrations, his achievement was remarkable.

Key to his work was how slow and meticulous he was. After we secured transfers to conventional videotape, Arnie locked himself into a tiny edit room in the AFI Sony Center and hacked away. When I discovered that Terry had him on an hourly wage, I almost had a coronary; I feared this might become a lifetime effort and a permanent career. But after nearly a year, and in close consultation with Todd and Terry, we began to see rough-cuts that made us ecstatic. Arnie proved the old Hollywood maxim that a film is written three times: first by the writer, then by the director, and then finally by the editor. Once the delightful score from Debussy's "Carnival of the Animals" was added, we knew this would be a very special finished piece.

A Documentary Finds Its Audience

NHK was also delighted with the finished piece, but of course for their domestic audiences, they had the same problem with *Visions of Light* that they'd had with *Hollywood Mavericks*: foreign movies, and foreign figures discussing esoteric concepts. I also later discovered that, when screening at international festivals, cinematography is often seen as a low-level craft in moviemaking, not to be taken terribly seriously and under the complete control of the all-powerful director. I had to become adept at selling: explaining the grammar of the screen and visual storytelling as the art and heart of cinematography.

Visions of Light had a limited distribution release initially. The HDTV analog format was in such limited use, and playback was rarely available; copies had to be down-converted to conventional video for most purposes. The loss of the crisp, rich screen image in true high definition was painful, given the visual banquet that the cinematographers and their work were serving up. Sony was helpful in finding equipment for festivals and special events, but it was frustrating to know what a treasure-trove of images was largely hidden to the world.

We then began discussions about tackling the expensive process of converting the HDTV *Visions of Light* to 35mm film for wide release. While this seemed counter-intuitive to the whole point of the project—bridging these two universes—it seemed like the only practical way to get *Visions of Light* to a wider world. In the early '90s, digital cinema was only a promise, and film still ruled. What I did not realize was that a 35mm release print would require a re-edit in film of all the elements, so Arnie went back to work on a Steenbeck editing table. So much for the glories of new technology.

The stunning results were well worth the effort, and the film print was gorgeous. We immediately began to explore a theatrical release for the film of *Visions of Light* and to look for other wider release venues. Many inquiries were coming in from Europe. Major distributors like Canal+ and the British Channel 4 were eager to get their hands on it, as were many festivals. But it was then that we discovered that NHK had neither the willingness nor the interest to market *Visions of Light* in these sometimes lucrative arrangements. I was astounded. Later, I learned that NHK had no experience or confidence in selling product in Europe, and were afraid of being cheated or embarrassed. To this day, *Visions of Light* remains a tantalizing rumor among European distributors, audiences, and film buffs.

The major public moment in *Visions of Light*'s life came when Kino, a relatively large arthouse theatrical distributor, acquired it for targeted large-market theatrical release and for the burgeoning videocassette market. Their advance covered our HDTV-to-film expenses, and there was even the potential for profits if the release was commercially successful.

And it was! More than a year in art-house release and playing widely throughout the country, *Visions of Light* grossed over $1 million dollars. It played for over six months in my own local arthouse in Santa Monica, California. We had a fifty-fifty split with Kino, but prints and advertising expenses came out of AFI's fifty percent. At the end of the day, our "profit" came out to $50,000—a painful lesson in the historic harsh realities of the film business. When I wanted to demand an audit of the books on the deal, friends from the studio world only smiled.

The critical response was overwhelming. My favorite from the glowing tributes the film received nationally may have been that of Vincent Canby, who described *Visions of Light* as "the vibrant, gloriously documented tale of the evolution of motion-picture photography." Siskel and Ebert loved it, and the National Society of Film Critics gave it the Best Documentary of the Year award in 1994. It was also chosen by the New York and the Boston Critics as Best Non-Fiction Film in 1993. It went on to various premium cable and public television releases and to a healthy commercial life in the videocassette and DVD markets.

Conversations began with NHK about possible sequels. For example, I was eager to take on editing as an unappreciated art form. But the push to promote HDTV was over, and funds were drying up as the Japanese economy deteriorated. Creative contributors to *Visions of Light* moved on to other projects, and I became enmeshed in other major initiatives at AFI.

Through *Visions of Light*, AFI re-committed to a large-scale public education role, bringing major attention as only it could to the rich and remarkable heritage of cinematic art. With the approach of film's centennial several years after *Visions of Light*'s release, AFI would launch its largest public education venture ever, *AFI's 100 Years...100 Movies*. It was a logical next step, following a through line from *Starring the Actor* to *Hollywood Mavericks* to *Visions of Light* and beyond.

Patricia Doyle Wise Lecture at AFI

Jean Picker Firstenberg

The Patricia Doyle Wise Lecture series was created by a bequest from the late wife of director-producer Robert Wise. The series focused on original thinkers' conception of the impact of film and television within a larger social and cultural context. Inaugurated in 1981, the Patricia Doyle Wise Lecture brought leading academic minds to the AFI. Each lecture brought an interdisciplinary perspective to questions and topics related to the role of film and television in contemporary society.

The bequest arrived soon after I joined the AFI. Bob Wise's beloved wife, who passed away in 1975, had left an $80,000 donation to the National Endowment for the Arts, and they hadn't decided how it should be spent. Bob asked me to determine how best to use it. It was a tricky period because Bob had mixed feelings about AFI's priorities, so I proposed an annual lectureship.

The series continued through 1994, with most lectures presented at the AFI Theater in the Kennedy Center in Washington, DC. In its penultimate year, Librarian of Congress James Billington's lecture titled "Is Alexandria Burning?" examined major threats to American heritage in the form of impermanence and physical decay of books and moving images, and the indifference of public leaders and the general public to the urgency of this crisis of culture. In this context, he termed the moving picture "not so much the art form as the language of the twentieth century."

PATRICIA DOYLE WISE LECTURERS

1981	Bruno Bettleheim, child psychologist
1982	Stanley Cavell, philosopher
1983	Arthur M. Schlesinger Jr., historian, author, political activist
1984	Natalie Zemon Davis, historian
1986	William Arrowsmith, child psychologist
1988	Reese Jenkins, historian
1989	Daniel Boorstin, Librarian of Congress Emeritus, historian
1990	Orlando Patterson, historical and cultural sociologist
1991	Elizabeth Hardwick, literary critic, novelist, and short story writer
1992	Hayden White, professor of comparative literature at Stanford University
1993	James H. Billington, historian and Librarian of Congress
1994	Wole Soyinka, Nigerian author and Nobel Laureate

Maya Deren Awards

In 1985, AFI acknowledged the significance and achievements of independent film and video artists by establishing an award named in honor of the pioneer independent filmmaker Maya Deren, whose experimental work in the 1940s signaled the birth of American avant-garde filmmaking. The board action, with strong support from trustees Ted Perry and Karen Cooper, created the AFI Award for Independent Film and Video Artists, thereby drawing a direct line from the early days of experimental film to the work of today's artists. The respected Amos Vogel, founder of Cinema 16, said:

> *By naming the award "Maya Deren," the AFI sets itself a standard of excellence and commitment; for Maya Deren was a fierce partisan, a catalyst of American avant-garde cinema who, in stubborn loneliness and without compromising, yoked her entire life and being to the cause of a new vision—the creation and promotion of personal cinema.*

Three recipients were to be honored each year and awarded $5,000. It was clear that even this relatively small grant could make a huge difference in the lives of these distinctive artists. AFI held events in New York City with some reluctance, because we could be perceived as encroaching on the media organizations based there. But we attempted to avoid this territorial question by holding the ceremonial part of the evening at a significant New York cinema culture site, like the Anthology Film Archive. Everyone in the film community was invited. A private reception at the Manhattan home of a trustee followed.

All of this was made possible by the support of Fred Henry of the Bohen Foundation and of New York trustees Larry Herbert and Jill Sackler. Fred Henry had just become president of the Bohen Foundation, and his goal was to commission new works of art with an emphasis on film, video, new media, and installations. Fred felt this was a strong way to introduce the foundation to the artistic community, and he provided $30,000 a year for eight years, with the sum of $5,000 being given to each of the three recipients every year.

To supplement this support, trustee Larry Herbert underwrote many of the receptions before the awards presentation. Jill Sackler hosted the post-reception dinner at their magnificent maisonette, where Arthur Sackler, one of the greatest collectors of Asian art in the world, welcomed independent artists to their residence. Masters' paintings graced their museum-like walls, and his classic toast illustrated his appreciation for all forms of creative expression: "All artists are welcome in this home."

My favorite honoree response was during the first year, when the pioneer video artist Nam June Paik was handed his $5,000 award and proclaimed, "Oh, this is so exciting. Now I can pay my phone bill!"

MAYA DEREN AWARD WINNERS

1986	Stan Brakhage, Sally Cruikshank, Nam June Paik
1988	Bruce Conner, Yvonne Rainer, Bill Viola; J. Hoberman received the Maya Deren Citation for Distinguished Service to the Field
1989	James Broughton, Shirley Clark, Joan Jonas
1990	Les Blank, Ernie Gehr, Edin Velez
1991	Bruce Baillie, Charles Burnett, Trinh T. Minh-ha
1992	George Kuchar, Marlon Riggs, Steina and Woody Vasulka
1993	Julie Dash, Pat O'Neill, Bruce and Norman Yonemoto
1994	Ken Jacobs, Barbara Kopple, Julie Zando
1995	Shigeko Kubota, Richard Leacock, Victor Masayesva Jr.

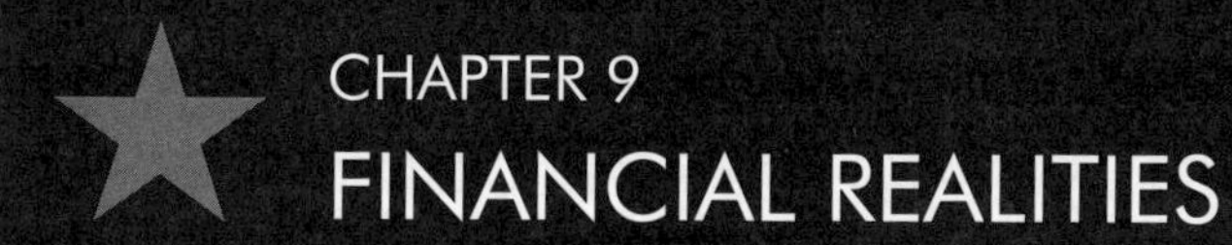

AFI Funding: Growing Up and Standing Tall

JEAN PICKER FIRSTENBERG

AFI's **early years** were an intense experience for everyone involved, as it defined its role, found its stride, and established its expertise. At the outset, with the first money committed by the federal treasury, AFI acted like a government-funded entity. Over the first three decades, the bottom line of NEA funding for general support of AFI was huge: a total of $47.7 million—some $1.5 million each year—went a long way toward making the AFI what it has become. In addition, another $15.4 million was passed through from NEA to AFI to artists and to other preservation centers. NEH grants of $4.37 million gave the *AFI Catalog* project prodigious boosts, and a matching NEA challenge grant of $750,000 was a wonderful, unexpected component of the Campus Campaign, as well as a $350,000 Challenge Grant for Preservation in 1993. In later years, there were additional grants, but always for special projects rather than general support.

Federal funding, however, was often secured in an atmosphere of extreme tension. Congress battled both endowments. The NEA itself had internal conflicts, always adjusting to the new occupant in the White House as well as shifting control of the powerful Congressional Appropriations Committee. Late in 1979, the NEA's Washburn Report (as discussed in Chapter 2) was created as an attempt to discredit AFI's fiscal practices and use of funds, pitting the NEA against the AFI and threatening AFI's very existence; however, large federal support through the NEA would continue for eighteen more years.

When I became AFI's new director and CEO in 1980, it was becoming clear that unpredictable federal funding had created a tenuous financial foundation, but it was really a question of defining our own identity clearly enough that our financial support structure would follow logically.

Friends and Foes

Although I was familiar with AFI prior to my appointment in 1980, now I needed to understand all its components and how they interrelated—in both overt and unspoken ways. I needed to understand what was behind the ugly Washburn Report, which seemed to be at the heart of the NEA-AFI conflict. I suspected that there was as much between the lines as on the page. How to understand it more fully? When in need, turn to friends.

Eamon Kelly was a brilliant thinker and PhD economist whose insights would have a profound effect on AFI's direction. We were introduced when he was at the Ford Foundation, where he built an entirely new philanthropic funding mechanism called Program Related Investments. In 1980, he was executive vice president at Tulane University (and was named president the following year). Kelly's razor-sharp mind could define structure and organization so that they fit with objectives, goals, and best practices. When we met at the Kennedy Center AFI offices in Washington, DC, and he realized that the Center for Advanced Film Studies was in Los Angeles, his response was immediate: "You cannot run an $8 million organization on two coasts." He was the first to suggest how difficult it was to be an effective bicoastal organization. As an outsider, Kelly brought a clear eye to the Washburn Report, together with AFI CFO Bruce Neiner. Between them, they dismantled and shredded every aspect of credibility it claimed to have.

While the Washburn Report had created a negative atmosphere that undermined our sense of forward momentum, it was the lesser of challenges in the NEA-AFI relationship. More daunting was the effort to find a way—year after year—to ensure that NEA's financial contribution was predictable and secure. From 1980 to 1997, NEA funding was the foundation of AFI's financial plan, but there was constant tension within AFI as we wondered how long federal support would last. Irony of ironies, it didn't end with a Republican administration, but in the middle of the Clinton years, under an NEA chair whom we thought was supportive of AFI (she was not only an artist herself but also the parent of an alumnus whom we also thought had had a great experience at the AFI Conservatory). But now, with a Republican-controlled Congress, the end of AFI's funding was clearly inevitable when, in 1996, the NEA budget was cut by roughly forty percent, and it lost forty-seven percent of its staff.

Some members of the National Council on the Arts were also always there to support AFI, meeting after meeting. Franklin Schaffner, Rosalind Wyman, Buddy Jacobs, Margot Albert, and George Schaefer championed the cause of film as art in an era when that question was all too easily unsettled.

The media arts program was led by Brian O'Doherty, together with other NEA staff who were smart, solid, and sometimes adversarial but always fair. O'Doherty is one of the most fascinating people I have ever met by far. At one time, he headed up both the NEA visual arts as well as its media arts program, while also remaining professionally fully engaged in the New York City art world. An original man and brilliant intellectual, he trained as an M.D. in Ireland, came to America to study at Harvard, and then gave up medicine to become a defining figure in the art world as artist, critic, and writer. His essay series "Inside the White Cube" in *ArtForum* is still as highly regarded today as when it first appeared in 1976. (In 2000, the essays were collected and reprinted as *Inside the White Cube: The Ideology of the Gallery Space, Expanded Edition.*) He was the perfect media arts leader to represent this new field, because he understood and respected all avenues of expression and vision.

O'Doherty was as politically astute as he was an incisive spokesperson for the cause of arts and culture. It was Brian who suggested to me, in February 1981, that it was time to move Bob Wise from chair of the NEA-AFI panel to the AFI board. The change in role was a positive for both Wise and AFI. In 1993, Brian wrote Bob and myself a letter of commendation about a presentation to the National Council on the Arts. We could dine out for months on his praise.

Brian was an advocate and adversary, insightful and honorable. Today, vibrant in his late eighties, he continues to make his art, and is as articulate and alive as he was when he gave NEA shape and direction. In May 2016, we visited in New York City and reminisced about all the good (and bad) guys (and gals), the ones that you could work with, and the ones who didn't know how to make the system work. There is no question that AFI's survival owes much to this gentleman's considerable skill and tenacity. In fact, all moving image artists are in his debt, because he made the case for this art form better than anyone. It was truly a privilege to have worked with him, and it was a thrill to reconnect. He also told me that the day AFI was informed of its final grant, he was informed that he was fired—an outrage, even today. We went through many tumultuous years together under various NEA chairs. Brian was the one

RECEIVED NOV 1 5 199

NATIONAL ENDOWMENT FOR THE ARTS

The Federal agency that supports the visual, literary and performing arts to benefit all Americans

Arts in Education
Challenge & Advancement
Dance
Design Arts
Expansion Arts
Folk Arts
International
Literature
Locals
Media Arts
Museum
Music
Opera/Musical Theater
Presenting & Commissioning
State & Regional
Theater
Visual Arts

The Nancy Hanks Center
1100 Pennsylvania Ave. NW
Washington, DC 20506
202/682-5400

November 8, 1993

Jean Firstenberg
Director
The American Film Institute
2021 North Western Avenue
Los Angeles, CA 90027

Dear Jean,

Rarely - in fact, not ever - has Film Preservation been so eloquently represented to the hydra-headed Council. The Council, made up of such diverse interests, is a hard sell - and you sold them. Several spoke to me later of Lawrence and yourself. Jane complimented _me_ on your performance. So I shine in the reflection of your light.

You and Bob Wise have an extraordinary act in common: you both inconvenienced yourselves to swoop down, give us of your wisdom and sweep off again without a moment's delay. Hard on the stamina, that. But your DNA proteins are obviously of the highest quality. I don't know how you can red-eye in and out without turning a hair. I'd be - as Sean O'Casey put it - in a "state of chassis."

So, many thanks for your generosity, so selflessly offered. The three crimson markers of the thirties stand over an open cornucopia of films tumbling upward to the (projector's) light. And one of them will, as you told us, star in the Kennedy Center affair. Let us know if we can help with that event.

The Thirties cost $2 million. I won't attempt to put a price on what you did for preservation. It was a splendid act of leadership. For which, much thanks.

Sincerely,

Brian

Brian O'Doherty
Director
Media Arts: Film/Radio/Television

constant, staying with the NEA just short of its last funding of AFI.

During the years when NEA funding was the AFI's primary support system, the cost in time and energy to secure that contribution was considerable. As soon as I arrived, quarterly reports were requested. Quarterly report after quarterly report, meeting after meeting, Congressional interactions, giving testimony and more testimony, time and time again . . . I began to wonder why the NEA funding always seemed like a battle. The NEA wasn't at all like a typical contributor taking pride in being part of the AFI's accomplishments, engaged as a stakeholder in our success.

John Ptak was a member of the NEA-AFI panel and chaired it for several years. John worked at AFI when Greystone opened, has had an illustrious career as an agent and manager and supporter of the individual artist, and is now a producer. He also shared the verbatim transcripts of the panel internal meetings that he has kept all these years. Reading these now clearly defines the conflict between the NEA and the AFI.

The primary funding battles inside the NEA stemmed from trying to strike a balance between supporting "establishment" arts organizations—performing art centers, opera companies, philharmonic orchestras, and theater companies—versus the young, new emerging art organizations. In the 1960s and 1970s, new entities were blossoming all over the country with the encouragement of the NEA (and the Ford Foundation). But funding discussions pitted the large vs. the small, the establishment vs. the fringe, the mainstream vs. the indie, and the old vs. the new. AFI was young, and a majority of its programs could be seen as more indie than establishment, but it was also seen as being connected to the big, commercial, mainstream film community. Discussions usually played out somewhere in the unpredictable middle ground of those contradictory perceptions.

What entities the NEA should or should not support was a hot issue throughout the 1980s and 1990s. This excerpt from AFI's five-year plan presented to the NEA in 1987 captured the organization's perspective, which led with a quote by NEA program director Bess Lomax Hayes: "ART ON THE ASCENT: The most notable examples of all arts and all art forms are not skyrockets but atolls, the tips of submerged mountains. And there is no way to say which is more important to a mountain—the base or the tip."

The origin and growth of the moving image as an art form is one of the notable aspects of the remarkable ascendance of art in America. With the sublime force of atolls emerging in the sea, the arts have surfaced in America in a way that is resplendent and cannot be ignored. There is a cultural nascence occurring throughout the United States, and it requires only a quick review of the cultural landscape of this nation twenty years ago, compared with the present, to make one realize how extensively art has reshaped the cultural terrain of the country.

Why and how this is occurring is not altogether clear. Gunther Schuller, a musical composer and director of Tanglewood, has argued that in order to make the arts flourish, attention must be paid to its entire social climate through the process of education—the bulk of the mountain, so to speak. Others such as Martin Friedman, director of the Walker Art Center, have eloquently expressed that when there are limited resources, it is necessary to cultivate the very tops of the artistic mountain peaks.

This debate continues unresolved, but still poses a practical dilemma for many arts organizations. The Institute itself has determined that its activities must be governed by supporting "excellence" whether through education, development, preservation, or presentation.

The Endowments' Fight for Survival

In 1980, the NEA and NEH faced their own issues. They were under attack from presidential candidate Ronald Reagan, who wanted to eliminate the endowments or significantly diminish their funding if he were elected. These annual fights for appropriation were basically a larger version of AFI's battle for support. If they were under siege, so were we.

The history of government funding of the arts has lots of heroes stretching back centuries, but the current era of organizations really began during the Eisenhower Administration. In 1954, undersecretary for the Department of Health, Education, and Welfare (HEW) Nelson Rockefeller wrote language for federal support of the arts. Commitment to that idea continued through the Kennedy and Johnson eras, and even into Nixon's administration, when lawyer and arts advocate Leonard Garment was an advisor. Garment was an unlikely close Nixon associate and friend, a liberal New York Jew who began his career as a jazz saxophonist with Woody Herman and who chaired the Brooklyn Academy of Music. He went on to have strong Republican ties and urged Nixon to surrender the Watergate tapes. The Congressional list of arts supporters is equally long on both sides of the aisle.

In 1965, President Johnson had signed the National Foundation on the Arts and the Humanities Act, which established the endowments:

> *Art is a nation's most precious heritage. For it is in our works of art that we reveal ourselves, and to others, the inner vision which guides us as a nation. And where there is no vision, the people perish.*

That inspiring vision led, two years later, to legislation that articulated the case for the moving image as a valid art form, and established AFI. Now, in 1981, the argument had been joined again at its most basic level, questioning whether the government should fund arts and artists and challenging the idea that John F. Kennedy had championed as part of building the New Frontier. In his words that are now engraved on the River Terrace of the Kennedy Center:

> *I look forward to an America which will reward achievement in the arts as we reward achievement in business or statecraft. I look forward to an America which will steadily raise the standards of artistic accomplishment and which will steadily*

enlarge cultural opportunities for all of our citizens. And I look forward to an America which commands respect throughout the world not only for its strength but for its civilization as well.

As soon as Reagan took office, the NEA and NEH knew they were facing a genuine fight for survival. On June 5, 1981, less than five months after his inauguration, President Ronald Reagan issued an executive order forming the Presidential Task Force on the Arts and Humanities to study the possibility of converting the NEA and NEH from government agencies into what was termed "public corporations."

We at AFI found out about it some weeks before, when Charlton Heston called me to say he would have to take a leave of absence from his position as AFI Board chair. He had been asked by President Reagan to be the arts chairman of the Presidential Task Force. He was joined by Hanna Gray, then the president of the University of Chicago and a nationally respected academic leader, as chairman for the Humanities and Daniel Terra, representative for the federal government. Terra turned out to be a great choice for the NEA, because he had been part of Reagan's inner circle as chair of his Campaign Finance Committee. In addition to being a very successful scientist-inventor-businessman, he had a huge art collection and loved the arts. Interestingly enough, Reagan named him Ambassador-at-Large for Cultural Affairs, and he is the only person to have ever served in that role. Franklin Schaffner, another AFI trustee and a member of the National Council for the Endowment, was also a member of the Task Force.

In many ways, this turned out to be an asset for AFI, because Heston was so committed to AFI and the arts in general. We became an extension of his team at work on the Task Force Report. You cannot imagine the amount of paper spent to provide detailed information about the endowments' fundamental objectives, how

---

"I was chair of the executive committee, and we went to Washington to talk to the National Endowment for the Arts, because they were giving us a couple of million dollars a year and keeping us alive. I decided that Chuck Heston, Greg Peck, and I should go visit with Congress members in their office space. I got there a little earlier than they did. And so I waited, and it was the quietest place I've ever seen. A couple of minutes later, Greg Peck comes up and suddenly everybody's running out of their offices to see him and get his autograph. Then Chuck Heston walks into the office, and you just couldn't get anything done. But it didn't seem to matter, because we got the $2.8 million."

—RICHARD BRANDT,
corporate executive and AFI board of trustees chair (1983–1986

---

they functioned, how they were organized and how they selected their grantees. In a marked change, the staff of the NEA began to see AFI as an ally. AFI earned its stripes during the battle to save the endowments, playing a positive role through Heston that helped them survive.

The Task Force Report issued in 1982 recommended that the endowments' existing structure and review systems be kept; that tax codes be adjusted to stimulate more private philanthropy; and that coordination among federal, state, and local arts agencies be strengthened. It basically affirmed the value and need for NEA and NEH endowments and ended contention (only too briefly) about the issue of their level of funding and appropriation.

Some in the administration were surprised by the strong support for arts and humanities from Reagan's Task Force. In spite of the reaffirmation of their value and purpose, there were plenty of indications that the NEA's structure and functioning would be different and more difficult going forward. It was also a clear sign that private philanthropy would have to play a larger role. That, of course, had profound ramifications for AFI, particularly for film preservation.

NEA had survived, but every step going forward was a potential battlefield. The next explosion came in 1989 with the Serrano-Mapplethorpe controversy. It stands as a classic case study testing the relationship between an artist's freedom and the perceived obligations that public funding imposes. In 1965, when President Lyndon Johnson had signed the legislation creating the NEA, he said, "We fully recognize that no government can call artistic excellence into existence. . . . Nor should any government seek to restrict the freedom of the artist to pursue his own goals in his own way." That idea was being tested by conservatives who considered Andres Serrano's and Robert Mapplethorpe's works immoral.

"Brouhaha" is too simple a term to describe the hot-button rhetoric that ignited a more widespread culture war that still has ongoing repercussions to this day. Members of Congress who stood up for artistic freedom in that politically charged atmosphere deserve medals of valor. Then, in 1995, the Republicans took control of Congress for the first time since the NEA-NEH legislation had been passed in 1965. Think about that tenure: Democrats controlled the House of Representatives, the authorizing entity, for thirty years in a row! And now, the Republican Contract with America called for the elimination of both endowments. This time, the huge frontal attack was on the NEH.

Sheldon Hackney was chair of the NEH from 1993 to 1997. In another example of those amazing intersections that sometimes happen in life, Sheldon had been provost at Princeton University when I was there. He had brought Eamon Kelly to Tulane when he was president there, and then moved on to be president at the University of Pennsylvania and finally to the NEH—a truly distinguished career for one of the very smart individuals I was fortunate to cross paths with professionally and then continue on as friends.

Both endowments survived, but with radically reduced funding: NEH's budget was cut by thirty-six percent, while the NEA's was reduced by forty percent. Pressures on NEA meant pressures on AFI. Two years later—1998—AFI received its last trickle ($200,000) of federal funds.

Several years later, I met Dana Gioia, NEA chair from 2003 to 2009 and a brilliant poet, thinker, stamp collector, and artist I feel honored to call my friend. We served together on the United States Post Office Citizens Stamp Advisory Committee—fifteen citizens who select the subjects and present designs for stamps to the Postmaster General, who has the final say. Dana had been appointed by President George W. Bush and invited to continue his public service by President Barack Obama. The NEA thrived under his leadership, but sadly, after being unable to write while serving his country, Dana resigned after six years to return to his forte. He joined the University of Southern California faculty as the Judge Widney Professor of Poetry and Public Culture. In 2015, he was named the State of California's Poet Laureate by Governor Jerry Brown, and his vision, leadership, and voice continue to be heard.

The Business of Nonprofits

I believe a nonprofit must be run in a businesslike way. It's a simple fact: if you can't balance your budget, you can't fulfill your mandate. But where should funds come from? Whose responsibility is it to support nonprofits? A wonderful trustee, Michael Forman, once said to me, "Always understand, just as I run my businesses, you are running the business of the AFI." He was absolutely right, and he echoed the wisdom I had learned growing up in a business-focused family.

As NEA funding faded away, AFI truly became stronger, evolving its own fundraising, development, and advancement programs. Through a disciplined approach, we eventually built a sound—though always challenging—fiscal process. I respect and appreciate the NEA and NEH and their mission; I believe a civilized nation must support its art, artists, and humanitarians. Privatizing the arts, as Reagan attempted, would have had troubling effects on the breadth of expression that enlivens the cultural landscape.

Of course, corporate sponsorship has always been a lifeline of the arts, but *it is not the business of corporate America to underwrite nonprofit entities in their entirety.* This opinion was a dividing line between the NEA's and AFI's funding expectations. It was also an issue where the power and culture divide between Washington, DC, and Hollywood became clear.

Because AFI was connected to film, the NEA felt that Hollywood should be its principal source of support. Because member companies of the Motion Picture Association of America were profitable, they therefore should fund the AFI to serve their own corporate interests. When Gregory Peck and Charlton Heston came to Washington on behalf of the new AFI, it was clear how much some figures in the NEA resented their star status, a symbol of the Hollywood adoration that Washington sometimes envied. Nancy Hanks, the otherwise highly regarded second chair of the NEA (serving 1969–1977) was uncharacteristically disrespectful, treating Peck and Heston not as artist-actors at the top of their profession, but as figures culturally beneath her. She used her behavior and attitude to let them know she was in charge—Washington politics at its most petty. (Just a few years later, Heston would be a savior of the NEA, making Hanks's actions even more indefensible.)

But perhaps NEA learned a lesson. In 1981, the NEA embraced Robert Redford and the Sundance Institute without hesitation. Sundance is both a for-profit corporation and a nonprofit institute, a combination that has allowed both sides to flourish with small but symbolic federal funding, and with strong commercial support.

Taking the National Stage

As NEA funding waned, AFI was finding its own identity on the national cultural stage. Enough supporters had called us a "best-kept secret" that we began to ask how we could use film and television to spread AFI's mission to millions of people across the country. This question would have a profound impact on AFI's ability to sustain itself financially, surviving without the annual fight for a shrinking government appropriation. The figures tell the story: fiscal year '96—$1,175,000; fiscal year '97—$725,000; fiscal year '98—$200,000.

AFI's last federal general funds were granted in 1998. After that, NEA supported several specific projects but never again granted funds for general support. Meanwhile, the international celebration of the 100th anniversary of film and the movies was at hand. It was fully appropriate that AFI should have a major role in helping the nation mark this milestone, which would also be a perfect opportunity to ignite the AFI brand and establish a higher profile in the American imagination. But how? What could we do that no one else could do as well?

The question had been asked a few years earlier by a new trustee and a brilliant brand and advertising executive, Liener Temerlin, when he asked a colleague to write a branding document on AFI. This document gave us a sense that we could see ourselves in a different way, but it took the disappearance of NEA money to push us forward boldly.

Why doesn't AFI name the best 100 movies of the first 100 years? Once it was said out loud, it sounded so simple. But in fact, it's an exceedingly complex idea to execute. How do we select an authoritative list of the 100 greatest movies? The list would have to bring people together in appreciation rather than divide them in argument. In a community famous for contention and litigation, how could we get everyone involved with those 100 movies to agree to participate—the companies that owned the movie copyrights as well as all the artists involved in front of and behind the camera? How could we produce a television special that would capture the attention of a primetime audience and attract sponsors?

Many questions. Many challenges. Many unknowns. We weren't sure if we would succeed. But we were sure that, of all the cultural and corporate entities around, AFI was the only one with the mandate, standing, and relationships to pull off something of this scale and complexity.

The television special was central to the financial plan. Trustee Fred Pierce, who had succeeded Gene Jankowski as board of trustees chair and knew all aspects of the television business and how the numbers worked, took off with the notion. It involved a basic buy-and-sell concept of the most complicated kind: buy the time from a major network at as good a price in as decent a primetime period as possible. Then, sell the advertising spots for more than the cost of the production and airtime. So simple, so brilliant, and so tough to actually do. Would sponsors pay a premium? Could all the spots be sold? Could we generate strong interest through the movie selection process and the countdown? Could the production be brought in on budget? Could the entire idea be fulfilled with the character and quality that the AFI stood for—and still be compelling enough to engage a primetime audience? It was a real gamble.

A project of this magnitude was unprecedented for AFI, but its sheer scale and audacity paid off. At first we thought it was a one-year, one-off effort, but for the next ten years, AFI's core NEA funding was replaced with what became the revenue from *AFI's 100 Years...* series of CBS telecasts. *AFI's 100 Years...100 Movies* also took AFI mainstream, making more Americans than ever aware of AFI and its role as a national institution with something to offer them. It was a sort of graduation from organizational adolescence to maturity, and its success would have an ongoing positive effect on every other effort to raise funds. (Read more about this landmark program in Chapter 10.)

Building a Fundraising Structure

The process of raising funds has some common truths, whatever the funding source—government (federal, state, county, city), individuals, foundations, corporations, sponsors, alumni, or members. Wherever the money comes from, securing it is an expensive process, because no two donors are alike. Whether the donation is $5 or $5 million, the donor becomes a stakeholder who needs to care about the organization they are giving to. It's expensive, because—done right—fundraising is a long process that requires structure, purpose, and strategy. It begins well before and continues long after the money is committed.

All giving is personal. Shaping the request, cultivating the donor, making the "ask," monitoring the process, caring for the donor, being proud of what was accomplished with the gift, and making the donor proud that they decided to give—all of this takes time and attention. There are no shortcuts. The gift is only successful if the donor believes the institution is worthy and responsible. President Johnson spoke the words in the Rose Garden that set the AFI in motion. Fifty years later, every donor and supporter can be proud of what was created, what it has achieved, and what it is poised to accomplish next.

Over the years, AFI had multiple campaigns, councils, associates, annual special events, premieres, and one-off events, as well as membership and alumni giving. We also had consultants undertake extensive and expensive studies of how much we could raise and how we should do it. You name it, we tried it.

I was guided by a strong personal belief that AFI was competing only against itself. There are no other organizations with AFI's mission. Today, there are other outstanding film schools in America, but AFI has its own distinctive approaches and philosophy on preparing the next generation of storytellers. And, of course, AFI supports much more than its Conservatory—the range of its work would give the Institute a multiplicity of roles: educator, technology incubator, convener, tastemaker, cultivator of artistic careers, award bestower, curator, festival producer, TV producer, and provider of standards and approbation.

I believed that if a potential funder understood the mission of the Institute and they respected its character, they would support it. The only reason our request or proposal might not be accepted was because we and the potential donor had different priorities.

THE DEVELOPMENT TEAM

When AFI kicked off the Campus Campaign in 1980, there was no development department to manage it. It took many years to build a fully functioning development team, recruit talented fundraising executives, organize volunteer support, field various programs, and ensure that everyone had the resources (or almost all the resources) they needed to do their job well.

For a CEO running a nonprofit, there is no more important colleague than the chief development/advancement officer (CDO/CAO). Over twenty-seven years, I worked with eight people in that position—the first person I saw when I arrived at the campus every morning and the last before turning off the office lights. I knew that if my CAO wasn't successful, the institution wouldn't be either. We went hand-in-glove.

Over time, I was privileged to work with outstanding fundraisers who taught me the art and science of raising money. Many went on to successful careers at even larger entities. Russ Mead, indispensable in the acquisition of the AFI campus, so impressed Chuck Heston that he was recruited for the Presidential Task Force on the Future of the Endowments staff in 1981.

We were in it as a team. My philosophy was that we worked as a team, and we succeeded or failed as a team. No one was out there alone, including me. I am eternally grateful to Russ Mead, Ken Scherer, Emily Laskin, Victoria Silverman, and John Campbell; without these development leaders, AFI would not have survived into this century.

BOARD LEADERSHIP AND CONTRIBUTIONS

Though it took some years to build a development department, I was truly fortunate to start out with a crucial inherited asset: AFI's dedicated board. Young organizations rely particularly heavily on their board members. Until an organizational structure takes shape, it is the board's involvement and participation that help it grow and find its future. Strong organizations remain strong because of the ongoing commitment of a board that is on the same page as the CEO.

There is nothing more satisfying than a board-nominating committee inviting someone to join a board. There are terms to any board membership: length of the term, quid pro quo, understandings, etc. Many boards have minimum "give or get" amounts; some do not. Some have a minimum amount plus tables or tickets to several events a year. Building a strong board takes much more than simply getting someone involved. Newcomers have to spend time at the organization and understand its goals and objectives and how it functions.

Actor-artists and creative professionals who are also activists can be great advocates for any organization or cause. When I arrived in 1980, such a guy, Billy Dee Williams, was on the board and often available. In 1983, Donald Sutherland called me—a cold call. He said he was moving to Los Angeles, and he wanted to get involved and join the AFI's board. He came to the campus and spent time visiting the programs. He went to Washington, DC, and saw what we were doing there. After his exploration, he said he had no idea AFI did so many things. He was a great trustee. If we asked him to do something (and he wasn't working), he was there. His name on an invitation was a powerful draw. He could talk about the Institute easily, because he knew firsthand what we did. Sidney Poitier, a founding trustee and founding vice chair, was a strong endorser. Marsha Mason was a great supporter (and friend) for many years, as was the always wonderful Debbie Allen. Franklin Schaffner, Robert Wise, Dan Petrie, and Frank Pierson gave us enormous creditability. And, of course, if I didn't mention Greg Peck and Chuck Heston again and again, I would be incredibly remiss.

"There's been a lot of glamorous financial news in the papers lately, multimedia conglomerates, billions of dollars in assets, and more such mergers are to come, or so we are told. Well, I would like to hear some glamorous talk about elevating the quality of films and television—entertainment that . . . enlarges the sympathies; that stimulates the mind and the spirit; that warms the heart; punctures the balloons of hypocrisy, greed, and sham; tickles the funny bone and leaves us with the glow that comes when we have been well entertained. *Making millions is not the whole ballgame, fellas.* Pride of workmanship is worth more. Artistry is worth more. The human imagination is a priceless resource. The public is ready for the best you can give them. It just may be that you can make a buck and at the same time encourage, foster, and commission work of quality and originality."

—GREGORY PECK,
actor and AFI board of trustees chair (1967–1969)

Gifts and Other Financial Support

INDIVIDUAL DONATIONS

Individual donor gifts can come from years of nurturing or spontaneously from unexpected places with a swiftness that can take your breath away. Board chair Bonita Granville Wrather once visited the campus with her close friend, Jack Haley Jr. It was the day that Metromedia had been sold to News Corp. (John Kluge took Metromedia private in a $1.1 billion leveraged buyout, then liquidated the company for $3.5 billion). Jack was stunned. He had worked for David Wolper on many documentaries and had been given stock when Wolper sold his company to Metromedia in 1964. Haley had put the stock certificates in a drawer. Now they were worth a lot of money. The next day, we got a check for $250,000, with a note: *Use this any way you like*. There were other examples of this kind of impulse philanthropy. After Adobe Systems Inc. acquired a competitor and considerably increased founder John Warnock's net worth, he sent an unsolicited gift of Adobe stock valued at nearly $200,000.

Windfalls are exhilarating, but they shouldn't be expected. Most donations from individuals come from careful nurturing—discovering what the donor cares about and identifying the intersections with the institution's needs. There is no more central component of any organization's success than the identification, research, planning, cultivation, and approach to individual donors. Board members are the first level of support; in many ways, their giving sets the tone for all giving. Historically, AFI has been very successful when a board member challenges other board members to match their grant—but only if every board member makes a personal contribution.

George Stevens did that in 1983 when he put forward a $10,000 challenge at a board meeting. No one knew he was going to do that, but exhibitor Hank Plitt matched it immediately, and soon thereafter everyone else pitched in. That round robin made for a dynamic meeting, but such giving is usually worked out in advance with the CEO and development team, who determine how to maximize the opportunity. That is what happened in 2005, when Bob Daly challenged the Institute to raise $9 million, to which he would add another $1 million. It took a few weeks, but every forty-eight hours Daly would call me and ask, "How we doing?"

ENDOWMENTS

Part of Bob Daly's motivation for the $10 million challenge was to build the AFI endowment. So, part of the challenge grant stipulated that $5 million would immediately go into the endowment; the second $5 million could be used at the discretion of the board. That's the way to challenge your colleagues to build the organization's financial backbone.

Many large academic institutions amass significant (read: huge) endowments that provide a nice (read: considerable) percentage of their annual budgets from the interest earned, rarely invading the principal. Donors who focus their contributions on endowments are thinking long-term. Up to now, AFI has reinvested the interest it has earned on its endowment rather than use it for general support. Hopefully, the AFI endowment will soon be large enough to take same of its interest earnings to cover annual expenses.

Some endowment funds are earmarked for special programs. The story of one of those small endowments is very personal. By the time I turned fifty, my circle of friends was so intertwined with the film community that my birthday became an AFI party. I celebrated a week early on March 6, 1986—a Friday. The previous night, we had honored Billy Wilder at the 14th AFI Life Achievement Award event. The next night, about 150 family members, friends and AFI trustees, colleagues, and alumni gathered at Dodger Stadium in the Stadium Club (recognizing another passion of mine—sports, and especially da Bums!). The tables were named for places in my childhood, like P.S. 6, Dalton School, Ebbets Field, Loews Capitol, Times Square, and Madison Square Garden.

It was a glorious event with lots of entertainment and a guest list that included George and Elizabeth Stevens, Roger and Catherine Stevens, Chuck and Lydia Heston, Bob and Millie Wise, Gene

Alfred P. Sloan Foundation
Creative Philanthropy

Founded in 1934, the Alfred P. Sloan Foundation, has had a clear and specific purpose: fund research and education in science, technology, engineering, mathematics, and economics. In 1996, recognizing the power of filmmaking, they initiated a program to influence the next generation of filmmakers, increasing the visibility of science and technology themes and depicting science accurately in feature films. This program, for example, helped the Academy Award–nominated film *Hidden Figures* find its way from novel to the screen.

The creative series of grants and programs were initiated through the leadership of Doron Weber, Sloan's VP of Programs. Since 1996, AFI has been the grateful recipient of nearly $2.5 million in support of seminars, festival events, and forty-three AFI Conservatory Fellows grants, testament to the Sloan Foundation's influence and Doron's foresight into the power of film to shape our sense of country and world.

and Sally Jankowski, Alan and Berte Hirschfield, Gordon and Helen Stulberg, Mike Frankovich and Binnie Barnes, Richard and Helen Brandt, Danny Selznick and Rita Gam, Jeanine Basinger, Norman Lear, Sherry Lansing, Jill Sackler, Nancy Malone, Linda Hope, Lesli Linka Glatter, and Peter Werner.

I paid for the festivities (this was my party), but in the meanwhile, my twenty-five-year-old son had gone to family, friends, and even trustees to raise $50,000 for a Directing Workshop for Women endowment in my name. I was deeply thrilled then and still am; every time a DWW short is presented, the end credits include, "Supported by the Jean Picker Firstenberg Endowment for the Directing Workshop for Women."

SPONSORSHIPS

Sponsorships are probably the trickiest support mechanism for a nonprofit. AFI began its outreach efforts in the early 1980s, searching for what were initially seen as donations or in-kind contributions from a corporation's foundation. To facilitate this kind of giving, companies would often set up its own foundation and define some parameters, and then the board, CEO, and other corporate leaders would determine where funds would be committed.

Of course, corporations realized that their marketing objectives could be furthered through these donations. The choice of sponsorships, rather than serving as a charitable commitment, became a marketing decision. Along the way, there were years and years of extraordinary support, friendships, commitments, and generosity before the marketing impressions became the measure of a successful sponsorship.

In fact, without the mechanism of sponsorship and corporate contributions, AFI would not have grown and become what it is. Among others, the support of ABC, Absolut Vodka, Adobe, American Express, American Airlines, Anheuser Busch, Apple, AT&T,

Audi of America, Best Buy, Blockbuster, CAA, CBS, Coca-Cola, Columbia, Condé Nast, Deloitte Consulting, Discovery, Walt Disney Company, Dreamworks, Eastman Kodak, Ernst & Young, General Motors, Google, HBO, Hewlett-Packard, Intel, Lifetime, MGM (MGM-UA), Microsoft, Micro Tech, NBC (NBC-Universal), Netflix, New Line Cinema, Oracle, Palm, Paramount, Penske, Pepsi, Remy Martin, Retrove, RKO Pictures, Sony, Twentieth Century Fox, Target, Turner Networks, Universal, USPS, Verizon, Village Roadshow, Vizio, Warner Bros. (Warner Communications/Time Warner), and Wells Fargo all helped AFI to create many programs, including the three major projects that have forged our national presence: eleven editions of *AFI's 100 Years...* series, three editions of *Target Presents AFI Night at the Movies*, and the AFI AWARDS, an annual event since 2000.

BOND ISSUES

The first Los Angeles campus bond issue came about out of sheer necessity. CFO Bruce Neiner worked diligently to find a way to renegotiate the Union Bank debt service that financed the initial purchase and partial renovation of the new campus during the early 1980s. Board minutes detail his various initiatives including a potential sale and lease-back of the property to Warner Communications, a creative way to lower the service costs, but for one reason or another, it never came about.

Financially, these were tough years. First, there was the never-ending battle to balance the Institute annual budget, which continued to have a carry-forward deficit in the neighborhood of $300,000 to $400,000. Second, there was the need to make interest and principal payments on the short-term bank loan we had acquired quickly to facilitate the purchase, just as 1980 interest rates rose from twelve percent to twenty percent. Third, we needed to raise funds to pay for the architect and contractor to make the new campus as ready as it could be. Quite a few challenges all at once.

We restructured the bank loan, requesting many extensions, asking board members to guarantee payments, getting a line of credit for the first time, and using it for the first time to pay the Institute bills so we could make bank payments with funds we raised. We followed all the rules and fulfilled all the requirements associated with federal grants, meanwhile feeling that we were always being squeezed by the NEA on what programs they would allow as appropriate to their funds and matching grants. The trustees were magnificent and hung in there throughout the arduous process of refinancing.

Several banks thought that, since AFI CAFS had received NASAD (National Association of Schools of Art and Design) accreditation in 1982, we could qualify to be part of the California Educational Facilities Bond Issue, an educational facilities entity chaired by Jesse Unruh, who was then treasurer of the state of California. But every time Bruce thought he had our application locked, there was a hiccup. What we needed was someone who could reach the state treasurer on our behalf.

Roz Wyman had been very helpful with the campus acquisition. As a prominent member of the Los Angeles political and cultural world, she could open many doors for AFI. Roz had become a major figure in 1953 when she ran for City Council at the age of twenty-two, the youngest person and the second woman ever elected to the council. She was also the acknowledged civic leader in the effort to bring the Dodgers to Los Angeles. After AFI purchased the campus, she introduced us to everyone in City Hall who could be helpful. She also knew everyone in Democratic politics and had just been named chair and CEO of the 1984 Democratic National Convention. So, with one phone call from Roz to Jesse, all the efforts to find a refinancing mechanism were achieved.

Unruh told Wyman that, if it qualified, AFI would be in the next CEFA bond issue. Unruh introduced Bruce Neiner to Grover

McKeon (then at Lazar Freres), who shepherded AFI into heady company indeed; with Stanford University, USC, Pepperdine, Pomona, University of the Pacific, Loyola Marymount, and the first NASAD-accredited art institute, AFI! In 2016, Grover McKeon reminded me that Stanford and USC were very displeased that a NASAD-accredited graduate program was in the bond issue. But Unruh told them that these state bond issues were for the small academic institutions who couldn't get their own bond issues, and if they weren't happy they could drop out. They didn't! Even more remarkable, AFI was the fourth largest recipient, with $6.7 million of this $60,935,000 bond issue. To celebrate, state treasurer Jesse Unruh came to the AFI campus early in 1985 for a press conference with Gregory Peck, a dozen board members, and L.A. City Council members Peggy Stevenson and Joel Wachs. It was a proud day for AFI.

Bruce Neiner went on to become a bond expert. With the team he had met through Grover McKeon (Jesse's guy), they refinanced the initial bond issue twice, in 1992 and 1999 (the legal limit), and lowered the interest rate each time. AFI was even able the second time to use the $1.5 quasi-endowment to begin a general endowment fund for the Institute. Trustee chair Richard Brandt often worked with Bruce and read every word of the bond issue, as did trustee Alan Hirschfield the first time, so when they recommended the board approve the bond issue, trustees knew one of their own had spent time making sure it was what it needed to be.

In-Kind Contributions

What a great day it was when Sony video equipment arrived on campus . . . when Kaypro and Wang computers arrived . . . when Apple and later HP computer boxes were delivered to the campus . . . when Microsoft software and Adobe licenses were donated . . . when cans of Pepsi were delivered for AFI events . . . and when they were changed out for Coca-Cola machines. General Motors sponsored the Life Achievement Awards for a short time, and Bob Wise (Life Achievement Award recipient in 1998) got the free use of a Cadillac for two years. In addition, these contributions helped the bottom line in the audited statement, because they had a real monetary value on the audited statement of a corporation and, therefore, also to the AFI.

Allen J. Bernstein was the chair and CEO of Morton's Restaurant Group, a gracious and generous man. He also loved movie stars and truly had a crush on Sherry Lansing. His respected public relations firm, Murphy O'Brien, introduced us to him, and a match was made in steak heaven. Karen Murphy O'Brien and Brett O'Brien went on to be great supporters of AFI and good friends of mine, whose company and interests are always ahead of the curve. Allen hosted numerous events at his restaurants—and I mean numerous, from Life Achievement Award recipient receptions, to fifty-person dinners in private rooms at Morton's, to dinner for six because we wanted to make a real connection with a potential donor, to closing the entire Beverly Hills Morton's for an AFI holiday party (an unprecedented thing to do during holiday season). Allen never cut corners and he was as happy with his relationship with AFI as we were thrilled with his significant in-kind contributions. He sat at the board table from 1999 until his untimely death in 2011. His friendship has been missed as much as his hospitality.

In terms of in-kind support, I must also acknowledge the great legal counsel AFI has been fortunate to have over fifty years. When I came to AFI, DC powerhouse attorney Harry McPherson was on the board, and a man of equal sagacity and charm. McPherson was President Lyndon Johnson's legal counsel (the equivalent of today's chief of staff) and wrote all of LBJ's speeches. He served as secretary and general counsel of the Kennedy Center for Roger Stevens as well as for George Stevens at AFI. Harry could make good things happen in Washington, DC. His young partner, Howell Begle, was doing much of the pro bono work (as he still does) and grew to be one of the most knowledgeable media rights negotiators in the country. As AFI counsel, Howell has been a wise advisor over the years, and is indeed a good friend.

When I came to AFI, the legendary Deane Johnson was the pro bono legal guru in California. Deane was everyone's attorney in those days, based at O'Melveny & Myers, but oddly enough, their real estate team (which we, of course, had to pay for the considerable services involved with a real estate purchase) were very close to the good sisters at Immaculate Heart College—so close that we felt they were representing them, more than us, their paying client. We were very worried. For a few weeks, we actually paid for two lawyers when Keenan Behrle at Pacht Ross came on board at the suggestion of Gordon Stulberg.

When Roz Wyman's son, Bob, graduated from Georgetown Law School and he wanted to provide pro bono legal work for AFI, the lawyers at his firm, Rosenfeld, Meyer, & Susman, another entertainment law giant, were good enough to let their young attorney do that, which is how Bob Wyman came to negotiate with Sheldon Adelson and the Interface Group for the Cinetex deal with AFI (an episode I try to pretend never happened). Bob soon left to start his own firm, but John Burke, a senior partner, took over the AFI pro bono account. When he moved to the international firm Akin Gump, John took AFI with him, and he has been a superb advisor, advocate, and connector to the likes of Todd Wagner, who has been a brilliant trustee and major advisor to AFI regarding the digital world. (Wagner was Mark Cuban's partner when they sold Broadcast.com to Yahoo in 1999 for over $5 billion.) John continues his pro bono contributions, negotiating some rather large projects for AFI, including the AFI Silver Theatre and Cultural Center with Montgomery County and the complex commitment from Sir Paul Getty for the *AFI Catalog*, among many others.

ADVERTISING AND BRANDING EXPERTISE

Several advertising, brand, and marketing professionals through the years helped AFI make the most of sponsorship and fundraising efforts.

Steve Frankfurt had been on the AFI board from 1969 to 1975, but I had met him over the years. He was a brilliant graphic designer and brand man who was equally respected for his creative and business acumen. An artist at heart, he had designed the movie credits for *To Kill a Mockingbird*. In 1968, he became the youngest person ever named president of Young & Rubicam. He knew everyone in the world of advertising and corporate sponsorships. Fortunately, he returned to the board in 1994, and he would lead AFI in thinking about refreshing our visual image to remain relevant in a new millennium.

A friend of longtime AFI counsel Howell Begle introduced us to Liener Temerlin of Dallas, Texas. Liener would teach us all the power of contacts and content. He ran a regional ad agency that was the first to get a national client, American Airlines. It was a coup for Liener and for AFI, and American Airlines remains AFI's official airline. But more than that, Liener Temerlin believed in the power of the moving image and its influence and contribution to our nation's culture. He made us believe in ourselves.

A Strategic Plan for AFI Campaign 2000 was presented to the board by Temerlin when he was a new trustee in 1989. It was a thirty-five-page document, the likes of which I had never seen before. It took quite a while to believe we could actually do anything that Temerlin and his team were suggesting, because basically it was an awareness campaign to make AFI a national entity with a business plan as well as the thesis to make this happen. The centerpiece was the 100th anniversary of the moving image and how to make that AFI's platform. It was audacious and farsighted and, believe it or not, within five or six years we were planning projects that in fact were exactly what Temerlin had suggested in 1989.

All these professionals came to AFI out of respect for the massive cultural influence of film and television, and because they were interested in sitting at the table with the heads of movie studios and television networks. That these leaders settled in and went to bat for AFI is a measure of their character and commitment. And it never hurt that every one of them loved the movies and the influence the big screen (and now, much smaller screens) had on them growing up.

> "When film in America needed an authoritative voice, AFI became that voice, calling generations of filmmakers to carry on the nation's film tradition and championing the preservation of our priceless film heritage. For a film lover like me, to be associated with AFI is one of life's great privileges. The opportunities to discuss with distinguished filmmakers and to learn what makes a great film have provided some of my most cherished memories."
>
> —LIENER TEMERLIN, *advertising executive and AFI trustee (1989–2000)*

LICENSING

In 1993, the board and staff spent an incredible amount of time trying to put together revenue programs involving licensing. In the minutes for March 11, 1993, trustee John DiBiaggio explained that museums and universities were raising substantial revenues through product placement and licensing without loss of prestige. DiBiaggio was president of Tufts University at that time. He had joined the AFI Board of Trustees on Gene Jankowski's nomination; they had met at Michigan State University, where John had been president and Gene had taught a class after he left CBS. John was impressive and instrumental in helping the board understand its new role as an accredited academic institution. He was a brilliant leader and served on the board from 1989 through 2007.

At that meeting in 1993, John reiterated what Mike Forman had told me: academic institutions have to be run in a business-like manner. Dollars were drying up, and other opportunities for funding had to be explored. He also thought there could be major international opportunities. The executive committee even went so far as to pass a motion to authorize a pilot licensing program utilizing an ad hoc committee of studio licensing professionals, but asked us to proceed with caution. We spent considerable time working on this idea, without success, just to say, finally, that you have to try every possible idea.

Events and Perks

AFI LIFE ACHIEVEMENT AWARD

The AFI Life Achievement Award was established in 1973 by George Stevens Jr. and immediately brought attention to artists in front of and behind the camera. Its continuing presence has been a benchmark for AFI—a standard of class, quality, and pride. It is usually AFI's largest fundraiser of the year and has always been telecast, thanks over the years to Bob Daly's great negotiating skills (see Chapter 10 for full details).

THE COUNCIL OF 100 AND THE SECOND DECADE COUNCIL

The Council of 100, formed in 1974, were individuals who donated $1,000 a year. They were invited four times a year to Greystone for a screening of a classic film, a discussion with the filmmakers, and a reception. The cost of these benefits was extraordinary, but a young organization is wary of not providing value for early donors. In 1977, a Second Decade Council (SDC) was formed at the same giving level. Besides the screenings, they also received two tickets to the Life Achievement Award dinner. It was a real bargain for sure.

As with most early AFI fundraisers, it was like dipping a toe in the Pacific Ocean to see how cold it was.

Over the years and through several experiments, we began to understand the appropriate balance between donation levels and perks. The SDC would eventually rise to a $1,500 annual level, without the LAA ticket perk but with lots of wonderful events that were really fun. But we had lots of giving structures as well, like a President's Council for a donation of $25,000 a year and a $25 membership for people anywhere who cared about movies and especially movie history.

We came to realize that it really doesn't matter what you call the group. These folks are your first line of defense. They believe in the cause, they care about the objectives, and they want to be more involved. I was grateful for every single one of them and did my best to get to know them, their interests, and their families. We always had a chair of the SDC whose job was to ask their friends and colleagues to join. (They also knew that if their friends joined, they would have to join whatever organization their friends chaired next time around.) George Chasin, David Begelman, Bob Daly, Brandon Tartikoff, and Sherry Lansing were great SDC chairs. And just look at the numbers: over twenty-seven years, there were over 1,150 members with different levels of annual commitment, raising more than $7.5 million. Impressive and appreciated!

THIRD DECADE COUNCIL

The Third Decade Council (TDC) was founded in 1988 by younger members of the film community. Mark Canton was instrumental in its establishment and early success. Mark Stein and David Greenblatt (class of 1978) followed in good stead. TDC gave up-and-coming individuals from all sectors of the community the opportunity to come together to support AFI and to create an influential peer group in support of the film arts. For over a decade, the Third Decade Council provided energy and remarkable reunion events that enticed some leading members of a younger generation to first experience the satisfactions of arts philanthropy.

TDC events were always enthusiastic while also demanding a good deal of staff support. The results were well worth the effort. During their fifteen-year span, they raised over $1 million and held several remarkable events annually. My favorite event was held in 1993 at the then-new Sony lot, coming about when Sony bought Columbia Pictures from Coca-Cola and then hired Peter Guber and Jon Peters, who were under contract with Warner Bros. To avoid multiple lawsuits, a variety of transitions resulted in the site of the former MGM Studios becoming the home of Sony Entertainment. Members of the creative team that produced *The Graduate* in 1967 gathered, including director Mike Nichols, screenwriter Buck Henry, and actors Dustin Hoffman and Anne Bancroft. Mike Nichols (honored with a Life Achievement Award in 2010) was beloved by many members of the creative community, none more so than the myriad of actors who had worked with him. But Anne did not fall into that category, and twenty years later she came to tell Mike that she still remembered how difficult a shoot it was and how she did not appreciate how he treated her on the set. Rarely—and I mean rarely—do you ever see such pent-up raw emotions unveiled in public. It was a night to remember. (Six years later, in 1999, AFI presented its Life Achievement Award to Dustin Hoffman, and Anne Bancroft attended but Mike Nichols wasn't there.)

As AFI became more involved with Silicon Valley, we borrowed these models to create additional giving groups of companies and individuals under the banner of the AFI Advanced Technology Council and later the AFI Millennium Council. The groups gave AFI the opportunity to bring creative and technical leaders together in social settings, not only to raise money, as all such groups do, but to raise awareness of an additional leadership role AFI was stepping into.

AFI ASSOCIATES

By the 1980s, the relevance and appeal of women's volunteer groups was waning. Personally, I had never belonged to one, though I remember my mother's tales about how difficult the internal politics could be. Nevertheless, in 1984, trustee Bonita "Bunny" Granville Wrather suggested we co-write a letter to prominent women in the entertainment community. Some were career women, but most were wives of successful leaders in movies and television. The response was incredibly strong, except for one letter from Peg Yorkin, founder of the Feminist Majority who would become a dear friend. She told me in no uncertain terms that women should not be involved in such frivolous groups.

The Associates were initially led by actress Patricia Barry and became a force from the get-go. While I thought the women were (as my mother had warned) very hard on each other, they raised over $5 million for AFI between 1984 and 2008. They also required more staff time and energy than most groups. While I believe every group must be respected, supported, and made to feel they are essential and special, I don't think I often succeeded with the Associates. We included the president of the AFI Associates as an ex officio member of the AFI Board of Trustees, a mark of respect the group deserved.

Ava Fries, Helene Tobias, Joan Ransohoff, Helen Stansbury, Dolly Gillin, Bunny Stivers, Barbara Tannenbaum, Carole Mitchell, and Joan Barton all dedicated real service as president of the Associates. I enjoyed working with all of them, especially their historian, Jean Schaffner, wife of Franklin Schaffner; never was there a better or funnier friend.

PREMIERES

Premieres come in all shapes and sizes. They can be great fundraisers and great fun. They can also be hard and sometimes painful.

They are often memorable. Occasionally, they sell themselves and nothing goes wrong—or right. Over the years, premieres have become valuable fundraisers for many nonprofits. Both the event and the proceeds can be dramatically exciting. As a kid, I had gone to premieres at Loews Capital and State Theatres in Times Square, and I'm still enchanted by those glamorous memories. When I joined AFI on January 1, 1980, I hadn't been to a premiere in years. On February 1, AFI held a premiere at the Kennedy Center in Washington, DC. My brother, David Picker, had joined Lorimar in 1979 to head up their moviemaking venture, hoping to match Lorimar founders Merv Adelson and Lee Rich's incredible success in television. Lorimar had a fitting Peter Sellers DC-based story, *Being There*. David had arranged the premiere for AFI, knowing I might be the new director.

I had to introduce the film—my first moment of public speaking, and I wasn't ready. I *prepared*, but I wasn't *ready*. So these were the first words out of my mouth: "Good evening, ladies and gentlemen. Welcome to the AFI premiere of *Being Here*." Not *Being There*. But the title was so odd that I think only a few people in the 1,000-seat theater knew I had gotten it dead wrong.

The first AFI premiere in Los Angeles was *On Golden Pond*, starring Katharine Hepburn, Henry Fonda, and Jane Fonda. What a beautiful, classic Hollywood way to start. The second L.A. premiere was Alan Pakula's *Sophie's Choice* with Meryl Streep and Kevin Kline. Not a bad follow-up.

The October 16, 1983, premiere of *The Right Stuff* in Washington, DC, was memorable for completely different reasons. This event was organized by an amazing colleague, Marcia Mitchell, who served as AFI associate director from 1981 to 1985, based in Washington, DC. She was truly a remarkable executive and an even better writer and person who taught me a great deal about management and team-building when I needed it most. Bob Daly was running Warner Bros.; the fact that he remained an AFI supporter after this event is a testimony to his fortitude. From AFI's perspective, there was never better timing to premiere the story of America's first attempt at a manned space flight. Astronaut John Glenn had become Senator John Glenn, running for the 1984 Democratic nomination for President.

Marcia Mitchell had put together an unbelievable event, with a five-fold square invitation that featured NASA and the spacecraft everywhere. There was a National Honorary Committee, plus a Washington Honorary Committee with dozens of Cabinet members, senators, congressmen, and ambassadors. You name them, they were on a committee. Before the premiere, there were several days of events, including a Potomac River flyover led by pioneer test pilot Chuck Yeager. Every event had a corporate sponsor. As soon as we mailed the invitations, everyone—and I mean everyone—in DC wanted to go to the premiere.

Then came a catastrophic phone call. Bob Daly said they needed to pull the premiere. Their research said the marketing was all wrong. They had a great movie, but no one wanted to see it because they were confused about what the movie was about.

Pull the premiere? What could the AFI do? We'd mailed our invitations, and DC was hyper-ready, even if Warner Bros.' marketing knew the rest of America wasn't. Somehow, we prevailed on Bob Daly's generosity and had our premiere—1,100 people in the Kennedy Center's Eisenhower Theater and 1,500 people at the after-party in a Washington National Airport hangar. (The USAir chairman gave AFI its hangar to use gratis and also made a large donation in exchange for having lunch with Patricia Neal. This was 1983.)

The movie was one of the best films of 1983, nominated for eight Academy Awards, including Best Picture, and winning four. Its thirtieth anniversary screenings in 2013 showed that it's still brilliant—a triumph of moviemaking shot by Caleb Deschanel (class of 1969) before digital breakthroughs in cinematography and all aspects of filmmaking. It cost around $30 million to make and grossed about $20 million, a take that surely would have been greater had the premiere been delayed and the marketing campaign adjusted. Warner Bros. didn't have any charity premieres for many years after this. And Bob Daly, though he remained the staunchest AFI supporter, has never forgotten how AFI ruined his great movie at the box office.

BACK TO THE ROSE GARDEN

The NEA celebrated its twenty-fifth anniversary in 1989; AFI's quarter-century milestone came two years later. As those dates approached, AFI chair Gene Jankowski (who had succeeded Bonita Granville Wrather as chair after she passed away in 1988) had an idea: Back to the Rose Garden. It would be a return to the site where President Johnson signed the legislation that brought AFI into existence. Thanks to several key trustees, AFI organized one of its most brilliant one-off events, celebrating both AFI and NEA.

Jankowski, a very respected former president of CBS, knew everyone in DC and Hollywood. He and Jack Valenti thought that if President and Mrs. George H. W. Bush would attend, we could build a glamorous evening and effective fundraiser. Jack chaired the event with his intense attention to every detail, not only delivering the President and First Lady, but also an outstanding event. David Wolper stepped up as executive producer for the evening's show. David was used to producing big events, including the opening and closing nights of the 1984 Summer Olympics in Los Angeles and the Statue of Liberty Rededication in 1986.

What a team to work with! Actually, I just stood in their wake, though I did move back to DC for six straight weeks to focus on every aspect surrounding the gala, including several trustee events. And a board meeting.

We invited everyone else—the heads of every independent group, every museum doing preservation work, major university film school deans, every sister organization. Like the premiere of *The Right Stuff*, it was the place to be. Everyone wanted to participate in the show, which made sponsorships an easy ask. Every studio and network bought a table. Every CEO attended, including Cabinet members, senators, and congressional leaders.

Wolper's evening show didn't disappoint. Steve Martin did his Great Flydini act. While guests ate dinner, Wolper walked around the tables, inviting members of the DC and Hollywood elite to recite memorable film lines: Secretary of Defense Dick Cheney intoned, "May the Force be with you." Barbara Walters and then-husband Merv Adelson, echoed immortal lines from *Gone with the Wind* as Scarlett and Rhett. NBC Entertainment chief Brandon

---

"To fund [the Back to the Rose Garden gala] we decided to charge the unheard-of price of $25,000 a table. And we said, 'What better place to start selling the first table than to call on Steve Ross, a big supporter of AFI?' Warner Bros. had given nearly $2 million to help with the campus. So I called Stephen Ross, and I said, 'We're having this big gala. It's $25,000, and anybody who's anybody in Washington is going to show up.' And he said, 'Gene, if it was up to me, you know I'd give it to you in a second. But we just had this merger with *Time*, and in all fairness to my colleagues, I think Dick Munro needs to make that decision.' So I called Dick, and Dick said, 'Damn it, Gene, you guys at the networks are so rich. But we in the magazine business are nowhere where we're going to pay $25,000 dollars for a table. Thank you, and goodbye.' Well, fortunately, even back then, Bob Daly came through. He bought the table through the film division. Steve Ross showed up and sat with the President. Dick Munro wasn't invited."

—GENE JANKOWSKI,
broadcasting executive and AFI board of trustees chair (1988–2002)

Tartikoff recalled Peter Finch's speech from *Network*: "I'm mad as hell and I'm not gonna take it anymore!" Martin Scorsese dropped a Groucho Marx one-liner, and President Bush stole the show when he looked across to the First Lady and uttered Humphrey Bogart's unforgettable line from *Casablanca*: "Here's looking at you, kid." The segment concluded with a roar of audience approval as Walter Cronkite repeated his famous sign-off: "And, that's the way it was—Tuesday, September 26, 1989." But we were not done yet. Gene Siskel and Roger Ebert capped it all with a mock review of the one-liners.

No one knew the angst that preceded this lighthearted night. Among many other duties, Jack Valenti was in charge of seating the primary tables—never an easy task with so many heavyweights. Of course, everyone wanted to be at the President's table. Late on Friday night before our Tuesday event, Jack called me, his voice tense: "Jeannie, we have a problem—and I'm not kidding. All the heads of the studios want to sit at the President's table. There are too many of them. If we don't solve this problem, we're both going to lose our jobs."

He was talking about Bob Daly, Tom Pollock, Steve Ross (head of Warner Communications and owner of Warner Bros.), Michael Schulof (head of Sony America, which had just acquired Columbia Pictures), Barry Diller (head of Fox), Michael Eisner (head of Disney), Paramount's Frank Mancuso, MGM's Alan Ladd Jr., and Universal's Sid Sheinberg, not to mention ABC's Dan Burke, NBC's Brandon Tartikoff, et al.

I was stunned by the intensity of Jack's concern. But the next morning, the sun came up in the east, just like it does every day, and Jack solved the problem by putting the First Lady at a different table. Two head tables, with enough seats for all the studio heads. His solution was perfect. I suggested that I didn't need to sit at a head table. Why didn't I sit at the table with Steven Spielberg, George Lucas, and Martin Scorsese? "Great idea!" Jack replied.

And that's how I got to sit at the best table in the whole room.

The next day, the trustees held their sixty-seventh meeting in the beautiful Old Post Office building on Pennsylvania Avenue, where the NEA and NEH offices were housed (and where, in 2016, the new Trump Hotel was built). It was a grand occasion with everyone in high spirits, and it was at this meeting that the recipient of the 1990 Life Achievement Award would be selected. The board did this in executive session, and Steven Spielberg had brought Martin Scorsese to the meeting to speak on behalf of their candidate, Sir David Lean. The only trouble was that Marty wasn't a board member. As staff members and other visitors were leaving the room, George Stevens asked if I was going to ask Marty to leave the room before the executive session started. I replied that I wouldn't. And George didn't either. Guess what? Sir David Lean was elected, but not before there was a spirited nomination of Kirk Douglas led by the passionate Jack Valenti. Jack graciously conceded, but not before he went quickly around the room asking support of everyone for Kirk Douglas to be the honoree in 1991. If you look at the LAA list, you'll see Kirk Douglas's name next to the year 1991. Jack knew when to concede, and he knew how to close.

The Bottom Line

There is no president of an educational or cultural or nonprofit organization that doesn't think about fundraising 24/7. The annual budget, the endowment, the big gift, and the need to be constantly focused on the bottom line permeate everything. Having an involved, supportive board; having a smart, dedicated development team; and never ever being tired of asking or worrying about a request or getting down because of a "Sorry, cannot do it." Just keep getting back up—move on—keep going and enjoy the moments that secure the "Yes, I'm in." But steady as you go, never get too high, never get too low. There are no shortcuts. It is a steady, constant beat with the eye on the bottom line.

And it always helps to have special people by your side. George Stevens's first hire was his assistant, Adrian Borneman. By the time I arrived, Adrian was head of personnel (now human resources). In 2015, she passed away at the age of ninety-two. At memorial services held for her on both coasts, we all agreed she was the glue that held AFI together. I called her AFI's heart and soul. She could tell a fraud a mile away, but—more than that—she could see potential and nurture it until it matured. Just like AFI itself.

There is also no doubt that each and every component of the AFI fundraising masthead—be it the NEA, NEH, the Second Decade Council, Life Achievement Award, the Third Decade Council, board contributors, individual donors, memberships at every level, gifts to the endowment, sponsorships, bond issues, in-kind contributions, AFI Associates, or premieres—added not only to the bottom line but also to the culture of the AFI itself. And all I could ask of myself was to be sure AFI always conducted itself with the same measure of quality and professionalism, no matter what component was in play at any particular moment. Because all fundraising efforts were devoted to provide resources to support programs—the raison d'être for AFI itself.

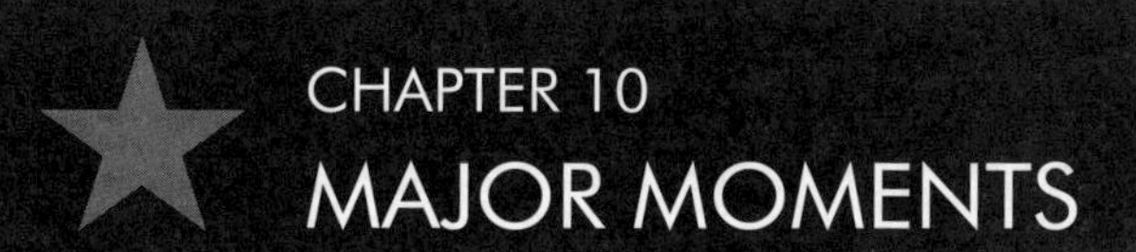

CHAPTER 10

MAJOR MOMENTS

Landmarks in AFI's Identity

Jean Picker Firstenberg

The people behind the American Film Institute have always exhibited a strong pioneering spirit. The Institute has had to forge its own path. There were no examples to emulate and no business models to follow. AFI had a mission, and it had prestigious beginnings in the White House Rose Garden. In bringing its mission to life, the AFI had to build programs and an identity within a national culture and a media universe that was changing rapidly. In this shifting landscape, the AFI strove to be a rallying point where the moving image could take its rightful place as a crucial part of America's living cultural heritage. An entrepreneurial commitment energized AFI's leadership, creating landmarks that have helped to celebrate and define the art of the moving image.

Over the years, AFI has mastered the art of producing the special event that can attract donors while maintaining a clear focus on mission and content. This chapter will describe several of the most dynamic, galvanizing projects that helped AFI develop enthusiastic national recognition and find fiscal balance, as it moved from dependence on government funding to fiscal independence. These initiatives and their evolution also demonstrate that not every idea leads to success, despite the energy, effort, and enthusiasm that might go into its design. As Steve Jobs often pointed out, when trying to innovate, you succeed some of the time but not all of the time. But that doesn't mean to say you aren't proud of the things you attempted. This chapter also illustrates the tension between nonprofit and for-profit culture, between mission and fundraising, finding exactly the fine line between what is appropriate and what isn't—and how, at the end of the day, what is at stake in every project is everything: the AFI's good name and reputation.

AFI Life Achievement Award

The AFI Life Achievement Award (LAA) has been central to the AFI annual calendar since 1973. It was a landmark idea initiated by George Stevens Jr., and this grand tradition continues every year with the award formally celebrating the career of one of America's great film artists. Since 1973, awardees had been male or female actors or directors, but in 2016, composer-conductor John Williams was honored, adding another discipline to the honor roll. In lauding Williams's accomplishment, Steven Spielberg captured the spirit and purpose of the LAA itself: "Without John Williams, bikes don't really fly. Nor do men in red capes. There is no Force. Dinosaurs do not walk the earth. We do not wonder. We do not weep. We do not believe."

As a national cultural institution, AFI was in a unique position to originate and leverage this award. In the early 1970s, the concept of celebrating an artist's life's work at an event taped for broadcast on a major television network was unique. Such programs constituted a new genre, and AFI's approach was both reverential and entertaining. Recollections from different people close to the honoree were interspersed with film clips of their work. Using clips in this way was a relatively new concept that made for some emotional moments. It was his sense of good taste and the strong writing and producing skills of George Stevens Jr. that set a high bar for the program. Trustee Jack Schneider, then head of CBS, also deserves recognition for his commitment to promote and air this new program idea in a time slot that helped it succeed. His confidence was well-placed and CBS well-served, with spectacular ratings for the time period for many of the early years.

Any number of refinements occurred over the years, especially on the telecast side. CBS carried the telecast for the first twelve years, but as the television landscape changed, the program stopped being the ratings standout it once was. In 1986, then-head of CBS Gene Jankowski told the executive committee that his programmers in L.A. did not want to carry the telecast on an exclusive basis. He suggested that the three major networks carry it on a rotating basis. Bob Daly stepped in and became the LAA's guardian angel, negotiating with the ever-changing roster of network power brokers to maintain LAA's place in the telecast pantheon.

Periods of flux in LAA network sponsorship align with AFI's underlying fiscal struggles, which were compounded when AFI's annual NEA funding appeared shaky. By late 1995, we knew that NEA funding would be phased out completely in 1998. At the same time, after twenty-seven years, the major networks told AFI they could no longer carry the telecast.

The board thought about every possible scenario and option. Cable carriage of the LAA, which would not have been a concept the board would have considered even five years before, was now seen as the best alternative. However, it was unclear if cable companies would pay the license fee necessary for a well-produced event. The board felt that if the telecast was able to continue, it would need

Life Achievement Award

RECIPIENT	YEAR	NETWORK	EXEC. PRODUCER
John Ford	1973	CBS	George Stevens Jr.
James Cagney	1974	CBS	George Stevens Jr.
Orson Welles	1975	CBS	George Stevens Jr.
William Wyler	1976	CBS	George Stevens Jr.
Bette Davis	1977	CBS	George Stevens Jr.
Henry Fonda	1978	CBS	George Stevens Jr.
Alfred Hitchcock	1979	CBS	George Stevens Jr.
James Stewart	1980	CBS	George Stevens Jr.
Fred Astaire	1981	CBS	George Stevens Jr.
Frank Capra	1982	CBS	George Stevens Jr.
John Huston	1983	CBS	George Stevens Jr.
Lillian Gish	1984	CBS	George Stevens Jr.
Gene Kelly	1985	CBS	George Stevens Jr.
Billy Wilder	1986	NBC	George Stevens Jr.
Barbara Stanwyck	1987	ABC	George Stevens Jr.
Jack Lemmon	1988	CBS	George Stevens Jr.
Gregory Peck	1989	NBC	George Stevens Jr.
David Lean	1990	ABC	George Stevens Jr.
Kirk Douglas	1991	CBS	George Stevens Jr.
Sidney Poitier	1992	NBC	George Stevens Jr.
Elizabeth Taylor	1993	ABC	George Stevens Jr.
Jack Nicholson	1994	CBS	George Stevens Jr.

Steven Spielberg	1995	NBC	George Stevens Jr.
Clint Eastwood	1996	ABC	George Stevens Jr.
Martin Scorsese	1997	CBS	George Stevens Jr.
Robert Wise	1998	NBC	George Stevens Jr.
Dustin Hoffman	1999	ABC	George Schlatter
Harrison Ford	2000	CBS	George Schlatter
Barbra Streisand	2001	FOX	Gary Smith
Tom Hanks	2002	USA	Gary Smith
Robert De Niro	2003	USA	Bob Gazzale
Meryl Streep	2004	USA	Bob Gazzale
George Lucas	2005	USA	Bob Gazzale
Sean Connery	2006	USA	Bob Gazzale
Al Pacino	2007	USA	Bob Gazzale
Warren Beatty	2008	USA	Bob Gazzale
Michael Douglas	2009	TV Land	Bob Gazzale
Mike Nichols	2010	TV Land	Bob Gazzale
Morgan Freeman	2011	TV Land	Bob Gazzale
Shirley MacLaine	2012	TV Land	Bob Gazzale
Mel Brooks	2013	TNT + TCM	Bob Gazzale
Jane Fonda	2014	TNT + TCM	Bob Gazzale
Steve Martin	2015	TNT + TCM	Bob Gazzale
John Williams	2016	TNT + TCM	Bob Gazzale
Diane Keaton	2017	TNT + TCM	Bob Gazzale

a refreshed format and different executive producer. Although such changes look inevitable now, believe me, they were not at the time.

How did the shift from network to cable happen? Just the way it always seems to: a personal contact between two people who respect each other. In this case, Howard Stringer, the former head of CBS, called Barry Diller, then head of USA Network, and asked if they would like to carry the AFI's LAA. Diller had been on the AFI board in 1973 when the initial LAA idea was first percolating. He was proud of that relationship and asked Doug Herzog, who was running the channel for him, if he would like to carry the AFI's LAA. Herzog reportedly shouted, "YES!" And so began a wonderful relationship with a brilliant executive whose aggressive support included extensive promotion and the very best type of sponsorship relationships possible. When Doug's career took him to TV Land as president, his USA Network successor Bonnie Hammer continued the association in a similar fashion for a total of seven years. After the USA Network's contract ended in 2008, Doug brought the Life Achievement Award to TV Land for four years. Not a bad run at all. Thank you, Doug Herzog!

When I came to AFI in 1980, the LAA was in its eighth year. George was fully in command of the LAA (he even had his own event planner) and continued to write and produce the next eighteen events, until 1998. At that point, the LAA came under my direct care. Special events are always very challenging—one-offs even more so—but recurring annual events take on a rhythm and a pressure that is different. From 1999 to 2002, two respected new executive producers took a turn. By then, it became clear that we had a young man on our senior management team who was an exceptional writer and was ready to take on the role of executive producer.

In 2003, at the age of thirty-eight (just a tad younger than George Stevens Jr. had been when he conceptualized this extraordinary program), Bob Gazzale took over to carry forward the great tradition begun in 1973. Although each year's LAA is shaped and propelled by the personality of the recipient, talented people respect talented people. Watching Bob establish a rapport with the honoree and support that person's comfort level has been a delight. With each event, he has more stories to tell (and some I'm sure he never will). His philosophy as executive producer and writer in framing the story of these remarkable careers and personal lives continues to bring new life to LAA. When Bob Gazzale succeeded me on November 1, 2007, he went on to not only assume the responsibilities of president and CEO but has also continued to be the executive

---

"When Sean Connery received the Life Achievement Award, my wife and I were at his table. He announced shortly before he was to go up and accept his award that he desperately needed to go to the bathroom. So my wife, in the spirit of this company, this institution, crawled across the hall to alert everybody that Sean had to go to the bathroom. She got, I think, as far as Bob Gazzale, who she didn't really know, and said, 'He needs to go to the bathroom.' Bob swiftly summons the Scottish pipers who were onstage and tells them to play 'Scotland the Brave' until their lungs collapse. I get Sean Connery to follow my wife to the bathroom. He later emerges triumphant—a long time later—after nine renditions of 'Scotland the Brave' and announces something even in Scotland I've never heard. He says, 'That was a double-flusher.' On the sublime side, Sean didn't really know much about the American Film Institute when we asked him to accept the award. For a man who's seen everything and done everything, the evening was something of a miracle. He's never stopped calling me, Jean, or Bob to explain how much that meant and did I realize how important it was that everybody know the power and magic of the American Film Institute?"

—SIR HOWARD STRINGER,
corporate executive and AFI board of trustees chair (2000–present)

---

producer and writer of the LAA and other productions. From my perspective, he is holding down not one job, but two!

Being both writer and executive producer has given Bob a perspective that has allowed him to add dimensions that showcase the honoree and personalize each presentation, all while maintaining the dignity of the event and adding a strong entertainment quotient. I think one could also argue that since Bob and his team have been involved, the AFI media clip and film packages used throughout the evening have set a new standard, made possible thanks to the *extraordinary* generosity of the studios, professional guilds, and actors who allow AFI to use these clips gratis. Movie clips and similar intellectual property are an incredible asset central to AFI's mission that make programs like the LAA as richly informative and entertaining as they can be. AFI has also been fortunate over the years to be represented by legal counsel Howell Begle, who is most adept at and respected in doing the elaborate legal choreography necessary to utilize these incredible resources.

To add a little financial perspective, during the 1980–2007 years, the Life Achievement events netted close to $45 million in support of AFI programs. Of that amount, about $8 million came through sponsorship, and the rest from ticket and table sales. As critical as the event is to AFI's mission, it has also been a key component of AFI's ability to support itself and maintain its independence.

Corporate Sponsorship

During the 1980s, event sponsorship became a hallmark of high-profile evenings like the LAA. Over the years, the AFI's LAA was the beneficiary of some spectacular corporate relationships.

Remy Martin was the first company to approach us with a sponsorship opportunity. It was 1985, and though George was executive producer, I was director and CEO and ultimately responsible for the AFI budget. Every financial opportunity had to be considered, but I was wary, concerned about whether a sponsorship could be supportive but not intrusive. We needed the funds, but we were in uncharted territory. What effect might a brand association have on AFI's reputation? How might it change people's perception of the LAA itself? What should the boundaries be—when was a sponsor asking for more than we thought appropriate? When was it time to demur? I was clearly aware of the high stakes behind a seemingly straightforward offer of financial support. AFI's reputation must always be protected.

The inauguration of the Remy Martin-LAA relationship was an extraordinary learning experience in how a corporate sponsor and cultural institution can strike fair and mutually respectful arrangements. I had a great teacher in New York communications guru Arthur Novell, who represented Remy Martin and thoughtfully explained both sides of the sponsorship relationship. (Arthur also represented Jim Henson, who came to the AFI Conservatory and gave several magnificent seminars.) For a decade, Remy sponsored the LAA event and donated well over $1 million, mostly in cash—but gifts of their wonderful cognac and Krug champagne were also received with great pleasure.

In these years, gift bags also became a new draw at glamorous events. We worked diligently to make sure that gifts were always appropriate and reflective of the honoree's work. In earlier days, it was VHS tapes of their movies, then DVDs donated by the studios, and now more likely digital media. These were boxed beautifully by the sponsors, who also sometimes provided handsome bags in which to carry them home. One year, a post-party sponsor provided director's chairs with the honoree's name on the back. One participating actor was seen carrying three of them to his hotel room at the end of the evening. Since he didn't live in L.A., I often wondered how he got them home to New York.

LAA Selection, Seating, and Other Details

The board chooses Life Achievement Award recipients through a secret ballot in executive session eight to nine months ahead of the event date. The selection requires a two-thirds vote of the present and voting trustees. An LAA trustee nominating committee presents at least three individuals for consideration (no nominations are allowed from the floor). The committee spends considerable time reviewing all possible recipients, and the board discusses at length all aspects of the choices before voting. Needless to say, a two-thirds vote of some forty trustees is often hard to secure on a first or second ballot.

After making the selection, the actual availability of the honoree is critical—for without the recipient, there is no event. Over the years, there have been a few brushes with potential disaster, such as when Barbara Stanwyck's back gave way and she actually came out of the hospital to attend the event, or when Kirk Douglas attended his event a few weeks after a serious helicopter crash, with heavy makeup covering deep bruises. In 1988, the board selected Burt Lancaster, who graciously but firmly declined. You will see the name Jack Lemmon on the list for 1988, another highly respected artist who had been nominated that year as well.

Every honoree has shown up, although Jack Nicholson did make his limo drive in circles until he had control of his anxiety attack, and then allowed the limo to pull up to the Beverly Hills Hotel entrance. To those of us anxiously awaiting the arrival of an honoree on whom an evening hangs, fifteen minutes can feel like an hour. As an attendee, on several occasions Jack was conflicted when the LAA event competed with his beloved Los Angeles Lakers playing in the NBA finals. He would arrive after the game ended. In fact, AFI LAA did well in the broadcast ratings every year except the evening we were bested by the seventh game in the NBA finals.

Tasting Luncheons with Pets

The best part of planning the evening, by far, is the tasting luncheon that precedes the evening. Back in the days when the event was at the Beverly Hilton Hotel, one of the more memorable luncheons featured Elizabeth Taylor, who attended with Sugar, her fluffy white Maltese, seated at the table (a first and last for the event).

No matter the location, the chef wants to show off, and working with the heads of catering is usually pleasant. These folks are used to making their clients happy, and they don't come much better than Barbara Brass at Wolfgang Puck, who handles all the catering at the Dolby Theatre at Hollywood & Highland, where the LAA has been held since 2002 except when the site was undergoing renovation.

Seating is by far the most challenging aspect of any event. Before computers, we designed our own process. With the advent of the computer, various seating programs have truly helped to meet the challenge of just making sure you've got the right people at the right locations with the right seatmates. I have always thought the Dolby Theatre in Hollywood (formerly known as the Kodak) is a great location, because it feels like you are in a concert hall. Bob Gazzale's production team built a wonderful structure that covers the stage and the front seating to build a perfect set. The other advantage to the Dolby are the balcony seats, which can be filled enthusiastically by AFI national members as well as alumni. Being able to include these folks in the theater was not possible at the Beverly Hilton Hotel.

How was it even possible for the AFI LAA to be held in the Dolby? At the time, the Academy of Motion Picture Arts and Sciences wanted to move the Oscars broadcast to the then-Kodak. Robert Rehme was responsible for negotiating with the Hollywood & Highland management on behalf of the Academy. Bob was also a wonderful AFI trustee. He negotiated on behalf of the Academy that no other movie award program could be held in the theater—except the AFI LAA. Thank you, Bob Rehme.

> "Since its inception in '73, the AFI Life Achievement Award has represented official recognition and celebration of the very basis of the American film art. This is the Golden Age of the Hollywood system—honoring as many of its past masters as possible. Many of the past recipients—Ford, Welles, Billy Wilder, Greg Peck, and Lemmon—made films that I love. In many ways, they shaped me as a person and, for better or worse, as a filmmaker."
>
> —MARTIN SCORSESE, filmmaker

Over the years, we missed the opportunity to honor several more-than-worthy actors and directors. Among the many I wish we had been able to honor are Charles Chaplin, Cary Grant, Katharine Hepburn, Audrey Hepburn, Charlton Heston, Elia Kazan, Laurence Olivier, and Paul Newman.

In 1990, the first Franklin J. Schaffner Alumni Medal was presented to David Lynch (class of 1970) at the LAA dinner. The Alumni Medal was a fitting tribute established after the loss of Schaffner, a longtime AFI trustee and national leader, with the support of his wife, Jean. The Alumni Medal has become a meaningful part of the evening that gives established AFI Conservatory alumni a moment in the sun. The list of recipients (see Chapter 3) highlights the AFI Conservatory's historic contribution in nurturing individual voices that tell meaningful stories.

Leading AFI in a More Independent Era

While the LAA provided a major part of AFI's annual income, it still left a major gap to be closed every year through a variety of creative ventures. Late in 1995, it was clear that federal funding was coming to an end, clearly expanding the income gap. It was just a matter of how federal funding in the final years would progressively diminish. It was time to face the future and take some radical steps.

We had left the Kennedy Center offices and given AFI a permanent home in Los Angeles. The AFI exhibition team still operated the AFI Theater in Washington, DC, but the heart of AFI was now on the West Coast. We still needed to clarify and define what AFI stood for and how the Institute should be perceived. The original AFI logo—the handsome celluloid strip—began to feel old-school. We were, after all, deeply in the age of television and video, with digital ever closer on the horizon. The celebration of the 100th anniversary of the motion picture was fast approaching. The logo became a literal image of the question we faced: Where was AFI's focus, on the future or on the past?

The world of moving images was undergoing a truly radical shift. We had seen this far earlier, and had been writing about it in various publications—thinking about how to prepare all the AFI programs to encompass the future while always respecting the past. We turned, as we always did, to the major figures on the board, whose expertise could help clarify the issue at hand. Steve Frankfurt suggested that we consult a young man, Darrell Hayden (son of actors Jeffrey Hayden and Oscar-winner Eva Marie Saint), who specialized in corporate and institutional identity. He took on the identity of the Institute as his assignment and did a major study on how AFI was perceived in New York City, Los Angeles, Washington, DC, and around the country. What was the perception of the Institute in the eyes of the trustees?

The senior management team and the board spent countless

hours discussing the way forward and coming to agreement. Change is hard, but the management team knew it was time to challenge the status quo or atrophy with the mindset of a previous era. This was one of those critical moments, and AFI chose to move on.

We debuted a new logo. Our new tagline became: *Advancing and preserving the art of the moving image.* Our updated mission statement read: "*The American Film Institute is dedicated to advancing and preserving the art of film, television, and other forms of the moving image.*" These changes reflected the deeper shifts that were evolving in the Institute. As I wrote in the *Annual Report 1994–1995:*

> *With the new contemporary AFI letter forms looking towards the future, while casting a star shadow that represents the foundation AFI was built upon, the logo alludes to the illustrious past that AFI works to protect and advance. As our consultants explained it, the choice was to position the Institute to move forward into the future. AFI is committed to change, but currently it is not perceived that way. It is critical to broaden the Institute's base of support to include television, new media, and technology. It must be more inclusive. The analogy is that AFI is like a moving train—moving toward advancing the art. The train is moving, but AFI is still in the station. The choice is whether AFI wants its corporate identity to convey what it is doing, or hang behind and exclude people.*

We had a new identity, and we had also assembled the team that would take AFI into its next era. Six individuals were responsible for the evolving redefinition of the AFI. James Hindman had not only strengthened the Institute's academic base but had also clarified our educational mission so it would grow and thrive and continue into the twenty-first-century, narrative storytelling world. Jamie had a creative's entrepreneurial approach that helped us to spot and make the most of new programs and opportunities.

Nick DeMartino was also a central player in repositioning the Institute, because he took us by the hand and showed us where the world of technology was moving. The way the digital world exploded was just overwhelming, and at its early beginnings, AFI was a real national player thanks to Nick and Jamie's initiatives. With an ever-evolving role, Nick was director of strategic planning and associate director for AFI by 1995, reporting to James Hindman, who was named co-director and COO at the time.

Bob Gazzale had the same trajectory. Having come to AFI in 1992, he spent a few years in New York City for us and then returned to L.A. with growing responsibilities for our national voice, always pushing for more activities to expand the Institute's vision of America's film history. By 1994, he had been named director of national programs.

In July 1995, we hired an experienced director of marketing, F. Lee Tomlinson, someone who knew how to design full-blown marketing plans with metrics-driven business plans to match, and assemble compelling presentation decks. He would create such a smart package that it helped to attract major, national sponsorships. Lee also made a brilliant presentation. He was tall and articulate, and he seemed to understand the nature and culture of AFI.

During the summer of 1995, AFI got really lucky when Seth Oster left U.S. senator Dianne Feinstein's office in Washington, DC, to take up the communications responsibilities for AFI. We really had not done a great deal to push our public relations, nor were we even very focused on how we were getting our message out—because, truth be told, we weren't getting our message out at all. I knew we were in good hands when I told Seth, "I cannot find any files to document what we've been doing," and he responded, "Don't worry about it at all. I'll be building my own files."

The last piece to this leadership puzzle was filled in November 1995, when Victoria Silverman joined AFI as director of development, another sterling fundraising leader who taught me so much.

Looking back, it is clear now that this team was the internal force that turned AFI from a federally funded entity into what it has become. Of course, none of us knew where that road would lead us at the time or how we were going to get there.

There was one other constant at the senior management table throughout all my years. CFO Bruce Neiner spent many hours (far more than he wanted) listening to lots of ideas, some in and some really out of the box, faithfully attending in case a notion or two took hold that might take us under. Then he would simply say, "Let's get real!"

We had been preparing for this major institutional change ever since Liener Temerlin had presented his forward-thinking paper, "A Strategic Plan for the AFI Campaign 2000," to the executive committee and the full board in May 1989. The crux of Temerlin's recommendations for AFI's future direction were to:

- Develop and market major national promotions that are attractive to corporations and consumers.
- Create new AFI-branded properties that utilize AFI's library of content and the assistance of its supporters.
- Leverage existing properties for maximum exposure and revenue.
- Own the 100th anniversary of American film history.

Yes, it took us close to six years to believe we could embrace efforts of this scale. But now we had the team that could be responsive to new ideas, and we aggressively invited a new AFI Board Entrepreneurial Advisory Committee (BEAC) to help us, which was convened to put these recommendations into action. The group met for the first time on February 27, 1996, with freewheeling discussions of many proposals from everyone at the table. Everyone understood the importance of establishing the AFI brand and finding connections with corporations looking for similar opportunities. Above all, every member acknowledged and appreciated

Board Entrepreneurial Advisory Committee Members

AFI BOARD MEMBERS

Richard Brandt, Chair and CEO, Trans-Lux Corp
Mark Canton, Chair, Columbia/Tri-Star Motion Picture Companies
Alfred A. Checchi, Co-Chair, Northwest Airlines
Stephen A. Frankfurt, President, Frankfurt Balkind
Frederick S. Pierce, Chair, the Frederick S. Pierce Company

NON-BOARD MEMBERS

Joerg Agin, Senior VP, New Technologies & Business, Eastman Kodak
John Burke, Rosenfeld, Meyer & Susman
Eric Ellenbogen, President, Broadway Video
Don Karl, Rosenfeld, Meyer & Susman
Herb Karltiz, Karlitz & Company, Inc.
Warren Lieberfarb, President, Warner Bros. Home Video
Gary Ross, President, Suncoast Stores
Scott Sassa, President, Turner Entertainment Group
Jonathan Seybold, Softbank Expos
Robert Sigman, President, Republic Entertainment
Michael Jay Solomon, Chair & CEO, Solomon International Enterprises
John Warnock, CEO Adobe Systems
Andrew Wing, Vice President, General Manager, Sports & Entertainment Services, American Express

that AFI was a nonprofit, educational institution with the highest ethical standards. Whatever we did had to be done with an integrity, dignity, and character that reflected those standards.

At that first meeting, the AFI team presented many projects, including an AFI Preview Night to be sponsored by American Express. This program would present new movies at college campuses nationwide—a way to introduce AFI to a younger generation. Another idea was opening the AFI Showcase at Walt Disney World with a ribbon cutting by Charlton Heston, an extraordinary opportunity to reach millions of people who would become aware of AFI.

AFI's 100 Years...100 Movies

The concepts for *AFI's 100 Years...100 Movies* were to evolve through many stages, but at the end of the first BEAC meeting, the management team left with a feeling of real momentum. The collective expertise and creativity at the table had promised to help us find the next steps in the process. And that they did. The basic idea kept evolving and changing until it worked—*big time*. Here are a few of its iterations along the way to becoming a classic (and just watch how the dollar amounts kept fluctuating):

- At the June 1996 board meeting, the core idea was an AFI Century Collection of classic and contemporary film titles. The business expectations were that it could generate over 1.5 billion impressions nationally and internationally, bring in between $2 million and $4 million in revenue, firmly establish the AFI brand, and position AFI as the definitive authority on movie-making excellence.
- By the October 1996 board meeting, Tomlinson had a $13 million plan that would net AFI $3 to $5 million. The plan sounded grand and unrealistic—so outside the realm of rationality—but he kept saying those numbers, and I kept wanting to believe them. Then reality came in

the form of trustee chair Fred Pierce actually structuring a practical program that could be successfully produced. Yes, it could change the identity and course of AFI. But it would also be a real financial risk.

- By March 1997, the idea had gone from Liener Temerlin to Lee Tomlinson to Fred Pierce, as well as Les Moonves, Phil Guarascio, and many others who contributed. But the person who always kept it real was Fred Pierce. Or, as Bruce Neiner put it, "Fred Pierce just took this notion and ran with it and made it work."
- By June 1997, the pitch was this simple and this daunting: *Celebrate the centennial of the motion picture by selecting the 100 greatest movies of the first 100 years, and announce these on network television.* Pierce went to Moonves, the head of CBS at the time, who made a commitment to a three-hour broadcast in late spring 1998, following the May sweeps. AFI would buy the overall time blocks from the network, with Stan Moger of SFM Entertainment seeking a range of sponsors/advertisers for the telecast in support of the effort. TNT agreed to program between ten and thirteen hours of documentaries to give full exposure to the 100 movies selected. Repeats of the CBS and Turner shows would bring AFI millions of dollars of recognition. Turner Classic Movies licensed as many of the 100 films as they could in order to broadcast them under the AFI Century Collection banner. An exhibition mounted in a semi-trailer would travel to major U.S. markets showing clips of the movies and memorabilia to excite interest in the telecast. *Newsweek* signed on as a media partner and would publish a single, special edition devoted to the century of the movies using *AFI's 100 Years...100 Movies* as the centerpiece.

The stakes were gigantic: nothing less than AFI's national standing and ongoing financial solvency. The cost to produce and deliver everything was $10 million. If AFI could secure *more* than $10 million in sponsors—and if everything worked—all costs would be covered, and the budget space formerly filled by the NEA could be offset.

Corporate partnerships were being secured at a premium price. Phil Guarascio made a $4.5 million commitment for General Motors, almost half of the sponsorship dollars needed to break even. If AFI could secure another $5 million-plus in sponsorship pledges, the costs of production would be covered, the risk would be acceptable, and the board would vote to move forward. The board members made these kinds of deals all the time and knew only too well how things can go wrong. Neither I nor my senior management team had this perspective. In 2016, Tom Pollock reflected that Fred Pierce convinced him to take an incredible risk. We were battling for the entire AFI existence on Stan Moger's ability to sell the time. Of course, we were on the hook for shortfalls, though we had Phil Guarascio and General Motors.

But, finally, we had no real choice. It was the biggest project we had ever attempted, with so many moving parts. These were good reasons for the board to be deeply involved with every nuance of the project, but there was one that was even bigger. For the first time, AFI would have to borrow funds for the pre-production costs. As Fred Pierce recalled on the conceptualization of *AFI's 100 Years...100 Movies:*

> *At the time, the NEA was deleting all the funds that were being provided to AFI. I kept thinking about how to celebrate 100 years of movies . . . how to monetize the idea. . . . I kept thinking about it, for maybe two years. . . . I was sitting next to Peter Lund, who at that time was a CBS representative on the board. I said to Peter, "Would you clear three hours of time for an AFI special that celebrates the movies?" And Peter said,*

"Sure, why not? If you buy the time, we'll clear it." Now Tom Pollock is AFI chair, and he asks, "Aren't we better off just licensing this to the network, instead of having all this obligation to sell advertising?" I said, "Well, the mechanics don't work. They're not going to pay us that kind of money going in, where we have a profit and they sell the advertising." By this time, Peter Lund had left CBS, and Les Moonves had replaced him on the board. And Les, again, was sitting next to me at one of the board meetings and I said, "I hope you're going to recognize Peter's commitment to us to clear three hours of time." He said, "You've got it." So I said to Tom, "We have no choice. We have to make the commitment. And we have to go out and sell it and hope we don't get killed. If we don't, AFI may not be in existence anymore." I convinced Tom, Gene, and the rest of the board at that time to give us the green light. So the board committed to over $10 million on blind faith, going in on year one. Because we owned the material, and we had foreign rights on the documentaries, we were able to produce a $2 million profit for AFI in that first year. The rest was history.

Once all the moving parts were put in motion, we were faced with the most challenging questions: How would we select the 100 movies? What were the criteria? Who got to weigh in? Hours went into defining this process. We wanted this list to stand the test of time and also satisfy the legions of passionate movie fans. AFI's integrity was on the line. The ten hours of documentaries would also help to communicate to audiences the enduring value we saw in the selected films. We didn't want this to be a static list but rather a gateway into knowing more about every movie selected.

With the remarkable leadership of Warner Bros. Home Video, led by Warren Lieberfarb, an unprecedented consortium of all major studios and companies agreed to have AFI market the 100 movies under the auspices of the AFI Century Collection. Some

15,000 video stores had AFI point-of-purchase displays for sixty to ninety days (and some even longer) after the TV special. I cannot stress how huge a commitment this was on the pre-digital movie world of 1998, when 7.5 million people visited video stores *every day*—a huge, built-in national audience. It's astonishing to realize that that was less than twenty years ago.

Between concept, approval, pre-production, production, and execution, the next year was something of a blur for me. Life was 24/7 for many times during my twenty-seven years and ten months as president and CEO, but none more so than when we were mounting *AFI's 100 Years...100 Movies*. Believe it or not, there were even more subsets and components to the concept. We tried too hard to prove that this centennial celebration was worthy of the 100 years of moviemaking and the 100 movies selected. What were we thinking? We clearly were trying to think of everything.

The concept of the program and the distribution of the ballots was announced with a bang in 1998 with a press conference on the AFI campus. Dustin Hoffman, Holly Hunter, and Chris O'Donnell announced the *AFI's 100 Years...100 Movies* program, while a U.S. Postal Service truck waited on campus to accept 1,500 ballots being mailed to the jury of members of the creative and professional community. Seth Oster, our brilliant communications VP, turned this relatively small event into something important, with six TV station cameras showing up. And it worked. National attention turned up the throttle to full speed. With the Centennial Celebration, AFI was setting the standard for recognizing greatness in American moviemaking.

> "In the last analysis, it doesn't really matter what movies are on [the *100 Years...100 Movies*] list. What matters is the movies on the list, voted by 1,500 above-average moviegoers who don't think *Citizen Kane* has aged one day."
>
> —ROGER EBERT, film critic

The final success of the 1998 program meant that AFI and CBS continued to produce annual specials through 2007, focusing on a different movie-related theme. Gary Smith and Dann Netter did a great job producing all these programs. Bob Gazzale was deeply involved in all the production decisions and was AFI's eyes on the ground as well as writer for all the shows. In those years, the Centennial was proof that Americans were passionate about their film history. It was an exciting time for American movie history, for those who respect and enjoy movie history, and for the AFI. And the *AFI's 100 Years...* series basically replaced NEA funding for the next decade.

AFI's 100 Years... Dimension and Character

1998	*AFI's 100 Years...100 Movies*
1999	*AFI's 100 Years...100 Stars*
2000	*AFI's 100 Years...100 Laughs*
2001	*AFI's 100 Years...100 Thrills*
2002	*AFI's 100 Years...100 Passions*
2003	*AFI's 100 Years...100 Heroes and Villains*
2004	*AFI's 100 Years...100 Songs*
2005	*AFI's 100 Years...100 Quotes: America's Greatest Quips, Comebacks, and Catchphrases*
2006	*AFI's 100 Years...100 Cheers: America's Most Inspiring Movies*
2007	*AFI's 100 Years...100 Movies: 10th Anniversary Edition*
2008	*AFI's 10 Top 10*

AFI Positioned for the New Millennium

With the advent of the digital era, the role and mission of AFI became more complex. The board was extremely focused on positioning AFI for relevance and longevity in the shifting landscape. This summary by board chair Tom Pollock, from a board retreat in April 2000 on this topic, explains the challenge:

> *When AFI was established thirty-two years ago, its primary goals were to celebrate and affirm the art of film, encourage film preservation, and foster film education. Film was not considered an art form at the time, but film is now considered to be America's greatest art form. Little film preservation was being done but considerable progress has been made. Film schools were few in numbers, but there has been tremendous growth in collegiate programs and student interest. The moving image is the language of the next Millennium. . . . Many of AFI's initial goals have now been met but the directors need to consider what AFI should do to ensure its continued value and significance over the next thirty-plus years. The Conservatory model is now being widely copied and imitated, as an example of AFI's success. AFI's role in film preservation has decreased over the past ten years. AFI is now more of a participant than a leader primarily because AFI lacks its own archive and firm source of funds for preservation. . . . The Internet will take on an almost infinite amount of content. What will AFI's role be in that? The Institute owns a substantial library, including short films, seminars, and panel discussions. It is only a matter of time before most education is distance learning. How AFI will respond to this challenge is the question on the table.*

Pollock was always on point. These were the correct questions to ask in 2000, and here we were, having just gone through a similar existential exercise five years earlier when we updated the logo, tagline, and mission statement. Pollock had other ideas for the future, including an annual almanac program in whatever format it might take.

AFI's Annual Almanac of Movies and TV was nurtured by the huge response to *AFI's 100 Years...* programs, so we felt emboldened and in the right place to take on another challenge: Could we appropriately assess annual artistic achievement? Not to rank films or televisions programs, but rather, to think about what were the best movies and television programs of the year, in aggregate?

An AFI annual awards TV show, or an AFI annual awards event was again a challenge to determine a selection process that was bulletproof and beyond reproach. Every project had to be built upon the unassailable integrity of AFI and based on our own standards of excellence. We discussed, with the board and in smaller groups, various structures, options, and challenges, as well as how to add to the awards season and not to duplicate it. Again, Fred Pierce went to Les Moonves; based on the success of *AFI's 100 Years...* series, there was a willingness to jump into the awards season with a two-year commitment to a two-hour live telecast with a firm starting date of January 10, 2001. (After year one, all the bumps and hiccups could be worked out in year two.) This was a new and hard challenge, but despite the fact that we had this verbal network commitment, the board was reluctant to move swiftly and so was the senior management team. We needed to be comfortable that we could make this something we could take pride in. So we postponed it a year, because we felt that we didn't have the concept quite right yet.

Instead, we did a limited version of the almanac idea in 2000 that was quite exciting. We put together *AFI 2000: Honoring a Year of Excellence in Motion Pictures*, bringing together a jury of twelve people: filmmakers, academics, critics, and AFI trustees. We had the best of the best, including *Newsweek* critic David Anson, academic and AFI trustee Jeanine Basinger, AFI alum and trustee Bill

Duke (class of 1978), film preservationist James Katz, *Washington Post* critic Rita Kempley, creative guru and AFI trustee Michael Nesmith, University of Texas film scholar Thomas Schatz, UCLA film historian and AFI trustee Vivian Sobchack, film journalist Anne Thompson, producer Saul Zaentz, filmmaker Steven Zaillian, and esteemed AFI chair and film producer Tom Pollock. It was an august group, and we met in the elegant penthouse of the St. Regis Hotel in Century City (long since torn down). The jury had seen all the movies either through special screenings or on DVDs where available. In addition to the ten best movies of the year, we asked the group to determine five noteworthy events of the year that had an impact on the world of the moving image in 2000.

We released the names of the ten films with a rationale for the selections. Between these statements and the noteworthy events, AFI's selections got the media's and readers' attention. We seemed to have caught something with the model, and impressed Moonves, who reaffirmed his original offer. Fred told me, "Jeannie, you need to learn to take *yes* for an answer." So several years after Tom started talking about an almanac, we agreed to produce a live CBS program called *AFI's Year in Review for 2001*. But when Fred told me that Les had given us the timeslot of Friday, January 3, 2002, at 9:00 PM, I vividly recall saying, "With that date, we'll be dead in the water." I don't know anything about programming television networks, but I know a lot about family vacation calendars. On the Friday at the end of the holiday season, no one has come home yet (at least not in L.A.). Television shows are on hiatus for the holiday. Schools don't start until the following Monday. No one would be home watching television on Friday night at 9:00 PM two days after the new year.

We did the show. It was well done, and it was respectable. And although we had some really great presenters, as anticipated, few of the honorees showed up because they were still on vacation. We didn't need a second year to work out the kinks. But we had the idea and, in fact, the basic structure for an annual event—just not an annual television program. That is how the AFI AWARDS came into the Institute's calendar of events. This annual affair is really AFI at its best, under the direction of that young man, Bob Gazzale.

Since 2003, we have had an absolutely delightful AFI AWARDS luncheon where there is *no* press, and where ten movies and ten television programs are represented and each has its own table with the creative teams—in front of and behind the camera—all attending. It is a highlight of the Golden Globes weekend because it is stress-free and so reverential. AFI secures sponsors every year to underwrite this marvelous event, and everyone attends because everyone is a winner. A distinguished member of the community closes the event with parting words that are part inspiration, part benediction.

Working with individuals in front of and behind the camera, it is also essential to have a relationship with their agents and publicists. During most of my years at AFI, Pat Kingsley was the publicity maven to the elite, a wise and respected counselor who was tough as nails in representing her clients. With time, we became friends, and then I could see why she was so successful and so respected. She got what she wanted for her clients. They came first, and they were all family to her. When it came to AFI business, Pat would deliver if she thought it was in her clients' best interest. Pat joined the AFI board in 2000, and her judgment at the table provided extraordinary insights that helped AFI achieve its objectives. If she were to write her memoir, it would be an instant bestseller, but Pat will never do that. She's too honorable.

"Let's hope that AFI's almanac will remind people, year by year, that it is not the technology or the delivery system, but the storytellers who show us the way."

—STEVEN SPIELBERG, filmmaker and AFI trustee (1986–2008, 2010–present)

Focus on Message

Looking back, it is easy to see how hard the AFI board and senior management team worked, not only to keep in sync with the new media world, but also to keep AFI relevant within it. We went through the process and changed the institutional identity in 1995, then revisited the mission again in 2000. In 2003, through the remarkable auspices and pro bono efforts of McKinsey and Co., we again sought to define, refine, and encourage a clarity of purpose and core programs. Again, the experts listened to stakeholders and came up with words to describe how AFI would be defined in this new millennium. And, once again, it took time to get the board to embrace the new language, albeit for the first time without the word "preservation." The statement said:

> *AFI is a national institute providing leadership in screen education and the recognition and celebration of excellence in the art of film, television, and digital media.*

At exactly this same time, AFI was trying to think even bigger about more ambitious projects, like a National Movie Week across America. The great Phil Guarascio had brought in another national marketing team to put such a large plan together. (Phil had now moved from GM to the NFL and was thinking—I kid you not—about how to build an AFI project of such stature, size, and visibility that it would garner the same kind of public excitement as the Super Bowl.)

Phil had made the initial *AFI's 100 Years...100 Movies* project a reality because of his GM sponsorships. He also sponsored Bud Yorkin's AFI Celebrity Golf Tournaments, a relatively new concept, which trustee Yorkin ran with because it combined two local passions (golf and movies). This event raised more than $4 million over eleven years. So National Movie Week was well within reason, given Phil's track record of making big things happen. Again, the studios and guilds stood tall, and all agreed to participate. And again, without studio and guild support with their movies, clips, and rights, there would be nothing to talk about. But we also needed the exhibitors. I had maintained a strong relationship with the exhibition community because of my paternal credentials. Movie theaters were facing rough times because of the avalanche of new ways to watch movies beyond the big screen. Nevertheless, they also joined the project. All hands were on deck, with the concept being driven by Condé Nast and their very strategic and dynamic marketing guru Richard Beckerman. We held innumerable meetings and spent hours crunching numbers. All this planning with Phil Guarascio left us aggressively prepared to move forward. Then, suddenly, the national economic slowdown caught up with publishing. Spending on advertising was pulled back, and *poof!* National Movie Week was gone.

At this same time, we were finalizing WASC accreditation for the Conservatory, and the Digital Content Lab was blooming. AFI was going 100 miles an hour in several different directions at once. With the fortieth anniversary approaching, I realized that it was time for me to step aside and for the board to find my successor. But before that, there was a slate of anniversary events to conceptualize and produce.

One of the most delightful adventures was *Target Presents AFI Night at the Movies*. We put together the idea with Target's local consultant, Gary Tobey, and then Bob Gazzale and I flew to Minneapolis in January 2007 to make the final pitch to Michael Francis, Target's famed marketing chief. The wind was blowing so strongly that we could barely walk across the street from the hotel to Target headquarters. But it was warm inside, when we got a $1 million commitment for *Target Presents AFI Night at the Movies*, thanks to the wonderful folks in frigid Minneapolis. Again, a simple concept: celebrating classic films by presenting them in their full stature on the big screen. Introduced by the artists who had made the films from behind or in front of the camera, these movies reached a new generation of film fans.

Transformation

From 1995 to 2005, AFI was transformed from a federally funded entity to a self-sustaining national-educational-cultural institution, always fulfilling its original mandate to celebrate the artistic achievements of moving images, affirming and celebrating all aspects of the ever-changing, ever-more-impactful, and engaging ways to tell and watch these stories.

Target Presents AFI Night at the Movies

AFI has always been fortunate to draw the support of actors and filmmakers working at the top of their craft. In 2007, the lineup at the fabulous ArcLight Cinemas in Hollywood the night before the AFI's Fortieth Anniversary Luncheon included:

- Julie Andrews presenting *The Sound of Music*
- Warren Beatty presenting *Bonnie and Clyde*
- Billy Crystal and Rob Reiner presenting *When Harry Met Sally . . .*
- Kirk Douglas presenting *Spartacus*
- Clint Eastwood presenting *Unforgiven*
- Morgan Freeman presenting *The Shawshank Redemption*
- Tippi Hedren presenting *The Birds*
- Angela Lansbury presenting *Beauty and the Beast*
- George Lucas presenting *Star Wars*
- Jack Nicholson presenting *One Flew Over the Cuckoo's Nest*
- Sylvester Stallone presenting *Rocky*

The board was strong in its leadership role, always cautious to protect the reputation of the Institute and believing in AFI's higher calling in a very noble way, while on a parallel track endorsing the highest accreditation for the AFI Conservatory. It all went hand-in-hand, as the true maturation of the Institute took firm root.

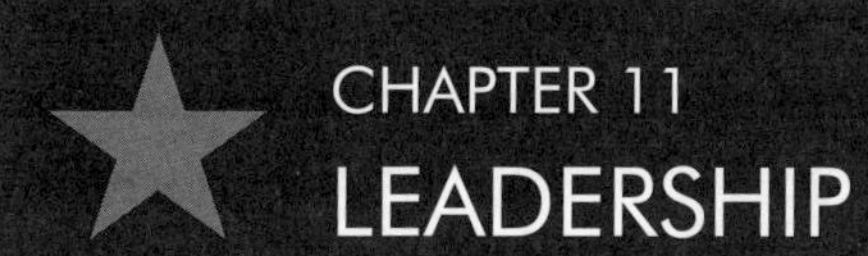

Ensuring the Future: The Role of AFI's Board of Trustees

JEAN PICKER FIRSTENBERG

There is no more essential component of a nonprofit institution than its board of trustees. A board's success being dependent upon the leadership at the head of the table, this chapter will tell the story of some of the men and women who played prominent roles throughout these years on the AFI Board of Trustees, as I experienced them.

Without an involved, committed, giving, and smart board, a nonprofit will not succeed. The evolving culture of a board, established by the ways it interacts and does its business, goes a long way in determining its effectiveness. It is quite clear to me why AFI was able to grow through its early years into organizational adulthood: definitive board leadership and strong board support across generations and platforms and changing leadership skill sets. This tradition was established early on and has never wavered.

The board's primary responsibility is to select and support the president and CEO. My first meeting with the AFI Board of Trustees as new AFI director and CEO was on the occasion of the organization's 38th meeting. My last was the 120th. In addition to these eighty-two meetings, there were executive committee meetings and a slew of retreats, committee meetings, and task force gatherings. Some of these were enormously energizing, others were effective, and all were exhausting.

AFI was a challenging organization to govern, in part because it was, from the start, something of a hybrid, founded with a national mandate to elevate film as an art form and headquartered in the nation's capital near its federal parents—yet rooted in the filmmaking capital of the world, Hollywood, and needing to respond to the burgeoning independent media arts community that was exploding around the country. Fortunately, AFI received significant funding for its first three decades from the federal government and then an ever-expanding group of major foundations, corporations, individuals, and entrepreneurial activities.

There are many trustees beyond those who served as chairs that also played key roles, and every trustee brings professional expertise of one kind or another. For example, Ernst & Young has been a remarkable corporate partner, represented on the AFI board first by Kelly Rose (1993–2003) and since then by Gary Birkenbeuel. They have provided insights and leadership on all financial matters, while also providing extensive advisory support when especially needed. Another example is Lawrence Herbert, founder and former chair and CEO of Pantone, the world standard for color across industries. Lawrence introduced himself to AFI out of a generous philanthropic spirit and has provided superb business and publishing advice, serving on the board almost continuously from 1987 until his last board meeting in June 2017. Space does not allow every trustee to be acknowledged in full, but every trustee is listed in the Appendix, and several are recognized throughout the book.

Since there was no other organization like it at the time, there was no blazed trail for AFI to follow. In re-reading the meeting minutes from my twenty-seven years—eighty-two trustee meetings and over a hundred executive committee or director meetings—I am overwhelmed by the memory of how hard it always seemed to be, and how remarkably patient and consistently supportive the board was. There were many meetings during the 1980s when the need to pay for the campus and its renovations, combined with the challenge of maintaining federal funding, required AFI to develop new strategic priorities and operational designs. And these challenges were met by the skills of a core group of trustee leaders.

But working with the trustees was also a challenge, because we had (and have) major figures in their fields. Since the 1990s, the board has included the heads of the major studios, networks, corporations, guilds, technologists, educators, philanthropists, and artists who work in front of and behind the camera—a group of individuals with strong opinions who are all very smart. Let me repeat that—*very* smart. (One trustee recently replied when I asked him how he thought a meeting went: "There are *too* many smart people at the table.") Therefore, arriving at a consensus . . . well . . . that could be hard. You never knew where a discussion might lead. This was the fascinating dynamic at the board table. This was the challenge, not only for me but for every board chair.

It was an absolute delight to write about the board leadership and all the trustees who made everything possible. They really deserve far more recognition than they have received. This chapter is only a small token of my regard and appreciation.

Board of Trustees Chairs

Board chairs have a particular role. Their command of the meetings, how they prepare for and organize the meetings, the respect their colleagues hold for them, and their knowledge of every issue on the agenda—each and every one of these elements is paramount.

The personalities of the board chair have shifted over the course of AFI history. The first three were strong personalities, and two were major movie stars at the time of their service (you don't get much bigger than Gregory Peck and Charlton Heston). And, serving briefly in between them was Washington, DC, power-broker Roger Stevens (no relation to George Stevens). Subsequent chairs were all business leaders and heads of television networks or movie studios (or companies that owned movie studios), except, of course, for the charming Bonita Granville Wrather (quite a sharp businessperson who served a short two years due to health reasons) and Richard Brandt (chair and CEO of a small exhibition chain). Their profiles speak to the nature of both the fiduciary responsibility of a board but also to the personalities of these individuals, who provided extraordinary insights into how best to leverage the board's relationships to the Institute's advantage. That, of course, is the purpose of a board: to provide insights into the future course that may be chartered, and to find the best way to pursue that direction.

In those eighty-two meetings when I sat next to the chair, there was never a meeting where the chair wasn't prepared. It is really hard to fake it in front of twenty, thirty, or sometimes even forty trustees. But personal caring also counts, especially since one never knew where a discussion might go. More often than not, there were surprises, in the most unlikely of subjects and especially when change was involved. Navigating these issues, such as updating the logo and mission statement, took considerable political skill at the head of the table. Talking through hard issues is always the best way to find some unanimity. All these chairs had the leadership chops to find the way through controversial and difficult issues.

Each board chair's strength was brought to bear in support of the Institute's needs at the time of their service. For example, Richard Brandt, a superb negotiator, represented AFI with other major entities, e.g., the NEA, the City of Beverly Hills, and the Atlantic Richfield company. Bonita Granville Wrather's relationship with President and Mrs. Reagan benefited AFI's situation

AFI Board of Trustees Chairs

Gregory Peck‡ (1967–1969)

Roger Stevens‡ (1970–1972)

Charlton Heston‡ (1972–1983)

George Stevens Jr. (1980–1983)

Richard Brandt (1983–1986)

Bonita Granville Wrather‡ (1986–1988)

Gene F. Jankowski (1988–1992)

Fred Pierce (1992–1996)

Tom Pollock (1996–2000)

Sir Howard Stringer (2000–Present)

‡Deceased

at the NEA and the Kennedy Center time after time. Gene Jankowski had the brilliant idea to celebrate the twenty-fifth anniversary of the NEA with an exceptional evening in Washington, DC, with forty-first President and Mrs. George H. W. Bush. Fred Pierce found a way for AFI to develop a national program that not only brought tremendous recognition for AFI worldwide but also developed a revenue stream to replace NEA funding when it ended completely in 1998. Tom Pollock transformed AFI into a self-sustaining entity with a myriad of new programs during his years. Sir Howard Stringer was the first American to head the giant Sony Corporation that not only provided AFI with breakthrough technology during its greatest years but also was one of the first foreign companies to acquire a major Hollywood studio. I must also salute our brilliant board guru, Bob Daly, who chaired Warner Bros. during multiple glory years and has never wavered in bringing both his network of contacts and his galaxy of friends into the AFI orbit.

Over the years, there have been twenty dedicated trustees who have served as vice chairs, starting with founding trustee Sidney Poitier in 1967. All of them were deeply involved with many aspects of the Institute and were particularly strong ambassadors, spreading AFI's goals and objectives with the authority of their own distinctive achievements and their peers' respect.

Board of Directors

(Formerly the Executive Committee)

It was Tom Pollock's idea to change the bylaws and create a board of directors (operating under the title of the executive committee

AFI Board of Directors Chairs (Executive Committee Chairs until 2000)
Arnold Picker‡ (1969–1972)
Richard Brandt (1972–1978)
Gordon Stulberg‡ (1978–1987)
Franklin J. Schaffner‡ (1987–1988)
Charles W. Fries (1989–1992)
Tony Thomopoulos (1993–1995)
Sir Howard Stringer (1996–2000)
Tom Pollock (2000–2002)
Jon Avnet and John F. Cooke (2002–2009)
Bob Daly (2009–Present)

‡Deceased

until 2000). Under either name, the group always spent an inordinate amount of time thinking about board structure and board membership, knowing what a huge difference these can make. It takes a lot of time to come to consensus. A new idea might have made sense and new board members may have been spectacular, but sometimes nothing we tried actually worked. Along the way, those who tried were truly the ones who deserved the applause, because if you hadn't come to the meetings, if you hadn't made the calls, if you hadn't gone to the lunches or dinners or breakfasts, if you hadn't thought about how to convince someone to believe in the cause, AFI wouldn't have survived for fifty years and wouldn't be looking ahead with confidence to the next fifty.

Leadership by Phase of Growth

AFI has gone through various phases of growth over its fifty-year history, with each phase demanding a particular character and set of skills of its trustees. I think of the shifts as characterized in five phases. In describing the individuals involved in each phase, it becomes apparent that each served at a time that paralleled the exact skills needed by the AFI.

THE INVENTORS (1967–1979)

Beyond just creating the institution, the Inventors are the people who made the organization work and gave it a formidable momentum. The Inventors who started AFI deserve dual credit for their work, because designing an institution from scratch is far more difficult than modifying the initial structure—and especially in this case, when there were no models to emulate.

THE INVESTORS (1980–1989)

The Investors saw what the Inventors had accomplished and, out of respect for their vision, gave an investor-type response by providing the connections and resources to give AFI deep roots. These were a determined group of individuals who brought stability to AFI by buying an established campus and gained accreditation that lent academic credibility to the young AFI.

THE CHANGE AGENTS (1990–1995)

Forced to restructure in a number of domains, the Change Agents and others came to terms with the inevitable elimination of AFI's federal funding and the huge challenges that accompanied them. This group took new steps to align the institution image with the foresight that embraced the new digital world.

THE NATIONAL VISIONARIES (1996–2000)

During this period, the Institute experienced its largest growth spurt in two decades—a growth that was fostered by the Centennial Celebration. This brought with it national recognition and visibility, signaling institutional independence and maturation. And, finally, they embraced full regional academic accreditation, the last step to ensuring a long-term vitality for the institution as an educational entity.

THE DIGITAL DYNAMOS (2001–2007)

Digital technology had reshaped the creative process for the profession, and the Digital Dynamos, building off the work of the Change Agents and others, prepared for the fitful transition to the twenty-first century.

EARLY TWENTY-FIRST-CENTURY HEROES (2008–2017)

Forced to face the harshest economic recession, these heroes regrouped, as always, to hold AFI's initiatives together. They not only maintained the Institute's priorities but also brilliantly renovated the campus and built programs where appropriate.

The Inventors (1967–1979)

GREGORY PECK
Board of Trustees Chair (1967–1969)
ROGER STEVENS
Board of Trustees Chair (1970–1972)

When I started my tenure as director on January 1, 1980, the pioneering board of trustees—I call them the Inventors—had already defined AFI's culture. The Inventors firmly believed there was a deep and real need for an American Film Institute, and that the mandate for the AFI was clearly ordained in the White House with the September 29, 1965, legislation that created the National Endowment for the Arts and the National Endowment for the Humanities. President Johnson's initial announcement that there would be "an American Film Institute, bringing together leading artists of the film industry, outstanding educators, and young men and women who wish to pursue this twentieth-century art form as their life's work" settled the issue permanently for them.

I did not serve when Greg Peck or Roger Stevens were chairs, but I spent considerable time with both, so I know how committed and engaged they were with the evolution of the Institute. What were those first board meetings like? Appointing George Stevens Jr., hiring a staff, getting legal counsel, designing stationery and a logo, opening a bank account—this slew of activities gave the first voice to AFI's goals and objectives, defining not only *why* but *how* this new thing called the "American Film Institute" would function and prosper. The culture of a board is central to the culture of the management of an institution. And it all starts from day one.

Greg Peck was a man of immense presence, stature, and character who carried himself with dignity and purpose. He was, by far, the best founding chair any organization could have had, because he took his responsibilities seriously and only associated himself with entities that he cared about.

Roger Stevens was certainly a major force in the establishment of AFI. He chaired the initial National Council on the Arts, of which Gregory Peck was also an original member. In all, Roger Stevens chaired three major cultural institutions in America: the National Endowment for the Arts, the American Film Institute, and the John F. Kennedy Center for the Performing Arts. What a legacy. As NEA chairman, Roger Stevens worked closely with George Stevens Jr. on the purpose, funding, and structure of the AFI. While George should certainly be identified as the principal inventor of AFI, he would agree that the leadership in those early days from Greg and Roger was also essential.

The first AFI trustees were deeply committed individuals who personally believed their values and reputations were aligned with the goals they would establish for AFI. They knew right up front that there would be financial challenges. Of the founding Inventors, only two—Jack Valenti and George Stevens Jr.—were on the board when I began twelve years later.

ARNOLD PICKER
Executive Committee Chair (1969–1972)

My uncle (my father's youngest brother) was a brilliant businessman; insightful and sharp, he didn't suffer fools. He wanted to retire at forty-five, but it took him to fifty-five, and then he moved to Golden Beach, Florida, a tiny town of less than 1,000 people just north of Miami. He ran for mayor, was elected, and resigned after a week—or so the family lore goes.

He was not only an AFI founding trustee but the first chair of the executive committee and primary fundraiser—without staff. As for AFI lore, there was a meeting in the early 1970s when finances were very tight. Arnold left the room to make a phone call, and when he returned, he said that $25,000 had been donated to AFI. As you can perhaps perceive, Arnold was a man of limited patience, and he resigned from the board in 1972. When he was involved, he

The Pick of the Enemies List

The Picker family's proudest moment was when Nixon's Enemies List was published in 1971. Nixon was a man with a lot of enemies, and the very first name on the list—the *first* name—was Arnold Picker. Arnold had supported Senator Edmund Muskie of Maine, who was thought to be Nixon's biggest potential rival before the Muskie campaign flamed out, and I had made the introduction.

In 1969, Muskie was thinking about running but did not believe he could be a real presidential contender, coming from such a small state where he had never had to raise money. (He once spent $8,000 on automobile bumper stickers, because he said he didn't need more—as long as they were on the right cars.) At the time, I was involved with the Democratic Party, and when we heard that Muskie needed campaign donors, we went to Arnold, who gave $25,000. Muskie then wanted to meet the man who had made such a contribution without a meeting or even a handshake. The likelihood of these two guys from totally different backgrounds getting along was unlikely, but Muskie and his wife Jane would fly down to Florida to visit Arnold and his wife Ruth. This Roman Catholic couple hit it off famously with my Jewish tante, Ruth, who peppered conversation with Yiddish and called my uncle *bubbeleh*.

When I called Arnold to tell him I wanted to throw my hat in the ring to succeed George Stevens Jr. as AFI director, he didn't beat about the bush, asking, "Why would you want that job?"

was all in, and when he moved on, he didn't look back.

GORDON STULBERG
Executive Committee Chair (1978–1987)

Gordon was the Canadian-born son of a labor organizer who worked his way through the University of Toronto, received his law degree from Cornell, and then moved to Los Angeles with a law firm that happened to represent the Writers Guild of America. Gordon was responsible for calling the first strike of the guild in 1954, which established for all future collective-bargaining agreements the concept of separation of rights and residuals, a crucial concept as digital media and Internet distribution entered the scene. A very successful AFI alumnus who has worked on many major TV series over the years told me that he is eternally grateful to Gordon; over this alumnus's career, his residuals have added up to more than $4.5 million.

Gordon went on to work at several studios, leading the turnaround of Twentieth Century Fox, where he was president and COO to chair and CEO Dennis Stanfill. Fox had previously greenlit *Star Wars* (after my brother turned it down at United Artists), but, in subsequent negotiations with Tom Pollock (on behalf of George Lucas), Fox also gave George Lucas the rights to own all the sequels, and then even gave Lucas back all the merchandising rights for *Star Wars* sequels. No one makes the right choice every time.

Gordon and his wife, Helen, were down-to-earth, kind people who had no airs. Many of those board meetings in the 1980s took place in the large pool house at their home on Comstock Avenue. Gordon suffered severely from diabetes but never complained. He was easy to work with, loved teaching at UCLA and USC, and was deeply involved with the formation of the California Community College Association, which he also chaired. After being central to the AFI campus acquisition, Gordon had to endure hard years at the helm before we secured the CEFA Bond Issue. His legal and fiscal acumen combined with his academic experiences meant so much for so long.

Even into the 1990s, Gordon still chaired a committee to ascertain whether a $15 million offer to purchase the campus was valid. (After several weeks of negotiating, the offer disappeared.) His expertise and commitment was always available to AFI.

The Investors (1980–1989)

Because the board is solely responsible for the selection of the CEO, I had met most of the current trustees by the time I started. And, because the acquisition of the campus occurred in the first eight months of my tenure, a lot happened so quickly that I was not really aware of the incredible dynamic of board participation. But over time, I became fascinated with the entire process of board management. As with the process of fundraising (described in Chapter 9) you try every possible way to engage board members—asking every member to be on a committee or committees, or subcommittees or holding retreats, or special task forces to solve specific, short-term issues. Effective board management requires enormous staff time. An inordinate amount of time over the years was consumed parsing who should be on the board, how large the board should be, who were the entities, corporations, and individuals whose representation could, should, and would make a real difference. Truth be told, these issues are discussed almost continually.

Gordon Stulberg, chair of the executive committee when I was selected, told me in one interview, "The board doesn't want to run the AFI. That's your job." But, the board and the CEO *must* be on the same page. The board must trust the CEO to use the resources of the organization appropriately—and, if not, the CEO will know about it.

Believe me, over the years there were many things I wanted to do that the board did not. But if I couldn't get the board's approval, I had to back off and try again at another time, if I still wanted to pursue another path. Over the first decade of my service, there were many decisions that were forced upon the Institute due to deep financial restrictions. These were particularly uncomfortable for my predecessor, whose own sweat and energy had started many programs that had to be reduced in size or even eliminated. Understandably, at board meetings, displeasure at changes was often expressed but only with respect and disappointment that the reality of the situation required such changes. It was neither easy nor pleasant when we had to close the DC office, or sell *American Film* magazine, or leave the AFI Theater at the Kennedy Center because the Kennedy Center management wanted to derive real income from the AFI space. Change can cause huge dissension. That is why a CEO who hopes to be around awhile needs to get the board fully involved before making big changes. You also better be right more often than not.

CHARLTON HESTON
Board of Trustees Chair (1972–1983) and President (1983–2006)

There was an odd phenomenon with the board chair role at the beginning of my tenure. When he resigned as director and CEO, George Stevens Jr. had been named as chair alongside Charlton Heston. Certainly Chuck had great respect for George, but Chuck saw himself as chair, not one of two chairs (and it was made very clear that they were not co-chairs). As Chuck would say, he carried Moses's staff with pride (and much better than anyone else).

Chuck Heston, a drama major at Northwestern University, loved theater and Shakespeare. He was a voracious reader and a beautiful writer who was always politically involved, first as a Democrat marching with Martin Luther King and then becoming a Republican to support his friend and fellow actor, Ronald Reagan, both of whom served as presidents of the Screen Actors Guild during their careers.

Eighteen months after I started, Chuck was tapped by then-President Reagan to chair his Presidential Task Force on the NEA and NEH. So, for the next eighteen months, the AFI board had no chair. George stood in, always gallant, but after twelve intense years, he really didn't want to be the only active, involved chair. We needed Chuck, but we didn't know how long his leave of absence would last.

By early 1982, Chuck's plans were still unclear, but he was so devoted that he wanted to find a different structure that worked for AFI and for him. The new position of AFI president solved this dilemma, a role Chuck took as seriously as he did chairman, until his health stole him from us in 2006.

Heston and I went on many trips on behalf of AFI. For instance, in 1983, we went to Atlanta to meet Ted Turner. CNN was just making its mark, and TNT and TCM especially were giving movie lovers wonderful choices 24/7, without commercial interruptions—a rare delight in an age before streaming video. Around Heston, Turner acted like a moonstruck teenager. He could not believe he was meeting Moses. A strong relationship evolved over the years between Heston and Turner and its multiple cable outlets.

GEORGE STEVENS JR.
Board of Trustees Chair (1980–1983)

As the founding director, George Stevens Jr. had a profound influence on what AFI has become. His founding passion and willingness to leverage his political and social relationships created a national entity to honor the motion picture arts. His concept for the AFI Conservatory (initially called the Center for Advanced Film Studies, then the Center for Advanced Film and Television Studies from 1985 until 2000) was spot-on. His twelve years fighting with the NEA for reliable funding was a form of hand-to-hand combat. His producing and writing abilities were brilliantly displayed during his twenty-four-year run as executive producer and writer of the AFI Life Achievement Awards. As the face of AFI during his years, George took the brunt of the attacks from the NEA, the archival community, and academic and indie world critics (perhaps more personal than they needed to be), but George never wavered. Despite how different AFI may look to him now than it did in 1979, George is still at the table to remind us how it all started when he was fighting the good fight that made all the next chapters possible.

RICHARD BRANDT
Board of Trustees Chair (1983–1986) and Executive Committee Chair (1972–1978)

With Heston not returning as chair, AFI needed to select a full-time chair. George said to me, "You have to choose: Bobby Wise or Richard Brandt." A tough choice, but at the fiftieth board meeting on March 3, 1983, Richard took the gavel. This was no disrespect to the wonderful Bobby Wise, but we had never had a businessman as chair, and given AFI's fiscal challenges at that time, we needed business acumen at the head of the table.

Richard wanted to examine every line on the AFI budget, and to know every aspect of our activities. He ran his own company in the same manner. Richard's AFI board meetings were punctuated with his detailed summary of what had been accomplished since the last meeting. He was one of the few trustees who read all the minutes and he became, over time, the only trustee who specifically asked if there are any corrections to the minutes. Richard suggested we hold board meetings at studios and networks offices all over town, a refreshing change of venue for trustees (hosts were always gracious).

During Richard's three years as chair, AFI accomplished a great deal, including accreditation by the National Association of Schools of Art and Design, securing the California Educational Facilities Authority Bond Issue, and navigating a wide range of NEA

"When I became chair in the mid '80s, Jack Lemmon was a board member. Jack was very helpful on the board — he really worked on a lot of different things. One day we were meeting in the CBS offices, and Jack Lemmon hadn't shown up yet. And since he was out of the room, we began to talk about the next nominee for the Life Achievement Award. Suddenly, there's some noise in the background, like a door creaking. Jack Lemmon was embarrassed about being late, and he was on his hands and knees, actually crawling across the room. Someone saw me wave a little bit, and then he popped up near his seat. We had to stop talking about the Life Achievement Award! Of course, a year and a half later, he got the Life Achievement Award."

—RICHARD BRANDT,
corporate executive and AFI board of trustees chair (1983–1986)

issues (always NEA issues). He was truly a superb negotiator, especially with the City of Beverly Hills and Atlantic Richfield when we were unable to fulfill our campus loan obligations, and Richard was always able to secure far more advantageous settlements for AFI.

Richard is a longtime family friend; our fathers were New York theater exhibitors who respected and liked each other. Without a doubt, Richard was instrumental in my being named director and CEO. While I had never worked with Richard, I learned his style quickly. And for someone who was such a micro-manager, I was stunned to know he also wrote poetry.

BONITA "BUNNY" GRANVILLE WRATHER
Board of Trustees Chair (1986–1988)

Soon after Ronald Reagan was elected U.S. President, one of the smartest things AFI did was invite Bunny Wrather to join the board. I was in awe of Bunny; she was so sharp and so classy, she knew everybody, and everyone loved and respected her.

She was married to Jack Wrather for thirty-six years, living a fabulous life as his partner in all facets of their world, including business dealings in oil, real estate, and entertainment. They owned a building on the corner of Canon Drive and Dayton Way in Beverly Hills. Bunny's office was painted a bright yellow, and I always thought that was because sunshine always seemed to surround her. She often drove a big, old Rolls-Royce, and I swear she could barely see over the steering wheel. Bunny had been a successful child actress who had had a brief performing career as a young woman. She had a great sense of business, and she and Jack built the Disneyland Hotel when it was a huge gamble in 1955, in a place no one knew then, called Anaheim. They also owned the rights to *Lassie* and *The Lone Ranger* and, best of all, they were close friends of "Nancy and Ronnie" and were prominent members of the Reagan Kitchen Cabinet (actually, everyone who was a member was prominent). Bunny was also appointed by the president to serve on the Kennedy Center board, and that was helpful to the AFI as well.

Bunny was thrilled to be invited to chair the AFI board; she had become active immediately when she joined the board and understood what AFI stood for. She was such a gracious soul but nobody's fool, and she often opened her home for AFI meetings and events. You never worried about anything that was being held on Delfern Drive, because Bunny's home was elegant and lively.

Unfortunately, our timing was less than perfect. Just as Bunny joined the board, Jack took ill with a rare form of lung cancer. He passed away in 1984, so Bunny assuming the chair role in 1986 seemed appropriate but, hard as it was to believe, she contracted the exact same form of cancer and was gone within two years of being diagnosed. However, she accomplished a great deal in her short tenure, especially because she ran into a young friend, believe it or not, in a seamstress shop. She had long known Suzanne Lloyd Hayes, Harold's Lloyd's granddaughter, who had been raised in his home. Sue has been the steward of Lloyd's legacy and became one of AFI's great benefactors when she donated over $1 million from the Harold Lloyd Foundation to name a wing in the Warner Bros. building and also to name the Conservatory Master Seminar program the Harold Lloyd Master Seminar. And that's how you get a million-dollar gift, we learned—you recognize someone's voice in the dressing room of a seamstress shop.

Before Bunny was finally hospitalized, we honored her at her last board meeting on campus and named the Bonita Granville Wrather Gallery in the Warner Bros. building in her honor. She deserved no less, and she passed with the dignity that she had lived with all her life.

FRANKLIN J. SCHAFFNER
Executive Committee Chair (1987–1988)

A prince of a guy, Franklin was the first man I ever saw who wore the classic Hollywood uniform for creatives: a navy-blue blazer with blue oxford shirt and blue jeans—and did he wear them well! Born in Tokyo, the son of missionaries in Japan, he first came to the U.S. at the age of five after his father died suddenly. He grew up in Lancaster, Pennsylvania, and went to Franklin & Marshall College, where he studied drama. While he was studying law at Columbia, he entered the Navy and served four years during WWII. Returning to New York City, he started working for a peace organization but then got a job as an assistant director for the documentary series *March of Time*. He joined CBS and rose to director of the new series of live dramas adapted from Broadway productions. Actually, he directed 150 hours of live television plays for CBS, including a number with war themes, such as *The Caine Mutiny Court-Martial* as well as *Twelve Angry Men*, many of which won Emmys and other awards.

Moving on to Hollywood and the movies in 1963, his inquisitive mind and political interests all came together in his movie storytelling, and he directed the remarkable *The Best Man*, *Planet of the Apes*, *Patton*, and *Papillon*, receiving numerous nominations and many awards (including an Oscar). Franklin was a prominent member of the National Council of the Arts and president of the Directors Guild of America, as well as a member of the AFI board and chair of the board advisory committee for the Center for Advanced Film Studies. Establishing this crucial committee to understand the Center's strengths and weaknesses was central to the growth and development of the Center into a full two-year Conservatory.

Franklin had a spectacular, wry sense of humor, though he credited his equally spectacular wife, Jean, with some of his best lines. They both became close friends when we traveled together to China in 1985 as part of an official U.S. delegation shortly after the end of the Chinese Cultural Revolution. Franklin was an elegant man with a dignified demeanor that commanded respect. Jean was a founding member of the AFI Associates, a woman of great wisdom. One day, I was pontificating on how making money was not my goal in life (clearly), but she advised, "Jeannie, remember to always have enough for a cab on a rainy day."

The Change Agents (1990–1996)

These leaders helped bring television into the totality of the moving image storytelling world that AFI represented. But the changes they oversaw were more than symbolic; the digital world was also evolving in ways few realized would be as profound as they have become.

GENE F. JANKOWSKI
Board of Trustees Chair (1988–1992)

Jankowski was born in Buffalo, New York. He went to Canisius College for undergrad, and then Michigan State University for a master's in radio, TV, and film. He started working at CBS in the sales department and worked his way up the ladder in 1970 to vice president, then controller, and then president in 1977, during Bill Paley's CBS heyday. He was chair and president of the CBS Broadcast Group for twelve years.

During his tenure as chair, Gene brought a great sensibility to the role and a great deal of New York involvement. He wanted every studio head and every network chief on the board. The only reprise of a Life Achievement Award came in 1992, when Sidney Poitier held a second event in NYC because Harry Belafonte had a conflict with the L.A. date. We got the second event completely underwritten by Ernst & Young, and it was as much fun the second time as it was the first. But Gene's most brilliant idea was one of the truly great nights in AFI history. The Back to the Rose Garden gala on September 26, 1989, was Gene's crowning moment; he made it happen. What we didn't quite realize that night was that, within months, technology would start changing the world of moving images with such speed that we would be stunned. But at that shining moment, classic American film history stood tall, and the art and artists received the recognition they so deserved.

In 1989, Gene invited the then-president of Michigan State, where he had gotten his graduate degree and where he taught a course after he left CBS, to join the board. John DiBiaggio was a wonderful trustee because he knew the world of academia so well, and the board really took its clues from him as accreditation became so significant. He chaired a mini-retreat with the board in 1994 that was extremely enlightening and helpful. He often explained that his success as a president of a university was dependent on his board. He felt that their counsel, guidance, and support were essential to his effectiveness. I certainly knew that was the case at AFI. I could point to every major step that had the board's total commitment and involvement that made it at all possible.

FRED PIERCE
Board of Trustees Chair (1992–1996)

Change was everywhere, but that was what made AFI so strong in those days, because we had steady hands on the wheel. Fred was a New York City guy; after attending CCNY, he began his career as a TV research analyst. He was the main architect in the growth of ABC from an also-ran to a full-fledged competitor with CBS and NBC. He conceptualized investment spending as a business strategy for the networks and established the event-driven concept for miniseries. Scheduling *Roots* for five straight nights on the ABC network changed television, as did combining sports and news in the 1970s. Fred identified and nurtured some of the most creative executives in the business, like Roone Arledge, Fred Silverman, Barry Diller, Michael Eisner, and Tony Thomopoulos.

Fred presided over great changes at AFI as NEA money was on its way out. And he prepared AFI for thinking in a new way, inviting new ideas and being strong and incisive as a decision-maker. It was a time of dramatic change—in film and television, all around us—and we had to make major changes. In the end, his chairmanship prepared him to find a way for AFI to become the national organization we sought to be.

There was great pressure from others on the board who thought AFI could only survive with federal funding because, to them, it was in AFI's DNA, and they could not deal with snipping the umbilical cord. No one realized at the time that it would be Fred Pierce who would develop the path for AFI to not only become a national entity, but also develop a large annual revenue stream for eleven years.

CHARLES W. FRIES
Executive Committee Chair (1989–1992)

Chuck Fries is another one of those true hands-on workers. Growing up in Cincinnati, Ohio, he is a proud graduate of Ohio State

"In the network business, you commit to your programming and then hope you can sell it and make a profit. AFI, being a nonprofit organization, would have to make the choice of committing to $10 million up front, and hopefully we would be able to sell the advertising time that would cover our exposure and our tails, and make a profit. All of this was transitioning during my four-year term, and I was pushing the idea, having come from a network where you make millions of dollars in commitments, like the Olympic Games, and then sell it. So, to me, it was a no-brainer. But to people on this board at that time, it might have been more challenging."

—FRED PIERCE,
network executive and AFI board of trustees chair (1992–1996)

University, but he moved to L.A. to work for a relative who was at Ziv TV. He knows everything about how to produce TV movies, miniseries, and features. After learning his vocation, he formed his own company, Chuck Fries Productions.

Early in his board term, Chuck worked hard to bring the TV world into AFI, especially by supporting the TV Writers Workshop sponsored by the networks in rotation for over fifteen years; lots of multitalented men and women came through this unique AFI program. He and his wife, Ava, who was an active member of the AFI Associates and served as their president, were very generous.

Chuck never gave less than 100 percent to any of his responsibilities. He was deeply committed to the AFI's K–12 National Education Program and worked diligently to get federal funding for it in the mid-1990s.

TONY THOMOPOULOS
Executive Committee Chair (1993–1995)

Like every television studio head, Tony Thomopolous was a great executive. It came with the territory. He was also handsome and charming. He married Cristina Ferrare in 1985, and they were gracious hosts. More than that, Tony was deeply loyal. He did an amazing thing for AFI as he was being shown the door as a result of ABC merging with Capital Cities in 1985.

In the mid-1980s, Gene Jankowski told the board that his CBS colleagues in Los Angeles didn't want to carry the Life Achievement Award telecast exclusively, suggesting that it be rotated between the three major networks. (As noted earlier, there were only three major networks at the time, although that would change within five years.)

So, Bob Daly began the process that he would continue to this day: he negotiated the AFI LAA telecast partnership in the most positive way because it was and is so central to AFI's fiscal health. And Tony agreed that ABC would be one of the partners in a six-year deal rotating between the three major networks at the time. However, he had to step down, and forty-eight hours before he had to vacate his office he called and told me he was sending over the contract for ABC to broadcast two LAAs. I should sign it and return the executed copy immediately, he said. With all the things he had to do as he was leaving, that was an expression of friendship you don't always see or ever forget. It was a pleasure to welcome Tony to the board in 1983 and to the leadership role in 1993.

In 1991, we invited Tony and Cristina to a small dinner that Mark Goodson was hosting for AFI at the Beverly Hills Hotel, where Mark kept a small apartment. It was in honor of Patricia Kluge, then-wife of John Kluge, the billionaire owner of Orion Pictures, and underwriter of the Virginia Festival of American Film in Charlottesville (run by a young UVA graduate by the name of Bob Gazzale). They were visiting L.A. and wanted to meet people in town. Patricia always wanted to have breakfast-lunch-dinner with stars. Chuck Heston had gone to the festival on behalf of AFI, and so he and Lydia were there as well. It was sort of a strange mix of people, but we were turning out the stars for Kluge. That is how I found myself standing next to Cristina Ferrare and Patricia Kluge as they were talking about John DeLorean—one had had an affair with him, and one had married and then divorced him. It was at that moment that I thought, "This job has its amazing moments." That same night, I was sitting at the far end of the table near Bob Gazzale as a group sang "Happy Birthday" to someone in the large area of the Polo Lounge; we were in the small, intimate back room. And with that, Gazzale pulled out his driver's license and noted that it was April 30, his twenty-sixth birthday. (He would celebrate his twenty-seventh birthday at AFI and has been here ever since!)

> "The moving image of film, television, video, and computer screens reveals in fine detail the culture and conscience of our times and ourselves. AFI, like a close and trusted friend, points out what belongs in our legacy and our future by identifying and honoring the best, and the most important qualities, of those images. What a treasure it is for us all. What a privilege it has been to have had a part in it."
>
> —MICHAEL NESMITH, musician, philanthropist, and AFI trustee (1992–2004)

The National Visionaries (1996–2000)

This phase was dominated by change. New thinking and creative analysis challenged the AFI identity. Charge is hard and often frightening; it took considerable persuasion to build the required consensus, but that is exactly what transpired during this era. And AFI's national voice was about to become truly strong. It was a very exciting era.

TOM POLLOCK
Board of Trustees Chair (1996–2000) and Board of Directors Chair (2000–2002)

Tom Pollock's background was quite different from his predecessors. The son of a prominent doctor, Tom grew up in Beverly Hills and went to prep school in Ojai, California. After graduating from Stanford, he went to Columbia Law School, where he was editor of the *Law Review.* Returning to L.A., he started his career as assistant to George Stevens Jr. at the newly founded AFI. In 1969, he became the manager of business affairs for the new Center for Advanced Film Studies. By 1970, he had started a new entertainment law firm, Pollock, Rigrod, and Bloom (later Pollock, Bloom, and Dekom, and now Bloom Hergott). Without any established clients, Pollock recruited film students from AFI, USC, and UCLA. By the early 1980s, Pollock, Bloom, and Dekom had become the prominent boutique entertainment firm in L.A.

I remember Jon Avnet (class of 1972) telling me that, after he graduated from AFI, he sat in his one-room office and the only people who called him were his wife and his lawyer, Tom Pollock. A young George Lucas was among Tom's first clients. Tom negotiated all the legal deals for *American Graffiti,* as well as the *Star Wars* and *Indiana Jones* franchises. As I got to know Tom, he told me that the only studio he ever wanted to run was Universal—and, in 1986, he left his firm to become executive vice president of MCA and chair of its motion picture group, Universal Pictures. Tom's nine years at the helm of Universal were spectacular. Fortunately, just after he moved on from Universal, he picked up the AFI baton, and I got my studio management education. Tom commuted from Montecito several days a week, working from a van converted into an office (in those early days of the car phone, but not the smartphone). When he stayed in town, he lived at the Beverly Hills Hotel. Every two weeks, we would have breakfast there and he would explain why something had happened in the

"I was chair of Universal, and Bob Daly, Steven Spielberg, and Jon Avnet came to my office and kidnapped me into being chair of AFI. I sort of knew the financial situation was tough, but we were still getting $2 million a year from the NEA. And, of course, the year I came in as chair, the NEA decided to pull the plug entirely. It was a financial crisis, and it was the *100 Years...100 Movies* show that saved our bacon.

"But there was something else. During my tenure as chair, AFI had a whole cultural change in its mentality, from being the recipient of money, to a more entrepreneurial culture. That change was really accomplished because of Jean [Picker Firstenberg], who saw the need and the opportunity. As a non-profit organization, it's not easy to change an entire mindset into taking the initiative to do things. . . . I see my tenure as a time of transition into Sir Howard [Stringer]. But it's really about Jean and how she changed the way the organization thinks of itself and how it operated."

—TOM POLLOCK,
studio executive, producer, and AFI board of trustees chair (1996–2000)

business, how it had happened, and what would happen next. It was like a B-school case study course.

I had become friends with Tom when he joined the board in 1989, so I knew how dedicated he was to AFI. Tom ran the AFI board meetings in a distinct style. He prepared until he knew everything about the issue on the table, and would then go through it with us, point by point. His analogies were brilliant—you had to listen to him and in the end, agree with his logic.

AFI took some humongous steps during his tenure—steps without precedence, steps with great risk, and steps that led to some astonishing accomplishments. Many other trustees were instrumental in helping these projects succeed, but it is no wonder they were initiated and proved successful during Tom's tenure:

- A new AFI logo and Institute identity plan.
- *AFI's 100 Years...100 Movies* series.
- The AFI AWARDS, recognizing the ten best movies and ten best television programs of the year, for which Tom continues to serve as movie jury chair.
- The AFI Silver Theatre and Cultural Center.
- A new board structure, with the executive committee replaced by a board of directors with expanded responsibilities.

Yes, NEA funding also ended during Tom's tour, but AFI's growth was exponential between 1996 and 2000, and much of this was because Tom was at the helm. He would provide major guidance as the digital revolution led to numerous partnership opportunities with technology companies.

The Digital Dynamos (2000–2007) and Early Twenty-First-Century Heroes (2008–2017)

The dramatic changes under Tom Pollock's trustee leadership continued with the change of the century and the truly dynamic changes in the media world. Everything about the field seemed to be upside down and no one knew where it would go, creatively or from a corporate point of view. The board took on new members from the technology world along with marketing gurus. It was a time of shifting priorities, and AFI shifted with the time in order to have a stronger structure that would empower the board of directors to deal with the operations in more detail, while a larger board of trustees was needed to be inclusive of all the new avenues of expression that should be represented at the table.

SIR HOWARD STRINGER
Executive Committee Chair (1996–2000) and Board of Trustees Chair (2000–Present)

Then came Howard Stringer, who had joined the board in 1989 before we had to bow and scrape when he got the best millennium gift ever (on December 31, 1999, he was awarded his KBE, dubbing him our Sir Howard). He had previously served for five years as executive committee chair and had been at the heart of AFI's world when he became head of CBS and joined the board in 1989.

Born in Wales, Howard's father was an English sergeant in the Royal Air Force and his mother was a Welsh schoolteacher. He got his master's from Merton College at Oxford.

Howard Stringer loves movies—particularly American movies. He grew up watching American movies, and right after he graduated, he moved to America because of these movies. As soon as he arrived, he was drafted while answering phones backstage at *The Ed Sullivan Show*. In the U.S. Army, he served in Vietnam as a military policeman in Saigon. Welcome to America, young man!

> "When I was a small boy growing up in England, I never knew I would come to America. For me, the West was *Shane, High Noon,* and *Red River*. All those vistas said to me: *What an extraordinary place. What an extraordinary opportunity. And maybe one day I'll get there.* So when I joined this board for the very first time and looked around this room, I was speechless. To some extent, I will always be speechless—not just by the commitment of all of you, but by the spirit you all represent and the American movies which, for me, are America's greatest export."
>
> —SIR HOWARD STRINGER, corporate executive and AFI board of trustees chair (2000–present)

After returning to New York, Howard's career at CBS spanned thirty years. He earned nine Emmys as a writer, director, and producer for CBS News, and was president of CBS from 1988 to 1995, after Larry Tisch had bought the corporation in 1988. His last corporate journey took him to Sony in 1997 as president of the U.S. operational unit and chair and then CEO of Sony Worldwide. He was the only non-Japanese executive to hold this position.

Howard was a great journalist and a great communicator. His ability to articulate his ideas, combined with his analytical mind, sense of humor, and dignity, make him a compelling figure. He has few peers when it comes to chairing a meeting.

There was never more fun than dining with Sir Howard and his pal, Sir Sean Connery, before he received the AFI Life Achievement Award in 2006. Friends for decades, they could spin a yarn with the best of them. My brother, David Picker, was president of United Artists when Connery was cast as James Bond. Everyone was thrilled to be included at the dinner that night, because we knew we were eating with royalty.

The Sony Video Center was already on campus when Howard went to Sony, but it was renamed the Sony Digital Arts Center, outfitted with its newest, most extraordinary equipment, year after year. Howard delivered both professionally and personally, with major gifts of every possible kind.

At my retirement luncheon, Sir Howard introduced me as a combination of Madame Curie, Joan of Arc, and Myrna Loy. Sure! He was also full of blarney.

When Sir Howard got his AFI honorary degree in 2007 on the AFI's fortieth anniversary, Bob Gazzale produced the presentation, with Connery flying to L.A. as a surprise. Connery walked down the center aisle at commencement, following a bagpiper and wearing a Scottish kilt. Sir Howard, who was standing at the podium, could not yet see Connery and exclaimed, "I'm Welsh—not Scottish." He howled with delight when he saw his friend following the bagpiper.

JON AVNET AND JOHN F. COOKE
Board of Directors Co-Chairs (2002–2009)

When the board structure changed, Tom Pollock made the adjustment incredibly smooth by swapping roles with Howard. Tom was close to Jon Avnet, who was deeply committed to AFI and had been a strong leader of the board advisory committee for the Center for Advanced Film Studies. Jon was a busy filmmaker, and his schedule was completely dependent upon his own pre-production, production, and post-production schedule, so I suggested that perhaps we could find a complementary co-chair with different skills.

John Cooke had made a huge impression on the board when he succeeded Rich Frank as the Disney representative on the board. Cooke had made the execution of the AFI Showcase at the Disney-MGM Studio theme park a delight, and he had hosted a marvelous meeting of the board at its dedication in Orlando. The idea of a filmmaker-alumnus and a major executive as co-chairs of the new directors' board was exciting. So, the three of us had lunch to see how it might work; from day one, there was mutual respect and complementary assets that only benefited AFI for years to follow.

In 1974, Avnet had an intense experience while at the Center for Advanced Film Studies. Remember, this was during the years of protests on campuses across America against the Vietnam War, and most young people were angry at visible authority figures. Avnet had led a mini-rebellion of AFI Fellows, and he flew to New York City representing the CAFS administration and the Fellows to meet with AFI board representatives at the office of Jack Schneider, the head of CBS at the time. I remember Jack telling me that the meeting was called for 5:00 PM, and CBS was famous for its gracious service of coffee, tea, cold drinks (and, no doubt, other options), and great chocolate chip cookies. But Jack told his assistant he didn't want the meeting to last long, so nothing should be served. He later told me that they were there till midnight without a glass of water.

This was one of those tough moments that occur in the lifespan of every institution; changes were made at CAFS, and for many years, Avnet saw himself as an AFI outsider. But then Tom told me that Avnet wanted to meet me, we hit it off, and Jon has been one of the most involved, passionate members of the AFI family ever since.

Jon Avnet is just one of those people who, when he is in, he is *all* in. One of his recent projects was to read all the biographies of U.S. presidents—*all* U.S. presidents. It took him five years. Actively involved in Democratic politics, we walked the halls of Congress together on many occasions to raise support for AFI from another agency of government, the Health, Education, and Welfare Agency for a K–12 education program in media. Chuck Fries had organized one of those trips because of his connections to the Republicans who had control of Congress, and we needed strong bipartisan support. Let me tell you, it takes all the passion you can muster to walk those granite floors—they are really hard on your feet and your back. It is a young person's game for sure.

John Cooke is a great executive and a fervent public servant. After a decade at Times Mirror, he built the Disney Channel into a powerhouse. Michael Eisner made him EVP for corporate affairs at Disney, where he created many corporate alliances and was, without a doubt, one of the most active members of an astonishing variety of nonprofit boards: Johns Hopkins University, the Thomas Jefferson Foundation, the Los Angeles Public Library Foundation, the Huntington Library, the Library of Congress, LACMA, Skirball, and the J. Paul Getty Trust, as well as the USC Annenberg Center on Communications Leadership and Policy and the UCLA School of Public Affairs Advisory Board, his alma mater. Thanks to John's contacts, from 2003 to 2004, McKinsey & Company were at work on a five-year, pro bono strategic plan for AFI. (The lead McKinsey Media partner, Luis Ubinas, soon thereafter became president of the Ford Foundation.)

Cooke is truly an American history scholar and has visited sites across this country, meeting with scholars who are specialists in the area. It therefore is not a surprise that he is incredibly well-connected to a broad range of influential members of the political and philanthropic worlds that he so easily and successfully relates to.

BOB DALY
Board of Directors Chair (2009–Present)

Bob Daly joined the board in 1981 and has been active and involved ever since. He always speaks his mind and provides leadership, and that leadership takes form in many ways, whether it's negotiating the Life Achievement Awards telecast with networks and cable companies for the last thirty years, making annual donations both personally and corporately, making challenge grants to the board to bring in annual or endowment support, talking about AFI's goals and objectives with everyone and anyone, and most of all, bringing a rationality and common sense to the board table that is balanced with passion and dedication—an awesome combination. When Bob Daly received an honorary degree from AFI in 1999, he said:

> *I just would like to say a few words to the 125 graduates. You form what you want to do in life. I had a couple of rules. First, I made up my mind I was going to love what I did. Every day. I wasn't going to make a decision because of money, just what I wanted to do. I also had another rule. I could be the poster boy on that. I worked hard. I worked harder than anybody, to try to get over the fact that I wasn't a college graduate. I also realized that you have to treat people very nicely. And respect everybody you deal with, in the world and certainly in business. And, the one thing that I didn't learn until I was much older is that you have to keep your priorities in order. And your priorities are your family and friends.*

Thank you, Bob Daly, for being the most decent person any of us have ever known and for making AFI part of your life for over thirty-five years. In large measure, you have made AFI what it is today.

And let me again thank all the chairs, not only for their board

Alumni Trustees

When any alumnus is invited to join the board of their college or graduate school, it is symbolic for the trustee. It is even more symbolic, I would argue, for the institution. This is certainly true for two guys who were in AFI's class of 1975 and since then have been partners telling stories worth telling and breaking ground in remarkable TV series. They are respected throughout the community as artists and leaders, and nowhere more so than at the AFI board table, where Marshall Herskovitz and Ed Zwick sat almost continuously since 2003, and then signed on for another term starting in 2013. They also have served the larger community, with Ed on the board of the Academy of Motion Picture Arts and Sciences and Marshall as president of the Producers Guild of America when it made gigantic strides in the recognition of the producers' role in the creative process. For AFI, they have given of their experience, their hearts, and their pocketbooks to make AFI all it strives to be. They set the standard for all of us. At the 2017 AFI Conservatory Commencement, I was pleased to present well-deserved honorary degrees to Marshall and Ed in recognition of their service to the Institute.

leadership but also for their giving leadership. The board chairs have also always been amongst the most generous board members—perhaps it comes with the territory. There are not enough words to describe all that the trustees have done over the years, including those that space does not allow me to name and brag about. It cannot be said often enough: a board goes a long way in determining if a new institution is going to survive and then thrive. As AFI marks fifty years, we must all thank this board for making AFI what we dreamed it could be.

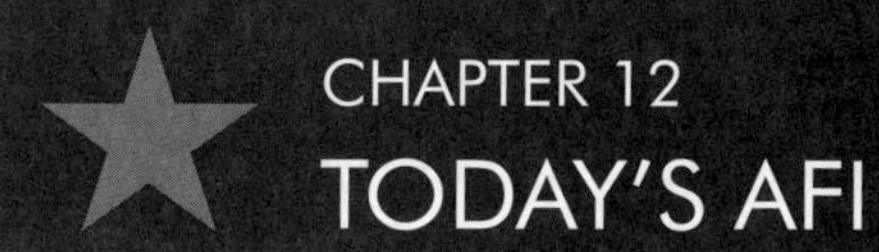

To 50 and Beyond

JEAN PICKER FIRSTENBERG

After you've been in any workplace for a long time, and especially when you've been at the helm, you always have this question in the back of your mind: When is the right time to leave? My philosophy was, better to leave a little early than stay too long; you never want to hang on so long that others need to push you out. When I sat in a theater on campus and realized I was the oldest person in the room, it hit me. But more than that, change in technology was rampant, and it wasn't easy being a "Digital Grandmother" (as Nick DeMartino dubbed me).

In mid-2006, I told the trustees it was time to find my successor. But just think about the digital explosions that took place between the time I announced my departure and the following year, when Bob Gazzale took the helm: Apple introduced the iPhone, launching the smartphone-apps revolution (remember life without an app?); Facebook expanded its reach beyond students (remember life without social media?); Google redefined the search engine (remember looking things up on paper?); Twitter was launched (remember life before the 140-character influence?); Amazon came out with Kindle; and Airbnb launched. Enough said. It was time for the next chapter.

Luckily, there was a talented young man, Bob Gazzale, ready to pick up the torch. A devoted film historian, Bob has become renowned for his brilliant writing, producing, and entrepreneurial skills. He has since taken AFI through hard economic times, as his stature as a spokesperson and institutional representative has grown.

The Transition

As Bob Gazzale's first day as AFI's third leader approached on November 1, 2007, it had been an exciting four months since the board had unanimously selected him on June 27. Bob was a popular choice with anyone who knew him. He was well-known to most of the board and the creative community, having produced the Life Achievement Awards since 2003. He was respected not only for his intelligence and considerable talents but also for his work ethic and sense of humor. He had been part of the AFI work-family for fifteen years and had married another AFIer.

Nevertheless, the choice of CEO for a national nonprofit is never easy. The presidential search committee had presented their choice to the board of directors a day before the special board of trustees meeting, and the directors were thrilled. With the directors on board, now we needed the trustees' support. We had urged all trustees to attend the special meeting, either in person or on the phone. Many questions were asked and answered. One trustee who didn't know Bob was particularly prickly about the choice of an "internal" candidate, wanting to know why we did not have more high-profile candidates. Then he breached board etiquette, asking about the second- and third-choice candidates. (Disclosing the name of additional candidates not under discussion is unethical, because it can jeopardize a person's current employment or reputation. One trustee sent a note to Bob Daly: "#2 Jon Peters, #3 Peter Guber"—truly Hollywood humor, for sure.) Finally, the concerns were quelled, and the selection of Bob Gazzale was unanimous. As the nimble Sir Howard Stringer put it, "We realized we had a Renaissance man lurking in the basement. And I've seen so many bright people given the wrong job because they had to go outside the organization."

We took pains to keep the board decision absolutely secret after the decisive meeting until we could get to campus, inform the staff, and then release the announcement. At the staff meeting where I announced the board's selection of Bob, the staff cheered wildly that it was not only someone they knew but also someone they liked and respected. For me, this made the transition really pleasant.

After the June 27 announcement, we turned our attention to the fortieth anniversary events slated for the first week of October and the transition of leadership on November 1. But we were also aware of the impending economic issues. I remember using the wrong term—*depression* rather than *recession*—at my last board meeting as CEO and being taken to task immediately by trustee Jim Gianopulos.

Unfortunately, the choice of word didn't soften the blow to AFI's finances. Starting in early 2008, AFI was hit with the impact of the market downturn and financial instability. Support from individuals, corporations, foundations, and sponsors receded. This led to necessary cutbacks—never an easy situation, but truthfully, I was glad not to be in the position to make those hard decisions after so many years with the AFI team.

At the board level, Bob enjoyed the continuing good fortune of Sir Howard's leadership as chair of the board of trustees. Then the remarkable Bob Daly assumed chairmanship of the board of directors. They have been at the head of the table since Bob became CEO, acknowledged across the board for their commitment, leadership, and integrity.

No leader achieves everything she or he hopes to accomplish. I know that. So it was exciting when the two Bobs—Daly and Gazzale—made campus renovation a priority and brought the magnificent site up to the standard it deserves. In 2010, AFI used a $5 million bond issue to finance campus improvements and invested another $2 million from operating surpluses (!) in the effort, and it really shows. The quality and taste of the project are impressive across the campus, from the monument sign at the entrance, to the handsome restroom fixtures. (Think about it: in 1980, we bought the campus for $4.7 million, and thirty years later, we spent another $7 million to make it what it should have always been.)

Evolutions

THE CONSERVATORY

Soon after AFI received WASC accreditation in 2004, James Hindman resigned to venture far and wide, designing other film academic programs. Dean Sam Grogg also moved on to become dean of the School of Communications at the University of Miami in 2005. Just as I was thinking about the timing of my retirement, I faced two searches for senior positions that are always filled under pressure, especially such two major posts. One worked out well, the other not so well; that is about the best you can hope for when you have been at the helm for many years.

Sometimes you get lucky. Trustee emerita Sherry Lansing called me with a recommendation for a strong candidate for the post of dean—Bob Mandel. She had worked with him, respected him, and found him talented, thoughtful, smart, and professional through and through. They had become close friends and—a bonus—he was an AFI alumnus.

But for Bob Mandel, the world of AFI in 2006 was quite a different place from what he had known as a 1977 CAFS Fellow on the Greystone campus. It was a leap of faith for Mandel and for AFI, but the alumnus credential was significant. (Bob asked that I negotiate his AFI contract with his agent. I explained that we didn't do that, but, of course, he could review any offer with his attorney of choice.) Adjusting immediately, he used his extensive range of relationships to build a strong faculty. Meanwhile, he and Bob Gazzale had to deal with WASC requirements, something that was not a part of the culture or requirements in the Greystone years. The two Bobs faced an impending WASC review (truth be told, there are always WASC reviews on the calendar), an event with high stakes for the future of AFI's accredited status. No one on staff had been involved with writing any of the prior WASC reports, though WASC had now raised the bar for even more specificity. No one on staff had participated with previous WASC visiting site committee experiences. The NASAD review was also on the calendar—not simply a double whammy, but more like a perfect storm. I know they were challenged, because I received many phone calls asking for advice.

They figured it out, with focus and intelligence and no small amount of stress. Their efforts are attested to in a particularly gratifying WASC statement from the February 2011 interim report committee's commendations:

> *The Team commends the unifying passion of the Institute and its Conservatory to educate the next generation of storytellers. AFI clearly defines its essential values and character. There is little doubt that an AFI education is much more than an accumulation of courses or credits.*

The WASC team understood the underlying AFI Conservatory vision and mission. One of the most reassuring aspects of the

Conservatory faculty was the continuing involvement of other former alumni: Tom Rickman (class of 1969) as chair of Screenwriting and Gill Dennis's (class of 1969) Special Workshops or Creative Advisor on Thesis Projects, both members of the original class at Greystone. (The memorial service for Gill in June 2015 was deeply moving and demonstrated the compassion and commitment among the Fellows from the first class at Greystone.) In 2011, the remarkable Frank Pierson retired as Distinguished Filmmaker-in-Residence and artistic director. He and Roger Birnbaum, who had joined him as artistic director in 2004, were succeeded as artistic director by the respected producer-director James L. Brooks in 2013.

After another special visit in September 2012, it was suggested that the Conservatory hire a vice dean, dedicated in part to integrating the WASC valuable learning concepts into the fabric of the AFI Conservatory structure. This resulted in the hiring of vice dean David Chase, making all subsequent (and frequent) WASC reports and visits far more effective. As demanding as the WASC process is, it has made the Conservatory stronger in the face of the ever-evolving world of moving images. The rationale for what the Conservatory does is balanced with sharp attention to the Fellows and what they need.

In 2013, after nine years, Bob Mandel decided he wanted to return to his directing career (to the great pleasure of his agent), and Bob Gazzale was faced with another one of those difficult searches. Late in 2013, Jan Schuette joined the AFI Conservatory from Germany, continuing the European tradition of the earlier leaders. The class of 2014 senior thesis films received the AFI Conservatory's greatest recognition, with all three Student Oscar nominations going to AFI Conservatory shorts. This is the first time any film training program has achieved this distinction. The three films are a capsule of the diversity and range of the storytelling that AFI committed to when CAFS first launched:

- *Day One*: Written and directed by Henry Hughes and produced by Michael Steiner, with cinematography by Kee Sun Kyung, editing by Anisha Acharya, and production design by Benjamin Cox (all class of 2014). Explores the story of the first day of a U.S. Army interpreter in Afghanistan who is forced to deliver the child of an enemy bomb-maker.
- *This Way Up*: Directed by Jeremy Cloe, written by Cloe, Michael Langer, and Ed Lee, and produced by Michael Langer, with cinematography by Cory Warner, editing by Steven Pristin, and production design by Ying-Te Julie Chen (all class of 2014). Tells the story of a homeless man living in a Las Vegas storm drain who creates a fake life to hide the truth from his daughter.
- *Stealth*: Directed by Bennett Lasseter, written by Melissa Hoppe, and produced by Melissa Hoppe and Muhua Yang, with cinematography by Andressa Cordeiro and editing by Leo Chan (all class of 2014). Tells the heartwarming story of a brave transgender tween.

In addition, Bob Daly has made scholarships a priority and has raised the amount available for AFI Fellows every year by a substantial degree, ensuring that AFI can compete for the best applicants. WASC was particularly impressed by the increase in scholarship funds and the campus upgrade.

Another impressive change Gazzale brought to the Conservatory academic year was moving commencement off campus to the great theatrical icon, Grauman's Chinese Theatre, now called the TCL Chinese Theatre. The program is truly inspirational, incorporating film clips of the graduates and honorary degree recipients walking along Hollywood Boulevard. The experience for graduates and their families has been significantly enhanced.

In 2016, just before the November WASC Site Visit Committee

evaluation, Jan Schuette announced his resignation as dean, effective at the end of the academic year. Sometimes, as I often experienced, things don't work out the way one hopes. The WASC visit was chaired once again by the estimable Lorne Buchman (now president of Art Center College of Design in Pasadena), who had chaired the 1999 committee. The committee included Patricia Prado-Olmos, VP for community engagement at California State University San Marcos; Brian Harlan, associate provost for academic affairs at CalArts; and Thomas Hannen, VP of finance and administration at Notre Dame de Namur University. The committee reported:

> "American film is one of the most cherished assets to our culture and the human race. It encompasses just about every discipline that is used on the planet. . . . For me coming from the streets of this city, just to be here at AFI today, I am truly humbled."
>
> —EDWARD JAMES OLMOS, actor, honorary degree recipient (1993), and AFI trustee (2015–present)

> "The AFI Conservatory is a special place. . . . The Conservatory's educational objectives are focused on graduating Fellows with exceptional leadership and collaborative skills, a deep understanding of the historical context of film, and a solid foundation in the techniques of storytelling that enable them to create and convey stories through an authentic voice. . . . The Conservatory's core pedagogy is well-known, and the Fellows report that the process "rocks their soul to the core." In other words, Fellows find the program challenging, rigorous and 'the best program I've ever been a part of.' . . . The team found the leadership of both AFI and the Conservatory is characterized by integrity at all levels and that leadership was candid and open in its presentation of all materials and conversations . . ."

DIRECTING WORKSHOP FOR WOMEN

The Directing Workshop for Women still remains as relevant and needed as ever—unfortunately. But fortunately, its range and impact continue to grow. It was run effectively by Patty West (class of 2006) for several years and now by a former participant and the first film director to run it, the dynamic 2014 DWW alum Tessa Blake. Support for women directors is alive, evidenced by Jada Pinkett Smith, Donna Langley at Universal, Google, Broad Focus at Lifetime, and Twentieth Century Fox Film franchise properties, thanks to Stacey Snider. All of these, combined with Nancy Malone's largest individual gift, symbolize the movement for women to take their place behind the camera.

Is the workshop effective? A film created through DWW with an interdisciplinary AFI crew won the Cinéfondation First Prize at 2015's Cannes Film Festival. *Share*, written and directed by 2014 DWW alum Pippa Bianco, with cinematography by Ava Berkofsky (class of 2013), editing by Oliver Harwood (class of 2013), production design by Andrea Arce Duval (class of 2015), and art direction by Mari Lappalainen (class of 2015), tells the story of a fifteen-year-old girl who attempts to restore her privacy after a sexually explicit video of her goes viral on the Internet from a night she doesn't remember.

EXHIBITION AND EVENTS

Particularly over the last decade, AFI FEST presented by Audi has defined a viable position in the L.A. cultural calendar by sharpening its focus and making all screenings available at no cost on a first-come, first-served basis for the community. In truth, since 2004, AFI FEST presented by Audi has brought a consistency of sponsorship support in the best and strongest way possible, resulting in a remarkable relationship with a special company. On the other coast, AFI DOCS has made inroads with the cultural communities of Washington, DC. This mission to connect governmental and elected officials with filmmakers in relevant and meaningful ways resulted in the *Washington Post* calling it the best documentary festival in the U.S. AFI has also been a partner of the White House Student Film Festival, with K–12 students submitting film shorts online that are truly inspiring.

In 2012, the White House screened *To Kill a Mockingbird*, celebrating the film's fiftieth anniversary. It was an intimate event, and I felt honored to attend with the Gregory Peck family. Other AFI trustees in attendance included Ron Meyer, chair of Universal, which distributed the movie in 1962, and good friends Bonnie

Target Presents AFI Night at the Movies

In 2008, the lineup of presenters for *Target Presents AFI Night at the Movies* included:

Sean Connery presenting *The Man Who Would Be King*
Annette Bening presenting *American Beauty*
Jim Carrey presenting *Eternal Sunshine of the Spotless Mind*
Cameron Diaz presenting *There's Something About Mary*
Jodie Foster presenting *The Silence of the Lambs*
Dustin Hoffman presenting *Tootsie*
Shirley MacLaine presenting *The Apartment*
Steve Martin presenting *The Jerk*
Rita Moreno presenting *West Side Story*
Mike Myers presenting *Austin Powers*
Keanu Reeves presenting *The Matrix*
Denzel Washington presenting *Glory*

Hammer and Jeff Wachtel from USA Network, which also broadcast the movie.

Target Presents AFI Night at the Movies continued in 2008 and 2013 to equally triumphant evenings. There is just something magical about having an entire complex as brilliantly designed as Arclight Hollywood entirely devoted to film history, with representatives of every film proud to present their particular moment in film history. Twice, I introduced a film—Steve Martin and *The Jerk* (a film my brother produced) in 2008 and Sally Field and *Norma Rae* in 2013. Both times, it was truly an honor and great fun.

In 2013, the lineup included:

Kathy Bates presenting *Misery*
Cher presenting *Moonstruck*
Sally Field presenting *Norma Rae*
Peter Fonda presenting *Easy Rider*
Harrison Ford presenting *Blade Runner*
Samuel L. Jackson presenting *Pulp Fiction*
Shirley MacLaine presenting *Terms of Endearment*
Sally Field and Shirley MacLaine presenting *Steel Magnolias*
Demi Moore presenting *Ghost*
Mike Myers presenting *Shrek*
Sidney Poitier presenting *In the Heat of the Night*
Kurt Russell presenting *The Thing*
Kevin Spacey presenting *The Usual Suspects*

Annual events continue at their highest standards. The Life Achievement Award had to find a new venue when the Kodak Theatre (now the Dolby Theatre) was undergoing renovations. The estimable Sir Howard provided Sony's iconic Stage 15 (where *The Wizard of Oz* was shot) for the event from 2009 to 2012. Everyone enjoyed the venue (especially those driving from L.A.'s Westside), but I love the Dolby Theatre's sense of grandeur (even if driving anywhere in Los Angeles these days is an endurance test). In 2016, AFI honored composer-conductor John Williams with an AFI Life Achievement Award, breaking the streak of actor-or-director honorees. Because producer Gazzale sets such a high standard, he literally reinvented the structure of the evening to recognize the genius of the recipient.

AFI CATALOG

As this book fully describes, AFI's founding priority to preserve cinema's heritage was realized early on with the launch of the *AFI Catalog of Feature Films*—an exhaustive effort to provide an accurate and comprehensive listing of American film's first 100 years. Publication began in 1971 with an inaugural print volume highlighting movies released from 1921 to 1930, and today the completed catalog is available online and consists of more than 55,000 entries—every film produced in the United States from 1893 to 1993. Every searchable record includes detailed information on cast and crew, as well as extensively researched production notes.

Today, the *AFI Catalog: The First 100 Years of American Film (1893–1993)* is available for free on AFI.com as part of AFIdb, a state-of-the-art online database with robust search capabilities and research tools. AFIdb is launching a Premium Records series that will feature historical audio-visual treasures from the AFI Archive, including interviews with filmmakers recorded at AFI events and seminars and digitized assets from AFI Special Collections. These advancements mean that the *AFI Catalog* is instantly accessible throughout the world, and the new possibilities are endless.

The Bottom Line

Today, AFI has an exceptional advancement team led by Tom West, with a new national council of motivated members providing financial and intellectual resources. They renew the perpetual need for entrepreneurial energy to embody AFI's mission in today's context, for today's needs. Sponsorship relationships have been maintained, expanded, and initiated with great finesse. The annual budget has been balanced since 2009, with operating surpluses in many years—a most powerful statement about the Institute's fiscal health on its fiftieth anniversary.

I think about AFI's reach—its impact on our nation, our world. And I think about what it will be like in another fifty years. How will it be celebrating a 100th anniversary? How will it renew itself? How will it stay responsive to audiences and relevant to the culture, especially as technology changes the way we relate and create with moving images? Where will the vision, passion, and persistence to reach 2067 come from? It's hard to imagine our nation without cultural institutions like AFI, which celebrate the artists whose visions provide all of us with a deeper understanding of ourselves and the world we live in.

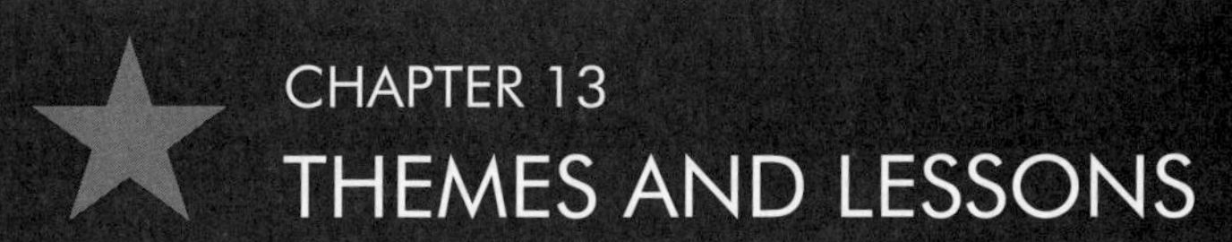

Looking Back to Look Forward

JAMES HINDMAN

What an elaborate, exhaustive, and often delightful process it has been, putting this book together: reviewing acres of paper, memos, reports, and publications; collecting stories and anecdotes from colleagues; and endlessly chewing it through with my thirty-five-year partner-in-crime, Jean Firstenberg. Memories are elusive things, and there was always a lot going on at AFI.

The looming, difficult question was always—*why* write a history of our time at AFI? Of course, we wanted to celebrate what was a fantastic life-adventure, and to thank a horde of remarkable people who played critical roles in getting this giant mobile circus down the highway over nearly thirty years as we attempted to be ringmasters. But what would the value of such a project be? We knew it was important to have a record of *what* actually happened and *why*, as best it could be determined.

But what emerged over the three-year process of putting

together a memoir of AFI at fifty was something quite interesting, something more than an institutional history. Battling through the trees, fighting each day's dramas, you don't see much of the forest. With hindsight (my students back in my university teaching days used to call me "Dr. Hindsight"), patterns and trends we only had a vague inkling of began to emerge. In fact, there were a lot of forests to be seen, and they have provided the arc of this book.

The beginning of the arc, we were reminded, was *why* there came to be an AFI in the first place. Movies lay close to the beating American heart, but in the 1960s there were few ways to have access to them beyond tired movie theaters. People who wanted to work in movies—to make them, study them, and often even just see them—had few ways in. AFI was created to be a bridge between the public and this most public of art forms, by ensuring cinema—stories on a screen—could be valued as an art form.

Now, as AFI reaches the half-century mark in 2017, the question persists: How did the AFI go from a small, embattled government program to a self-sustaining arts authority with national reach and international stature? A cultural institution can be created with the stroke of a pen, but it takes decades to define its lasting contributions—and determine whether it will survive.

AFI's leadership made the crucial difference. George Stevens Jr. charted the territory with a range of original initiatives. From 1980 to 2007, the years of Jean Picker Firstenberg's tenure at the helm, AFI evolved dramatically before being handed off to Bob Gazzale, the Renaissance man lurking in the basement. AFI left its childhood behind, survived a lively

"Let us raise our cups then standing, as some of us do, on opposite sides of the river and drink together to what really matters to all of us—to our crazy and beloved profession. To movies—to good movies—of every possible kind."

—ORSON WELLES, filmmaker

adolescence, and matured into the respected educational, cultural, national institution it is today. This book is a broad look at the highlights of those fifty years, while focusing on the largely untold story of the middle years. It is a testament to the leadership's passionate determination and collective diplomacy, which turned a set of aspirational ideals into a sustainable institution.

Mission Issues

The only thing certain is change, and AFI and the art of the screen have changed profoundly over these many years. The arc of this book documents much of that change. Certain "mission issues" that were present at AFI's founding still persist, and we're still seeking answers:

- The ambivalence of government funding for the arts—if not the government, who? (And how? And why?)
- The role of a service organization in a public, business-driven art—whom to serve? How to fund it?
- Film (now media arts) education—hugely popular, hard to deliver.
- Technology and film art—tracking and understanding their elaborate dance together.
- Achievement and recognition—approbation, mapping our past, setting the standards of excellence for the future.

Since the past is usually prologue, in researching this book we constantly confronted the question of what the future might be for AFI. The circumstances of its birth and film art itself have changed so profoundly—where might it go from here? Predictions are not very useful, but the good news is that there are certain carry-forwards in AFI's assets, and programs that are smart, useful, and enduring, and they bode well for AFI's existential value well into the future:

- The AFI campus, marking its strength as a major educational venture in cinematic arts.
- The *AFI Catalog of Feature Films*, the enduring map and formal record of this evanescent art form.
- The AFI Silver Theatre and Cultural Center, creating an ideal community experience for this most public art.
- The various AFI recognition programs (for example, the AFI Life Achievement Award, the AFI AWARDS), setting standards and finding benchmarks, and elevating the field.
- Education and public and professional service to communities, audiences, the professions, students and scholars, technologists and businesses, and artists and craftspeople.

Through programs and priorities, over time we created various answers to the then-prevailing challenges—cultural, institutional, financial, technological, and more. That is what we did over those many years, and those necessities set AFI on a very lively road. But rather than document every twist and turn (of interest to a very few), we chose to make this a human story, a memoir of AFI as personal history, based on our own experiences in that incredible environment. Along the way, we have attempted to depict the efforts of a wide range of mission-driven people, committed to America's dreams—at the movies.

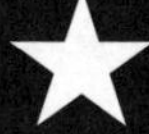

AFTERWORD

A Personal Tribute from David Lynch

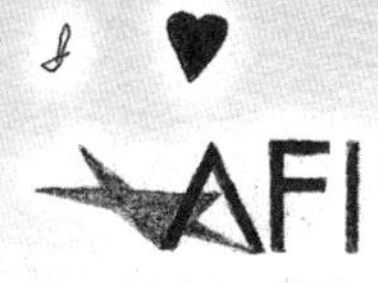

and I  Jeannie!

As in JEAN PICKER FIRSTENBERG

. Jeannie is A great person. Jeannie has a great and beautiful face.

Her face is warm — welcoming - intelligent - and Strong.
This was the shining face of AFI for 27 years.
from 1980 -

☆ ☆ ☆ ☆ ☆ ☆ ☆ ☆ ☆

☆ ☆ ☆ ☆ ☆ ☆ ☆ ☆ ☆ ⟸ many years

☆ ☆ ☆ ☆ ☆ ☆ ☆ ☆ ☆

until 2007.

In this Book Jeannie and James Hindman will bring us stories — many stories of those 27 years — how AFI has not only survived through a myriad of challenges but in addition! — has gloriously evolved to become what it is today —
A respected and loved educational and cultural institution !!! — A successful National Arts Treasure !!!

David Lynch!

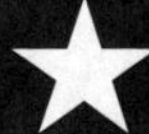

APPENDIX

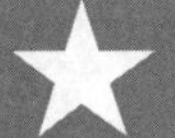

AFI'S FIRST 50 YEARS: A TIMELINE

1935

The National Council on Education calls for a government-supported American Film Institute, primarily to encourage the use of film as a teaching aid in the classroom.

1961

Based in Los Angeles, British film educator Colin Young serves as spokesperson for a group of more than 100 prominent educators and critics that issues a detailed call for a federally mandated American Film Institute to support a wide range of cultural, educational, and preservation efforts.

1965

In the White House Rose Garden, President Lyndon B. Johnson signs into law the National Foundation on the Arts and the Humanities Act of 1965. In his remarks, the President says, "We will create an American Film Institute bringing together leading artists of the film industry, outstanding educators and young men and women who wish to pursue this twentieth-century art form as their life's work."

1966

The National Council on the Arts commissions a report from the Stanford Research Institute to define the functions of AFI, and appoints a Film Advisory Board.

1967

National Council of Arts chair Roger L. Stevens announces the establishment of AFI with headquarters in Washington, DC. The twenty-two-member AFI Board of Trustees is led by Gregory Peck as chair and Sidney Poitier as vice chair. George Stevens Jr. is named director and CEO.

AFI's founders define "motion picture" in the broadest terms: "The moving image, whether it be projected in a theater, museum, classroom, or on a living room television set."

Initial funding of $5.2 million comes in equal parts from the National Endowment of the Arts and the Ford Foundation, member companies of the Motion Picture Association of America and AFI.

1968

AFI sends out the clarion call to save America's film heritage and begins work to locate and preserve rare and historically significant American films, an effort coordinated with the Library of Congress, the George Eastman House, and the Museum of Modern Art and funded by the National Endowment for the Arts. AFI initiates a major national film catalog project separately funded by the National Endowment for the Humanities.

AFI begins awarding Independent Filmmaker Grants, funded by the National Endowment for the Arts, to aspiring independent filmmakers.

1969

Roger L. Stevens is elected second chair of the AFI Board of Trustees.

AFI establishes the Center for Advanced Film Studies (CAFS) in Beverly Hills, with eighteen Fellows in the first class.

1970

The AFI Theater opens at the National Gallery in Washington, DC, then moves to a full-time exhibition operation at L'Enfant Plaza Theater showing American classics and international films.

1971

Czech screenwriter and educator Frank Daniel, who came to the Center for Advanced Film Studies in 1969, is named dean. Antonio Vellani is named associate dean.

The first volume of the *AFI Catalog of Feature Films, 1921–1930* is published, quickly establishing the project as an authoritative reference for film history, with the majority of the funding coming from the National Endowment for the Humanities.

1972

Charlton Heston is elected third chair of the AFI Board of Trustees.

1973

The AFI Board of Trustees creates the annual AFI Life Achievement Award to recognize the highest standards of enduring excellence in cinematic arts. Its first recipient is director John Ford. President Richard Nixon attends and presents Ford with the Presidential Medal of Freedom after Ford receives the AFI honor. The gala is televised on CBS, and written and produced by George Stevens Jr.

The AFI Theater exhibition program relocates to the John F. Kennedy Center for the Performing Arts, in a 224-seat theater built with funds donated by Jack Warner.

1974

AFI establishes the Directing Workshop for Women, a program championed by Mathilde Krim to give more opportunities to women, who are historically underrepresented in the field of directing.

Antonio Vellani is named chair of the faculty at the Center for Advanced Film Studies.

1975

AFI's national magazine on cinema, *American Film*, debuts with Hollis Alpert as editor and AFI national director of publications.

Hungarian filmmaker Jan Kadar, director of the Oscar-nominated *Lies My Father Told Me*, becomes the first Center for Advanced Film Studies filmmaker-in-residence.

1976

The second volume of *AFI Catalog of Feature Films, 1961–1970* is published.

AFI produces a feature-length documentary, *America at the Movies*, for the American Revolution bicentennial.

1977

To celebrate its tenth anniversary, AFI hosts a twelve-day film festival at the Kennedy Center. A White House reception with President and Mrs. Jimmy Carter precedes a gala benefit in the Kennedy Center's Eisenhower Theater, attended by luminaries from Hollywood and Washington, DC. The event salutes the ten greatest American movies as chosen by AFI members. George Stevens Jr. produces and writes the gala for broadcast on CBS.

The John and Mary R. Markle Foundation awards the Directing Workshop for Women a $154,000 grant through the efforts of program officer for the Markle Foundation Jean Picker Firstenberg.

1978

AFI begins to hold public service programs throughout the country to explore current artistic and technical issues the film community faces.

1979

After establishing the initial direction and definition of the Institute, George Stevens Jr. resigns as AFI director and CEO and is elected board chair with Charlton Heston. He is also named founding director and lifetime trustee.

1980

Jean Picker Firstenberg becomes AFI's second director and CEO.

AFI purchases the campus of Immaculate Heart College near the Griffith Observatory in Hollywood for $4.7 million to establish its permanent home and programmatic center.

1981

The first AFI National Video Festival and Student Competition is held at the Kennedy Center in Washington, DC. Sponsored by Sony Corporation of America, it summarizes a decade of new and innovative work for the small screen.

1982

The AFI Center for Advanced Film Studies becomes the first film program to receive academic accreditation from the National Association of Schools of Art and Design.

Academy Award–winning producer/director Robert Wise becomes chair of the Center for Advanced Film Studies.

James Hindman joins AFI, beginning a twenty-four-year career that will include serving as deputy director, co-director, COO, and provost.
AFI receives a $750,000 challenge grant from the NEA. The grant provides additional support for the purchase and renovation of the campus.

The Sony Corporation donates $350,000 to create the Sony Video Center on the AFI campus. Included in the renovated facility is more than $1.5 million in equipment, including state-of-the-art editing consoles for the Fellows' use at the Center for Advanced Film Studies.

1983

Richard Brandt is elected fifth chair of the AFI Board of Trustees.

A campaign to increase public awareness about the value of film preservation, "A Decade of Preservation: 1983–1993," is declared by the AFI Board of Trustees.

1984

AFI and the NEA announce the creation of the National Center for Film and Video Preservation at AFI. One of six U.S. members of the International Federation of Film Archives, the Center's mission is to coordinate and implement national efforts to find and restore lost and decaying film prints.

The AFI Associates, a women's group whose goal is to provide financial and human resources to the Institute, is formed. The Associates will raise more than $5 million over the next twenty-three years.

1985

The AFI Center for Advanced Film Studies is included in a California Education Facilities Authority Pooled Bond Program, the first arts institution to be so awarded. The bond provides AFI with $6.7 million in tax-exempt funds.

The AFI Television Writers Summer Workshop is established through the leadership of trustee Grant Tinker, chair and CEO of NBC Television, with rotating sponsorship by the three major television networks.

The AFI Award for Independent Film and Video Artists, also known as the Maya Deren Award, is established and presented in New York City at an annual event for the next ten years.

1986

Bonita Granville Wrather is elected sixth chair of the AFI Board of Trustees.

The Center for Advanced Film Studies is renamed the Center for Advanced Film and Television Studies, acknowledging the expanding scope of AFI's educational mission.

1987

The first AFI Los Angeles International Film Festival is held, soon to become one of the major annual festivals in Los Angeles, now known as AFI FEST presented by Audi.

The Directing Workshop for Women continues through the Gale Anne Hurd Productions Grant and matching funds.

1988

AFI holds the Preservation Ball in Washington, DC, honoring President and Mrs. Ronald Reagan and paying tribute to Fred Astaire. The event raises significant funds for AFI's film preservation program.

The ongoing program of master seminars, inaugurated in 1969 by Harold Lloyd on the Center for Advanced Film Studies' opening day, is renamed in his honor: the Harold Lloyd Master Seminar series.

Gene F. Jankowski, former president and chairman of the CBS Broadcast Group, is elected seventh chair of the AFI Board of Trustees following the death of Bonita Granville Wrather.

AFI Catalog of Feature Films, 1911–1920, is produced under the direction of executive editor Patricia King Hanson, with principal funding from the National Endowment for the Humanities.

1989

Antonio Vellani is named director emeritus and master filmmaker-in-residence of the Center for Advanced Film and Television Studies. Later this year, he passes away and is mourned by hundreds of alumni.

Dezsö Magyar becomes director of the Center for Advanced Film and Television Studies; Daniel Petrie is named chair. The CAFTS Board Advisory Committee is led by Robert Wise as chair and Jon Avnet (class of 1972) as vice chair.

Honorary degrees in the arts and in service to the Institute are conferred for the first time at the Center for Advanced Film and Television Studies commencement ceremonies.

AFI hosts special screenings of David Lean's newly restored 1962 classic *Lawrence of Arabia* in New York, Washington, DC, and Los Angeles. The film's restoration is funded by Columbia Pictures.

The Back to the Rose Garden gala in Washington, DC, celebrates the twenty-fifth anniversary of the signing of legislation enabling creation of the National Endowment of the Arts and the National Endowment of the Humanities. President and Mrs. George H. W. Bush attend alongside a galaxy of film and television artists, as well as cultural, education, business, and government leaders.

1990

The AFI–Apple Computer Center for Film and Videomakers is announced. Apple pledges to donate more than $1 million in Macintosh equipment to the Center. It will open in 1991.

1991

AFI establishes the Franklin J. Schaffner Alumni Medal in honor of the late filmmaker and AFI trustee. Director David Lynch (class of 1970) receives the first medal.

In a presentation at AFI, Apple launches QuickTime, its new application for viewing video and animation.

1992

Frederick S. Pierce, former president of ABC Television, is elected the eighth chair of the AFI Board of Trustees.

The feature-length documentary *Visions of Light: The Art of Cinematography*, a co-production of NHK Broadcasting and AFI, premieres at Cannes International Film Festival.

AFI hosts "Breaking the Cycle: The Business of African American Filmmaking in the '90s," a seminar in collaboration with Paramount, Sony, and Warner Bros. that is attended by filmmakers and studio executives.

1993

AFI founds the Advanced Technology Council with filmmaker James Cameron and Adobe Systems cofounder Dr. John E. Warnock as cochairs. The Council's mission is to "celebrate, understand, and influence the digital revolution for moving image artists."

1994

AFI hosts a screening of the 1933 horror classic *King Kong* at the AFI Theater in Washington, DC. The gala event celebrates the release of *AFI Catalog of Feature Films, 1931–1940*.

1995

Writer-director Frank Pierson is named master teacher and artistic director of the Center for Advanced Film Studies.

AFI Catalog of Feature Films: Beginnings, 1893–1910 is published, covering American cinema's earliest years.

AFI's new logo is unveiled, an image that reflects the evolving nature of moving image arts.

AFI launches its website: AFIonline.org.

1996

Tom Pollock is elected the ninth chair of the AFI Board of Trustees.

The AFI Showcase opens at the Disney–MGM Studios theme park in Orlando, Florida, through the board leadership of Rich Frank and John F. Cooke.

AFI National Center for Film and Video Preservation receives a donated original nitrate print of *Richard III*, a 1912 film believed to be the earliest American feature adaptation of a Shakespearean work and the oldest surviving dramatic feature produced in the U.S.

AFI presents Charlie Chaplin's *The Rink* (1916) to an online audience of 100,000—the first time a classic Hollywood film is streamed on the Internet.

1997

AFI announces a national celebration of cinema's centennial, *AFI's 100 Years...100 Movies*. More than 1,500 members of the greater film community—artists, scholars, critics, and historians—are invited to select the century's best 100 movies.

1998

AFI's 100 Years...100 Movies airs on CBS as a three-hour, prime-time special. AFI also produces ten one-hour broadcasts for Turner Network Television documenting cinema history by theme and genre, executive-produced for AFI by trustee Fred Pierce.

AFI receives its last federal funds. Going forward, the Institute will be fully self- supporting.

Sam L. Grogg, who led AFI's Education Program in the 1970s, returns to the Institute as the new director of education and training and dean of the AFI Center for Advanced Film and Television Studies.

AFI and Montgomery County, Maryland, announce an extraordinary arrangement to restore a long-shuttered and historic movie palace in Silver Spring, to be called the AFI Silver Theatre and Cultural Center.

1999

Sir Howard Stringer is elected the tenth chair of the AFI Board of Trustees. A board of directors is formed to replace the executive committee, with Tom Pollock named chair.

AFI Catalog of Feature Films, 1941–1950 is published, the largest volume to date. It receives rave reviews and is selected by *Los Angeles Times* movie critic Kenneth Turan as one of the top 100 books of 1999.

AFI relaunches its website after acquiring the domain names AFI.com and AFI.edu.

2000

The Center for Advanced Film and Television Studies is renamed the AFI Conservatory, a reflection of its unique approach to developing the emerging filmmaker as an artist.

2001

The Institute announces selections for AFI AWARDS 2000, a new annual program that honors "excellence in the moving image during the twenty-first century."

The AFI K–12 Screen Education Center launches its pilot program, a video-based course that familiarizes teachers with filmmaking techniques that can be used by K–12 students to master core subjects from literature to math and science.

2002

The AFI Conservatory receives formal accreditation as a graduate school from the Accrediting Commission for Senior Colleges and Universities of the Western Association of Schools and Colleges.

Jon Avnet and John F. Cooke are elected co-chairs of the AFI Board of Directors.

In its thirtieth year, the AFI Life Achievement Award gala moves to the new Kodak Theatre at Hollywood & Highland for a tribute to Tom Hanks.

2003

The AFI Silver Theatre and Cultural Center opens with a sixtieth-anniversary screening of *The Ox-Bow Incident*, with Clint Eastwood selecting the film and cutting the ribbon to open the three-theater complex.

The thirty-first AFI Life Achievement Award, honoring Robert De Niro, is executive-produced and written by AFI's Bob Gazzale and broadcast on USA Network.

SILVERDOCS: AFI/Discovery Channel Documentary Festival debuts at the AFI Silver Theatre and Cultural Center, screening seventy documentaries from sixty-eight countries.

The AFI AWARDS moves to the Four Seasons Hotel in Beverly Hills as an annual luncheon honoring the year's outstanding movies, television shows, and significant moments.

The AFI-Intel Enhanced TV Workshop is renamed AFI Digital Content Lab to reflect the wider range of platforms for the distribution of digital media.

2004

Producer Roger Birnbaum joins Frank Pierson as artistic director of the AFI Conservatory.

Co-director and provost James Hindman resigns, going on to design film schools in New Mexico and Jordan.

2005

Award-winning director Robert Mandel (class of 1977) is named dean of the AFI Conservatory, becoming the first Conservatory alumnus to hold the position.

AFI Catalog of Feature Films, 1951–1960 is released electronically. Previously published *Catalog* volumes also become available online, providing a carefully curated database of searchable film entries that sets the highest national standard for information on American feature films.

2006

After serving twenty-seven years as CEO, director, and president, Jean Picker Firstenberg announces she will retire. The search for her successor begins.

The first group of short films from the AFI Conservatory and Directing Workshop for Women library is selected for distribution on Apple iTunes.

In the aftermath of Hurricane Katrina, AFI Fellows, faculty, and staff travel to the University of New Orleans, the first of continuing multiple annual visits to support the university's film program.

2007

AFI's 100 Years...100 Movies—10th Anniversary Edition celebrates ten years of the popular program with a special edition, counting down the 100 greatest movies of all time in a three-hour television event on CBS.

AFI celebrates its fortieth anniversary with *Target Presents AFI Night at the Movies*, a public showcase at Arclight Cinemas in Hollywood screening ten classic American films, introduced by their stars and filmmakers.

At the Fortieth Anniversary Luncheon, retiring president and CEO Jean Picker Firstenberg is presented with an AFI Life Achievement Award for Service to the Institute by Kirk Douglas, the 2004 recipient of the award. She is named president emerita and lifetime trustee.

After working at AFI for fifteen years, film historian and Emmy-nominated television producer and writer Bob Gazzale is named president and CEO of the Institute.

2008

AFI creates spin-offs of the popular *AFI's 100 Years...100 Movies* series, counting down the top ten films from ten classic American film genres.

The second installment of *Target Presents AFI Night at the Movies* is held at Arclight Cinemas.

2009

Bob Daly is elected chair of the AFI Board of Directors.

AFI embarks on a $7 million campus renovation, funded by a $5 million bond issue plus $2 million from operating surpluses.

The AFI Conservatory receives reaccreditation from the Accrediting Commission for Senior Colleges and Universities of the Western Association of Schools and Colleges.

2010

Producer-director James L. Brooks becomes artistic director of the AFI Conservatory.

AFI FEST presented by Audi establishes the role of guest artistic director as an opportunity to shine a light on great artists and the films that inspire them. AFI Conservatory alumnus David Lynch is the first to take the position.

2011

AFI Conservatory tops *The Hollywood Reporter*'s first ranking of the best American film schools.

AFI and the Los Angeles Philharmonic Association partner in *The Big Picture: AFI's Great American Movie Quiz*. The live movie trivia experience held at the sold-out Hollywood Bowl is emceed by *Jeopardy* host Alex Trebek.

AFI and Turner Classic Movies launch AFI's *Master Class: The Art of Collaboration*. The series premiere features participants Steven Spielberg and John Williams.

2012

An AFI-sponsored White House screening of *To Kill a Mockingbird* (1962), introduced by President Barack Obama, celebrates the film's fiftieth anniversary. The new digital restoration film is also screened on USA Network.

American Film relaunches as a digital magazine with feature stories, trivia quizzes, archival material, and more.

2013

Jan Schuette, filmmaker and dean of the German Film and TV Academy, is named dean of the AFI Conservatory.

AFI DOCS, the next evolution of SILVERDOCS, launches. The program honors the spirit of the documentary art form, and the Washington, DC, location brings together the nation's leaders and the nation's leading documentary film practitioners.

2014

The White House and AFI co-sponsor the first-ever White House Student Film Festival. Selected films are screened in the White House, with President Barack Obama providing opening remarks.

At the AFI AWARDS 2014 luncheon, surprise guest Kirk Douglas announces the establishment of the Kirk Douglas Fellowship—a biennial, full-tuition scholarship—at the AFI Conservatory.

2015

AFI Conservatory Fellows receive all three nominations for the Oscars Student Academy Awards in the Narrative category—the first time all nominations go to one film training program.

The second annual AFI-sponsored White House Student Film Festival theme explores "The Impact of Giving Back." President Barack Obama announces that the Screen Actors Guild–American Federation of Television and Radio Artists will answer his call to action with an unprecedented mentorship pledge, working toward a goal of 1 million mentor hours over the next three years.

2016

For the first time in its forty-four-year history, the AFI Life Achievement Award is presented to a composer-conductor, John Williams.

AFI Conservatory Fellow David Henry Gerson (class of 2016) wins the Oscar in the Student Academy Awards Alternative category for *All These Voices.*

AFI Conservatory dean Jan Schuette announces his resignation, effective at the end of the academic year.

2017

AFI Catalog of Feature Films completes volumes covering the first 100 years of filmmaking, from 1893 to 1993, available online.

The AFI Conservatory receives re-accreditation from the Accrediting Commission for Senior Colleges and Universities of the Western Association of Schools and Colleges, whose visiting committee states in its assessment: "The AFI Conservatory is a special place."

Oscar-nominated producer Richard Gladstein is named dean of the AFI Conservatory.

AFI celebrates its fiftieth anniversary.

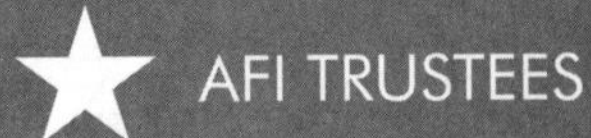

AFI TRUSTEES

Debra Lee (2016–Present)
Lori Lee (2014–Present)
Eva Longoria (2015–Present)
Bryan Lourd (2010–Present)
Michael Lynton (2013–Present)
Lori McCreary (2010–Present)
Ron Meyer (1988–1995, 1996–2009, 2010–Present)
Jonathan Miller (2005–2014, 2015–Present)
Jim Moffatt (2013–Present)
Leslie Moonves (1997–2008, 2009–Present)
Edward James Olmos (2015–Present)
Frederick S. Pierce* (1978–1983, 1992–Present)
Cecilia DeMille Presley (2009–Present)
Kevin Reilly (2015–Present)
Shonda Rhimes (2010–Present)
Jay Roach (2003–2012, 2013–Present)
Howard A. Rodman (2016–Present)
Rich Ross (2010–Present)
Jill Sackler* (1986–2008, 2009–Present)
Josh Sapan (2015–Present)
Ted Sarandos (2014–Present)
Chris Silbermann (2010–Present)
Stacey Snider (2002–2011, 2017–Present)
Steven Spielberg (1986–2008, 2010–Present)
Kevin Tsujihara (2014–Present)
Todd Wagner* (2003–2012, 2013–Present)
William Wang (2015–Present)
Hayma Washington (2017–Present)

Founding Director
George Stevens Jr.* (1967–Present)

President Emerita
Jean Picker Firstenberg* (1980–Present)

President & CEO
Bob Gazzale* (2008–Present)

Chairs Emeriti

Gregory Peck‡ (1967–1969)
Roger L. Stevens‡ (1970–1972)
Charlton Heston‡ (1972–1983)
George Stevens Jr. (1980–1983)
Richard Brandt (1983–1986)
Bonita Granville Wrather‡ (1986–1988)
Gene F. Jankowski (1988–1992)
Fred Pierce (1992–1996)
Tom Pollock (1996–1999)
Jon Avnet (2001–2009)
John F. Cooke (2001–2009)

AFI Trustees Emeriti

Berle Adams‡ (1973–1979)
Merv Adelson‡ (1987–2008)
Chris Albrecht (2003–2011)
Shana Alexander‡ (1973–1978)
Debbie Allen (1992–2008)
Herbert Allen (1969–1971)
Gil Amelio (1996–2009, 2010–2014)
Maya Angelou‡ (1975–1981)
John Antioco (1999–2004)
Anna Bing Arnold‡ (1972–1973)
Lisa Arpey (2005–2014)
Elizabeth Ashley (1967–1969)
Ted Ashley‡ (1971–1980)
Norbert T. Auerbach‡ (1981–1983)
Paris Barclay (2014–2017)
Sidney Barlow‡ (1969–1971)
Ting Barrow (1978–1978)
Joan Barton (2001–2003)
Katherine J. Bayne (2012– 2015)
Warren Beatty (1973–1975)
David Begelman‡ (1975–1982)
Bob Bennett‡ (1983–2008, 2009–2017)
Charles Benton‡ (1967–1971)
Jeff Berg (1992–2005)
Allen Bernstein‡ (1999–2008, 2010–2011)
James Billington‡ (1991–2007)
Richard L. Bloch‡ (1977–1983)
Daniel J. Boorstein‡ (1972–1975)
Todd Bradley (2008–2014)
Steven Broidy‡ (1979–1982)
David Brown‡ (1972–1984)
Dan Burke‡ (1986–1994)
John Calley‡ (1997–2003)
Mark Canton (1991–2009)
George Chasin‡ (1978–1983)
Alfred A. Checchi (1996–2000)
Peter Chernin (1993–2004)
Henry Cisneros (2001–2004)
John F. Cooke (1995–2011)
Martha Coolidge (1992–2008)
Joan Ganz Cooney (1971–1977)
Karen Cooper (1984–1990)
Peggy Cooper–Cafritz (1971–1973)
Francis Ford Coppola (1967–1971)
Bruce Corwin (1980–1988)
Sherrill Corwin‡ (1967–1971)

John Costello (2005–2011)
Cathy Coughlin‡ (2009–2013)
John Culkin‡ (1967–1972)
Massimo d'Amore (2008–2012)
William Daniels (2000–2001)
Martin S. Davis‡ (1969–1972)
Suzanne de Passe (1986–2008)
John DiBiaggio (1989–2007)
Barry Diller (1972–1976, 1986, 2001–2003)
Garth Drabinsky (1986–1991)
Dominique Heriard Dubreuil (1991–1993)
Bill Duke (2000–2009)
Tracey Edmonds (2006–2015)
Michael Eisner (1978–1986)
William Ellinghaus (1981–1983)
Ari Emanuel (2004–2010)
Ed Emshwiller‡ (1969–1975)
Roger Enrico‡ (2005–2016)
Robert Evans (1977–1980)
Raymond Fielding (1972–1979)
Freddie Fields‡ (1982–1984)
Robert L. Fitzpatrick (1984–1987)
Christopher Forman (2006–2015)
Michael Forman (1984–2006)
Richard Fox (1985–1986)
Stephen O. Frankfurt‡ (1969–1975, 1994–2007)
M.J. Frankovich‡ (1976–1984)
A. Alan Friedberg (1979–1980)
William Friedkin (1972–1975)
Charles Fries (1985–2008)
Michael Fuchs (1982–2000)
Richard Gallop‡ (1984–1985)
Emanuel Gerard‡ (1971–1975)
Dolly Gillin (1994–1996)
Ina Ginsburg‡ (1979–2008)
Marvin Goldman‡ (1976–1979)
Samuel Goldwyn Jr. (1979–1982)
Douglas Gomery (1986–1988)
Mark Goodson‡ (1975–1992)
Larry Gordon (1985–1986)
Brad Grey (2005–2014, 2015–2017)
Edward Grebow (2001–2002)
J. Ronald Green (1983–1986)
David Greenblatt (1999–2008)
Philip Guarascio (1997–2008)
Peter Guber (1990–1992)
Andre Guttfreund (1978–1981)
Dee Dee Halleck (1978–1979)
John Hancock‡ (1973–1978)
Sidney Harman‡ (1982–1988)
Salah M. Hassanein‡ (1975–1977)
Lawrence Herbert (1987–2009, 2010–2017)
Charlton Heston‡ (1998–2000)
Alan Hirschfield‡ (1978–1978, 1982–1988)
Dustin Hoffman (1998–2000)
Ken Howard‡ (2010–2016)
Gale Anne Hurd (1989–1996)
Robert Iger (1994–2008)
Cheryl Boone Isaacs (2014–2017)
Alan Jacobs (1980–1983)
Leo Jaffe‡ (1978–1981)
Jon Jashni (2014–2017)
Deane F. Johnson‡ (1971–1982)
Robert Johnson (1992–2006)
Larry Jordan (1973–1977)
Vernon E. Jordan Jr. (1988–1990)
Marvin Josephson‡ (1972–1978)
Fay Kanin‡ (1975–2009)
Lawrence Kasdan (1990–1999)
Jeffrey Katzenberg (1986–1986)
Jerry Katzman (1991–2000)
Francis Keppel‡ (1967–1969)

James Kimsey‡ (1999–2008)
Patricia Kingsley (2000–2009)
Arthur Knight‡ (1967–1971)
Howard W. Koch‡ (1977–1979)
Barbara Kopple (2001–2010)
John Korty (1971–1976)
Alan Ladd Jr.‡ (1978–1980, 1985–1988)
Melvin R. Laird (1977–1980)
Sherry Lansing (1980–1985, 1993–2006)
Mary W. Lawrence‡ (1971–1972)
Richard Leacock (1967–1969)
Jack Lemmon‡ (1984–1987)
Joseph E. Levine‡ (1979–1982)
Warren Lieberfarb (2000–2009)
Suzanne Lloyd (1988–2008)
Peter Lund (1995–1997)
David Lynch (1981–1982)
Shirley MacLaine (1969–1975)
John W. Macy Jr.‡ (1971–1975)
David Mallery‡ (1967–1979)
Frank Mancuso (1984–1993)
Brad Martin (2001–2004)
Marsha Mason (1978–1980, 1984–2004)
Richard Masur (1998–1999)
David Matalon (1989–1991)
Guy McElwaine‡ (1985–1986)
Donald H. McGannon‡ (1967–1969)
Harry McPherson‡ (1972–1975, 1977–1985)
Barry Meyer (1999–2008, 2010–2012)
Edward H. Meyer (1983–1992, 1996–2009)
Bernard Meyerson‡ (1973–1978)
Ronald W. Miller (1984–1984)
Walter Mirisch (1973–1977, 1978–1983)
Carole Mitchell (2005–2007)
Phil Molyneux (2013–2014)
Wendi Murdoch (2012–2015)
Janet Murray (2000–2009)
Michael Nesmith (1992–2004)
Mace Neufeld (1979–2008)
Paul Newman‡ (1969–1972)
Rick Nicita (1995–2009)
Richard Orear‡ (1981–1983)
Michael S. Ovitz (1981–1988)
Amy Pascal (2003–2012)
Gregory Peck‡ (1967–1973)
Charles Peebler Jr. (1985–1986)
Arthur Penn‡ (1969–1972)
William L. Pereira‡ (1967–1971)
Eleanor Perry‡ (1973–1979)
Ted Perry (1980–1988)
Daniel Petrie‡ (1990–2004)
Dan Petrie Jr. (1998–2000, 2004–2011)
Arnold Picker‡ (1967–1973)
David Picker (1972–1979)
Frank Pierson‡ (2006–2012)
Henry Plitt‡ (1989–1993)
Sidney Poitier (1967–1969)
Tony Ponturo (1999–2008)
Frank Price (1981–1987)
Michael Pulitzer (1981–1984)
David Puttnam (1986–1988)
Robert Rehme (1983–1990, 1996–2009)
Joel Resnick (1983–1985)
David Rips (2011–2013)
Victoria Riskin (2001–2004)
Jeff Robinov (2012–2013)
Henry C. Rogers‡ (1972–1979, 1982–1988)

*AFI Board of Directors
‡Deceased

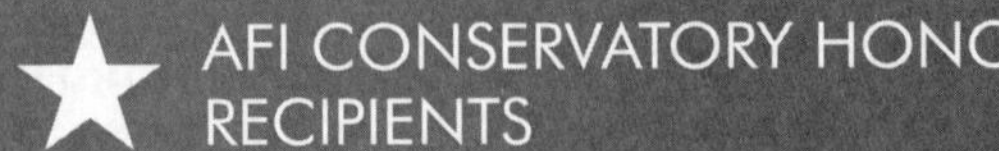

AFI CONSERVATORY HONORARY DEGREE RECIPIENTS

1989
Horton Foote
Bill Moyers
Martin Ritt

1990
Dede Allen
Norman Lear

1991
Charles Kuralt
Sven Nykvist
Roger L. Stevens

1992
Fay Kanin
Richard Sylbert

1993
Don Hewitt
Edward James Olmos

1994
Maya Angelou**
Saul Bass

1995
Michelangelo Antonioni
Karen Cooper
Robert Wise

1996
Robert Altman
Steven Bochco
Robert Boyle

1997
Chuck Jones
Quincy Jones
Haskell Wexler

1998
Kevin Brownlow
Roger Corman
Gena Rowlands

1999
Robert A. Daly
Ray Harryhausen
Alfre Woodard

2000
Karl Malden
Thelma Schoonmaker
Saul Zaentz

2001
Lee Grant**
John Lasseter
Jack Valenti

2002
Richard Brandt
Marcy Carsey
Daniel Petrie
John Williams

2003
Ken Burns
Sherry Lansing
Richard Schickel

2004
Roger Ebert
Frank Pierson
John Warnock

2005
David Brown
Nora Ephron
Fred Pierce

2006
Jeanine Basinger
Charles W. Fries
James Earl Jones
Sydney Pollack

2007
Tom Pollock
George Stevens Jr.
Sir Howard Stringer

2008
Caleb Deschanel*, ASC
Jean Picker Firstenberg
Norman Jewison

2009
Clint Eastwood

2010
Jeffrey Katzenberg
Kathleen Kennedy

2011
Richard H. Frank
Spike Lee
Helen Mirren

2012
Mel Brooks
David Lynch*

2013
Jon Avnet*
Kathryn Bigelow
Anne V. Coates

2015
Lawrence Kasdan
Angela Lansbury

2016
Rita Moreno
Quentin Tarantino

2017
Carol Burnett
Marshall Herskovitz*
Edward Zwick*

*AFI Conservatory Alumni
**AFI Conservatory Directing Workshop for Women Alumnae

★ ACKNOWLEDGMENTS

Jean Picker Firstenberg and James Hindman would like to give a deep thank you to those without whom there would not be a book. This is also the time to say thank you to so many of you who, over the years, have made us look good. There is this nonsense that when you are the "boss," you appear to take credit for everything that happened during your time at the head of the table. Well, there was a round table in Jean's office, and we needed not only the input of those at the table, but also their vision, tenacity, commitment, and leadership. So thanks to all of you, over the years. Together, you made the telling of this story not only *possible* but also a *pleasure*.

The process of writing this book continued that philosophy. None of it really came together without so many who made it happen. Deepest thanks to David Lynch, Patty Jenkins, and Dana Gioia for gracing this book with their insights. We thank our respected colleagues Nick, Pat, Larry, and Emily for their illuminating chapters. Without our personal editor, Jana Branch, there would certainly be no book, simple as that. Richard Bontems brought a long history with AFI to fact check and copyedit the book with speed and commitment. Mike Pepin (now AFI historian, having stepped incredibly well into the huge shoes of dear Adrian Borneman), Josh Kushins, Albert Diaz (who always responded to Jean's computer meltdowns with comments like, "Did you know I built computers when I was a teenager?"), Rachel Pepin, and Seth Pierson (who started as an AFI intern on the AFI fortieth anniversary book and is now photo editor extraordinaire) were also crucial. Seth Oster provided valuable insights. Without everyone in this paragraph, there would be no book. Most of all, we thank each other as colleagues, co-conspirators, and friends for so many decades. We have tolerated each other's nonsense for a long time. Special thanks to Bob Wyman, whose legal expertise was so helpful when we needed it most, and to Howell Begle for always being helpful with his insights and clearance advice.

Our thanks to everyone else at AFI up and down the halls who kept answering our questions with speed and accuracy. And to John Ptak, Arthur Novell, Vivian Sobchack, Brian O'Doherty, Bob Rosen, Eddie Richman, Greg Lukow, Robert Vaughn, Joe Petricca, and Joe Pichirallo, who spent time and thought remembering and reminding us of things long forgotten—"thank you" seems so inadequate.

To Jeffrey Goldman and Kate Murray at Santa Monica Press and Amy Inouye of Future Studio Design and Gallery, thank you. You are good people and have made a challenging project something like fun.

To Bob Gazzale, Tom Pollock, John Cooke, and Jeanine Basinger—thank you for your insights and guidance regarding the publication of this book.

In 1976, Jean left Princeton University's Publications Office because she could not bear the pressure of the final printing, knowing there would be errors in the publication (because there always are). So here she is again, apologizing ahead of time for any and all mistakes that there must be in the book, and just hoping they will not be egregious ones.

From Jeannie to the Wyman clan—thank you for not only giving me a home in California but also for your friendship and love, and also for including me in your world of California arts, culture, sports, and politics. To Roz; Betty and John; Bob (always great to have a lawyer in the family), Peggy and Sammi; and Brad, Eugene, and Oliver—you are an amazing group.

A special thank you to our personal editor, Jana Branch. When this book was just a budding idea, she gave us confidence to plow ahead. At every bend on the road, she steered us in the right direction. This book is a testimony to her strong support and expertise.

From Jamie to Elizabeth Daley—who runs the other great show in this town—thanks for the support and insight that kept me going for so many years.

From Jeannie, last but not least—what can be said about my daughter and her husband, my son and his wife, my six grandchildren and one great-grandchild? To Debbie and Mike; Doug and Suzanne; Rachel #1 and her Eric and little Elizabeth Jean; Christopher #2; Sara #3; Samantha #4; Lindy #5; Drew #6—thank you for your love and the joy you have brought to my life. And to my brother, David, and his Sandy, and my Mother and Father—thank you for making this story possible. Because of all of you, it has been (and continues to be) a wonderful life.

★ ABOUT THE AUTHORS AND CONTRIBUTORS

Jean Picker Firstenberg served as president and CEO of the American Film Institute from 1980 to 2007, overseeing the development of AFI as one of America's greatest national, cultural, and educational resources. She received an AFI Life Achievement Award for Service to the Institute and was named president emerita and a lifetime trustee.

In 2016, Firstenberg was named to the California State University Board of Trustees by Governor Jerry Brown, overseeing the largest four-year public university system in the United States, with twenty-three campuses educating the most diverse student body in the nation. Prior to serving at AFI, Firstenberg spent four years as a program officer at the John and Mary R. Markle Foundation. She also served as director of Princeton University's Publications Office.

Firstenberg is a summa cum laude graduate of Boston University's College of Communications. She has served on several boards, including that of Boston University (1984–1996), the George Foster Peabody Awards at Georgia University (1985–1997; board chair 1991–1997); and the United States Postal Service Citizens' Stamp Advisory Committee (2002–2014; committee chair 2008–2014). She has won numerous awards and honorary degrees.

James Hindman, PhD, has spent his career in cinema and performing arts, creating and leading professional and public education programs at major institutions. During his twenty-four years at the American Film Institute, where he served as co-director and chief operating officer, he was provost of the AFI Conservatory, which he nurtured through WASC accreditation. He was also the uncredited producer of the award-winning feature documentary *Visions of Light* and the television series *Starring the Actor*. He developed the AFI Silver Theatre and Cultural Center in Silver Springs, Maryland, as well as numerous television projects and international film and television festivals.

Subsequent to AFI, he developed and led film schools in the U.S. and internationally, including the Red Sea School of Cinematic Arts in Aqaba, Jordan, and New Mexico State University's Creative Media Institute in Las Cruces. He is currently on the board of the New Mexico School for the Arts in Santa Fe, charged with creating a new cinematic and media arts program and facilities for the school. Prior to AFI, he served as head of graduate studies in the Performing Arts Department at American University in Washington, DC, having previously taught at the University of North Carolina.

Hindman holds a PhD in drama from the University of Georgia and has served on the boards of the AIDS Service Center and LAMP in Los Angeles. He currently splits his time between Santa Monica, California, and Taos, New Mexico.

Nick DeMartino is a Los Angeles-based media and technology consultant who advises companies on strategy, content distribution, strategic partnerships, and marketing. He is chairman of the advisory board and senior advisor for the Toronto-based digital media accelerator IDEA-BOOST, and advisor to POV Partners, a private investment and operating company in the entertainment and media sector.

Previously, DeMartino was the senior vice president for media and technology at the American Film Institute, where he created innovative programs like the AFI Digital Content Lab, which incubated more than ninety multiplatform applications with the biggest names in media. He was named No. 3 on the PGA/*The Hollywood Reporter*'s list of Digital 50 and was twice named among the most influential in broadband by the *L.A. Business Journal.*

DeMartino writes about current industry matters on his website, NickDeMartino.net, and across the web on such sites as IndieWire, The Wrap, Huffington Post, and MIPCOM. Follow him on Twitter @nick-demartino.

Bob Gazzale has served as president and CEO of the AFI since November 2007. He first joined the Institute in 1992, holding various positions including director of AFI programs in New York and director of AFI productions in L.A. Since 2003, he has been the writer and executive producer of the AFI Life Achievement Award telecasts. He also created the format for the AFI AWARDS, an annual almanac of excellence, as well as AFI Night at the Movies. Gazzale was a principal in the team that created, produced, and wrote the *AFI's 100 Years...* series, which has driven millions of people back to the classics of American film. Gazzale is a graduate of the University of Virginia, and served as director of the Virginia Festival of American Film before joining AFI.

DANA GIOIA was appointed Poet Laureate of the State of California in 2015 by Governor Jerry Brown. An award-winning poet who has published five collections of poetry, Gioia served as chair of the National Endowment for the Arts from 2003 to 2009, and was named a USC Judge Widney Professor in Poetry and Public Art in 2011.

PATRICIA KING HANSON served as executive editor and project director of the *AFI Catalog of Feature Films* from 1983 to 2009. Prior to coming to AFI, she was the associate editor of *Magill's Survey of Cinema*, *Magill's Bibliography of Literary Criticism*, and *Magill's Cinema Annual*. She has contributed dozens of articles on film to magazines, including British publications *Flics*, *Stills*, *The Listener*, and *Moving Pictures International*, and was a reviewer for the British trade publication *Screen International*.

In addition to contributing to a number of film reference books, she has co-authored other books, provided DVD audio commentary for a number of classic films, been an on-air expert on film for MSNBC, CNN, NPR, and numerous radio stations, and been quoted in a wide variety of print and online sources.

PATTY JENKINS made history in 2017 when she directed her second film, *Wonder Woman*, becoming the first woman to direct a studio superhero movie and earning the biggest domestic opening of all time for a woman director. Jenkins wrote and directed her first film, the crime drama *Monster*, in 2003, launching Charlize Theron's career with many awards, including an Oscar for Best Actress. Jenkins graduated from the Cooper Union for the Advancement of Science and Art in 1993 and the AFI Conservatory in 2000.

LARRY KIRKMAN is a professor of Film and Media Arts and dean emeritus of the School of Communication at American University. His pioneering work in public-purpose media has encompassed documentaries, social advertising campaigns, strategic communications for nonprofits, digital journalism, and communication policy. He is an executive producer in the Investigative Reporting Workshop and senior research fellow in the Center for Media and Social Impact.

EMILY LASKIN has held leadership positions in nonprofit organizations in Los Angeles for over thirty years. She has led talented teams at the American Film Institute, the L.A. Philharmonic, Art Center College of Design, Sundance Institute, and USC Marshall School of Business. She is currently senior vice president at Art Center College of Design. At AFI, Laskin supervised broad-based offerings of public programs held across the country and a wide range of national publications via the AFI Press, and was instrumental in securing the gift from Apple that created one of the first computer labs designed to explore applications appropriate to filmmaking.

David Lynch, born in 1946 in Missoula, Montana. Eagle Scout.

★ QUOTE CITATIONS

29 George Stevens Jr.—fortieth anniversary remembrances, trustee meeting, October 4, 2007

35 Robert Mandel—fortieth anniversary tribute book

38 Sir Howard Stringer— fortieth anniversary remembrances, trustee meeting, October 4, 2007

47 Barbara Kopple—from an interview with the author

64 George Stevens Jr.—first day, Center for Advanced Film Studies, September 23, 1969

68 David Lynch— fortieth anniversary remembrances, trustee meeting, October 4, 2007

73 Robert Mandel—Toni Vellani memorial service, February 1990

80 Bill Moyers—letter to Jean Picker Firstenberg upon her retirement, August 15, 2007

82 Edward Zwick—fortieth anniversary tribute book

85 Dezsö Magyar—fortieth anniversary tribute book

91 Darren Aronofsky—acceptance of Franklin J. Schaffner Alumni Medal, 2001

95 Carl Franklin—AFI Annual Report, 2004 and 2005

98 WASC–NASAD Capacity Visit Team—2002 initial findings report, repeated verbatim in 2007 report

111 Lesli Linka Glatter—fortieth anniversary tribute book

115 Maya Angelou—fortieth anniversary tribute book

119 Jeanine Basinger—fortieth anniversary tribute video

122 Frank Rich—*New York Times*, September 21, 1996

132 John Ptak—from an interview with the author

136 Dr. Carla D. Hayden—letter to Bob Daly, February 23, 2017

140 Martin Scorsese—AFI Annual Report, 2005

147 Kenneth Turan—*Los Angeles Times*, November 14, 1999

148 Jane Alexander—letter to Jean Picker Firstenberg, May 18, 1995

167 Ken Wlaschin—fortieth anniversary tribute book
180 William Friedkin—*The French Connection* screening at the AFI Silver Theatre, 2006
184 Ken Burns—AFI SILVERDOCS speech
230 Todd Wagner—fortieth anniversary tribute book
232 Dale Herigstad—AFI Annual Report, 2002
284 Richard Brandt—fortieth anniversary remembrances, trustee meeting, October 4, 2007
293 Gregory Peck—remarks on accepting Life Achievement Award, 1989
304 Liener Temerlin—remarks at last board meeting, November 1, 2000
312 Gene Jankowski—fortieth anniversary remembrances, trustee meeting, October 4, 2007
323 Sir Howard Stringer—fortieth anniversary remembrances, trustee meeting, October 4, 2007
328 Martin Scorsese—remarks on accepting Life Achievement Award, 1997
338 Roger Ebert—*Chicago Sun Times*, June 21, 2007
343 Steven Spielberg—2005 AFI Awards benediction
365 Richard Brandt—fortieth anniversary remembrances, trustee meeting, October 4, 2007
371 Fred Pierce—fortieth anniversary remembrances, trustee meeting, October 4, 2007
373 Michael Nesmith—fortieth anniversary tribute book
375 Tom Pollock—fortieth anniversary remembrances, trustee meeting, October 4, 2007
377 Sir Howard Stringer—fortieth anniversary remembrances, trustee meeting, October 4, 2007
392 Edward James Olmos—remarks upon receiving honorary degree, 1993
400 Orson Welles—remarks on accepting Life Achievement Award, 1974

★ PHOTO CREDITS

i: Courtesy of AFI (top); Courtesy of Jean Picker Firstenberg (bottom)
ii: Courtesy of AFI
iii: Courtesy of AFI (all)
iv: Courtesy of AFI
v: Courtesy of AFI/Yani Begakis
vi: Courtesy of AFI (all)
vii: Courtesy Kennedy Center
viii: Courtesy of AFI
ix: Courtesy of AFI (all)
x: Courtesy of AFI (top); Courtesy of AFI/Richard Bratten (bottom)
xi: Courtesy of AFI/James L. Miller
xii: Courtesy of AFI
xiii: Courtesy of AFI/Peter Borsari
xiv: Courtesy of AFI/Lee Salem
xv: Courtesy of AFI/Peter Borsari
xvi: Courtesy of AFI
xvii: Courtesy of AFI/Lee Salem (top); Courtesy of AFI/Joan Marcus (bottom)
xviii: Courtesy of Merlyn Rosenberg
xix: Courtesy of AFI
xx: Courtesy of AFI
xxi: Courtesy of AFI/Lee Salem (top); Courtesy of AFI (bottom)
xxii: Courtesy of AFI/Nancy Ostertag (top); Courtesy of AFI/Seth Pierson (bottom)
xxiii: Courtesy of AFI/Nancy Ostertag
xxiv: Courtesy of AFI
xxv: Courtesy of AFI (top); Courtesy AFI/Veronika Cernadas (bottom)
xxvi: Courtesy AFI/Veronika Cernadas (all)
xxvii: Courtesy of AFI
xxviii: Courtesy of AFI
xxix: Courtesy of AFI/Seth Pierson (top); Courtesy of AFI (bottom)
xxx: Courtesy of AFI/Doug Gifford (top); Courtesy of AFI/Michael Kovac (bottom)
xxxi: Courtesy of AFI
xxxii: Courtesy of AFI/Randall Michelson (all)

★ INDEX